Reinventing Citizenship

Black Los Angeles, Korean Kawasaki, and Community Participation

Kazuyo Tsuchiya

Critical American Studies

University of Minnesota Press
Minneapolis
London

Portions of chapter 1 were published in Japanese in "1964 nen Amerika keizai kikaihō ni okeru hōsetsu to haijo: 'Kanō na kagiri saidaigen no sanka' jōkō o megutte," *Rekshigaku kenkyū* 858 (October 2009): 18–32. Portions of chapter 4 were previously published in "Race, Class, and Gender in America's 'War on Poverty': The Case of Opal C. Jones in Los Angeles, 1964–1968," *Japanese Journal of American Studies* 15 (2004): 213–36, and "'Jobs or Income Now!': Work, Welfare, and Citizenship in Johnnie Tillmon's Struggles for Welfare Rights," *Japanese Journal of American Studies* 22 (2011): 151–70.

Published by the University of Minnesota Press
111 Third Avenue South, Suite 290
Minneapolis, MN 55401-2520
http://www.upress.umn.edu

Library of Congress Cataloging-in-Publication Data
Tsuchiya, Kazuyo.
Reinventing citizenship : Black Los Angeles, Korean Kawasaki, and community participation / Kazuyo Tsuchiya.
(Critical American Studies series) Includes bibliographical references and index.
ISBN 978-0-8166-8111-2 (hc : alk. paper)—ISBN 978-0-8166-8112-9 (pb : alk. paper)
1. Community development—California—Los Angeles—History—20th century. 2. Social service—California—Los Angeles—History—20th century. 3. African Americans—California—Los Angeles—Politics and government—20th century. 4. Community Action Program (U.S.)—History. 5. Community development—Japan—Kawasaki-shi—History—20th century. 6. Social service—Japan—Kawasaki-shi—History—20th century. 7. Koreans—Japan—Kawasaki-shi—Politics and government—20th century. I. Title.

HN80.L7T78 2014
307.1'40979494—dc23 2013028366

Printed in the United States of America on acid-free paper

20 19 18 17 16 15 14 10 9 8 7 6 5 4 3 2 1

Reinventing Citizenship

CRITICAL AMERICAN STUDIES SERIES

George Lipsitz, University of California–Santa Barbara, Series Editor

Contents

Abbreviations vii

Introduction: Los Angeles and Kawasaki as Arenas of Struggle over Citizenship 1

1. Between Inclusion and Exclusion: The Origins of the U.S. Community Action Program 15
2. Fostering Community and Nationhood: Japan's Model Community Program 43
3. Struggling for Political Voice: Race and the Politics of Welfare in Los Angeles 59
4. Recasting the Community Action Program: The Pursuit of Race, Class, and Gender Equality in Los Angeles 81
5. Translating Black Theology into Korean Activism: The Hitachi Employment Discrimination Trial 117
6. Voicing Alternative Visions of Citizenship: The "Kawasaki System" of Welfare 139

Conclusion: The Interconnectedness of Oppression and Freedom 163

Acknowledgments 171

Notes 175

Bibliography 225

Index 257

Abbreviations

ADC	Aid to Dependent Children
AFDC	Aid to Families with Dependent Children
AFL-CIO	American Federation of Labor and Congress of Industrial Organizations
ANC	Aid to Needy Children
CAP	Community Action Program
CCAP	Citizens' Crusade against Poverty
CCC	Community Conservation Corps
CEA	Council of Economic Advisers
COINTELPRO	Counterintelligence Program
EOF	Economic Opportunity Federation
EYOA	Economic and Youth Opportunities Agency of Greater Los Angeles
FEPC	Fair Employment Practices Commission
HEW	U.S. Department of Health, Education, and Welfare
KCCJ	Korean Christian Church in Japan (Zainichi Daikan Kirisuto Kyōkai)
LAPD	Los Angeles Police Department
LBJ	Lyndon Baines Johnson
LDP	Liberal Democratic Party (Jiyūminshutō)
MCP	Model Community Program
MLK	Martin Luther King Jr.
NAACP	National Association for the Advancement of Colored People
NAPP	Neighborhood Adult Participation Project
NCC	National Council of Churches
NCNC	National Committee of Negro Churchmen (later the NCBC, the National Committee of Black Churchmen, and then the National Conference of Black Christians)
NKK	Nihon Kōkan Kabushikigaisha (NKK Corporation)
NOW	National Organization for Women

NWRO	National Welfare Rights Organization
OEO	Office of Economic Opportunity
PCJD	President's Committee on Juvenile Delinquency and Youth Crime
PCR	Program to Combat Racism (World Council of Churches)
RAIK	Research-Action Institute for the Koreans in Japan (Zainichi Kankokujin Mondai Kenkyūjo)
SCAP	Supreme Commander for the Allied Powers
UAW	United Auto Workers
UCLA	University of California, Los Angeles
USC	University of Southern California
VISTA	Volunteers in Service to America
WCC	World Council of Churches
WIN	Work Incentive Program
WLCAC	Watts Labor Community Action Committee
YOB	Youth Opportunities Board

Los Angeles and Kawasaki as Arenas of Struggle over Citizenship

On April 3, 1966, three hundred fifty people gathered to protest the dismissal of African American social worker and activist Opal C. Jones from her position as the executive director of the Neighborhood Adult Participation Project (NAPP), one of the most popular and influential antipoverty programs in Los Angeles.[1] Throughout the operation of its programs, NAPP aimed at providing training and employment opportunities for adults, as well as making the voices of "the poor" heard. Jones worked closely with African American politicians like Augustus Hawkins, who was elected to the U.S. Congress in 1962, and Thomas Bradley, who won the election for city council in the following year. Together with black politicians, activists, and her black and brown colleagues, Jones carried on the struggle against the official Community Action Agency, the Economic and Youth Opportunities Agency of Greater Los Angeles (EYOA). Jones demanded that the EYOA incorporate voices from the poor into the program. NAPP indeed transformed into a unique social space for nurturing local leadership among the poor. One of those leaders was a mother from Watts, Johnnie Tillmon, who ultimately became a chairperson of the National Welfare Rights Organization. Yet as Jones became a "principal watchdog of the representation of the poor," she also became a political threat to the EYOA and city hall.[2] At the demonstration, protestors rallied behind Jones, demanding her reinstatement. Armed with the "maximum feasible participation" clause of the 1964 Economic Opportunity Act, they also insisted on their economic, educational, and welfare rights—not only de jure but also de facto rights—to participate in and enjoy the benefits of the expanding American welfare state.

Almost seven years later, on April 28, 1974, Koreans living in the city of Kawasaki, Japan, gathered in support of Park Jong Seok, who filed a lawsuit against Japanese electronics company Hitachi for dismissing him due to his ethnic origin.[3] After four years of struggles, Park and his supporters were about to win a major victory over Hitachi, thus setting in motion an epoch-making trial in the history of the *zainichi* Koreans' battle for citizenship.[4] Park and his supporters received financial and moral support from both national and transnational church organizations, especially through the World Council of Churches (WCC). Black liberation struggles and theology, in particular, offered a significant framework around which *zainichi* Koreans constructed their own challenge to narrow definitions of citizenship. At the gathering, some of the participants questioned why *zainichi* Koreans were denied the right to apply for the city's allowance for dependent children. *Zainichi* mothers, led by Song Puja, pushed this question further: Why were they—former colonial subjects and their descendants—classified as "noncitizens" and stripped of their educational and welfare rights? In fact, they were about to initiate a long struggle for their rights as citizens in the expanding Japanese welfare state.

Reinventing Citizenship compares African American welfare activism in Los Angeles with Korean battles for welfare rights in Kawasaki during the 1960s and 1970s. A comparison of these two struggles reveals unique insights into the contested nature of citizenship during the period of welfare state expansion in the United States and Japan.[5] Based on a wide range of sources, which include archival documents, oral histories, and newspapers, I investigate both institutional discourses and the ways in which they were challenged by grassroots organizations.[6] In the working-class and poor neighborhoods of both locations, local activists brought to the forefront race-, gender-, or nationality-based exclusions that were deeply embedded in each welfare state. They sought not only their recognition as legitimate constituting members of "communities" but also actual resources, including jobs, job training, promotions, day care, allowances for children, health care, and better schools. Both cases involved grassroots mobilization, brought new leaders to the vanguard, and demanded that the policy makers rethink previously accepted distinctions between "us" and "them," the "deserving" and the "undeserving," "producer" and "parasite," wages and reproductive labor, citizen and noncitizen. *Reinventing Citizenship* also argues that black liberation theology provided a valuable language for *zainichi* activists in Kawasaki. It delineates the interactions, exchanges, and translations that emerged between black liberation struggles and the *zainichi* Korean pursuit of citizenship rights.[7]

The Politics of Participation in the Community Action Program in the United States

The Community Action Program (CAP), along with its famous and controversial goal of securing the "maximum feasible participation" of residents, was created as a core program of President Lyndon B. Johnson's "War on Poverty." The War on Poverty was officially launched in August 1964 with the signing of the Economic Opportunity Act and the establishment of the Office of Economic Opportunity (OEO). The War on Poverty led to the creation and administration of many novel programs, but CAP, designed to "help urban and rural communities to coordinate and mobilize their resources to combat poverty," was its most important and unique feature. CAP established more than one thousand Community Action Agencies (CAAs) and required the involvement of not only representatives of public and private agencies involved in antipoverty programs but also representatives of the poor themselves in policy planning and execution. Title II of the Economic Opportunity Act specified that CAP could be administered by either a public or private nonprofit agency but that it must be "developed, conducted, and administered with the maximum feasible participation of residents of the areas and members of the groups served."[8]

Scholars have debated what the Community Action Program—especially its famous phrase, "maximum feasible participation"—signified. They have argued whether the inclusion of that phrase in the Economic Opportunity Act (1964) was merely a strategy developed by Democratic Party leaders to accumulate urban African American votes.[9] Since the 1990s, however, scholars have explored the origins and implications of CAP from different perspectives. For political scientist Barbara Cruikshank, it is the participation of the poor in federal welfare programs itself that should be carefully examined. Cruikshank insists that, whether Democratic leaders created CAP with such an intention or not, democratic self-government was still a mode of exercising power. Power, in her view, only works by requiring the active participation of the poor in programs on the local level, programs that transform the poor into "self-sufficient, active, productive, and participatory citizens." These "technologies of citizenship" are the means by which "government works *through* rather than against the subjectivities of citizens" and can be traced back to the War on Poverty programs of the 1960s. In other words, Cruikshank argues that the participation of the poor in the decision-making processes itself was a strategy of the government to transform them into productive and useful citizens.[10]

Other scholars have emphasized the crucial connections between CAP and the fight for racial and gender equality. According to Jill Quadagno, Nancy A. Naples, Rhonda Y. Williams, Christina Greene, Annelise Orleck, Noel A. Cazenave, Susan Youngblood Ashmore, Robert Bauman, Lisa Levenstein, and Alyosha Goldstein, what needs to be examined is not only the intention of the Democratic Party but also the results CAP produced.[11] They have shown how CAP brought about enduring change by fostering the participation of people of color (especially African Americans) and women in local politics. In the anthology *The War on Poverty: A New Grassroots History, 1964–1980,* one of the editors, Annelise Orleck, has observed that CAP, especially its call for "maximum feasible participation" by the poor, "sparked two decades of community activism and political struggle across the United States, engaging and empowering people who had rarely been heard in American politics."[12] Following the course of this new scholarship, I first discuss how CAP was created based on racialized and gendered definitions of citizenship. I then analyze how African American activists in Los Angeles appropriated CAP, invested it with new definitions, and transformed it into a vehicle for social change. I regard CAP as a contested political terrain across which multiple political actors fought for their visions of the War on Poverty. Scholars have demonstrated how race and gender relations have played a critical role in the history of the U.S. welfare state.[13] I, too, place the question of race and gender, as well as class, at the center of both welfare policy discourse and welfare activism.

Chapter 1 provides an analysis of how CAP and its doctrine of the "maximum feasible participation" of the poor emerged in the early 1960s. It first examines the question of CAP's origins. It explores how CAP and the War on Poverty became part of America's Cold War strategies to demonstrate the nation's dedication to equality and justice.[14] It then analyzes how the War on Poverty programs defined women's roles in the programs in volunteer terms, stressing their support roles. The War on Poverty also muted the question of race rather than linking the issue of racial inequality with the problem of poverty. I argue that this was because the policy makers who created CAP were divided as to the extent to which the poor and people of color were to be incorporated into state programs. Consequently, the original concept of CAP was caught between schemes of inclusion and exclusion.[15]

The Creation of "National Communities": Transnational Perspectives

Reinventing Citizenship also puts CAP in a transnational context and analyzes it from a new angle. There has been little attempt to assess CAP from a comparative and global perspective. It is only possible, however, to completely understand the following questions through comparative and transnational investigations: How did participation tactics become a main strategy for the War on Poverty? Why did CAP eventually open up a space where African American and other activists of color could intervene? How could these activists address the inadequacies of the American welfare system from *inside* the welfare state and revise the New Deal legacy that reinforced racial and gender inequality? And finally, how did CAP carve out a political path for African Americans and other subjugated people of color?

In chapter 2 I introduce the case of another country, Japan, as a way to examine how different capitalist countries employed similar technologies relating to community action and citizen participation. CAP was not exceptional in producing racialized and gendered meanings of citizenship. Similar to CAP in the United States, "communities" became the main target of social welfare enterprises in Japan during late 1960s and early 1970s. In April 1971, the Ministry of Home Affairs initiated the Model Community Program (*Moderu komyunitī shisaku* or *keikaku*), establishing community centers in eighty-three local areas by 1973. Other ministries followed the example of MCP, creating similar types of community programs. The "community" approach acquired a cardinal significance in the expanding Japanese welfare state in the early 1970s. It was not a mere coincidence that policies resembling community programs were created in Japan in the late 1960s and early 1970s. Political scientists and sociologists affiliated with the Japanese Ministry of Home Affairs translated and implemented American technologies for the purpose of reconstructing "communities" during a period of a perceived national crisis. They reshaped these technologies to meet different political ends in Japan.

Scholars in Japan have debated why local and national governments turned their attention to these community programs in the late 1960s.[16] I contend that the Liberal Democratic Party (LDP) created community programs to counter the ascendancy of residents' movements as well as oppositional left-wing power. They sought to create "a sense of nationhood" among divided residents through the Model Community Program.

Residents' movements—which had expanded significantly since the 1960s and had pressured the LDP into committing to issues like *kōgai* (environmental pollution), prices, and welfare—exercised a huge influence on both national and local politics. According to Yamaguchi Yasushi and Shimada Shuichi, the Model Community Program was developed to deal with the Japanese people's criticisms of increased social chaos brought about by the government's policies of high economic growth.[17] Like CAP in the United States, these policy makers and scholars regarded the Model Community Program as an apparatus designed to co-opt radical residents' movements and transform them into "negotiable" local organizations.

Both community programs were thus initiated by the Japanese and American governments to counteract movements from below. In fact, as historian Alice O'Connor explains, OEO official John Wofford later noted that CAP was an attempt to "reach community consensus at a time when race, politics and poverty were pulling communities and the nation apart."[18] I argue that CAP and the MCP can be understood as part of the larger movement toward state re-creation of the "national community" and that it was a reaction to a perceived national "crisis" brought about by social movements in the 1960s.[19]

Reinventing Citizenship: Black Los Angeles and Korean Kawasaki

The complexity of race and gender relations in both U.S. and Japanese welfare policies, however, cannot be fully understood without incorporating the experiences and the everyday tactics of welfare activists at the local level. This book focuses on the role played by these welfare activists in particular cities: African Americans in Los Angeles and Koreans in Kawasaki. It combines local narratives—the cases of Los Angeles and Kawasaki in the late 1960s and the 1970s—with national and even transnational stories.

I focus my investigation first on Los Angeles. *Reinventing Citizenship* emphasizes, as do earlier studies that explored race relations in twentieth-century Los Angeles, the question of race and its spatial dimensions in the history of the City of Angels.[20] Los Angeles was at the forefront of the antipoverty struggles of the 1960s. Los Angeles was unlike New York, where the poor exercised a substantial influence over the local antipoverty programs, nor was it like Chicago, where city officials appointed the representatives of the poor, thus retaining a controlling power over CAP.[21] Los Angeles became an arena of intense struggle over the meaning of "maximum feasible participation," citizenship, and welfare rights.[22] I demonstrate that African American activists were at the heart of the Los Angeles War on Poverty and illustrate how they transformed antipoverty efforts into a battle for racial, class, and gender equality.

The Los Angeles Community Action Program formally started soon after the Watts uprising in 1965. The central task force of the Los Angeles War on Poverty, the Economic and Youth Opportunities Agency of Greater Los Angeles (EYOA), was established in September 1965. In chapter 3, I investigate how African American leaders forcefully challenged the city government and insisted on the right to realize the participation of the poor in the Los Angeles War on Poverty by establishing their organization, the Economic Opportunity Federation, and providing opportunities for residents to join the Community Action Agency. These same individuals used the antipoverty program as a way to politically confront Mayor Samuel Yorty and other government officials who sought to secure control of the antipoverty programs at the expense of poor people themselves. I contend that these efforts resulted in a crucial change in the political status of African American residents in Los Angeles.

In chapter 4, I focus on the Neighborhood Adult Participation Project, which became a major point of contestation regarding the participation of "the poor," people of color, and women in the Los Angeles Community Action Program. It was one of the few programs targeted at adults, and it was directed by a female African American social worker, Opal C. Jones. Through NAPP, Jones attacked racial discrimination, criticized middle-class "experts" for muting the voices of "the poor," and contested notions of what constituted "appropriate female roles," practiced by the federal antipoverty agency, the OEO, and the EYOA. Moreover, Jones constituted a challenge to the EYOA's perception of the programs as being dominated by the local antipoverty agency rather than the local residents. I argue that Jones transformed the Neighborhood Adult Participation Project into something sharply different from the project originally set up by the OEO or the EYOA, making it into a weapon in a battle over the meaning of "maximum feasible participation." In chapter 4, I also discuss interracial coalitions and conflicts between black and Latino Angelenos in relation to the Neighborhood Adult Participation Project in particular and the War on Poverty in general. Both groups, each in their own way, searched for representation and actual resources in their struggles against poverty.

I then examine two organizations that sought to foster the political participation of the poor in the Watts neighborhood and addressed the inadequacies of the welfare system: the Watts Labor Community Action Committee (WLCAC) and Aid to Needy Children (ANC) Mothers Anonymous. I pay particular attention to activists Ted Watkins of the WLCAC and Johnnie Tillmon of ANC Mothers Anonymous, who played critical roles in each organization.

The WLCAC was organized early in 1965 by labor union members living in the Watts area, with financial support from the OEO, the AFL-CIO, and the Department of Labor. The WLCAC emerged from a campaign to bring a hospital to Watts. I analyze how these unionists in the WLCAC created oppositional discourses against negative representations of Watts and refashioned the War on Poverty to bring the programs closer to the neighborhood residents. I also examine the criticism the WLCAC received from within South Central, thereby uncovering the intricacy of their antipoverty efforts. Johnnie Tillmon established one of the first organizations in the nation created by and for welfare recipients, ANC Mothers Anonymous, in 1963. Tillmon joined the Neighborhood Adult Participation Project, and through NAPP, she found a new opportunity. She expanded her activism from the local level to the national level, from ANC Mothers Anonymous in Watts to the National Welfare Rights Organization (NWRO) in Washington, DC. In both ANC Mothers Anonymous and the NWRO, Tillmon struggled to establish a system that guaranteed women's autonomy in controlling their own lives—whether they preferred working outside the house, remaining at home to devote themselves to child rearing and housework, or doing both.[23] The examples of Ted Watkins and Johnnie Tillmon show how African American activists in Watts interpreted the "maximum feasible participation" concept and redefined it to suit their needs.

Rethinking the rise of African American political power in Los Angeles leads to the reassessment of the postwar history of American cities. Scholars have debated why American cities became entangled with numerous social and economic "crises," such as poverty, unemployment, and residential segregation. These studies offer a significant framework within which to understand the reconfiguration of the ghettos in postwar urban America. As historian Heather Ann Thompson has demonstrated, however, urban historians' exclusive focus on "urban decline" has rendered unclear other "equally important" postwar urban experiences and has resulted in the dismissal of inner cities from postwar urban history.[24] While it is certainly undeniable that inner cities faced economic decay and physical deterioration, these same cities had also become places where African Americans could gain political and economic control after World War II, especially during the 1960s.

Reinventing Citizenship sheds more light on the role of black leaders in shaping the future of postwar cities. By taking the role of African American leaders seriously, it considers them as historical actors rather than as passive victims of "urban deterioration." This emphasis on the agency of African American activists does not necessarily mean ignoring the issues they could not untangle or even the problems they themselves created. Emancipatory social movements often depend on what Miranda Joseph has called "fantasies of community" in order to "mobilize constituents and validate their cause to a broader public," and this idealization of community needs to be critically examined.[25] I contend, however, that crucial shifts in African American political power occurred during the 1960s. African American activists appropriated and reshaped the principle of "maximum feasible participation" that had been the foundation of CAP. They radically questioned the meaning of poverty and refashioned the War on Poverty into a struggle against inequalities based on race, class, and gender.

In the case of the Japanese Model Community Program, while "Japanese" citizens were provided with a new political space, "minority" residents remained outside of assumed "communities." The MCP in Japan shared a similar goal with CAP in the United States—that of reconstructing "communities" through the active participation of local residents in a period of perceived national "crises" and massive reform. In addition, both programs failed to address the question of racial and ethnic inequality. However, there was one significant difference between CAP and the MCP. While CAP eventually created new terrain where local welfare activists of color could intervene, Japanese community programs in the early 1970s consistently excluded non-Japanese residents from these functioning communities, thereby reinforcing the equation of ethnonational identity with citizenship.[26] In fact, the MCP turned out to be only one in a long line of welfare programs that redefined the boundary between "citizen" and "noncitizen."

This does not mean that resident non-nationals did not challenge the government's exclusionary welfare policies. Koreans in Japan (*zainichi* Koreans) contested this limited notion of citizenship. After Japan concluded the San Francisco Peace Treaty with the Allied Powers, the government of Japan, free to use its own discretion regarding domestic and international matters, formally declared its Korean residents to be "aliens." Korean residents, who had rendered service to Imperial Japan and who had been considered Japanese nationals during the colonial period, were deprived of legal rights.[27] Thereafter, the Japanese government constantly used citizenship as a pretext for the exclusion of Koreans from social security programs. By the early 1970s, however, the new generation of Koreans initiated a series of political struggles against the Japanese government and major Japanese companies, demanding their rights as citizens.

I have focused my investigation on Kawasaki (Figure I.1). Kawasaki City, a hub for the defense industry before and during World War II, was home to a large number of Korean workers and their descendants, who were enlisted by the Japanese government to construct military factories. After the war, Kawasaki City became the center of the Keihin industrial belt, ranking third (after Tokyo and Osaka) in the value of shipped manufactured goods by 1960. It developed diversified neighborhoods and a multiethnic work force. It also evolved into a major working-class town with strong roots of labor activism. When Ito Saburo, a chairperson of the city officials' labor union, won the mayorship in 1971, he called for the "creation of a humanitarian city (*Ningen toshi no sōzō*)." Ito's "progressive" policies placed great emphasis on welfare, antipollution measures, and the rights of resident non-nationals.[28] Korean activists appropriated Mayor Ito's "progressive" narratives to advance their education and welfare rights. After they achieved a victory in the Hitachi Employment Discrimination Trial, Kawasaki became a center for *zainichi* Korean welfare struggles and an arena of struggle over citizenship.

Chapters 5 and 6 focus on the *zainichi* Koreans' struggles in Kawasaki City. Chapter 5 discusses how the coastal areas of Kawasaki emerged as a major *zainichi* Korean district and later as the center of *zainichi* activism in the late 1960s and the early 1970s. The Kawasaki Korean Christian Church, and the nursery school that opened inside the chapel, provided *zainichi* activists with a social space to contest the racialized processes of differentiation by the Hitachi company, one of the largest electronics corporations in Japan and the world. They eventually founded a social welfare organization called Seikyusha (Green Hill Association) in 1974.

Chapter 5 also explores the exchanges and interconnections between black liberation struggles and the efforts of Koreans in Japan to pursue citizenship rights. I examine how Korean activists in the Kawasaki

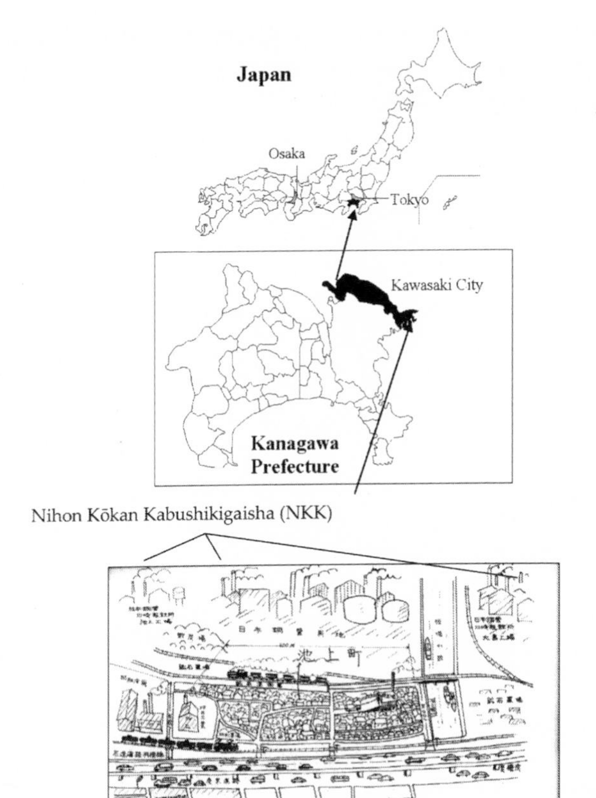

Figure I.1. Coastal areas of Kawasaki City. Bottom figure courtesy of Kanagawaken Daini Aisen Hōmu, Kawasaki City.

Korean Christian Church were influenced by black theology and invested it with new meaning, how they encountered African and African American leaders through worldwide religious organizations such as the World Council of Churches and searched for common ground, and how *zainichi* Koreans won a victory in the Hitachi Employment Discrimination Trial—a watershed in the history of the Korean struggle in Japan during the postwar period—with help from black leaders.

Chapter 6 shows how Kawasaki Koreans challenged the city's and the nation's exclusionary local and national welfare policies, asserted their welfare rights, and voiced alternative visions of citizenship. Seikyusha's determination to advance citizenship rights for resident non-nationals resulted in the formation of the Kawasaki Association for Promoting Zainichi Koreans' Education (Zainichi Kankoku Chōsenjin Kyōiku o Susumeru Kai) in 1982 and the establishment of a "community" center for both Korean and Japanese residents in 1988, called Fureaikan. Seikyusha not only succeeded in changing Kawasaki City's welfare policies toward *zainichi* Koreans but also had a great impact on other local governments' programs for "minority" citizens. They created an alternative vision of a "model" community. Korean residents succeeded in transforming Kawasaki into a bastion of equal rights, forging the "Kawasaki system (Kawasaki *hōshiki*)," whereby the city government preceded the central government in abolishing the nationality clause (or *kokuseki jōkō*), which was used as a pretext for the exclusion of Koreans and other former colonial subjects from welfare programs. In addition to stressing how they reshaped the city's welfare policies, the chapter describes the criticism they endured from within Korean Kawasaki, indicating the complexity of their struggle for citizenship.

Through the examination of *zainichi* Koreans' struggles in Kawasaki, this book explores how the status of Koreans in Japan stood at the center of a great national debate regarding the parameters of citizenship in the postwar period. Until the 1960s, most of the scholarly work on *zainichi* history concentrated on the prewar period, exploring how Koreans were subjugated under Japanese colonial rule as well as the ways in which they resisted and fought for their liberation.[29] Since the late 1960s, however, scholars have moved beyond the colonial period and have focused increasingly on the postwar period, scrutinizing how ethnicity became the grounds for citizenship in postwar Japan and how Koreans were stripped of their legal and welfare rights.[30]

Since the 1990s, several studies have shed light on the multilayered and evolving lives of the *zainichi* in postwar Japan. By the mid-1970s more than three-fourths of the Koreans in Japan were Japanese born, and this new generation of Koreans was engaged in a series of political struggles. While both the Japanese government and leading Korean organizations such as the pro–South Korea organization Mindan (Zai Nihon Daikanminkoku Mindan, or Korean Residents Association in Japan) and the pro–North Korea organization Chongryun or in Japanese Sōren (Zai Nihon Chōsenjin Sōrengōkai, or General Association of Korean Residents in Japan) considered Koreans in Japan as either foreigners or sojourners, younger Koreans born and raised in Japan contested the narrow definition of citizenship, contending that they were entitled to social security by right. These studies demonstrate that, as a result of the struggles fought by the younger generation of Koreans, crucial shifts had occurred in Japan's political consciousness regarding Koreans and also in the government's position on the *zainichi* during the 1970s and 1980s.[31]

Furthermore, several scholars complicated the understanding of the trajectory of citizenship in postwar Japan. They critically reexamined the link between ethnonational identity and citizenship after World War II. Takashi Fujitani has explained that it became imperative for Japanese elites to deter overt acts of racism during the war. In order to mobilize Koreans for the war effort and to wage total war, they felt increasingly bound to disavow racist practices and proclaim equality, acting as if they regarded Koreans as the equals of Japanese.[32] When the war was over, according to Oguma Eiji, the Japanese nation's primary discourse was converted from a militaristic, multinational empire to a "peace-loving homogeneous state." The myth of the "homogeneous" nation became a dominant discourse in postwar Japan.[33] Koreans came to be classified as "sojourners, nomads, the homeless, and blockade runners" as they lost citizenship in the postwar regime. Yoon Keun Cha, Kang Sang-jung, Tessa Morris-Suzuki, and others demonstrated how the status of Koreans was of cardinal significance in the remapping of citizenship in postwar Japan.[34] In addition, a number of studies sought to rescue women from invisibility, considering Korean women as historical actors in the drama of *zainichi* empowerment. Sonia Ryang, Jung Yeong-hae, Song Eoun-ok, and Kim Puja have argued that Korean women's stories did not fit easily into the standard narrative of *zainichi* history and analyzed how these women simultaneously opposed racism *and* sexism.[35] *Reinventing Citizenship* locates *zainichi* Koreans at the heart of the contestations over Japanese citizenship in the 1970s and the 1980s. It also sheds light on the role of Korean women, especially second-generation *zainichi* mothers, in the history of this pursuit of citizenship.

These Koreans in Japan mobilized alternative visions of citizenship, where national state membership would not be the rule for determining citizenship rights. They problematized not only the equation of citizenship with race but also citizenship with nationality in postwar Japan. By so doing, their struggles produced a radical critique of the postwar Japanese dichotomy between citizens/nationals and noncitizens/non-nationals.

* * *

Following scholars who emphasize that the struggles over racial equality and citizenship rights take place not only in formal politics but also in streets, churches, schools, and local community organizations, in this book I stress the everyday forms of protest developed by welfare activists and the new social visions they created in Los Angeles and Kawasaki.[36] I examine how local activists, both in Los Angeles and in Kawasaki, forcefully challenged the official welfare institutions, created oppositional discourses and movements, and reinvented citizenship. By so doing, I try to rescue local activists from invisibility and consider them as historical actors rather than as passive victims of a racist and sexist state.

This book also documents the interconnected histories of African Americans and *zainichi* Koreans in their pursuit of citizenship rights. By writing a transnational history of grassroots counterhegemonic struggles against racial and ethnic inequality, I explore what George Lipsitz has called "interethnic antiracist alliances" and delineate how activists with "similar but nonidentical experiences" were able to forge a transborder network.[37] Scholars have begun to challenge the assumed centrality of the nation-state and stress the significance of transnational perspectives on American studies, American history, and the history profession itself. Even though transnational history and comparative American studies are becoming increasingly popular, few scholars have actually carried out the task. By introducing the case of the Model Community Program in Japan in comparison with the Community Action Program, I try to overcome the paradigm of "exceptionalism" and interrogate how "different" welfare states employ similar techniques of producing racialized and gendered notions of citizenship. Furthermore, I explore the linkages between black liberation struggles and the *zainichi* Koreans' quest for their rights. Black theology and liberation struggles offered Koreans in Japan a ray of light, a framework for understanding the meaning of oppression and liberation, and they became a bulwark against racial and ethnic discrimination. This history of interactions, exchanges, and translations is truly an example of transnational antiracist networking that historians and American/Japanese studies scholars have not yet fully uncovered. The stories of both African American and *zainichi* Korean mobilization powerfully show why it is necessary for scholars to overcome the nation-centered approach and write a transnational history of grassroots antiracist alliances.

1

Between Inclusion and Exclusion

The Origins of the U.S. Community Action Program

Chapter 1 examines the ways in which the Community Action Program (CAP) and its doctrine of "maximum feasible participation" of the poor emerged. It analyzes how the goals of CAP have changed over time, up until the 1964 passage of the Economic Opportunity Act.[1] At that time the War on Poverty became an apparatus for transforming the poor into productive and participatory citizens for the sake of the development of economic wealth and the war against Communism. CAP and the War on Poverty were attractive to the architects of the Economic Opportunity Act because they could be effective tools to expand the number of poor, especially the African American poor, who qualified for military service; they could serve as useful anti-Communist propaganda; and they could even create jobs—calming down the angered ghettos—for African American military veterans. It also analyzes how the War on Poverty saw the role of women as being supportive volunteers. By keeping women in a marginal position, the War on Poverty assigned women to what historian Alice Kessler-Harris has called "a secondary citizenship" based on their roles as family members and dependents.[2] Finally, it shows how CAP triggered tension between city hall and the Community Action Agencies by fostering the political participation of the poor. The specific goals of CAP were left ambiguous because there was no clear consensus among policy makers as to the extent to which the poor and people of color were to be incorporated into the state. Accordingly, the original concept of CAP was suspended between the rubrics of inclusion and exclusion. Local activists made the best of this ambiguous character of CAP. Yet precisely because the poor started asserting more control over the programs through CAP, the Office of Economic Opportunity (OEO) came under fierce attack. CAP was increasingly cast in a negative light as urban uprisings erupted throughout the nation and as the assumed connection between the War on Poverty and urban insurrections grew in critics' minds.

Transforming the Poor into Productive and Participatory Citizens

"The poor" became an object of U.S. social policy in the early 1960s. The problem of poverty was largely ignored during the post–World War II period. Social welfare legislation held low priority during the years after the war, and no important laws were enacted except modification in minimum wages, extension of coverage under unemployment insurance, and the establishment of Old-Age, Survivors, and Disability Insurance. In fact, until 1964, the word "poverty" did not appear as a heading in the index of the Congressional Record or the Public Papers of the President. Yet the problem of poverty, along with the category of "the poor," suddenly attracted enormous attention.[3]

The so-called rediscovery of poverty had its origin in the publication of several books and articles. Most prominent in the 1950s was John Kenneth Galbraith's *The Affluent Society*. Galbraith argued that there were two main components of the "new poverty": case poverty and insular poverty. Case poverty existed in any community, rural or urban, however prosperous that community or the times may be. Galbraith called attention to another type of poverty that he called "insular poverty," located in areas such as the Appalachians or the West Virginia coal fields, where an entire region had become economically obsolete. Here the "community" perpetuated its problems through "poor schools, evil neighborhood influences, and bad preparation for life." By discussing the new character of modern poverty, Galbraith called for taking steps to reduce poverty, such as investment in schools.[4]

Influenced by Galbraith's work, Michael Harrington published *The Other America* in 1962, which had a significant impact on the Kennedy administration. *The Other America* described the poverty of unskilled workers, migrant farm workers, the aged, minorities, and others who lived in the "economic underworld" of American life. His work reached the White House. Charles L. Schultze, who served as assistant director of the Bureau of the Budget from September 1962 to February 1965, later noted that President Kennedy had read Harrington's book and that "it impressed him."[5] Harrington certainly succeeded in appealing to readers' "ethical" positions by arguing that in a nation with technology that could provide every citizen with a decent life, it was "an outrage and a scandal" that there should be such social misery. Yet Harrington's book also contributed to isolating the poor as "the other America." Harrington argued that the real explanation of poverty lay in the fact that the poor made the mistake of "being born to the wrong parents, in the wrong section of the country, in the wrong industry, or in the wrong racial or ethnic group." And once the "mistake" has been made, they would never have a chance to get out of "the other America." "The poor" were caught in "a vicious circle," in other words, "a culture of poverty."[6] Here poverty was depicted as a "culture, institution, a way of life." As Barbara Cruikshank discusses, Harrington did more than anyone to identify the poor as a group and define their subjectivity.[7] According to Harrington, only the larger society, with its help and resources, could really make it possible for the poor to emerge out of "the other America."

In addition to the two books noted previously, an article by Dwight MacDonald that appeared in the January 1963 edition of the *New Yorker* contributed to the "rediscovery of poverty." The article, "Our Invisible Poor," reviewed the major literature on poverty issues, including Galbraith's and Harrington's books. As Harrington did, MacDonald identified the poor as a group by arguing that the poor were different "both physically and psychologically." He contended that the extent of poverty had "suddenly become visible" and that the federal government was the "only purposeful force" that could reduce the numbers of the poor and make their lives more bearable. Through MacDonald's article, as well as Galbraith's and Harrington's books, the phenomenon of "mass poverty in a prosperous country" received increased national attention.[8]

Along with the publication of a series of books and articles that contributed to the "rediscovery of poverty," community-based projects were launched by private foundations and government agencies. The "community approach" became central to the antipoverty efforts through two antecedent models. They were Gray Areas projects funded by the Ford Foundation and antipoverty initiatives sponsored by the President's Committee on Juvenile Delinquency and Youth Crime (PCJD). The Ford Foundation initiated the Community Development Program in New Haven, Oakland, Boston, Philadelphia, and the state of North Carolina from 1959 to 1963 under the leadership of Paul N. Ylvisaker, the head of the Ford Foundation's Public Affairs Program. The PCJD also had a significant impact on the later community action programs. Kennedy asked an old friend and campaign associate, David Hackett, to organize the PCJD in 1961. The PCJD awarded research grants to organizations such as Mobilization for Youth (MFY)—developed by Richard Cloward and Lloyd Ohlin of Columbia University's School of Social Work—for developing comprehensive plans of community organization to attack the causes of juvenile delinquency and youth crime. The PCJD increasingly became involved in antipoverty programs. Jule Sugarman, who served as chief of budget and management planning at the Department of State's Bureau of Inter-American Affairs from 1962 to 1964 and later became associate director of Head Start, noted that the original concern with the problem of juvenile delinquency broadened into a larger strategy because of the relationship between "juvenile delinquency and the much broader problem of poverty." In fact, Sugarman argued that many of the basic concepts of CAP did grow out of the PCJD.[9] The ground rules for the later community action programs would be created out of the Ford Foundation's Gray Areas projects and the PCJD programs.

Both the PCJD and the Ford Foundation were greatly influenced by Cloward and Ohlin, who published *Delinquency and Opportunity*, which laid the theoretical base for the "community organization approach." Cloward and Ohlin analyzed juvenile delinquency not as an individual problem but as *community* pathology. For them, the focus of remedial public policy had to be "the social setting" that gave rise to delinquency. Through their theoretical framework, "community" was destined to be the primary target of antipoverty programs.[10]

Theories of cultural deprivation became the backbone of a series of research projects on poverty and community-based programs and later became a theoretical foundation for the War on Poverty. Historian Alice O'Connor has shown how poverty came to be represented as a sign of cultural deprivation and pathology in the 1930s and 1940s. Theories of cultural deviance and social disorganization were first synthesized by Chicago sociologists such as Charles S. Johnson and E. Franklin Frazier and then later reformulated by scholars including sociologist Gunnar Myrdal, anthropologist Oscar Lewis, journalist Michael Harrington, and assistant secretary of labor Daniel P. Moynihan.[11] These analyses of poverty as a cultural pathology had several theses in common. First, poverty was supposedly perpetuated by family. Black poverty, in particular, was assumed to be caused and reinforced by a matriarchal family structure, which was interpreted as an accommodation to slavery and the joblessness of black males. Finding jobs for men would thus be the first step in alleviating poverty. Men could then take up their "proper" positions as the heads of patriarchal families. Second, once people found themselves in poverty, they would be caught up in a "vicious circle"—one that passed poverty on from generation to generation—and its psychological effects. In order to break this "vicious circle" of cultural deficiencies, the government was required to intervene and alter the psyches of the poor so that they could partake of the opportunities enjoyed by an affluent society. As poverty and juvenile delinquency were thus increasingly viewed as "community pathology," the government was assumed to have an obligation to initiate programs not only for individual families but also for communities as a whole. Theories of cultural deprivation therefore cast the poor as "deviants," different from "normal" mainstream America. Historians Michael B. Katz and Alice O'Connor have shown how these views focused on the internalized psyches of individual families and communities, drawing attention away from such structural barriers as the lack of job opportunities, the gendered division of labor, and racial segregation.[12]

The question of racial barriers was largely omitted in President Kennedy's PCJD. Black liberation struggles had an impact on the Kennedy administration, certainly since economic deprivation was a significant part of the overall discrimination African Americans and other people of color experienced. Charles L. Schultze noted that in addition to the rediscovery of pockets of poverty, there was "the recognition on the part of the civil rights people that legal remedies were not going to be enough." In order to understand why the Kennedy administration paid increased attention to issues of poverty, one needs to take a closer look at the Democratic Party of the 1960s. As Frances Fox Piven and Richard A. Cloward have demonstrated, 90 percent of all African Americans were concentrated in ten of the most populous northern states in 1960, and as a result black voting power in national elections grew steadily. At the same time, black liberation struggles resulted in the dissolution of the north-south Democratic coalition. By 1960, the disarray in the southern wing of the party had become visible, since in the three previous presidential elections, only three southern states had consistently given their electoral votes to the Democratic presidential candidate. While southern support declined, the political importance of the big cities in the North in presidential contests increased. In this way, Kennedy made a vigorous appeal to the African American vote in the North by pledging to deal with civil rights and poverty.[13]

Appealing to the African American vote did not necessarily mean, however, that the Kennedy administration tackled the issues of civil rights immediately. Kennedy signed an executive order barring discrimination in federally subsidized housing but did not do anything to implement it, nor did he send substantial civil rights legislation to Congress. In fact, as Piven, Cloward, and other scholars have pointed out, while the Democrats attempted to solidify the loyalty of African American voters, it was important for them that white voters not be alienated. Antipoverty programs initiated by the Democrats had to be ambiguous on the question of race. Democratic Party leaders thus muted the question of race rather than linking issues of racial inequality with the problem of poverty.[14]

The discussion within the Kennedy administration concerning what later became the War on Poverty began in the spring of 1963. Robert Lampman, who was a staff member on the Council of Economic Advisers (CEA) and "one of the distinguished experts in the field of income distribution," performed a significant role in bringing poverty to the attention of the administration at an early stage. On April 25, 1963, Lampman wrote a memorandum to Walter Heller, chairperson of the CEA, on changes in the distribution of wealth and income through 1961 to 1962. Lampman called the attention of Heller and others to the fact that past or pending administrative measures would do little to help "the poor." He also demonstrated that a decline in poverty had stopped after 1956. They were influenced by the so-called human capital theory, which stressed the significance of individual investments for improving productivity and creating economic growth. For Lampman and Heller, attacking poverty was part of their strategy for developing economic wealth. The memorandum sent to President Kennedy on May 1 started a wide discussion about antipoverty programs.[15]

The discussions were soon divided on the very point of the definition of poverty. The discussions, led by Lampman, first took place during informal Saturday "brown bag" lunches. These meetings included members from various agencies and departments, such as the CEA; the Labor Department; the Department of Health, Education, and Welfare (HEW); the Housing and Home Finance Agency; and the Bureau of the Budget. According to Lampman, these agencies had very different approaches to the question of poverty. Some people said poverty obviously meant a "lack of money income." Yet for others, it was "a participation-in-government concept," it was "a lack of some kind of self-esteem," or it really had to do with race or a "lack of opportunity" in general. Yet all immediately recognized that poverty was not *a* problem. These varied definitions were intertwined with one another in some way.[16] As William M. Capron, then a staff member with the CEA and later the assistant director of the Bureau of the Budget, recalled, poverty was "a whole constellation of problems with very different sources."[17] Yet the ambiguous definition of poverty had lingering effects on the creation of what later became community action programs, since as Lampman pointed out, "difference in concept was also later on reflected in the kinds of remedies that people would come up with."[18]

There was another division among the administration's advisers with regard to the political appeal of antipoverty programs. Several believed that fighting poverty would lack political appeal and hence should be delayed until after the 1964 election campaign. Kennedy's close political advisers pointed out that "the poor don't vote"—and that probably many of those who did voted Democratic anyway. Kennedy refrained from committing himself to such a program until his last meeting with Heller, on November 19, 1963, because of this "advice."[19] On November 5, Heller circulated a memorandum titled "Widening Participation in Prosperity" to the heads of the major departments and agencies involved in administering antipoverty programs. This November 5 memorandum marked a major turning point, since it shifted responsibility from the CEA to the Bureau of the Budget and led to the first consideration of "community action."[20]

At this early stage, "community action" meant bringing various antipoverty programs together for the sake of greater efficiency. The Community Action Program was originally created under the leadership of the Bureau of the Budget as a new administrative device to coordinate diverse existing and proposed federal programs under one umbrella, which later became the War on Poverty. In a memorandum dated December 28, the most important new ingredient of the proposed program to attack poverty, "the development of a coordinated 'community action plan,'" was announced. Through this plan, the resources of existing public and private organizations could be committed in a "coordinated long range effort to improve educational, training, health, and other services for the poor." These community action programs were to be concentrated in certain "target areas" and controlled by local governments.[21] Capron recalled that part of the problem was that existing antipoverty programs were terribly "unintegrated." They were "little bits and pieces that didn't really hang together." Capron said, "What we'd struggled for through November of 1963 was an organizing theme . . . it was the Community Action Program, which we viewed as a device to focus many different federal local programs to match the needs in particular localities."[22] William Cannon, the assistant chief of the Legislative Reference Division, the Bureau of the Budget, also noted that the Community Action Program was originally created "to put a legislative package together and try to figure out a way to unify, politically and intellectually, things that were very different—and organizing it around a political appeal that I thought would be very effective and would sell on the Hill, which was localism." In other words, in this early period, the Community Action Program had less to do with organizing the poor than coordinating diverse federal programs for greater "efficiency."[23]

On November 19, Kennedy gave Heller a yes to the question whether antipoverty programs would be in the 1964 legislative agenda. According to Heller, he said, "Yes, Walter, I am definitely going to have something in the line of an attack on poverty in my program. I don't know what yet. But yes, keep your boys at work, and come back to me in a couple of weeks." It was a few days before his tragic death.[24]

Kennedy's death did not arrest the development of the antipoverty program. The new president's response was "favorable and immediate." President Lyndon B. Johnson told Heller, "That's my kind of program . . . I'll find money for it one way or another."[25] As many scholars have argued, the new president had a significant impact on the design of the Community Action Program. Johnson wanted to make the program as visible as possible. He had endured the "pro-longed post-assassination worship of Kennedy" and needed to establish an identity. The antipoverty efforts were perfect for someone like Johnson, who was "a Roosevelt type of liberal."[26]

While Johnson wanted the program to be large, he also wanted it to be frugal. In contrast to Johnson's promises of an "unconditional war," the outlay suggested by the Bureau of the Budget was only $500 million. One solution was that single-purpose programs, then pending before Congress, could be included in the newly created antipoverty programs. According to Richard Blumenthal, this "legerdemain" would not only increase the apparent size of the program at no extra cost but also broaden its appeal (for funds from other new legislation and existing programs, see Table 1.1).

Johnson also transformed the Community Action Program from pilot projects concentrated in a few targeted areas to major new programs that spread throughout the country. Capron later noted that "we were not talking about a massive War on Poverty that fall at all . . . that was

Table 1.1. Estimated Funds in 1965 Budget for Use in the U.S. Poverty Program

EXPENDITURES (IN MILLIONS OF DOLLARS)	
Antipoverty bill	250
Funds from other new legislation	98
Funds from existing programs	238
Total	586

Source: Memo, Kermit Gordon to Lyndon B. Johnson, January 22, 1964, Executive File, WE 9, Box 25, Lyndon B. Johnson Library.

very much the Johnsonian impact." Johnson emphasized that poverty was a "national problem—a problem which need[ed] to be attacked and conquered in every private home, in every public office, in every local community throughout the Nation." As a result, the Community Action Program became a set of huge nationwide programs that even included single-purpose programs.[27]

Furthermore, departmental infighting had an enduring effect on the concept of the program. One question arose over the components of the Community Action Program. Sar A. Levitan explains that once the decision to ask Congress for an appropriation of $500 million was reached by January 4, 1964, departments and agencies intensified their lobbying for the maximum feasible share of the program.[28] A more significant issue was over the administrative structure of the new program. Capron later recalled that the big debate that went on through that fall was "whether or not you did some restructuring of programs and agencies, within particularly Labor and HEW [U.S. Department of Health, Education, and Welfare], or whether you needed something bureaucratically separate from those." Heller leaned toward the second in order to give a public "visibility and distinctiveness" to CAP as well as to be clearly identifiable as the "Johnson Attack on Poverty."[29]

All these controversies, along with the transformation of the meaning of CAP under President Johnson, made the contents of CAP increasingly unclear. Kermit Gordon, then the director of the Bureau of the Budget, and Heller wrote the "Outline of a Proposed Poverty Program" and circulated it through the secretaries of the departments involved in the antipoverty programs in January 1964. In it, they just mentioned that the central purpose of the new poverty program was to "launch an intensive and coordinated attack upon basic causes of poverty in specific local areas, urban and rural."

The basic concept would be a "locally-initiated, comprehensive community action program." The specific programs that would be operated through CAP were left unexamined.[30]

Ironically enough, this ambiguous design of CAP was exactly what some members of the original task force wanted. Frederick O'R. Hayes, then an assistant commissioner in the Urban Renewal Administration and later the assistant director of CAP, noted that "the definition of Community Action was purposely not spelled out" so that it would remain flexible.[31] Hayes certainly wanted to leave CAP open-ended in order to maximize local initiatives once the programs began operating. This unclear nature of CAP helped to conceal divisions among departments involved in the antipoverty programs as well as the distance between Johnson's promises of an "unconditional war" and the minimal budget available. As I will discuss in detail, the ambiguous character of CAP also masked the connection between welfare and warfare, as well as inconsistencies in the drafters' treatment of the extent to which the poor and people of color were to be incorporated into the state.

Since the contents of CAP remained vague, it would be vital to have "a strong federal agency" that could set a clear policy. Sundquist noted that the CEA had reached the conclusion independently that "we needed someone with stature and political appeal to handle the salesmanship of this program to the Congress."[32] On February 1, 1964, Johnson announced that he was appointing R. Sargent Shriver, President Kennedy's brother-in-law and the organizer and first director of the Peace Corps, to resolve the controversies and plan the War on Poverty.[33]

The appointment of Shriver had a significant impact on the nature of the Community Action Program. First of all, in spite of opposition from the Bureau of the Budget, Shriver succeeded in establishing the War on Poverty agency in the Executive Office.[34] Furthermore, Shriver contended that community action was not enough. Adam Yarmolinsky, special assistant to the Secretary of Defense, later recalled that Shriver's immediate reaction was that "this just wouldn't fly," since they wouldn't get results "soon enough, clear enough, to be able to carry it forward in the successive years and get appropriations the second year."[35] Cannon agreed with Yarmolinsky that Shriver wanted something "glamorous, easily understood, apparent in its workings, and which you could succeed at."[36] The concept of community action was "much too complex and diffuse." Shriver searched for additional suggestions from departments and agencies, state and local governments, and business and private organizations. As a result, five more titles were added to the draft, including youth employment programs such as the Job Corps, the Neighborhood Youth Corps, and Volunteers for America (subsequently changed to Volunteers in Service to America, or VISTA). CAP, which was originally meant to be the only program in the War on Poverty, was squeezed into Title II of the draft of the Economic Opportunity Act.[37]

On February 4, the Shriver task force began drafting the Economic Opportunity Act. The writers left the provisions as flexible as possible. John Steadman, who helped author the Economic Opportunity Act, recalled that he was told by Shriver to "make the language as general as possible." Steadman wrote them in "extraordinarily general language," with the preamble to say, "We're going to do all kinds of good things."[38] James L. Sundquist also noted that the bill was "deliberately drafted to grant the broadest possible discretion to the administrator." As the original design of CAP was left vague, so were the contents of the Economic Opportunity Act.[39]

The task force members also neglected to discuss the provision that caused the most controversy—the "maximum feasible participation" clause. One of the three criteria in Section 202 (a)(3) stated that the program must be "developed, conducted, and administered with the maximum feasible participation of residents of the areas and members of the groups served." While Cannon and Schlei argued that these phrases came from the pen of Harold Horowitz, there was no consensus regarding the origin of the phrase.[40]

Although the provenance of these words was not clear, it was evident that the member most responsible for the inclusion of the "maximum feasible participation" provision was Richard Boone of the PCJD. Boone noted that CAP was "an attempt to move administrative authority closer to people directly affected by federal legislation." According to Boone, concern over neglect of the poor by public and private programs, their oppression by political design, and the "insensitivity of service systems" were some of the reasons for the creation of CAP.[41] Frank Mankiewicz, then the director of the Peace Corps in Peru and a member of the Shriver task force, shared Boone's opinion. Mankiewicz later noted that one of the things of which they were conscious when they were drafting the legislation was "to keep it *out* of city hall," since municipal governments were "in large part responsible for the problem." Mankiewicz saw an analogy between the poor in the United States and "underdeveloped society" in Latin America where he was assigned as a Peace Corps director and where, he believed, decision making hardly came from the bottom up.[42] Through his involvement in the Peace Corps, Mankiewicz came to realize that the poor understood their own priorities and that programs targeted at them would not be successful without following their ideas and suggestions. He understood that the poor themselves, not the outside agency, should make decisions regarding their own matters, and that was the goal of "maximum feasible participation." Mankiewicz argued that this concept of CAP as an "essentially revolutionary activity" was "pretty clearly understood by us."[43] In other words, for some drafters such as Boone and Mankiewicz, the chief goal of CAP was to encourage the participation of the poor so that they could challenge and reform the established public/private welfare institutions.

Whereas some members interpreted CAP as a revolutionary activity, there were many drafters who later argued that they did not envision the extent to which CAP would be under the control of "the poor." Frederick O'R. Hayes, one of the chief authors of the bill, argued that the "maximum feasible participation" requirement was not seen, at that point, as potentially controversial. Hayes noted that "we were not talking about any radical shift of authority to the poor." For him, the clause simply meant improving what business would call "'customer relations' by doing a better job of listening to, responding to, and communicating with their clients." Hayes contended that the task force members were inclined to regard the participation of the poor as a "more symbolic than substantive form." This view was shared among other task force members.[44] Schlei, who drafted Title II with Horowitz, argued that he did not envision the extent to which these programs would wind up being under the control of "the poor." For him, the key idea of CAP was to coordinate diverse antipoverty programs, not putting "the whole thing under the control of poor people."[45] Yarmolinsky also contended that "it never occurred to us that local government would get into a big fight with the community." His conception of what the maximum feasible participation meant was that "you involved poor people in the process, not that you put them in charge."[46] Even President Johnson did not clearly understand the meaning of this clause. Through the analysis of telephone conversations recorded during the Johnson presidency, Guian A. McKee explains that the president "never embraced a grassroots version of community action."[47] President Johnson and the task force members were clearly divided on the matter of the participation of the poor in CAP.

There was also no consensus on the impact of black liberation struggles among the War on Poverty task force members. On the one hand, Richard Boone, for example, argued that all those working in Washington were "keenly aware of the civil rights struggle and growing demands by blacks and their allies for first-class citizenship." According to Boone, those responsible for the inclusion of the "maximum feasible participation" in the act were "deeply influenced by the movement."[48] Yet on the other hand, members like William B. Cannon emphasized that CAP and the War on Poverty in general were "not black-designed, minority-designed programs. . . . They weren't designed to deal with that problem specifically."[49] Policy makers were divided and opposed to each other regarding the question of race.

Although there was no agreement on that matter, both sides shared one trait: they did not discuss the relationship between poverty and racism. Task force members avoided explicit mention of racial discrimination as a cause of poverty. By so doing, they redefined racial inequality simply as an economic problem.[50]

The antipoverty bill was introduced in Congress on March 16, 1964. The proposed Economic Opportunity Act of 1964 consisted of six titles (Table 1.2). The task force members were firmly confident of the bill's passage from the start.[51] In fact, the proposed act was enacted within five months and signed into law on August 20. President Johnson proclaimed, "Today for the first time in all the history of the human race, a great nation is able to make and is willing to make a commitment to eradicate poverty among its people."[52] There were some significant amendments to CAP, such as the agreement to allow funds for parochial schools and the elimination of comprehensive plans. The Republicans attempted to splinter the proposed act by denouncing it as a "throwback to the 1930s," calling Shriver an authoritarian "poverty czar." Peter H. B. Frelinghuysen of New Jersey drafted a substitute, which was a state-run program costing half of the estimated amount, yet it attracted little support. Shriver knew that the antipoverty bill contained "a number of errors which [had to] be corrected by amendment." Far from being disempowered, Shriver showed "extraordinary achievement, skill, imagination, and energy" in talking down the opponents. Both houses of Congress approved the act by wide margins: the Senate in July, 61 to 34, and the House of Representatives in August, 226 to 185.[53]

Table 1.2. OEO Requests and Congressional Authorization, Fiscal 1965

PROGRAMS BY TITLE		ADMINISTRATION REQUEST (IN MILLIONS)	CONGRESSIONAL AUTHORIZATION (IN MILLIONS)
Title I	Youth Opportunity Programs	412.5	412.5
	A Job Corps (OEO)	190.0	190.0
	B Work-Training Program (Dept. of Labor)	150.0	150.0
	C Work-Study Program (HEW)	72.5	72.5
Title II	Community Action Program (CAP) (OEO, local communities)	315.0	340.0
Title III	Rural Economic Opportunity Programs (Dept. of Agriculture)	50.0	35.0
Title IV	Employment and Investment Incentives (Small Business Administration)	25.0	*
Title V	Family Unity Through Jobs (HEW)	150.0	150.0
Title VI	Volunteers in Service to America (VISTA) (OEO)	10.0	10.0
Total		962.5	947.5

*No special funds were authorized.

Source: Office of the White House Press Secretary, "The White House, Economic Opportunity Act of 1964: A Summary," March 16, 1964, Subject File, FG11–15, Box124, Lyndon B. Johnson Library; "A Summary of the Economic Opportunity Act of 1964," August 26, 1964, Executive File, WE 9, Box 25, Lyndon B. Johnson Library; Sar A. Levitan, *The Great Society's Poor Law: A New Approach to Poverty* (Baltimore: Johns Hopkins University Press, 1969), 46.

Yet one significant issue was never resolved on the Hill: the objectives of the Community Action Program. Many task force members later recalled that the "maximum feasible participation" clause was ignored entirely. Donald M. Baker, then the counsel to the Senate Select Subcommittee on Poverty, later thought if the members had read community action and understood what it meant, it would never have gotten through. Sundquist also wrote that one could search the hearings and debates in their entirety and find "no reference to the controversial language regarding the participation of the poor in CAP."[54] Not only the Shriver task force but also Congress never clarified the meaning of the participation of the poor in CAP.

One of the most significant clauses was neglected because many did not envision that CAP would leave their control. According to C. Robert Perrin, who later became acting deputy director of the OEO, the bill was generally straightforward except for the part on community action, which he didn't think "anyone really fully understood then" other than some ideas that were "floating around." The participation of the poor never became the subject of much discussion during the legislative process. Perrin explained that it was because "every time you use the word 'feasible,' you have the option of going as far as you want to or stopping as short as you want to. . . . 'feasible' would control how far you had to go." Put differently, task force members left the definitions of CAP vague so that they could bring the programs under control whenever necessary.[55]

Between Inclusion and Exclusion: Race, Gender, and Citizenship

Welfare and Warfare

The ambiguous character of CAP also had the effect of obscuring linkages between the War on Poverty and the war against Communism. Both the welfare state and the warfare state expanded under the slogan of "guns and butter," considering these elements as two sides of the same coin. David Zarefsky has discussed how the military imagery penetrated public discourse and the war metaphor sustained national interest and participation for the War on Poverty. It was certainly the case that President Johnson repeatedly deployed the war metaphor both in the framing of the War on Poverty and in his speeches.[56] Yet the link between the War on Poverty and the military was not just at the metaphorical level. Some members of the Johnson administration intended to employ CAP in order to educate the poor who were unqualified for military service.

In January 1964, the Task Force on Manpower Conservation, originally appointed by President Kennedy in September 1963, released a controversial report demonstrating that one-third of the youth who reached draft age would be found unqualified on the basis of the standards set up for military service. When the Department of Defense carefully studied records between August 1958 and June 1960, it found that the actual "overall" rejection rate was 31.7 percent. In May 1963, however, the department modified the mental aptitude test criteria and estimated that the rejection rate had increased to about 35 or 36 percent. Of these, about one-half were rejected for medical reasons. The remainder failed through the inability to qualify on the mental and medical tests. The mental test included questions on word knowledge, arithmetic, mechanical understanding, and the ability to distinguish forms and patterns. All men who scored below the "10th percentile" on this test—roughly corresponding to a fifth-grade level of educational attainment—were disqualified for military service. The report concluded that the majority appeared to be "victims of inadequate education and insufficient health services." Especially regarding the persons who failed the mental test, a major proportion of these young men were the "products of poverty." W. Willard Wirtz, the chairperson of the task force and the secretary of labor, wrote to the president saying that "this level of failure stands as a symbol of the unfinished business of the Nation." President Johnson expressed "utmost concern," quickly making a statement that he would present to the Congress a program designed to attack the roots of poverty so that "no young person, whatever the circumstances, shall reach the age of twenty-one without the health, education, skills that will give him an opportunity to be an effective citizen and a self-supporting individual." The War on Poverty would be a perfect means to educate the poor and mobilize them for the war effort.[57]

There was one public official who was particularly interested in making use of the War on Poverty in order to decrease the military rejection rates among poor youth: Daniel Patrick Moynihan. Robert Lampman noted that Moynihan was interested in using "the Department of Defense to some extent . . . as a kind of recovery device for kids who were really ineligible for the draft." He had done research on "the percentage of rejectees who were in some sense from very disadvantaged backgrounds."[58] William Canon understood that Moynihan envisioned making more youths eligible for the draft in order to "shape them up into citizenship so that they could carry on the roles of a citizen"—in other words, "rejuvenate them physically, mentally."[59] According to Lampman, this idea of using the antipoverty programs to increase the draftable among the poor in fact "attracted a lot of people" in the initial task force. Moynihan continued to argue that the administration should utilize the War on Poverty to expand the number of the poor—especially the African American poor—who could qualify for service. Moynihan wrote to Harry McPherson as follows: "It seems clear what we should do. First say nothing. Second, quietly adjust the Armed Forces Qualifications Test in order to compensate for the general difficulty of Negroes (and Southerners generally) to handle such questions . . . Third, start a hard, steady Manpower Development and Training Program and Job Corps program to qualify men for the Armed Forces." The warfare state and the welfare state were clearly linked in the minds of President Johnson and some task force members such as Moynihan.[60]

In addition, the administration engaged in a continuous effort to project the Great Society to an international audience as part of its anti-Communist agenda. Historian Mary L. Dudziak has shown how race matters became a matter of international concern in postwar America. She argues that the federal government attempted to tell a "particular story . . . a story of U.S. moral superiority" regarding civil rights during the 1960s. The Great Society could also make an impact on Cold War affairs. A memorandum with the title "Why Should Conservatives Support the War on Poverty?," for instance, stated that one of the reasons was "because it is *American*" (emphasis added). It contended that the War on Poverty would preserve "our basic national principles of equal opportunity, local initiative, voluntary service, federal-state-local cooperation, and of public and private cooperation." Therefore, it was "one of our most effective tools in the war against Communism." The memorandum emphasized that "our international stature will be immeasurable enhanced if we succeed in becoming the first great nation to enter the anti-poverty race." The War on Poverty was part of America's Cold War strategy to make capitalism look superior. The U.S. Information Agency also suggested that the administration make the Great Society "meaningful to foreign audience groups" because an understanding of the Great Society was "fundamental to an understanding of the U.S. of today and of the future." The Great Society, including the War on Poverty, would be an effective propaganda tool because it could convince the foreign audience that "a nation so committed to the Great Society could not strive less energetically for peace or refrain more steadfastly from aggression or aspirations for territorial gain or political domination." The U.S. Information Agency, however, gave the following caution to the administration: "Never suggest that the United States promises to bring the fruits of the Great Society to all people, everywhere, lest the Great Society be interpreted as some sort of vast foreign aid project." "Use extreme care in projecting 'the American standard of living' as requiring improvement, for that standard is considered beyond the hopes and expectations of numerous peoples especially in the developing countries." With caution in mind, the federal government was advised to publicize the Great Society as a proof of America's commitment to equality and justice. Once again, a linkage between welfare and warfare was forged.[61]

Finally, there was an idea of making use of the War on Poverty not only to mobilize the poor into warfare but also to send Vietnam veterans, especially black officers, to the Community Action Agencies in urban ghettos. While the military's share of the national budget was on the rise from 43.2 percent in 1966 to 45.99 percent in 1968, the percentage devoted to Social Security decreased from 15.38 percent to 13.39 percent.[62] While the Vietnam War expanded and consumed more and more of the nation's resources, urban uprisings flared throughout the major cities, bringing on a severe backlash against the antipoverty programs. In these situations, a confidential report titled *Political Stability, National Goals and [the] Negro Veteran*, prepared by the National Strategy Information Center, suggested that the administration make plans to retrain and employ as many as one thousand selected African American Vietnam veterans in diversified Community Action Programs at the grass roots level. It listed five objectives: (1) to open the doors of civilian opportunity for those "who have served their country so well in Vietnam"; (2) to seed into metropolitan slum areas mature "father figures" and symbols of authority; (3) to "generate (informally) a new source of Civic Initiative whose natural leaders, as they identify themselves in constructive service, will not be inclined to link the cause of civil rights in America with the Communist doctrine of 'anti-imperialist wars of national liberation'"; (4) to dispel the widespread myth that military service and patriotism were incompatible with humanitarian ideals and concern for the poor; and (5) to prevent the "Maoists from driving more wedges between whites and Negroes and harnessing unemployed Negro servicemen to sinister causes." It emphasized that it was imperative for the Johnson administration to "break the link" between the War on Poverty and "defense against Communist aggression" since Communists and their allies were seeking to forge a connection. The War on Poverty was linked up with actual warfare, not only because it would decrease the number of poor unqualified for military service and reconstitute them as productive citizens for the sake of the war against Communism, but also because it could provide services for discharged veterans seeking reentry into civilian life. These discharged veterans were then supposed to infuse the urban ghettos with patriotism.[63] This idea of mobilizing African American veterans into ghettos was not put to practical use. It shows, however, how the Johnson administration perceived the black ghettos where uprisings flared, how transnational anti-imperialist networks could be forged as a threat to the normative order, and how government officials tried to co-opt radical youth through the War on Poverty. Also, seeing as the Moynihan report (titled *The Negro Family: The Case for National Action*) represented the matriarchal black family as the "fundamental problem" causing poverty and "restoring the Negro American Family" as the solution to the "tangle of pathology," it is no surprise that its authors emphasized the significance of establishing a "normal" and stable family structure by sending "father-figures" back to the ghettos.[64]

The War on Poverty was entangled with the war on Communism in several ways. It was regarded as an apparatus to decrease military rejection rates among the poor youth. It was utilized as propaganda for U.S. moral supremacy. There was even an idea of mobilizing discharged veterans in the urban ghettos to sever linkages between black liberation struggles and anti-imperialist movements. Whereas the extant literature on the War on Poverty seldom discusses how the anti-Communist agenda was embedded in the architecture of the antipoverty programs, it is imperative to understand how the Johnson administration intended to transform the poor into self-sufficient and productive citizens through the War on Poverty. In this sense, the welfare state and the warfare state were inherently linked.

Incorporating Women as Volunteers

Neither the staff members on the Council of Economic Advisers nor the Shriver task force discussed gender as dimension of poverty. They muted the question not only of race but also of gender. The "feminization of poverty," however, was already taking place in the 1960s and the early 1970s. According to Diane Pearce, the "feminization of poverty" was under way even though other trends, such as the increase in women's labor force participation, the mandating of affirmative action, and the increasing employment of better educated women, would suggest the potential for improving women's economic status. In 1976, nearly two out of three of the fifteen million poor persons over sixteen were women.[65] Yet policy makers failed to understand this trend, and as a result, gender was not considered as a significant analytical framework.

While policy makers passed over the issue of gender in silence during their discussions regarding poverty, the OEO attempted to incorporate women (mainly white middle-class women) into the War on Poverty through various techniques once the programs began. When feminist theorists such as Jill Quadagno and Catherine Fobes analyzed how the welfare state influenced gender relations, they explained that there were three ways of reproducing male dominance. Welfare policies could reinforce gender inequality by recreating market inequality through eligibility rules that closely connected benefits to wages. They might also reproduce inequality by providing greater rewards for benefits earned through paid work than for those granted on the basis of family membership. Finally, they could recreate the subordination of women by failing to intervene—by excluding women from welfare programs because women were less competitive in the labor market if they could not find child care or take paid leave when they had children. Quadagno and Fobes emphasized that the welfare state reinforced the gendered division of labor in the household as well as in the market through these mechanisms.[66]

The OEO's strategy for defining women's roles in the War on Poverty was based not on the exclusion of women but rather on their mobilization. Techniques of "mobilization," as well as those of "exclusion," played an important role in recreating the subordination of women. The OEO held conferences in Washington, DC, in May 1967 and 1968 in order to clarify the roles of women in the antipoverty programs. At the 1967 conference, Sargent Shriver, the director of the OEO, emphasized how indispensable women were to that "war." Shriver pointed out that fifty thousand women served on local community boards and advisory councils in the War on Poverty and that more than ten thousand women volunteers from all religious and racial groups had joined an organization called Women in Community Service. But he quickly added that, despite this record of participation and involvement by women, the OEO had only begun to "scratch the surface." Put differently, with Head Start, the OEO was reaching only 30 percent of the poor children who needed that program; with the Neighborhood Youth Corps and Job Corps combined, only 32 percent of the teenagers who needed job training were covered by the War on Poverty. Therefore, Shriver contended that women's involvement in the antipoverty programs was absolutely necessary. He noted that "these statistics show you how large the need actually is and from that you can easily see why we have called you to Washington." Bill Crook, the director of VISTA, also emphasized the important roles of women in the War on Poverty. At the conference, Crook noted, "I believe that the feminine influence upon the national character of this country has been a dominant factor in the conception of the War on Poverty and it should be, I think, a driving force behind its application." Both Shriver and Crook repeatedly referred to the importance of women's roles in the War on Poverty.[67]

The OEO aimed at mobilizing women into the antipoverty efforts through these conferences because the OEO needed strong support from women in order to pass the War on Poverty legislation. In a memo to President Johnson in 1967, Shriver clearly noted that one of the purposes of this daylong conference was "mobilizing the various women's organizations for legislative backing." At the conference, Theodore Berry, the director of the Community Action Program, called on women to "tell your congressman back home that you are interested . . . and you support OEO."[68] These conferences were designed by the OEO to organize women for the antipoverty programs.

In 1969, the OEO published a report titled *Women in the War on Poverty*. In this report too, the OEO emphasized that American women had long been active in efforts to help the poor, as individuals and through various organizations. The report declared that many kinds of antipoverty programs, such as CAP, Head Start, and the Job Corps, offered the chance for women to use "their ingenuity and creative talents, to reinspire and reshape lives, and to participate in an urgent challenge to wipe out poverty."[69]

There are two significant themes in this report. First, the report stressed that women of all ages and from all walks of life volunteered for the antipoverty programs. It did not specify the differences among "women" in the antipoverty efforts. At the conference, too, OEO officials had emphasized that women of all kinds were vigorously involved in the War on Poverty. Yet some women who participated in the conference objected to this notion of women as a coherent group. For example, Frances Flores, a delegate from the League of Mexican-American Women, suggested that most of the women who were at the conference were members of established organizations dominated by white females. She pointed out that Mexican American women were not part of some of the established general groups and that, consequently, they usually did not receive the opportunity to attend the War on Poverty conferences. Dorothy Height, a delegate from the National Council of Negro Women, also stressed the particular conditions for women of color, mostly African American women. She suggested that for the African American woman, poverty was "a condition that has plagued her all her life." Height added that although she spoke primarily of African American women, what she said had bearing for "all women of minority groups." While the OEO looked at women as a coherent group disregarding racial/class differences, these women on the floor questioned whether all women were suffering poverty problems on the same level and whether they were equally involved in antipoverty programs.[70]

Second, although the OEO endeavored to mobilize women in the War on Poverty, it tried to incorporate women not as paid workers but as volunteers. Sociologist Nancy A. Naples also suggested that the OEO continued to define women's roles in the War on Poverty in volunteer terms, stressing their important support roles, not their leadership roles. In the report, the OEO emphasized that more than twenty million women volunteers, either individually or as part of an organization, had participated in programs related to the War on Poverty. Of the more than five hundred thousand individuals who had volunteered for Head Start, for example, the majority had been women. Why did the OEO stress the roles of women as volunteers? Naples pointed out that by constructing the pathway to prevention of poverty through expanding employment opportunities for poor men, women's employment needs and their actual contributions needed to be ignored or marginalized.[71] As I have discussed, theories of cultural pathology, which became the philosophical backbone of the War on Poverty, interpreted "matriarchy" as a major factor in perpetuating poverty among the lower class. Securing jobs for males was thus viewed as the first step in the fight against poverty, as it would help reconstitute "proper" patriarchal families. In other words, it was important for the OEO to keep women as volunteers in order to secure the paid jobs for poor men.

In order to reinforce the role of women as volunteers, the OEO invented a "homemaker program" in which women were trained in homemaking skills. The goal of this program was to train about ten thousand local women as "sub-professional homemaker aides." These women would go to the homes of the "poorest of the poor" to instruct them in nutrition, sewing, home management, and the like.[72] The creation of the "homemaker program" shows that the OEO not only attempted to limit women's roles to domestic matters but also tried to reformulate women's subordination by assigning women the role of aides. The OEO thus designated women as dependents, not as main agents in the War on Poverty. By so doing, it assigned women to what Alice Kessler-Harris termed "a secondary citizenship."[73] Women involved in CAP, however, refused to passively accept these racialized/gendered visions. Once the programs began, some of the women, such as Opal C. Jones and Johnnie Tillmon, struggled against them and asserted their rights in the Community Action Program.

Contradictions, Backlash, and New Openings in CAP

The ambiguous aspects of CAP were the necessary outcomes of the contradictory attitudes policy makers had toward the poor and black liberation struggles. Sociologists Kenneth J. Neubeck and Noel A. Cazenave pointed out that a significant change occurred in the racialization of the poor in the mid-1960s. As for Aid to Families with Dependent Children (AFDC), Neubeck and Cazenave explained that both eligibility rules and benefits for AFDC recipients were liberalized in the late 1960s. In this way, "racial exclusion" from the rolls began to be increasingly replaced with "racial inclusion."[74] CAP and the War on Poverty were in the middle of a transition, and policy makers could not resolve several dilemmas. On the one hand, CAP was regarded as an apparatus to transform the poor into active, productive, and participatory citizens for the sake of the development of economic wealth and the war against Communism. Yet on the other hand, task force members were not sure of the extent to which the poor would control CAP. Some policy makers mentioned that they were clearly influenced by black liberation struggles, whereas others denied its impact and completely neglected to mention the relationship between racial inequality and poverty. Rather than being consistent on CAP, these policy makers were divided and constantly changing their views—on the extent to which the poor and people of color were to be incorporated into state programs.

Local welfare activists kept their eyes on precisely this ambiguous characteristic of CAP. As Quadagno has argued, the crucial linkages developed among the War on Poverty, black liberation struggles, the Chicano movement, and the women's movement once the antipoverty programs began. The appointment of Jack Conway as director of CAP strengthened these linkages between the antipoverty programs and social movements. Conway, a labor organizer in Detroit during the early days of the United Automobile Workers (UAW), used the phrase "maximum feasible participation" for more radical purposes. Later, Conway noted that he foresaw the degree of the conflict between CAP and local governments.[75] With support from Conway, local welfare activists created counterhegemonic movements against policy makers who were caught between inclusion and exclusion and could not articulate the significance of racism and sexism in the poverty issue. The CAP program guide, distributed in July 1964 and published in February 1965, suggested that the poor not only would participate in the antipoverty programs but also would challenge and revise some of the decisions made by the board. It stated that residents would be provided with "meaningful" opportunities, either as individuals or in groups, to "protest or propose additions to or changes" in the ways in which a Community Action Program was being planned or undertaken. In places such as Los Angeles, local welfare activists would not overlook the chances to express objections and recast antipoverty programs endorsed by the CAP program guide.[76]

It was precisely this aspect of CAP—fostering the political participation of the poor—that triggered tension between local public officials and the Community Action Agencies. Many mayors asserted that CAP was setting up a competing political organization in their own backyards with help from the OEO. The mayors believed that they were being bypassed in the implementation of antipoverty activities. Mayors' organizations, such as the United States Conference of Mayors, with its 600 affiliated cities and mayors, and the National League of Cities, with its 13,000 members, adopted resolutions urging the OEO to recognize agencies endorsed by city hall as the proper channel for the War on Poverty programs. As a result, the OEO took several actions to calm down the angered mayors. The administration appointed Vice President Hubert Humphrey as their liaison to local officials. The OEO created the Public Officials Advisory Council, where mayors, governors, county officials, and city managers would meet with OEO personnel to review the agency's guidelines, publications, pending amendments to the Economic Opportunity Act, and so on. The OEO also tightened up its administrative control over the Community Action Agencies by setting up "national emphasis programs." For example, appropriations for Head Start, one of the "national emphasis programs," increased from $180,000,000 (27.5 percent of the total funds for CAP) to $327,117,000 (40.6 percent) in 1967. Appropriations where the funds for major programs were deducted—open to utilization for each Community Action Agency—on the other hand, were decreased from $315,202,000 (48.2 percent) to $255,796, 000 (31.7 percent). All these changes in the management of CAP resulted in stripping the Community Action Agencies of their power to foster the political participation of the poor.[77]

It was not local public officials' opposition alone, however, that caused disfavor with CAP and that eventually limited its scope. The representation of CAP as a facilitator not only of the participation of the poor but also of the urban uprisings in major cities brought on a severe backlash against the program. As massive uprisings occurred in almost all the major cities—more than 329 instances in 257 cities between 1964 and 1968—the OEO tried to respond to the needs and grievances of residents in the ghettos, although their programs were severely underfunded and increasingly limited in scope. As political scientist James W. Button has suggested, the uprisings, after all, were directed not only at the local repressive officers and city halls but also at the federal government. And they were successful to a certain degree, at least in their early years. The OEO reacted to the uprisings, which were interpreted as cries of despair from the urban ghettos and requiring immediate response. The City of Los Angeles, for instance, received more than a sixfold increase in funds from the OEO in the year following the Watts uprising. As the escalation of the uprisings became a national security crisis in the 1960s, and as the OEO directed more and more attention to the needs of the residents in the areas, however, it was bombarded with criticisms from mayors, Southern Democrats, and Republicans. All these critics were concerned that the War on Poverty, especially CAP, was "rewarding violence."[78]

The OEO faced severe criticism as the uprisings intensified. The big-city mayors especially blamed CAP for its assumed role in fomenting the outbursts. Mayor Hugh J. Addonizio of Newark made a statement on August 22, 1967, that "the cities were flat on their backs and the OEO came along and instead of helping us, as Congress intended, it decided we were a bunch of bullies and it gave a club to the so-called powerless to help beat us as we lay on the ground." Some Republicans and Southern Democrats joined the mayors in attacking the War on Poverty. By quoting an article in a local newspaper in Greenville, South Carolina, Republican senator Strom Thurmond, for example, argued that the riots had been "tolerated" and even "encouraged" by persons in high places on the national level and in many state and local governments. The OEO also faced allegations that CAP workers helped to provoke the outburst throughout the United States.[79] Moynihan described the assumed connection between CAP and the uprisings as follows: "As Negro rioting grew endemic, the association between community action and violence also grew in the minds of the legislators . . . In no time at all, the antipoverty program was in trouble in Congress, and the focus of this trouble was community action and the provision for 'maximum feasible participation' of the poor." The more the OEO tried to fund the antipoverty programs in the curfew areas to alleviate the causes of the uprisings, the more it was bombarded with criticisms that it was supporting "rioters" and "disrespect for law and order."[80]

The OEO investigated 32 cities that experienced the uprisings in the summer of 1967 and found that only 16 out of 30,565 workers were arrested. It insisted that "not one mayor or police chief . . . accused antipoverty workers of stirring up trouble, or of encouraging violence." Instead, the office found that the antipoverty programs "helped reduce tensions and played an important role in preventing or minimizing racial disturbances." The OEO continuously published reports, such as *OEO and the Riots* and *Myths and Facts about OEO*, and made desperate efforts to prove the value of the antipoverty programs in alleviating urban tensions. In order to rebuff the attack against CAP and the War on Poverty, the OEO constantly made a statement that the poverty workers were "cooling off" the urban tensions instead of aggravating them and that the poverty program was still a very small effort in relationship to the needs of the cities.[81]

Nonetheless, the OEO took actions to set a limit to fostering the participation of the poor. As I have already discussed, under the pressure of mayors' organizations, it set up a Public Officials Advisory Council and established "national emphasis programs," reducing CAP's risk-taking nature. Having dim prospects for authorization and facing their dismantlement, the OEO made a behind-the-scenes effort to pass an amendment proposed by Democrat representative Edith Green for their survival. The so-called Green Amendment placed CAP under the control of a state or local government (as later modified, it provided that a public or private nonprofit agency could be designated by a state or political subdivision of a state). On the surface the OEO stood in opposition to the amendment, but in reality, it was eager to keep CAP within bounds to satisfy big-city mayors, who were concerned with CAP's assumed role in instigating the uprisings, and Southern Democrats, who feared the participation of African Americans in local politics through CAP. Bertrand Harding, who became deputy director of the OEO in May 1966 and acting director in March 1968, later recalled that the Green Amendment was a "conscious effort" on the part of the OEO to satisfy criticisms against the agency. Harding felt that unless "some sort of compromise" was put into the bill, the OEO would have come to a screeching halt. Thus as the criticism took its toll, CAP no longer worked as a vehicle for organizing the poor—it became a part of the regular local government structure. Ironically enough, big-city mayors, who staunchly opposed CAP at the earlier stage, now expressed "deep concern" with the cutbacks in CAP spending and demanded "adequate funding" of the antipoverty program.[82]

In the preceding argument, I have discussed the processes through which poverty was rediscovered and how theories of cultural pathology came to the forefront of policymaking in the early 1960s. I have analyzed how the Community Action Program, along with its famous doctrine of "maximum feasible participation," was invented by scholars and officials. The specific goals of CAP were left inherently vague. The ambiguous aspect of CAP concealed not only divisions among government departments and agencies involved in the antipoverty programs as well as the distance between Johnson's promises of an "unconditional war" and the minimal budget available but also the close connection between the welfare state and the warfare state. CAP was deployed in order to educate the poor unqualified for military service. CAP and the War on Poverty became part of America's Cold War strategies and proof of America's commitment to equality and justice. It could also provide jobs for discharged veterans seeking reentry into civilian life, who were assumed to infuse the urban ghettos with patriotism.

The sometimes confused workings of CAP masked the linkage between racial and gender inequality and poverty. The OEO emphasized the role played by women in the War on Poverty and endeavored to mobilize women's support for the antipoverty efforts. While the OEO stressed that women were indispensable to the antipoverty efforts, it located women as volunteers and dismissed racial and class differences among them.

I have also demonstrated that the concept of CAP was left ambiguous because there was no consensus among policy makers as to the extent to which the poor and people of color were to be part of the American welfare state. The original concept of CAP was suspended between inclusion and exclusion. CAP provoked a furious backlash from city hall precisely because it fostered the participation of the poor (especially the black poor) in local politics and carved out a social space for the activists to challenge and transgress the boundaries of citizenship. Also, CAP and the War on Poverty increasingly came under attack precisely because the participation of the poor posed a grave threat to city hall and the critics of the

OEO, as CAP was linked to the uprisings in the cities. As I will show in the next chapter, by opening up new terrain in which the poor and people of color could intervene, CAP in the United States would take a different trajectory from Japanese "community programs," which, in contrast with the American case, would become an apparatus to reinforce a racialized national identity.

Before assessing the legacy of the War on Poverty, one needs to see why CAP became so contested and controversial. Chapters 3 and 4 focus on Los Angeles and explore how the city of Angeles became an arena of struggle over the meaning of welfare and citizenship. They examine how local activists came to exploit openings in CAP and assert their welfare rights when the programs actually began.

2

Fostering Community and Nationhood

Japan's Model Community Program

I now introduce the case of Japan and analyze the ways in which the participatory schemes produced different results when transplanted to Japan. In response to the ascendancy of residents' movements and oppositional left-wing parties, the Liberal Democratic Party (LDP)-controlled national government created the Model Community Program (*Moderu komyunitī shisaku* or *keikaku*). The residents' movements that had been expanding since the mid-1960s and that had been dealing with various kinds of issues such as *kōgai* (environmental pollution), industrial development, prices, and welfare had a great impact on both national and local politics.[1] Indeed, during times of perceived national crises, the Ministry of Home Affairs and affiliated scholars reinvented the tactics of citizen participation, trying to foster "a sense of nationhood" in the masses through the Model Community Program.

Reinventing the Tactics of Citizen Participation

While the so-called rediscovery of poverty provided a foundation for the conceptualization of the Community Action Program in the United States, it was the rediscovery of "community disintegration" that became the pretext for the inception of MCP in Japan. The architects of MCP repeatedly emphasized that rapid urbanization had resulted in a profound deterioration of the living environment and the "disintegration of community," which caused numerous social problems in the nation's cities.[2]

It was certainly the case that the rapid expansion of the Japanese economy in the postwar period—especially in the 1960s—transformed people's everyday lives. Between 1955 and 1973, the real GNP expanded at an annual rate of 10 percent in Japan, increasing more rapidly than in any other industrial economy in the world. People rushed into major cities such as Tokyo, Yokohama, Osaka, Nagoya, Kyoto, and Kobe searching for new employment opportunities. Such dramatic urbanization processes caused several changes in family life. The average family size, which remained at a little under five persons from the 1920s down through the mid-1950s, dropped to 3.45 in 1975. The nuclear family now became widespread, due to the fall in birth rate after the initial postwar "baby boom" and the decline in the number of three-generation households.[3]

As Ochiai Emiko and Ueno Chizuko argued, the prevalence of the nuclear family did not weaken the concept of the family as a continuing corporate household (*ie*). They contended that the emergent nuclear family coexisted with the traditional notion of the hierarchical household.[4] Furthermore, the separation of workplace and living space, along with the limited employment opportunities outside the home and the lack of day-care facilities, confined women to the domestic sphere. In fact, the percentage of women who became housewives increased during the era of the "economic miracle." Women were assumed to sustain high-priced male labor, which in turn supported rapid economic growth.[5]

Changing family structures, however, heightened the sense of an emergent social crisis. According to the architects of MCP, the rapid changes in family life caused by urbanization made families more isolated and anonymous, resulting in a weakening sense of "community." The policy makers of MCP argued that in order to counteract the effects of urbanization, especially on families, the central government had to take initiative in rebuilding these disintegrating "communities."

Equally significant in the creation of MCP were the ways in which the surge of residents' movements (*jūmin undō*) had transformed the national political landscape. The reputed Big Four Pollution Diseases cases ignited fury among the public.[6] The conflict surrounding the "Minamata disease" (caused by mercury-filled effluents from a Nippon Chisso Corporation plant in Kumamoto Prefecture), along with the Sanrizuka struggle (where Narita farmers and their supporters fought against the government's decision to appropriate their land for the construction of an airport), became representative examples of the numerous "residents' movements" occurring around the nation. Popular discontent was manifested in residents' movements, where pollution victims, farmers, residents, and their allies used demonstrations, sit-ins, local election campaigns, and court struggles to pressure the government into taking remedial action. Countless people, many of whom had not led politically active lives before, joined these residents' movements as locals, consumers, and ordinary citizens, casting doubt on the ways capitalist corporations and the government prioritized industrial development and belittled local people's lives in the name of "public benefit" (*kōkyōsei*).[7]

The supporters of these residents' movements turned away from LDP candidates and helped send "progressive" (*kakushin*) left-wing governors into office in major prefectures like Tokyo, Osaka, and Kanagawa. While the LDP received 61.16 percent of the total vote in the 1958 general elections, only 48.91 percent of votes went to the party in 1976.[8] Minobe Ryokichi—a professor at the Tokyo University of Education and a son of the famous constitutionalist Minobe Tatsukichi—won the election for governor of Tokyo by a landslide, which exemplified this power shift from the LDP to the progressive governors and mayors.[9] As environmental pollution began catching public attention, left-wing governors and mayors who attacked the LDP for its "economism" policy and neglect of people's everyday lives were elected in the metropolitan areas, winning positions in more than 120 of the nation's 639 cities.

The newly elected governors and mayors like Minobe expanded welfare, medical, and education programs. For instance, they increased the number of day nurseries, utilizing the slogan "Create as many nurseries as mailboxes," and in addition provided free health care for the elderly. They organized an association in 1964, proposing that *kakushin* local governments "encircle" the central government controlled by the LDP. They urged the LDP to change its economy-centered policy, foster political participation of the residents, and pay more attention to their welfare needs in order for both capitalists *and* workers to reap the benefits from the "economic miracle." And even after the progressive governors and mayors took their offices, some advocates of the residents' movements continued to question the meaning of "public benefit," pressuring them to take active roles in resolving the cases.

As a result of the criticisms made by the residents' movements as well as by progressive governors and mayors, the LDP-controlled central government was forced to respond to them by advancing its welfare policy. The cabinet, headed by Tanaka Kakuei, made an announcement that they would establish the Ministry of the Environment and improve environmental policy, provide free health care for the elderly who were older than sixty-five years old, and set up aid for children. It called 1973 "the first year of welfare (*fukushi gannen*)," a watershed in the history of the Japanese welfare state. It came to assert the significance of "citizen participation" in the implementation of welfare policies.[10]

It was thus not only a "disintegration of community" but also a political shift brought about by urbanization and residents' movements that provoked policy makers to consider inventing a new MCP during the early 1970s.[11] "Community" programs would be an effective technology not only to meet the welfare needs of the residents but also to reunite societies divided by oppositional movements from below.

Similar to CAP in the United States, community programs became one of the major social welfare enterprises in Japan during the late 1960s and early 1970s. The creation of community programs in Japan had its origin in 1967, with official statements by the Tokyo metropolitan government and the Ministry of Home Affairs. The Social Welfare Council of the Tokyo metropolitan government released a document titled *On the Development of Community Care in Tokyo* in September 1969. It emphasized the significance of supporting "communities" as a whole in order to implement welfare programs geared toward children and elderly people rather than confining these groups to institutions such as kindergartens and homes for the elderly. It called for an "active participation of residents in local areas" to promote such "community care" programs.[12]

Inspired by the Tokyo metropolitan government's initiative, the National Life Council of the Ministry of Home Affairs published a famous document, *Community: The Recovery of Humanity in Everyday Life*. In January 1968 Prime Minister Sato Eisaku reorganized the National Life Council in order to secure "healthy Japanese people's lives." The chairperson of the council, Matsukuma Hideo, declared that "now was the time to recognize the necessity of building communities and making efforts to develop them." The National Life Council expanded the notion of "community" from a term that encompassed mainly children and the elderly to a much broader concept targeted toward all residents in designated areas.[13]

In the same fashion as CAP, the community approach became a primary mechanism. *Community: The Recovery of Humanity in Everyday Life* defined "community" as a group designed to meet the residents' various demands and creative impulses based on "residents' willingness and responsibility."[14] According to the document, there existed four obstacles to community action: (1) the residents' lack of interest in local activities, (2) the scarcity of community facilities, (3) the problems created by rapid urbanization, and (4) the "connection" between some neighborhood self-governing bodies and "particular political parties" (meaning the Japan Socialist Party and the Japan Communist Party). It emphasized that "the more a community broke down, the more people recognize[d] its necessity." In other words, community programs were crucial precisely because "communities" were crumbling in the late 1960s. "Community" was regarded as "the last place to recover humanity"—a space in which to solve a wide range of problems, including issues of environmental protection, juvenile delinquency, children's safety, the need for leisure, the issues of the elderly, and the status of women.[15]

It was not pure coincidence that similar types of community programs were brought into existence in Japan during the late 1960s and early 1970s. Leading scholars in political science, such as Omori Wataru and Nishio Masaru, conducted research on CAP at the time it was implemented in the United States.[16] Omori published a detailed account of CAP in 1974. According to Omori, CAP functioned less as a program of allocating welfare services and more as a function of transforming the traditional way of understanding poverty and challenging prejudice against the poor. The significance of CAP lay in the ways in which it problematized the system that had deprived the poor of their confidence, self-esteem, and identities; in the process, it shook the power base of political elites. CAP came under attack, and it was easy, argued Omori, to see why. CAP came to be regarded as a program targeting African Americans while failing to gain support from the white poor. CAP also experienced an internal dilemma of fighting against the (local) government with financial help from the (federal) government. The federal government maintained the power of allocating and withdrawing funds, as well as deciding how the funds were going to be used. Having less and less room available for each Community Action Agency, the representatives of the poor were disenchanted and frustrated with CAP. Omori demonstrated that regardless of its innovative policies, CAP was caught up in insoluble political contradictions and foundered in the end.[17]

Nishio's *Power and Participation* also made reference to CAP. According to Nishio, CAP exemplified programs aiming to foster the participation of residents and in the process produced complicated conflicts and rivalries. It "emerged from turmoil and enlarged turmoil," yet it also fostered the "development of the organizations and cultivated the leaders at the bottom of the black community." Through his examination of CAP and other programs aimed at fostering the participation of residents, Nishio tried to capture "what was unique to America," such as the impact of black liberation struggles on the concept of the participation, and "universal trends," that would be applicable to the Japanese case.[18]

Omori and Nishio published their articles with Sato Atsushi, a core member of the Community Study Group charged with designing the Model Community Program in Japan. Sato served as a chairperson of the Tokyo Model Community Program's Committee on Citizen Participation from 1973 to 1977. Nishio became a chairperson of the same committee in 1982.[19] Omori and Nishio introduced CAP and by doing so suggested to other political scientists the states' technologies for recreating "communities."

It was not only these political scientists who turned their attention to CAP. Okuda Michihiro, an urban sociologist and one of the members of the subcommittee on community problems in the National Life Council, referred directly to CAP's "maximum feasible participation" clause when fleshing out his ideas for the Model Community Program. He stressed that the goal of community policy in Japan boiled down to how the "participation of residents" could be realized. According to Okuda, there were three stages in the realization of participation of residents. The first stage was simply providing information concerning the role of the government in community programs; the second stage was allowing residents to commit themselves to the decision-making processes; the third and final stage was letting the residents not only make decisions but also administer and manage the programs. Okuda argued that "whereas in our country, the third stage was still at its planning stages, it was no longer at the experimental level in the U.S.—it was called 'maximum feasible participation,' and in the middle of being implemented in several cities."[20] For Okuda, CAP in the United States was therefore an excellent example to follow. In fact, as Majima Masahide argues, CAP was one of the models used for the conceptualization of the Japanese Model Community Program—it demonstrated how the federal government could seize the initiative in fostering the political participation of residents through community programs.[21]

In addition, Okuda contended that while CAP dealt with "African American issues that were specific to the U.S.," the expansion and institutionalization of residents' participation could be understood as a government's response to the "rise of citizens' power (including black power)."[22] Okuda's argument showed how the architects of the Japanese Model Community Program construed the issue of race as something relevant only to the American society and how they interpreted CAP's "maximum feasible participation" clause as a reasonable government response to the challenge posed by movements from below.

There was, however, a notable difference between CAP in the United States and the MCP in Japan regarding the technology of participation. Whereas in the United States fostering the participation of the residents was perceived as a "revolutionary" activity by some of the "radical" members of the War on Poverty task force, there was nothing revolutionary about it in the Japanese case. As Omori Wataru made clear in the interview, the MCP was so embedded in the power structure that it did not become a site of contestation.[23] While CAP generated a conflict, provoking controversy throughout the nation, the later-developed MCP would turn out to be a moderate community-building project. It is well worth examining why.

In April 1971, the Ministry of Home Affairs officially announced that it would launch the Model Community Program throughout the nation, and as a result, community centers were established in eighty-three local areas by 1973. The MCP turned out to be a program focusing on establishing a wide range of facilities and centers for the designated districts: (1) facilities that would secure traffic safety (such as pedestrian roads, bicycle tracks, and street lights) with side trees and flowers along the streets; (2) places that would conserve the environment in areas such as pastures, public restrooms, junkyards, facilities for crime/fire prevention, and evacuation areas; (3) cultural centers such as meeting places, citizens' public halls (*kōminkan*), libraries, centers for children (*jidōkan*), and training centers; (4) clinics and health centers; (5) social welfare facilities, such as child and elder daycare centers and nursing homes for the elderly; (5) recreational sites, such as parks, playgrounds for children, recreational grounds, gyms, pools, and recreational farms; and finally, (6) community centers that would be the epitome of the MCP. The local governments were charged with the tasks of conferring with their residents and creating these facilities. Each designated "model community" received an average amount of ¥100 million as municipal bonds in three years. By the spring of 1977, 410 facilities were established in the "model communities" throughout the nation (Table 2.1).[24]

In the same year that it launched the MCP, the Ministry of Home Affairs established the Community Study Group, its main task force. Seven scholars in various fields such as public administration, sociology,

Table 2.1. Types and Numbers of Facilities Created through the Model Community Program by Spring 1977

TYPES OF FACILITIES	NUMBER OF AREAS THAT ESTABLISHED THESE FACILITIES
Community centers and citizens' public halls	81
Centers for children	3
Centers for the elderly	9
Community streets	48
Facilities to enhance traffic safety	28
Street lights	23
Facilities for fire prevention	19
Lights for crime prevention	13
Public restrooms	8
Side trees and flowers for streets	12
Junkyards	5
Day-care centers and preschools	27
Parks and recreational ground (larger than 2,500 m^2)	58
Parks and playgrounds for children (smaller than 2,500 m^2)	47
Pools	12
Gyms	17

Source: Morimura Michiyoshi, *Komyunitī no keikaku gihō* (Tokyo: Shokokusha, 1978), 25.

urban engineering, and urban/rural planning joined the group. Together with public officials in the Ministry of Home Affairs, they did intensive research on the MCP and shaped the contours of the program.[25] Their discourses on "resident participation" and "community" offer crucial insights into the MCP.

Some architects of the MCP did not hide their intentions to use it as an apparatus to co-opt residents' movements. They rationalized the MCP by contending that residents' movements were too egoistic in nature. In the report *Community: The Recovery of Humanity in Everyday Life*, Shimizu Keihachiro stressed that the raison d'être of community was to build organizations in which residents would make demands not only for self-government but also for a relationship that would make clear both their "rights and obligations."[26] Sociologist Matsubara Haruo and political scientist Sato Atsushi, both members of the Community Study Group, agreed with Shimizu. Matsubara contended that community building should overcome the egoism demonstrated by residents' movements and advance cooperativeness. Sato explained as follows: "Through cooperation in the community, residents are expected to go into training in order to be responsible governmental subjects or agents. The isolation of residents, the rise of the egoistic nature of residents' demands, and their increased dependency on the government—egoism and regionalism like this prevailed among the local and national politics, turning residents into irresponsible beneficiaries easily influenced by others."[27] For these scholars, the creation of the community programs was an urgent matter because they would transform residents into subjects or agents willing to take responsibility rather than simply making "unreasonable" demands.

According to these architects, residents' movements became egoistic due to their isolation and alienation from society. The following statement by Miyazawa Hiroshi, at the time chief of the administrative office of the Ministry of Home Affairs, was a typical example of their interpretations: "Nowadays, there is a lack of communication, or mutual understanding, among people, as words like 'alienation,' 'rupture,' and 'loneliness' illustrate. Community should be the place where people recover their humanity and their sense of social solidarity."[28] One of the members of the Community Study Group, Kurasawa Susumu, knew that this justification of the MCP was under attack. According to the critics of the MCP, the lack of mutual understanding did not exist, the Home Ministry officials and the Community Study Group put too much emphasis on the emotional aspects of the community programs, and their programs would nurture artificial cooperation among residents.[29] The architects, however, explained the rise of the residents' movements as an indicator of the lack of community consciousness among the residents rather than of systemic problems posed by the policy of "economism" adopted by LDP government. Elevating community consciousness was the tactical response to the rise of the oppositional movements. According to Matsubara Haruo, the real intention of the MCP was to "channel residents' voluntary power" into the development of community. The MCP was a "strategy to let residents internalize a sense of community." He suggested that the groundwork for residents' movements was basically the same foundation on which the MCP could be built.[30]

Turning to "community consciousness" was not necessarily a new technology for the Ministry of Home Affairs. Historian Sheldon Garon examined the "century of the moral suasion behavior," demonstrating how government officials made "extraordinary efforts" to transform the Japanese into active participants in the state's projects.[31] According to Garon, they fostered "a sense of nation" in the masses and created a national orthodoxy with help from "popular" (*minkan*) ideologues during the prewar and postwar periods.[32] The MCP found itself echoed in other campaigns initiated by the Ministry of Home Affairs that also targeted the Japanese masses and sought to transform them into active, productive, and participatory subjects.

It is thus clear that the Model Community Program was developed to deal with the Japanese people's criticisms of increased social chaos brought about by the government's policies of high economic growth. In other words, these programs were created to solve such problems by promoting mutual understanding and cooperation among residents at the community level. The program performed the function of "dividing and restraining a sense of rights and autonomy among residents" so that consciousness among residents would remain at the local level without pressuring the national government.[33] Sato Atsushi has stressed that the local governments needed to keep the residents' movements "negotiable," "adopt" the criticisms raised by the residents, and "co-opt" their efforts. These policy makers and scholars regarded the Model Community Program as an apparatus designed to co-opt radical residents' movements and transform them into "negotiable" local organizations.[34]

As a new technology focused on internalizing a "sense of community" in the Japanese masses, the MCP became a model for numerous programs in the early 1970s. According to Matsubara, other ministries and agencies rushed to create and reinforce similar types of community programs.[35] The community approach emerged as the key concept of Japanese social welfare programs in the early 1970s.[36]

The technology of participation had different consequences when translated into the Japanese Model Community Program. Policy makers invented the MCP to respond to the criticisms made by the advocates of the residents' movements and to counteract progressive governors and mayors and their supporters. It became an effective tactic for fostering "a sense of nationhood" in times of perceived crises. While CAP generated a conflict that shook the nation, the MCP did not become an arena of contestation. It would turn out to be another community-building program initiated by the Ministry of Home Affairs.

Redrawing the Boundaries of Communities: Race, Gender, and Citizenship

Disconnection and Continuity with World War II

While there were some members who openly endorsed the idea of the MCP as a means to co-opt residents' movements, others were anxious about the criticisms made by opponents of the MCP. They made desperate attempts to assuage the critics, promising them that MCP would not become a type of program where the government simply exhorted the masses to do what it wanted them to do.[37] Kimura Hitoshi, at the time assistant section chief of the administrative office of the Ministry of Home Affairs, acknowledged that it would be dangerous to have a fixed idea about a model community and the way it should be created. He contended, however, that "our nation is far behind other countries in maintaining the local environment" and that it would be "extremely effective for the local government to present some idea of a community and develop facilities that would improve the local environment."[38] Sociologist Kurasawa Susumu agreed with Kimura. He argued that while the government "should not normally get involved in this," the MCP "required the government to stimulate the program and sprinkle water on what is already growing." Both stressed that what mattered most was that the residents make the decisions, not the government. The MCP conditioned residents to vigorously participate in the programs and act in their own interest.[39] These members took great pains to differentiate the MCP from the top-down militaristic program mounted by the Home Ministry in the prewar period. The "notorious" *chōnaikai/burakukai* (neighborhood and/or village associations) were still fresh in the memories of the critics of the MCP. Not surprisingly, the issue of neighborhood/village associations was a "taboo subject" in the Home Ministry.

The *chōnaikai/burakukai* became widespread during World War II. In 1940, the Ministry of Home Affairs officially became involved in organizing them, and in 1942 they were put under the control of the *Taisei yokusan kai* (Imperial Rule Assistance Association, which was created by the second Konoe Fumimaro cabinet in 1940). Occupying the lowest level of Imperial Japan's government hierarchy, they were utilized for mobilizing the Japanese masses for the war effort as well as disciplining their behaviors with help from the police and local "bosses." Since the *chōnaikai/burakukai* were closely related to Japanese imperialism, they were regarded as a barrier to the democratization of Japan during the occupation period. While the Ministry of Home Affairs desperately tried to keep them alive, the General Headquarters of the Supreme Commander for the Allied Powers (GHQ-SCAP) issued more and more stringent guidelines for the *chōnaikai/burakukai*: first, they purged the heads of the associations and promoted elections; second, they demanded the abolishment of the associations; finally, they began to punish those who still attempted to get involved with them. The *chōnaikai/burakukai*, however, continued to exist by taking on a different name and shape.[40] That was precisely why the critics were skeptical of the "new" program initiated by the Ministry of Home Affairs and why the architects felt the need to use the *katakana* word (i.e., a foreign loan word) for "community" (*komyunitī*) instead of a Japanese word like *chōnaikai/burakukai*. This was in order to signify that the new program was not "indigenous" to Japan.[41] It was imperative for the architects of the MCP to demonstrate that their project was completely different from old, top-down organizations like neighborhood/village associations.

Kimura emphasized that new community organizations should be open and based on the "residents' voluntary wills and responsibilities." He also added that anyone trying to reorganize the old neighborhood/village associations that lacked initiative should be punished.[42] Kurasawa also stressed the difference between the MCP's new "community" and the old, militaristic neighborhood/village associations. In the MCP, he claimed, members should follow their own ideas and participate "voluntarily and spontaneously—and this was a new type of community, different from the old Japanese *mura* [village]."[43] That was why he insisted the government should limit its participation to building physical facilities. Another member of the Community Study Group, Higasa Tadashi, agreed with Kimura and Kurasawa. The government, he argued, should never impose a community program from above. It should care only about providing information regarding the development of communities and helping residents indirectly. Higasa contended that while there was such a thing as "denying the private and obeying the public (*messhi hōkō*) during WWII, what people need today is to respect and make oneself a useful member of society, which was respecting the private and obeying the public (*risshi hōkō*)."[44] It was crucial that the government should not force residents to participate and instead should step back as residents joined voluntarily and actively. Involved residents would participate and act in their own interest—in other words, residents could be led to act as participatory citizens.

In contrast to these explanations, however, some wondered if anything really distinguished the postwar community-building campaigns from their prewar roots. Some observers noted that *chōnaikai/burakukai* controlled the MCP in several cities. As Omori noted, people had the old neighborhood and/or village associations in mind when they involved themselves with the MCP.[45] Formally, the MCP was supposed to represent all the residents served by a given area; in reality, it was dependent on the neighborhood and/or village associations, preventing residents not affiliated with these organizations from participating in the projects.[46] It was immensely ironic that the architects had to differentiate the MCP from the *chōnaikai/burakukai* precisely because the MCP not only reminded the critics of these militaristic associations but also depended on them for their actual operations.

Incorporating Women as Volunteers

The architects of the MCP recognized the value of women as guardians of "communities." The report *Community: The Recovery of Humanity in Everyday Life* represented women as the "moving force" behind the MCP. The report claimed that through their involvement in the MCP, women would be able to "locate themselves and their families in the context of the broader society and take pleasure in social activities."[47] Here, women were assigned a political significance as wives and mothers. Matsubara Haruo explained that the destruction of traditional local communities led to two different types of communities: the "metropolitan community" and the "neighborhood community." The "metropolitan community" was a "husbands'/fathers' community, or an eccentric-circle community," which was diffused in one's workplace, the production center. Neighborhood community was a "wives'/children's community, or a concentric-circle community," which tended to converge on one's permanent home, the consumption center.[48] In this vision, husbands/fathers were the primary breadwinners, and women were simply identified as wives/mothers, bearers of fragmented neighborhood communities.

This highly gendered concept of family and work was represented as a "healthy" guide to the construction of community. Washimi Takeshi wrote that the establishment of "healthy families" was the basis for a "community" and one of the chief goals of the MCP.[49] As wives and mothers, women were supposed to take care of their homes, nurture male labor, and support the MCP, whose efforts targeted the "wives'/children's community." The pursuit of "healthy" families was not unique to the MCP. The 1967 *Economic and Social Development Plan* report, prepared by the *Keizai shingi kai* (Economic Council) stressed the "necessity of building a warm-hearted society with a strong sense of solidarity, based on a regional society surrounding healthy families." Strengthening a nuclear family headed by *sararīman* (company employees) was the core of the social security policy during the era of high economic growth.[50] The "community," then, was interpreted as an extension and a complement to the nuclear family, which was founded on a traditional sense of family and work. Policy makers stressed the significance of "healthy families"—in which women were expected to perform traditional gender roles—as a prerequisite for the construction of a new "community."

While women were regarded as the mainstays of families and new "communities," they were regarded as volunteers, not as principal agents of social programs. This resembled CAP, which stressed the role of females as aides in its programs. As Omori Wataru and Kimura Hitoshi made clear in interviews, women were involved in the operation of the programs—Omori noted that "without their assistance, most of the programs could not exist"—yet almost all the leadership positions were taken by men. The policy makers were not interested in challenging traditional images of family.[51] In fact, since 1973—"the first year of welfare"—the Tanaka cabinet promoted the idea of "self-help" based on families and communities instead of expanding expenditures on social welfare programs. They sought to incorporate women as volunteers in the "Japanese-style welfare state."[52]

The Boundaries of Communities

In the case of the Japanese Model Community Program, opening up new terrain for "Japanese" citizens meant closing the door to "minority" residents. Community programs in Japan not only shared a similar goal with CAP in the United States—that of reconstructing "communities" through the active participation of residents and an ambiguous definition of "community"—but also similarly muted and avoided the question of racial/ethnic inequality. There was, however, one significant difference between CAP in the United States and the MCP in Japan. While CAP eventually opened up space where local welfare activists of color could intervene, Japanese community programs in the late 1960s and early 1970s consistently excluded non-Japanese citizens from community efforts by equating the term "residents" with "Japanese people." Policy makers asserted that the nation was "not only the aggregate of Japanese people but also the aggregate of communities."[53] These community programs were literally created to make Japanese people's lives the first priority; therefore, they completely dismissed the fact that there were many non-Japanese residents, mostly former colonial subjects and their descendants, living in these supposed "communities."[54]

More than 87 percent of resident "noncitizens" in Japan identified themselves as "Koreans" in 1965.[55] As discussed in the introduction, these Korean residents, who had once rendered services to Imperial Japan, were deprived of legal rights in the postwar period. As I explain in detail in chapters 5 and 6, when the San Francisco Peace Treaty ended the Allied occupation and gave Japan full sovereignty in 1952, the government declared its Korean residents to be aliens and put them under the surveillance of the Alien Registration Law. The Japanese government thereafter used citizenship as an excuse to ensure the exclusion of resident Koreans and other "noncitizens" (with some exceptions) from major social security programs, including National Health Insurance, state pensions, public housing, the House Loan Corporation, and allowances for dependent children.[56]

Community programs in Japan, by implicitly equating "residents" with "Japanese people," became another social welfare program that marginalized resident non-nationals. The architects appeared to not even have considered their exclusion of former colonial subjects and their descendants. As both Omori and Kimura explained in their interviews, non-Japanese residents were simply "out of the realm of concern" for the policy makers.[57]

The MCP was based on the notion that Japan was a "mono-ethnic" country. In Miyazawa Hiroshi's words, "the community" could and should be interpreted as a place where "the majority of the Japanese people (*kokumin*) could calm down and live in peace."[58] Endo Fumio, former chief of the administrative office of the Ministry of Home Affairs, wrote that it would not be difficult for local government officials to collect residents' opinions through assemblies since "we, as a mono-ethnic people, share similar feelings and our local societies do not have conflicts of interest." According to Endo, however, the Japanese still lacked a sense of public spirit. He stressed that, in order to strengthen public spirit among the Japanese, there was no other way than disciplining the public through the development of community programs.[59] The Model Community Program reinforced a discourse of a "homogeneous" nation by regarding "the Japanese" as the only worthy residents.

In this chapter, I have shown how the MCP conditioned (Japanese) residents to commit to the residents' own decision-making processes and to act in their own interest. By doing so, it claimed to be different from top-down, militaristic organizations like neighborhood and/or village associations, although it relied on them for its actual operations. It assigned (Japanese) women a political significance as wives and mothers and tried to incorporate them into the programs as volunteers and aides. Finally, it strengthened a myth of a "mono-ethnic" country by equating "residents" with "Japanese nationals" and marginalizing former colonial subjects and their descendants, especially Koreans in Japan.

I do not mean to argue that there were no community programs among Koreans in Japan. Koreans in Japan engaged in battles for equal rights and eventually made demands for alternative visions of citizenship and community. In chapters 5 and 6, I focus on the *zainichi* Koreans' struggles in Kawasaki City, one of the major Korean residents' districts around the Kanto area. I will show how Korean activists like them, who remained outside of the states' community programs, struggled to carve out a unique social space and thus challenged government authority in a welfare state that pursued projects of "progressive" mobilization and manipulative co-optation of purported inclusion as well as tacit yet obstinate exclusion.

3

Struggling for Political Voice

Race and the Politics of Welfare in Los Angeles

Through a case study of the War on Poverty in Los Angeles, I investigate how African American leaders forcefully challenged city government and voiced alternative visions of citizenship in the 1960s.[1] During this time, black middle-class leaders transformed the War on Poverty programs, especially the Community Action Program, into a significant channel through which new political opportunities could be pursued. These efforts resulted in a change in the political status of African American residents in Los Angeles. While analyzing how these African American leaders embraced and reshaped the War on Poverty, I also discuss such issues as divisions among the black residents and the feminization of poverty in Los Angeles. By so doing, I shed light on the complexity of the struggle for political access in Los Angeles. Los Angeles would be a contested political space where multiple political actors would fight for their visions of the War on Poverty.

Revisiting Black Los Angeles in the 1960s

In the field of African American urban history, northern and northeastern cities such as New York and Chicago have been treated as the epitome of the American city. Yet in terms of the impact the 1965 uprising made on the civil rights movement, the OEO, and the Johnson administration, Los Angeles was far from marginal. Los Angeles provides a significant case study for the black urban experience in the 1960s.

In the early twentieth century, Los Angeles was labeled a city called "heaven" for African Americans. In 1913, W. E. B. Du Bois, the senior officer in the National Association for the Advancement of Colored People (NAACP), wrote that "Los Angeles is wonderful. Nowhere in the United States is the Negro so well and beautifully housed, nor the average efficiency and intelligence in the colored population so high." In fact, in 1910,

Los Angeles showed one of the highest percentages of homeownership for African Americans. While 36.1 percent of black Angelenos owned their own homes in the City of Angels, only 2.4 percent of black residents in New York City were homeowners. Central Avenue became a "hub" for black residents, providing space for black businesses, the offices of black physicians and dentists, jazz clubs, and the famous Hotel Somerville, later renamed the Dunbar Hotel. Historian Lonnie G. Bunch thought of Los Angeles from 1900 to the stock market crash in 1929 as a "golden era" for black Angelenos, explaining that the "quantity and quality of the black owned homes" was one of the key elements in the high reputation of Los Angeles.[2]

As historian Douglas Flamming argues, however, black Los Angeles was only "half-free and locked in struggle."[3] Racial discrimination was persistent in the City of Angels, and in fact, with the large-scale influx of black and white migrants from the South, residential segregation hardened. Du Bois noted that "Los Angeles is not paradise . . . the color line is there and sharply drawn."[4] In 1926, a local court decided to take no action on a Los Angeles city policy that restricted the use of bathhouses and pools by "colored groups." In 1929, the California Supreme Court declared that residential restrictions were valid, legitimizing restrictive covenants that were widely used to keep people of color out of white neighborhoods. While the 1920s was a remarkable period in the musical and literary movement, it was also a time of spatial segregation for black Angelenos.[5]

The 1930s and 1940s saw a massive increase in the African American population in Los Angeles. During the Great Depression, many black migrants joined in the journey to California, searching for better economic opportunities. In Los Angeles County, the black population increased from 46,425 (2.1 percent of the total population) in 1930 to 75,209 (2.7 percent) in 1940. The number of migrants continued to grow when A. Philip Randolph organized the March on Washington to protest job discrimination by defense industries. As a result, President Franklin D. Roosevelt issued Executive Order 8802, which ordered defense contractors to eliminate discrimination in their hiring practices. Since Los Angeles was a regional center for defense production, black workers pursued opportunities there. Between 1940 and 1950, 130,000 black migrants headed to Los Angeles. In 1950, the number of African American residents in Los Angeles County rapidly increased to 217,881 (5.2 percent). Yet Los Angeles became at the same time a much more highly segregated place in the 1950s. The African American population in Los Angeles County rose to

461,546 (7.6 percent) in 1960, with 334,916 people (13.5 percent) in the City of Los Angeles alone. According to the Los Angeles County Commission on Human Relations, in the City of Los Angeles, 93.7 percent of these residents lived in one of four districts. By 1970, the City of Los Angeles was rated as one of the nation's most segregated cities, following Chicago and Gary, Indiana (Figure 3.1).[6]

During the early 1960s, residential segregation was renewed and reinforced in the Golden State. Even so, in California, a fair housing act was made law on June 21, 1963, a year before the War on Poverty started. A decisive victory of the California Democratic Party in the 1958 general election and the 1962 reelection of Democratic governor Edmund G. "Pat" Brown—a man who stressed the need for legislation to combat discrimination—enabled state politicians to enact the fair housing code. On February 14, 1963, one of the state's leading African American politicians, W. Byron Rumford, introduced the fair housing bill with other assembly members.[7] The Rumford Act was intended to extend the ban on discrimination beyond publicly assisted housing and to secure administrative enforcement of the act through the Fair Employment Practices Commission (FEPC).[8]

Yet as soon as the Rumford Act was passed, it came under fierce attack from the California Real Estate Association and the California Apartment Owner's Association. These two groups formed the Committee for Home Protection to sponsor an initiative for a constitutional amendment, Proposition 14.[9] While civil rights groups, the American Federation of Labor and Congress of Industrial Organizations (AFL-CIO), and numerous other organizations formed a statewide anti–Proposition 14 group, they were defeated. Proposition 14 was approved by voters in the November 3 election by a 2–1 margin. The passage of Proposition 14 was a clear message to black Los Angeles that left many residents filled with anger and disappointment.[10]

Whereas spatial segregation made it difficult for black Angelenos to find homes in the suburbs, black workers were also facing fewer job opportunities in and around their neighborhoods. Deindustrialization was already under way in Los Angeles during the early 1960s because of the rise of overseas competition. Reacting to intense competition from overseas, manufacturing firms had started leaving the central city to reduce their tax burden, extend their plant size, and explore new markets. In South Los Angeles, which includes Watts, Central, Avalon, Florence, Green Meadow, Exposition, and Willowbrook, the unemployment rate was markedly higher than in the city as a whole throughout the 1960s.

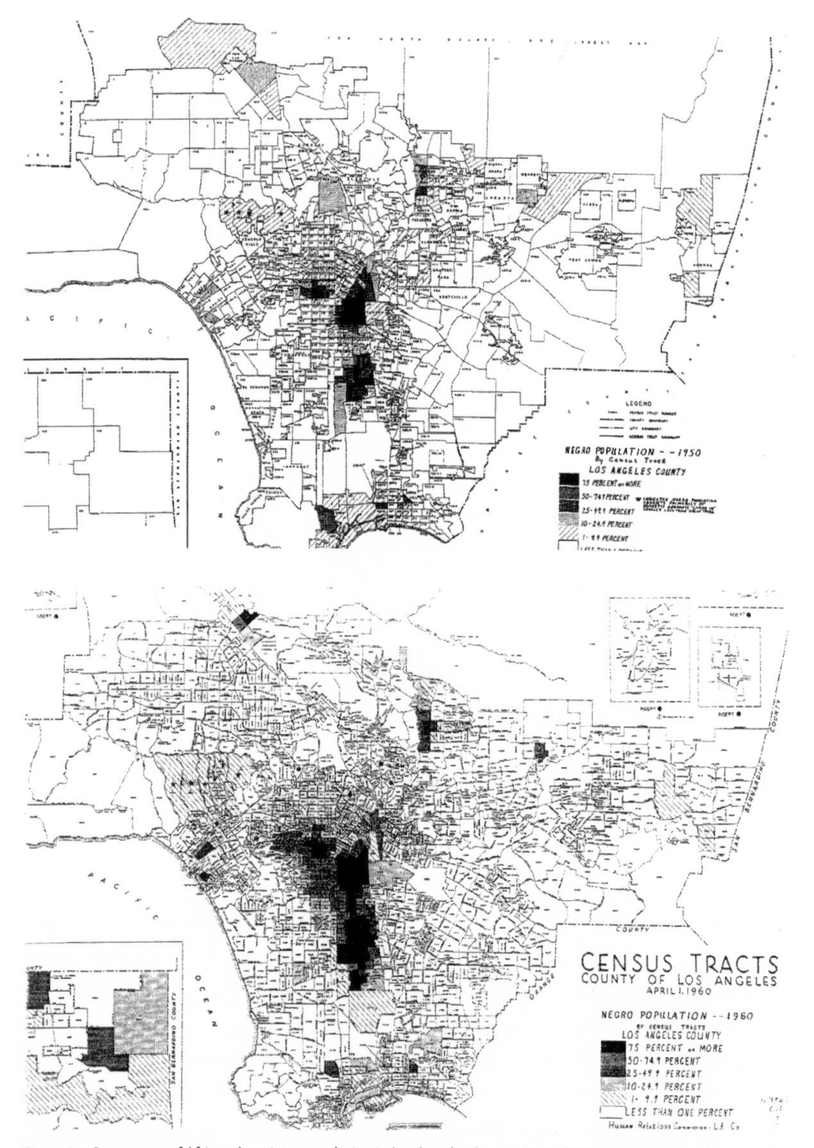

Figure 3.1. Percentage of African American population in Los Angeles County, 1950, 1960, 1970. Courtesy of Los Angeles County Commission of Human Relations.

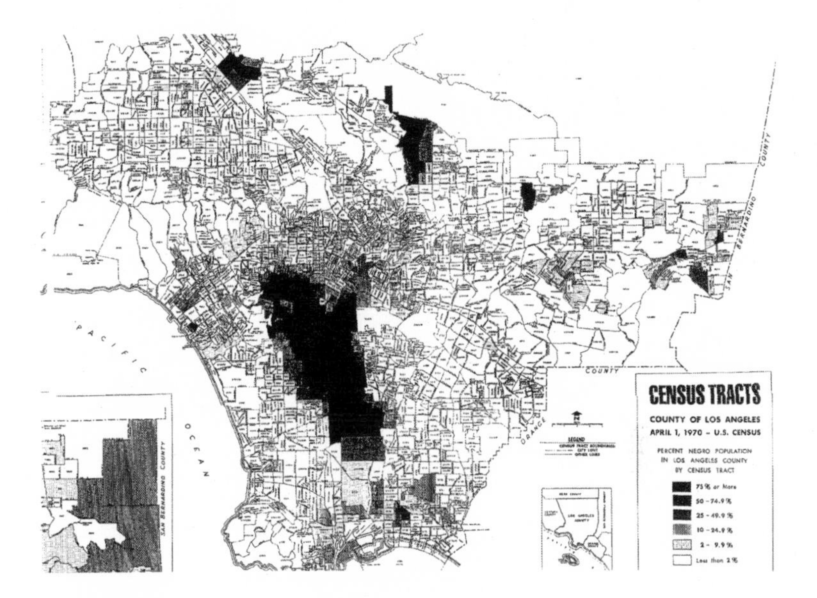

According to an analysis prepared by the State of California, the unemployment rate for males in South Los Angeles in 1960 was 11.3 percent while the rate for males residing in the whole city was 5.3 percent (Table 3.1). In 1965, the unemployment rate dropped 1 percent to 10.3 percent, yet it remained much higher than the rest of the city. More than one-quarter of all families in South Los Angeles, 26.8 percent, had incomes below the "poverty level" ($3,130 per year for a family of four). In the Watts area in particular, 41.5 percent of all families had incomes below the poverty level. All these statistics show why South Los Angeles, especially Watts, would become a major "target area" for the Los Angeles War on Poverty when the programs began.[11]

One needs to take, however, a closer look at these records of unemployment and poverty in South Los Angeles. It was certainly the case that both the unemployment and poverty rates for black Angelenos were much higher than those for white residents. Yet those statistics were marked not only by race but also by gender. The analysis by the State of California did not forget to point out that the proportion of families headed by women was on the rise, from 19 percent in 1960 to 26 percent in 1965. While the unemployment rate for men fell 1 percent, among women the rate actually increased from 10.4 to 11.5 percent. It was also the case that the poverty rate was much higher among families headed by women. While 18.2 percent of persons living in families headed by a man had incomes below the poverty level, 58.9 percent of those in families headed by a woman were in poverty (Table 3.2).[12] These statistics show that what Diana Pearce would later call "feminization of poverty" was already taking place in South Los Angeles in the early 1960s.[13] In other words, female-headed families formed an increasingly large proportion of all poor families.

Many black Angelenos could not expect unions and traditional civil rights organizations to support their daily struggles against residential segregation, unemployment, and poverty in the early 1960s. According to historian Gerald Horne, Red Scare restrictions, exemplified by the

Table 3.1. Percentage of African American Population and Joblessness in South Los Angeles, 1960–65

	LOS ANGELES CITY, 1960	SOUTH LOS ANGELES	
		1960	*1965*
African American population as a percentage of total population	13.5	69.7	81.0
Unemployed persons as a percentage of civilian labor force:			
Males	5.3	11.3	10.1
Females	NA	10.4	11.5

Source: U.S. Senate Committee on Labor and Public Welfare, Subcommittee on Employment, Manpower, and Poverty, *Examination of the War on Poverty,* 90th Cong., 1st sess., May 12, 1967, 3780–81, 3784.

Table 3.2. Income of Families in South Los Angeles, 1960–65

AREA	FAMILIES		PERCENTAGE WITH INCOME BELOW POVERTY LEVEL	
	MEDIAN INCOME IN $ (1965)	*PERCENTAGE BELOW POVERTY LEVEL*	*MALE HEAD OF FAMILY*	*FEMALE HEAD OF FAMILY*
South Los Angeles	4,736	26.8	18.2	58.9
Watts	3,803	41.5	27.1	66.6

Source: U.S. Senate Committee on Labor and Public Welfare, Subcommittee on Employment, Manpower, and Poverty, *Examination of the War on Poverty,* 90th Cong., 1st sess., May 12, 1967, 3786.

Taft-Hartley Act, made it difficult for unions to organize the black migrants from the South. COINTELPRO, the Counterintelligence Program of the Federal Bureau of Investigation, launched in 1956 and designed to obliterate radical political organizations, made the situation worse. Horne argued that many black Angelenos were out of touch with trade union politics by 1965. Furthermore, traditional civil rights organizations like the NAACP failed to win popularity among black residents. Membership in the local chapter dropped from 14,000 in 1945 to 2,500 by 1950. There was a slight increase in the membership during the 1950s (5,800 members in 1961), yet the NAACP continued to be deemed a middle-class organization. This issue of the failure of unions and civil rights groups to reach the "masses" in South Central came to the forefront when the Watts uprising occurred in 1965.[14]

Furthermore, black residents could not expect much from Mayor Samuel Yorty, a "renegade Democrat rapidly moving toward the right," who served as mayor of Los Angeles from 1961 to 1973.[15] In his 1961 campaign, Yorty formed a coalition of San Fernando Valley homeowners and people of color in central cities. On the one hand, he tried to gain suburban homeowners' votes by assuring them that he would end the separation of trash. On the other hand, Yorty promised to fight the police violence against people of color when he ran for election. However, the mayor would soon disappoint black Angelenos by standing behind Chief William Parker of the Los Angeles Police Department (LAPD), who openly made racist comments about African Americans and other people of color. As a Democrat who backed Republican Richard Nixon for president in 1960 instead of John F. Kennedy, the mayor had a strained relationship with Johnson-Kennedy Democrats, especially "the Kennedy group left" in the Johnson administration, exemplified by people in the OEO.[16] As I explain later, Yorty, who tried to take control of the local War on Poverty, was at odds with people in the OEO, who criticized the lack of representation of the poor and people of color in the Los Angeles antipoverty efforts.

Yet there was also a sign of change for black Angelenos in the early 1960s. Augustus F. Hawkins, the first black Democratic Party member of the California State Legislature, was elected to the U.S. Congress in 1962. Hawkins, a graduate of Jefferson High School and the University of California, Los Angeles (UCLA), represented the 29th Congressional District of California, which included South Central. A black candidate, Mervyn Dymally, replaced Hawkins in the California State Legislature in 1962. The year 1963 was also a watershed for black Los Angeles: three African American representatives were elected to the city council. Thomas Bradley, a UCLA and Southwestern University School of Law graduate and former police officer, was elected in the 10th District, a residential area northwest of South Central and primarily inhabited by the black middle class and liberal whites. In 1968, Bradley ran against Mayor Yorty. He was not successful in this first attempt. However, with help from a strong biracial coalition network, he became the city's first African American mayor in 1973. Bradley's success in the earlier city council election was soon followed by the election of two other African American candidates. Billy Mills, who attended Compton College and UCLA, represented the 8th District, which consisted mainly of the black working class in South Central. Gilbert Lindsay was elected in the 9th District, an area northeast of South Central, which was evenly divided between its African American and Latino populations. Lindsay was chosen as candidate when Edward Roybal, a Latino council member, resigned to run successfully for U.S. Congress in 1962. These African American elected officials, especially Hawkins, Bradley, and Mills, would have a strong influence over the implementation of the Los Angeles War on Poverty.[17]

The execution of the Los Angeles antipoverty programs would soon show that the African American political leadership in Los Angeles was far from monolithic. Hawkins and Bradley would work together, stressing the role of representatives of poverty areas and grassroots activists. Dymally and Mills, on the other hand, were close to powerful California State Legislative leader Jesse Unruh, who at that time shared Mayor Yorty's opposition to Governor Brown. The implementation of the local War on Poverty, especially the Community Action Program, would soon become a major site of dispute for these black and white politicians in Los Angeles, Sacramento, and Washington, DC.[18]

Contestations over the Los Angeles War on Poverty

In order to understand debates about the Los Angeles antipoverty programs, one needs to review the history of the Youth Opportunities Board (YOB). The YOB was established in April 1962 as one of fifteen urban centers across the nation to receive a federal grant from the President's Committee on Juvenile Delinquency and Youth Crime. The PCJD had been set up by President Kennedy in May 1961. The idea of establishing an organization targeted at youth was proposed by Robert Goe, executive assistant to Mayor Yorty, at a conference on youth called by County Supervisor Ernest Debs. The YOB was known for the "peculiar governmental structure" that brought it into existence. The "five powers"—the City of Los Angeles, the city schools, the County of Los Angeles, the county schools, and the State of California—operated the YOB together under a "Joint Powers Agreement," an agreement that in California law enabled various government bodies to work together. The YOB conducted various kinds of programs targeted at youth, such as youth training and employment projects, education, community development, volunteer programs, the establishment of a "delinquency prevention clinic," and recreation services. The federal government provided most of the funding for the operation of these programs: in October 1962, the YOB received $252,906 from the Federal Department of Health, Education, and Welfare (HEW) and $88,621 from participating agencies.[19]

The YOB was established with a clear purpose—to discipline unemployed and out-of-school youth and attack juvenile delinquency. According to a statement prepared by the YOB, the YOB came into existence because of increasing concern throughout the nation and within the Los Angeles area about problems associated with large numbers of unemployed and out-of-school youth and rapidly increasing rates of juvenile delinquency and youth crime. The number of juvenile court referrals for delinquency reasons increased more than 57 percent in the period from 1955 to 1960. The YOB emphasized that young people were disproportionately represented in incidences of crime and delinquency and that there was a "direct relationship" between the "idleness" of school-age youth and delinquency.[20] According to the YOB, this demanded coordinated government action because these young people were the ones who would retain a pattern of job instability in later life, who would "fail as human beings" to realize their maximum potential, and who would tend to "perpetuate problems" of deprived social and economic status into a later generation.[21] Whereas the YOB stressed that their programs were conducted with the participation of a wide range of voluntary community youth-serving agencies, government bodies were in full control of the YOB. They regarded it as a training ground in which to transform these youth into self-sufficient and productive citizens. Mayor Yorty would attempt to gain control of the Los Angeles War on Poverty through the YOB.[22]

When the Economic Opportunity Act was enacted and antipoverty programs officially began in August 1964, local African American leaders fought for their visions of the War on Poverty. As early as in April 1964, Hawkins stressed the significance of bringing the War on Poverty to the grassroots level and fostering local leadership. Tom Bradley did not take his eyes off the implications of participation in CAP either. In August, Bradley made a statement that "we have to work cooperatively with community agencies which are active in the neighborhood front lines of the war on poverty."[23] The major newspaper for black Los Angeles, the *Los Angeles Sentinel*, agreed: it stressed that "we have to make sure that some of its benefits come to communities like ours where its objectives are vitally needed."[24] A group of African American leaders began to meet at 1122 Manchester Street, the home of Opal C. Jones, an African American social worker at the Avalon-Carver Community Center (Figure 3.2). As I discuss in the next chapter, Jones, who was what the OEO called a "principal watchdog of the representation of the poor" in Los Angeles, would

Figure 3.2. Los Angeles activist Opal C. Jones (left) at the Avalon Community Center. Courtesy of Security Pacific National Bank Collection, Los Angeles Public Library Photo Collection.

become one of the central figures in bringing the antipoverty programs to the grassroots level.[25] Concerned that Mayor Yorty might try to take control of the local antipoverty programs and hinder poor people from participating in the decision-making processes, these African American leaders decided to fight the Joint Powers board. They succeeded in persuading a local welfare agency, the Welfare Planning Council, to create an agency called the Economic Opportunity Federation (EOF) in September 1964 to compete with the YOB for the War on Poverty funds. Several Congress members from Los Angeles, such as Hawkins, Edward Roybal, James Roosevelt, and George Brown, supported the EOF. On September 3, 1964, James E. Ludlam, then president of the Welfare Planning Council, wrote to Mayor Yorty, arguing that there was "every indication" that the director of the OEO desired the creation of "a local group, broadly representative of public and private interests, to act as a screening and coordinating body."[26] When these leaders held a luncheon at the Los Angeles City Hall of Administration, more than eighty representatives of government and private agencies supported their plan to request $9 million in federal funds. A running battle over the implementation of the Community Action Program, a struggle that would have a tremendous impact on the future of local politics, had begun.[27]

Yorty was quick to fight back. Furious about the creation of the EOF, an organization that would compete with the YOB for the Los Angeles War on Poverty, Yorty wrote to Ludlam, contending that "it is my conviction that an appropriate structure has already been established to act as a coordinating agency."[28] Yorty insisted that there was no need to develop a new organization to administer the antipoverty programs. Yorty also complained to the White House. He wrote to President Johnson's assistant Walter Jenkins as follows: "This 'Umbrella' group is a thinly disguised effort to sabotage Los Angeles' advanced plans for the anti-poverty effort; and I would like the Administrator's cooperation to prevent obstruction to our plans for City effort if anti-poverty is to be kept a sincere effort and not just a political football."[29] In October, the YOB submitted proposals to the OEO, claiming that they should be the main Community Action Agency for Los Angeles.

The OEO intervened in the dispute in January 1965 by proposing the merger of the EOF and the YOB and the involving of more representatives of the poor on the board. The OEO proposed a new organization to expand the members of the board to twenty-two: ten from the government bodies, six from private organizations, and six from the representatives of the poor. While twelve members were going to be elected by ten persons appointed by the public agencies, the merger was still appealing to African American leaders like council member Bradley and Congress member Hawkins since a majority of the membership would be composed of persons who did not belong to government entities.[30]

On February 8, the YOB and the EOF approved the merger plan at a joint meeting and decided to form a new organization to be called the Economic and Youth Opportunity Agency (EYOA) of Los Angeles County. Meanwhile, Hawkins continued to stress the importance of community organizations and the involvement of local people in CAP. He took the initiative and organized a mass meeting for the implementation of the War on Poverty in February. It seemed like the dispute between the EOF and the YOB had been brought to a satisfactory settlement with the establishment of the EYOA.[31]

Yorty did not, however, accept the merger plan. Instead, he countered it with his own proposal, in which the board would have nine members, all from government bodies. Yorty especially resented the fact that more than half of the total members (twelve) on the board would be private citizens, whom Yorty regarded as "not responsible to the people as . . . elected officials."[32] Yorty, once again, argued that the YOB had served as a "nationwide model for later agencies in other areas" and therefore that it should be a central Community Action Agency for Los Angeles.[33]

The real question was who would gain control of the local antipoverty programs through CAP. As Gerald Horne has argued, African American leaders as well as Yorty were concerned with the question of "where money would flow, who would supervise the flow, and what strengthened constituencies would result."[34] The OEO knew that Yorty opposed the merger plan because the proposed new organization might move out from under his control and even be a challenge to city hall. A confidential memo noted that "Yorty [did not] really care how many people sit on the board—as long as he appoints the majority," and that if Yorty succeeded in making the YOB a Community Action Agency, he could "kill any program which might tend to build organizations." It concluded that the OEO had to find some way to "keep YOB under constant surveillance to insure that it does not become a political tool for Yorty."[35] The number of nonpublic officials on the Community Action Agency was a critical issue for both African American leaders and Mayor Yorty precisely because it would determine where the antipoverty funds would go.

Hawkins, Bradley, and other leaders expressed deep resentment of Yorty's opposition to the merger and his counter proposal. Bradley charged that Yorty was dragging his feet in implementing the antipoverty programs. The editors of the *Los Angeles Sentinel* criticized the underrepresentation of the poor, especially low-income people of color on the YOB board. Governor Brown also gave full support to the merger plan and criticized Yorty's new alternate plan of ruling out community participation. Hawkins and other members of Congress from the Los Angeles area strongly urged approval of the proposed merger agreement, noting that the idea was at least a workable beginning. In order to fight Yorty's new proposal, Hawkins, together with church and civil rights leaders such as Reverend Hamel Hartford Brookins of the United Civil Rights Committee and Tony Rios of the Community Service Organization, created an organization called the Community War on Poverty Committee. The committee, comprising more than three hundred local activists, proposed an alternative to Yorty's plan whereby the board would be expanded to thirty-two members, with sixteen from the poverty areas, ten from the public agencies, and six from private agencies. Leaders in the city, the state, and Congress were outraged by Yorty's resistance to the participation of the poor and the further delay in implementing antipoverty programs caused by his rejection of the merger plan.[36]

Overtaken by a storm of criticism, Yorty came up with another plan. He called for the enlargement of the YOB board to nineteen members, including six representatives from poverty areas. Furthermore, Yorty appointed African American city council member Billy G. Mills to replace Robert Goe as the city's representative on the YOB.[37] Mills was close to the state legislative leader Jesse Unruh, who stressed that "the poverty war . . . should be run through local government."[38] While Hawkins argued that the board would still be under city control, Mills ignored other leaders' criticisms and appealed to the OEO for the release of funds. Because of his stand in the antipoverty dispute, Mills would face a recall campaign in late July. Yorty's "divide and conquer" strategy caused further confusion and delay in the implementation of antipoverty programs.[39]

Almost a year had passed since the enactment of the Economic Opportunity Act; Los Angeles, however, was still without its own Community Action Agency. According to Hawkins, the situation had reached a "crisis stage."[40] Hawkins continued to argue that the involvement of the poor should be included at every stage of antipoverty activities. Yet, according to Hawkins, public officials were "grabbing federal money and channeling it into the old ways of doing business . . . these misguided officials see themselves threatened politically."[41] Members of Congress Hawkins, Roosevelt, Roybal, and George E. Brown Jr. urged the OEO to bypass the Community Action Agency and grant directly to projects in Los Angeles. The OEO followed their request. In June, they funded the Los Angeles Unified District directly in order to permit an urgent program to move forward. When the Los Angeles County Board of Supervisors passed Yorty's nineteen-member board plan on July 13, civil rights groups and Mexican representatives organized massive protest demonstrations under the leadership of Reverend H. H. Brookins. Brookins also received support from Martin Luther King Jr., who endorsed his thirty-two-member board plan.[42] The War on Poverty had indeed reached a crisis in Los Angeles—it was not until one of the nation's worst urban uprisings occurred that the City of Angels could finally establish its own antipoverty agency.

The Watts Uprising and the Establishment of the Economic and Youth Opportunities Agency of Greater Los Angeles

On August 11, 1965, a white California highway patrol officer asked Marquette Frye, a twenty-one-year-old African American driver, and his older brother, Ronald, a passenger, to pull their car over at 116th and Avalon near the Watts area. The officer suspected Frye of drunk driving. A scuffle involving Marquette and Ronald, their mother, and the patrolman followed, attracting a large crowd. When three more police officers arrived on the scene and put Frye and his brother and mother under arrest in a violent manner, anger in the crowd escalated. Many started throwing rocks at automobiles and attacking a police field command post. These events sparked an uprising that continued for five days, spreading throughout the Watts area and beyond. By the time the smoke had cleared, 34 people were dead, 1,032 injured, and 3,952 arrested. Approximately six hundred buildings were damaged and $40 million in property destroyed. The Watts uprising was a watershed in the history of Los Angeles as well as in the history of the black liberation struggle. It showed that the civil rights movement led by middle-class African American leaders had failed to reach the ghettos in northern and western cities. As Gerald Horne has argued, it would also soon be the case that in the wake of Watts, black Los Angeles would face the "two sharply contrasted tendencies" of Black Nationalism and a reactionary white backlash. The Watts revolt would also have a tremendous impact on the stalled Los Angeles War on Poverty.[43]

Politicians, scholars, and civil rights activists attempted to explain why the uprising occurred in Los Angeles. Governor Brown appointed John McCone, a former CIA director, to head a commission to make an "objective and dispassionate" study of the revolt. On December 2, the McCone Commission released its report titled "Violence in the City: An End or a Beginning?" The commission argued that the fundamental causes of the Watts uprising stemmed from the lack of job opportunities, the low level of scholastic attainment, and a resentment of the police as symbols of authority. In addition, there were a series of aggravating events, such as "unpunished violence and disobedience to law," the passage of Proposition 14, and controversy over the mechanisms for handling the antipoverty program in the city. According to the McCone Commission, all these factors together produced the "dull, devastating spiral of failure" in the ghettos.[44]

Civil rights activists and scholars, however, were quick to challenge the McCone Commission's findings and recommendations. According to historian Robert M. Fogelson, they criticized the McCone report for failing to understand that a much larger and more representative segment of the ghetto residents joined the uprising, that these people participated in it because they could not passively accept conditions any more, that the uprising was an articulation of genuine grievances and meaningful protest, and that to maintain public order in Los Angeles demanded fundamental changes not only in the segregated ghetto but also in the white metropolis. These civil rights activists and scholars argued that "Violence in the City" regarded people involved in the uprising as "lawless" criminals who were willing to take the "most extreme and even illegal remedies" and therefore ignored the deep resentment among Watts residents over the police in particular and life in the segregated ghetto in general.[45]

Other analysts questioned whether middle-class civil rights leaders might have reached the alienated residents in South Central Los Angeles at all. In this vein, Horne has pointed out that the Watts revolt was an uprising not only against a white elite but also against ineffective black leaders as well. Civil rights organizations had failed to play a major role in challenging Mayor Yorty and Police Chief Parker and improving life chances for black Angelenos. For example, when Martin Luther King Jr. visited Los Angeles after the revolt, he saw no "sensitive and determined leadership to solve the problem." King noted that while there were serious doubts about whether white Angelenos were in any way willing to accommodate their needs, there was also a "growing disillusionment and resentment toward the Negro middle class and the leadership it has produced."[46] When King had a stormy closed meeting with Mayor Yorty on August 19, he urged the mayor to acknowledge police brutality and asked for the resignation of Parker. What King received instead was an accusation. Yorty staunchly defended Parker, contending that there was "no excuse to find fault in law enforcement." The mayor severely criticized King for performing what he called "a great disservice to the people of Los Angeles and the Nation."[47] Visiting Los Angeles made King reconsider his understanding of civil rights. King admitted that "we as Negro leaders—and I include myself—have failed to take the civil rights movement to the masses of people" and that the "North, at best, stood still as the South caught up."[48] The Watts uprising showed that the civil rights movement, which was oriented toward the South, did not necessarily bring about a dramatic and discernible change in people's lives in the northern and western ghettos.

While civil rights leaders were in the middle of reconceptualizing their strategies, Los Angeles encountered Black Nationalism on the one hand and white backlash on the other. After the uprising, two "Black Nationalist" groups emerged. One was a group of "political nationalists" exemplified by Hakim Jamal and influenced by Malcolm X and the Black Panther Party. The other was a group of "cultural nationalists" represented by Maulana Karenga, which stressed the need for African Americans to recover their "African" heritage and emphasized that "cultural evolution was indispensable to the political struggle." The latter group, led by Karenga, would play a significant role in the local antipoverty programs, utilizing grants from the OEO for their own activities.[49]

The Watts revolt was also accompanied by a profound white backlash. According to the "White Reaction Study," 71 percent of the respondents thought that the uprising increased the gap between the races. In addition, 68 percent agreed that "Negroes should stop pushing so hard."[50] This reactionary tide turned in some politicians' favor. A prominent state legislative leader, Jesse M. Unruh, for example, tried to speak as the voice of "innocent Caucasians." Unruh contended that "unless the majority [was] protected and convinced that such protection is forthcoming from physical excesses of minorities," it would become difficult to convince these "innocent Caucasians" to pay the economic costs of wiping out "second-class citizenship."[51] Yet no one could beat Mayor Yorty in representing himself as an enforcer of laws and "anything but a coddler of criminals."[52] The mayor's staunch law-and-order position attracted many white Angelenos. Indeed, as Democratic National Committee Deputy Chair Louis Martin admitted, Yorty was a "maverick who knows how to divide and rule the various groups and communities that make up Los Angeles."[53] Yorty placed the blame not only on civil rights workers for provoking black residents' resentment but also on Governor Brown. The mayor announced a "growing sentiment in the Democratic Party to demand new leadership" and called for an end to "influence peddling, false promises, favoritism, and power politics."[54] Yorty's challenge to Brown in the Democratic primary, as well as the white backlash against the uprising, lent a hand to Republican gubernatorial candidate Ronald Reagan, who was a steadfast critic of civil rights measures. Reagan, who opposed not only the Rumford Fair Housing Act but also the 1964 federal civil rights laws, attracted hundreds of thousands of Democratic voters and won the election for governor.[55]

The repercussions of the Watts uprising went far beyond Southern California, reaching the White House. President Johnson would soon notice that his "close identification with the cause of black Americans" would accord him some responsibility for the revolt.[56] Yet the president stressed the significance of attacking the "deep-seated causes of riots" rather than appealing to "law and order."[57] Johnson announced the appointment of Deputy Attorney General Ramsey Clark to head a special task force to report on the causes and solutions for the Watts uprising. Then a week later, following the recommendations of the task force, the president authorized more than forty-five employment, health, education, and housing programs totaling $29 million for Los Angeles. After much delay, the Los Angeles War on Poverty had begun.[58]

The confusion over the establishment of the Community Action Agency, in fact, was one of the chief causes of the Watts revolt. As Nathan Cohen has noted, there were almost no resources available to alleviate unemployment in Watts before the uprising. As the battle between the YOB and the EOF continued, most funds for the local antipoverty programs were either withheld or delayed, while some educational programs were funded directly from the OEO.[59]

While it was Mayor Yorty's staunch refusal to agree to a merger plan that caused a serious delay in the implementation of the War on Poverty, some pointed their fingers at black middle-class leaders. The Watts Community Action Group, established by Earline A. Williams, a lifelong resident of Watts and an assistant librarian, complained to the OEO that there was no visible evidence of accomplishment and that some of the community leaders were self-seeking.[60] According to the *Los Angeles Times*, not only Yorty but also Hawkins earned blame for leaving the poor waiting outside, since they "accuse each other of attempting to seize political control of the program."[61] The *Los Angeles Sentinel* also reported that "distrust over political power" was one of the key issues leading to the Watts revolt.[62] While CAP certainly became a strategy for increasing black representation in Los Angeles, African American leaders were criticized for the length of time it took to reach an agreement about the Community Action Agency.

African American leaders were not simply standing around without taking any action. Bradley saw the uprising as an opportunity to struggle for better educational and economic opportunities for the poor. Together with King, Bradley harshly criticized Police Chief Parker and the LAPD. Soon after the revolt, Bradley helped the city council establish the Human Relations Board to improve the relationship between the police and black Angelenos. Bradley was not the only official to use the uprising to demand more educational and economic opportunities for the poor.[63] On August 17, Louis Martin, the deputy chairperson of the Democratic National Committee, had a meeting with elected black public officials including Hawkins, Dymally, Mills, and Maurice Weiner, one of Bradley's deputies. They agreed that unemployment was a major factor in the uprising, and most blamed lack of antipoverty funds on political conflicts among public officials, with some attacking Mayor Yorty in particular.[64] Hawkins, whose "leadership was generally acknowledged by the other officials," wrote to President Johnson that "if tensions are to be removed . . . those who live in the community and who are directly concerned have to be brought into decision making and planning."[65] Hawkins spoke most forcefully for the participation of the poor in the local antipoverty programs after the revolt.

Mayor Yorty, who had come under fire for his opposition to the merger plan, aimed attacks at Sargent Shriver, the director of the OEO. Yorty contended that the OEO's "deliberate and well-publicized cutting of poverty funds to the city" was one of the main contributing factors to the uprising. He claimed that the city continued to be subjected to "federal whims which are confusing, changing, and arbitrary."[66] Shriver was quick to challenge Yorty, calling the charge "intemperate and unfounded." Shriver argued that $17 million had already been approved for Los Angeles in spite of the city's inability to comply with the OEO guidelines for the participation of the poor. He maintained that Los Angeles was the only major city without a "well-rounded community action program because of the failure of local officials to establish a broad-based community action board representing all segments of the community." For Shriver, it was Yorty's resolute opposition to the participation of the poor and people of color that had brought about a serious delay in the allocations of the War on Poverty funds.[67]

On August 18, President Johnson dispatched Leroy Collins, undersecretary of commerce and former governor of Florida, to resolve the dispute over a Community Action Agency in Los Angeles and get antipoverty programs started. When Collins arrived in Los Angeles, he found the "air was more filled with tension than smog. Everyone was criticizing and blaming everyone else."[68] According to President Johnson's aide Joseph Califano, Mayor Yorty was again the "stumbling block." Califano reported to the president that it took all of Collins's skill and discussions with Jesse Unruh ("Yorty's man behind the scenes") to bring the parties together.[69] Collins managed to get agreement on a twenty-five-member board, the Economic and Youth Opportunities Agency of Greater Los Angeles (EYOA). EYOA would consist of twelve public agency members, seven community representatives elected by the poor, six private agency members, and two nonvoting members from the Los Angeles Chamber of Commerce and League of Cities. It was nothing but a compromise between the YOB and the EOF. The YOB side was satisfied, since Collins's plan would give public agency members dominance in voting power on the board, and the EOF side also succeeded by having community representatives be elected by the poor rather than appointed by government officials. The OEO approved the agreement and announced that grants amounting to $12,979,000 would be made in two weeks. The lingering contestation over the establishment of a Community Action Agency looked as if it were coming to an end.[70]

The establishment of the EYOA, however, was just the beginning of another battle, a battle over the implementation of the antipoverty programs. At first, the Community Anti-Poverty Committee, which included two thousand members of labor, church, and social groups, was not happy with Collins's proposal because he had consulted only with public agencies and then passed it on to them for mere approval.[71] Hawkins was not satisfied with the compromise either. He persuaded Collins to attend a meeting in the Watts area to discuss the future of the Los Angeles War on Poverty. While Hawkins agreed with the general thrust of Collins's proposal, he was also considering the possibility of advancing the participation of the poor by bypassing the EYOA. Based on Congressional hearings conducted in the Los Angeles area, Hawkins wrote to the OEO director Sargent Shriver that the image of city hall in Los Angeles was "at an all-time low" among people of color and that there existed "overwhelming sentiment" for resident involvement and self-determination. In the end, Hawkins made several recommendations, including the building of leadership through the Neighborhood Adult Participation Project directed by Opal C. Jones, more involvement of residents at the policy level, and recognition of other Community Action Agencies as well as single-purpose agencies. While Hawkins tried to increase the power of residents in the poor areas on the EYOA board, he also attempted to prevent the EYOA from taking full control of all the antipoverty programs in Los Angeles.[72] Yorty criticized Hawkins's attempts as a "phase of the strong arm tactics employed against us."[73] Shriver, on the other hand, welcomed his recommendations. Shriver agreed with Hawkins that there was a growing attitude in favor of resident participation and that Los Angeles was too large to have only one "octopus size" Community Action Agency.[74] Hawkins continued to argue that the people who were in poverty areas should be given a dominant role to play in the antipoverty program.

Struggles over the Los Angeles War on Poverty moved to another phase after the Watts uprising. The battles were no longer over the establishment of a Community Action Agency. They would be over the actual implementation of each antipoverty program. The struggles of African American leaders like Bradley, Hawkins, and Jones, however, continued. In fact, their fight for increasing the power of residents in poor areas and bringing the antipoverty programs to the grassroots level was about to begin.

* * *

In this chapter we have seen how African American leaders insisted on the right to realize the participation of the poor in the Los Angeles War on Poverty by establishing the EOF and providing opportunities for residents to join the Community Action Agency. These same individuals used the antipoverty program as a way to politically confront Mayor Yorty and other government officials who sought to secure control of the antipoverty programs at the expense of poor people themselves. While emphasizing the agency of the black middle class in voicing alternative visions of CAP, I argue that black leadership in Los Angeles was far from monolithic. Their struggles were intricate, in terms of both the differences within the leadership of black Los Angeles and their relationships with multiple political actors such as Mayor Yorty, Governor Brown, the OEO, and the Johnson administration. A new class of black leadership emerged within the context of electoral rivalries between the Yorty-Mills-Unruh coalition and the forces allied with Hawkins, Bradley, and Brown. Los Angeles black leaders transformed CAP into a contested political space where new political opportunities for the poor and African American residents could be pursued.

4

Recasting the Community Action Program

The Pursuit of Race, Class, and Gender Equality in Los Angeles

With the establishment of the Economic and Youth Opportunities Agency of Greater Los Angeles (EYOA), the War on Poverty officially began. In this chapter, I examine how local activists in South Central Los Angeles turned the concept of "maximum feasible participation" into a weapon in the battle for welfare rights. They forcefully challenged the official local/federal antipoverty institutions—EYOA and the Office of Economic Opportunity (OEO)—and created oppositional discourses that could work against them.

In the first section, I focus on one of the major antipoverty programs in Los Angeles: the Neighborhood Adult Participation Project (NAPP). NAPP was funded by the OEO through the EYOA and came to be at the center of a great debate over the implementation of the Los Angeles War on Poverty. A black female social worker, Opal C. Jones, served as the executive director of NAPP from its inception in April 1965. Soon, it became a major point of contestation regarding the participation of the poor and people of color in the Los Angeles Community Action Program. I analyze how Jones and NAPP became a political threat to Mayor Yorty and the EYOA. I also examine how she was actively engaged in recasting the Los Angeles War on Poverty programs by both stressing the role racial inequality played in creating poverty and providing an incisive critique of the role of assumed "professional" antipoverty workers.

Then I explore two organizations that insisted on realizing the participation of the poor: the Watts Labor Community Action Committee (WLCAC) and Aid to Needy Children (ANC) Mothers Anonymous. Watts was the source of both the WLCAC and ANC Mothers Anonymous. Both of these organizations were engaged in a campaign to bring a hospital to the area after the Watts uprising. I focus on activists Ted Watkins of the WLCAC and Johnnie Tillmon of ANC Mothers Anonymous, who played crucial roles in their respective organizations, and bring their discourses forward as representative voices of local welfare activists in South Central Los Angeles. These local activists creatively appropriated antipoverty programs and invested them with new meaning. The examples of Ted Watkins and Johnnie Tillmon give insight into the interaction of race, class, and gender relations in the War on Poverty programs.

Through examining the cases of NAPP, the WLCAC, and ANC Mothers Anonymous, I explore how these activists' efforts resulted in expanding the roles available to the poor, people of color, and women in the Los Angeles War on Poverty. They would provide a significant critique of the local and federal welfare systems that ignored race/class/gender differences and restore welfare activists to the status of fully empowered historical agents.

Recasting the Community Action Program: The Neighborhood Adult Participation Project

Before exploring how Opal C. Jones initiated her struggle against the Los Angeles Community Action Agency, I briefly discuss the characteristics of the EYOA and its antipoverty programs. The EYOA was made up of three parts: a board of directors that decided on EYOA policies, the director, and the employees who actually managed the programs. As I have explored in the preceding chapter, after the long battle over the implications of "maximum feasible participation" between the YOB side and the EOF side, the newly created EYOA required the participation of the poor on the board of directors. The board of directors originally consisted of three representatives from each of four public government bodies (the City of Los Angeles, the County of Los Angeles, the Los Angeles Unified School District, and the Los Angeles County Schools); one representative from each of six local organizations (United Way, the AFL-CIO, the Welfare Planning Council, the Los Angeles County Federation of Coordinating Council, the Chamber of Commerce, and the League of California Cities); and seven representatives elected by the residents of the poor areas. Joe Maldonado, a Mexican American with a background in social work and who had been the executive director of the Youth Opportunities Board, became the first executive director of the EYOA. On October 31, 1966, the number of employees stood at 245. The EYOA functioned as a comprehensive planning and coordinating body, thereby retaining certain administrative responsibilities for the programs.[1]

Although the EYOA required the participation of representatives of the poor in its decision-making process, the amount of actual power wielded by these representatives on the board of directors was severely limited. Dale Rogers Marshall participated on the board in 1968 and conducted interviews with the thirty-two board members. Marshall pointed out that while the participation of the poor had a significant influence on their careers, these representatives of the poor could not gain power over the decisions made by the board. In other words, whereas the increase in confidence, efficacy, participation, interest in community work, self-esteem, and leadership aspirations among the representatives of the poor certainly showed that they were motivated by their experiences on the board, they were unable to match the predominant influence on the board exercised by public agencies.[2] Thus the EYOA board was ultimately dominated by public officials. Opal C. Jones and other local leaders would criticize this point later on.

There were two significant aspects concerning the funding of the EYOA. First, almost half of the funds went to educational programs such as Head Start, which was a child-development program geared toward preschool-age children (Table 4.1). Second, the funding for job training and other employment programs was only 22 percent of the overall grant, and most of this money was aimed at youth, except in the Neighborhood Adult Participation Project. This was because the War on Poverty originally placed more emphasis on youth development as a measure "to prevent entry into poverty." Although the EYOA created 48,797 temporary and permanent jobs for poor people, providing the skills and experiences necessary for poor adults, NAPP was the only program geared toward adults who had already entered into poverty.[3] Overall, about 9 percent of the funds were aimed at adults. While most of the antipoverty funds were channeled into programs for teenagers, Opal C. Jones would launch significant critiques of the EYOA, using NAPP as a vehicle for social change.

How did the EYOA decide on the eligibility of its program participants? Based on the eligibility criteria issued by the OEO in its CAP program guide, the EYOA established its own standards for each program, but as for the definition of "poverty" in the election, the poor were defined as those with a family income of less than $4,000 a year regardless of the number of dependents. In 1960, "whites" made up 73 percent of those below the poverty line in Los Angeles County. But a strikingly different picture emerges when the statistics are analyzed by racial/ethnic group. Only

Table 4.1. EYOA Programs, Amount of Grant from the OEO, and Principal Delegate Agencies

PROGRAM	AMOUNT OF GRANT (MILLIONS OF DOLLARS)	PRINCIPAL DELEGATE AGENCIES
Educational	10.3	Los Angeles Unified School District, Los Angeles County Schools
Head Start	8.6	Los Angeles Unified School District, Los Angeles County Schools, Los Angeles Area Federation of Settlements and Neighborhood Centers Inc.
Neighborhood Adult Participation Project (NAPP)	2.9	EYOA, Los Angeles Area Federation of Settlements and Neighborhood Centers Inc.
Teen Post	3.6	Los Angeles Area Federation of Settlements and Neighborhood Centers Inc.
Training and employment for youth	2.3	Westminster Neighborhood Association Inc., etc.
Employment and vocational training	2.9	National Urban League, etc.
Community services	1.7	Westminster Neighborhood Association Inc., etc.
Legal services	0.5	Los Angeles Area Federation of Settlements and Neighborhood Centers Inc.
Cultural and recreational	0.6	
Administration and other	3.2	
Total	36.6	

Sources: U.S. General Accounting Office, *Review of the Community Action Program in the Los Angeles Area under the Economic Opportunity Act* (Washington, DC: U.S. Government Printing Office, 1968), 2–13; U.S. Senate Committee on Labor and Public Welfare., Subcommittee on Employment, Manpower, and Poverty, *Examination of the War on Poverty*, 90th Cong., 1st sess., May 12, 1967, 3865–94.

17 percent of "white families (excluding Spanish speakers)" were below the poverty line, while 34.7 percent of "non-white families" and 25.7 percent of "families with Spanish surnames" earned less than $4,000 annually.[4]

The main focus of the EYOA programs was not the white poor, who made up more than 70 percent of the poor, but the African American and Latino poor.[5] One of the major reasons why most of the antipoverty funds flowed toward people of color lay in the Watts uprising, which had led to the organization of the Los Angeles War on Poverty task force as well as to the provisioning of federal funds. As I discuss in detail later, Mexican American leaders demanded equal opportunities for Mexican Americans, and antipoverty money went into Latino areas as well. The other reason was that the EYOA didn't administer antipoverty programs directly to each poor family but instead identified "major poverty areas" (Figure 4.1 and Table 4.2). And it so happened that these "major poverty areas" were the predominantly African American and Latino neighborhoods.[6] The fact that the main focus of EYOA programs was on African American and Latino areas meant that the War on Poverty had to attack not only poverty

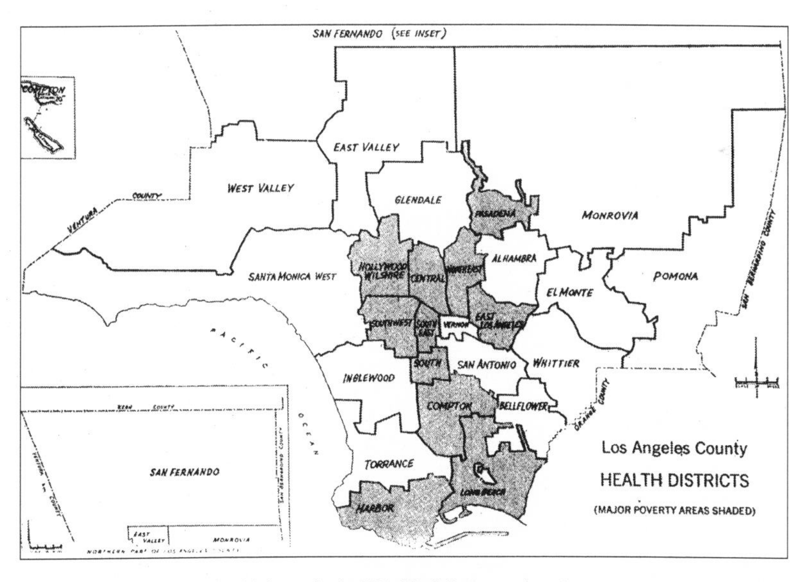

Figure 4.1. Los Angeles County health districts by the EYOA. (Shaded regions indicate "major poverty areas.") Source: U.S. Senate, Committee on Labor and Public Welfare, Subcommittee on Employment, Manpower, and Poverty, Examination of the War on Poverty, *90th Cong., 1st sess., May 12, 1967, 3900.*

Table 4.2. Population Characteristics of Los Angeles County, Total Funds from the EYOA, and Funds from the EYOA for Each Poor Family by Twenty-Five Health Districts

	TOTAL POPULATION	RACE/ETHNIC GROUPS (%)			PERCENTAGE OF FAMILIES WITH ANNUAL INCOME—LESS THAN $4,000 (%)	TOTAL FUNDS FROM EYOA (IN DOLLARS)	FUNDS FROM THE EYOA FOR EACH POOR FAMILY (IN DOLLARS)
		WHITE	*BLACK*	*SPANISH SURNAMES*			
Alhambra	234,332	91.01	0.11	7.82	15.57	962,619	95.5
Bellflower	304,940	91.84	0.24	7.41	14.02	532,611	61.0
Central	**201,733**	**70.95**	**5.41**	**15.28**	**33.82**	**5,234,106**	**353.5**
Compton	**221,626**	**63.06**	**27.25**	**8.73**	**21.39**	**5,738,030**	**513.2**
East Los Angeles	**145,146**	**40.98**	**0.31**	**55.89**	**25.12**	**3,821,227**	**425.5**
East Valley	255,963	87.87	3.60	7.39	15.05	1,590,544	151.2
El Monte	199,817	83.53	0.54	15.57	16.81	1,861,033	226.7
Glendale	363,367	95.59	0.60	3.93	15.44	122,275	9.1
Harbor	**117,982**	**76.10**	**4.42**	**16.81**	**23.63**	**1,659,376**	**236.2**
Hollywood-Wilshire	**340,491**	**88.70**	**4.09**	**3.91**	**22.54**	**580,711**	**28.0**
Inglewood	375,209	93.23	0.28	4.73	13.77	820,669	57.7
Long Beach	**247,104**	**91.25**	**3.51**	**3.54**	**24.67**	**2,037,080**	**90.8**
Monrovia	224,435	91.03	2.31	5.89	16.00	659,962	70.9
Northeast	**193,810**	**45.00**	**4.35**	**46.07**	**30.68**	**4,702,922**	**338.4**
Pasadena	**111,927**	**79.32**	**13.03**	**4.64**	**21.87**	**1,470,153**	**222.6**
Pomona	208,155	92.79	0.61	6.08	14.54	1,255,337	169.1

Table 4.2. (*continued*)

	TOTAL POPULATION	RACE/ETHNIC GROUPS (%)			PERCENTAGE OF FAMILIES WITH ANNUAL INCOME—LESS THAN $4,000 (%)	TOTAL FUNDS FROM EYOA (IN DOLLARS)	FUNDS FROM THE EYOA FOR EACH POOR FAMILY (IN DOLLARS)
		WHITE	*BLACK*	*SPANISH SURNAMES*			
San Antonio	255,181	93.39	0.55	6.70	17.92	654,962	51.7
San Fernando	184,855	88.92	1.51	8.69	12.40	1,020,331	183.3
Santa Monica, West	454,497	90.37	2.34	5.15	15.93	2,370,448	121.9
South Los Angeles	**139,164**	**19.19**	**65.69**	**14.11**	**37.79**	**6,594,273**	**526.1**
Southeast Los Angeles	**115,383**	**9.14**	**81.47**	**7.61**	**46.35**	**3,435,832**	**265.9**
Southwest Los Angeles	**291,292**	**44.13**	**40.83**	**6.91**	**26.02**	**3,346,504**	**160.1**
Torrance	244,694	93.39	0.53	5.18	12.69	584,991	74.3
West Valley	395,198	95.60	0.12	3.87	11.29	749,567	64.6
Whittier	234,380	86.19	0.65	3.09	10.69	1,032,281	163.6
Total	6,000,682	80.70	7.68	9.58	19.04	52,837,874	177.0

Notes: The EYOA used health districts for statistical measurement. The total districts were twenty-six, but the EYOA excluded the Vernon district, an area primarily devoted to industrial land uses. The districts in bold were the places the EYOA identified as "major poverty areas." The funding from the EYOA for each family is calculated based on the total number of families, the percentage of families with an annual income of less than $4,000, and total funds from the EYOA (figures are rounded to the first decimal place).

Source: U.S. Senate Committee on Labor and Public Welfare, Subcommittee on Employment, Manpower, and Poverty, *Examination of the War on Poverty*, 90th Cong., 1st sess., May 12, 1967, 3899–902.

problems in general but also the relationship between racial inequality and poverty.[7] However, the EYOA did not make clear how poverty issues and racial issues were intertwined but rather left local residents to tackle the racial issues by themselves. This would be another significant issue that Opal C. Jones would critique.

The executive director of the Neighborhood Adult Participation Project, Opal C. Jones, intended to bring the antipoverty programs closer to the people and to mobilize poor adults in their neighborhoods. Since the early 1950s, Jones had worked at the Avalon-Carver Community Center, established in 1940 to provide multiservice resources to low-income residents in South Central Los Angeles. Jones worked with distinguished social workers such as Mary Henry, who later founded the nation's first urban pediatric telemedicine center.[8] Having experience as a professional social worker in South Central, Jones was nominated as the executive director of NAPP.

NAPP started its operation on April 1, 1965, with ten neighborhood "outposts" located in Los Angeles County and four hundred aides trained there. Soon the number of "outposts" had grown to fifteen: Avalon, Boyle Heights, Canoga Park, Compton-Willowbrook, El Monte, Exposition, Florence-Graham, Lincoln Heights, Long Beach, Los Angeles Central, Pacoima, San Pedro, Venice-Mar Vista, Watts, and Wilmington-Harbor City. According to a NAPP pamphlet, the program's chief purpose was to link the antipoverty programs with the people who were served by the programs and to bring these antipoverty programs to the grassroots level so that people in poor communities could have a louder voice in the operation of the War on Poverty.[9]

The program of NAPP was threefold: career development, neighborhood development, and information and referral. Career development was established to provide job opportunities for neighborhood adults in poor areas as aides at NAPP "outposts." Through the career development program, these neighborhood adults were able to acquire careers and improve the agencies' services. The NAPP outposts helped neighborhood people find jobs and served as a liaison between the neighborhood adults and the antipoverty agencies. Neighborhood development was for organizing neighborhoods and their people to work on their own behalf "toward self-help, self-determination and total improvement." NAPP also helped people improve their neighborhoods through various kinds of activities: offering residents English classes, adult education classes, civil service instructions, and hot lunches for school children; helping neighborhood people install street/traffic lights and obtain crossing guards, boulevard stop signs, and pedestrian crosswalks; and establishing a Saturday clinic and expanding services in public health centers. Finally, an information and referral program was started to link neighbors with the services to which they were entitled. For adults in poor communities, NAPP acted as an important link to the EYOA in order to get these various services enacted. NAPP became one of the most popular programs for poor communities among the Los Angeles War on Poverty activities.[10]

NAPP, in fact, would stand at the heart of a great debate over political participation after the Watts uprising. As I have discussed, there were prolonged battles over the establishment of a Community Action Agency in Los Angeles. These struggles emerged between African American leaders like member of Congress Hawkins and Los Angeles city council member Bradley and government officials such as Mayor Yorty. With the EYOA in operation, the Hawkins-Bradley group sought to increase the power of residents in poor areas through the implementation of each antipoverty program, with particular emphasis on NAPP. Before scrutinizing how NAPP became a unique vehicle for the poor, I turn to the political biography of Opal C. Jones.

Opal C. Jones wrote various kinds of pamphlets to explain the character of NAPP.[11] Here I focus on three sites in which Jones sought to address poverty: the connection between poverty and racial discrimination, the importance of the role of the people who were served by the programs, and the critique of professional antipoverty workers. Jones did not explicitly discuss women's rights or women's roles in the antipoverty programs. What Jones achieved as one of few female directors of color, however, resulted in the expanding of women's roles in the Los Angeles War on Poverty programs. By raising these three critical issues, Jones forcefully challenged the EYOA's perceptions of what women should and should not do.

Jones paid particular attention to the connection between poverty and racial discrimination. She was invited to a hearing titled *Examination of the War on Poverty* held in Los Angeles in May 1967. In her statement, she criticized some people involved in the War on Poverty for ignoring the link between "poverty and discrimination" and "housing [discrimination] and other forms of segregation."[12] In a pamphlet titled "Strategy and Strategists," Jones wrote that antipoverty workers had to tackle "all of the forces at work in the neighborhood," including racism.[13] Jones was fully aware that the EYOA and public officials involved in the War on Poverty failed to confront issues of racial discrimination seriously, especially those regarding residential segregation. Even though many antipoverty programs targeted the districts inhabited by people of color, only poverty issues were discussed and issues of race were usually left unexamined. Jones repeatedly emphasized that the issue of racial discrimination could not be separated from the causes of poverty.

Jones also vigorously encouraged the participation of the poor and believed their involvement and their perspectives were indispensable to the effective functioning of the program. In a report titled *A New Look in Community Service*, she pointed out that there were plenty of nonprofessional and neighborhood staff—"ready, anxious, willing and able to work, to serve and become members" of the staffs of local social agencies or to serve as neighborhood workers in the schools. Jones wrote, "I have discovered that for a long time they [neighborhood residents] have wanted to work with us—side by side in our social institutions." Jones also conducted research on what neighborhood mothers wished their children's teachers would do and introduced these mothers' opinions into discussions of NAPP. For example, one mother wanted a teacher to educate her son in "the role of the Negro in world history, especially the history of the United States." Another mother hoped that teachers would become more involved in community activities.[14] Under the leadership of Jones, many mothers, including Johnnie Tillmon, developed their careers. Jones regarded the people who joined NAPP not only as recipients of the antipoverty programs but also as coworkers who would have innovative ideas and suggestions.

Finally, Jones was critical of the "experts" involved in antipoverty programs or the "professional" antipoverty workers who lacked "sincerity," as evidenced by her picture book titled *Guess Who's Coming to the Ghettos?* In the first segment, Jones provided a critique of the "experts" in "poverty problems," who were mostly middle-class, well-educated whites. Jones wrote,

> They saw us as problems—as clients, as the poor . . .
> They all became experts—with advice given free! . . .
> They soon made studies; They researched us to death . . .
> They kept up the old "maximum feasible line" . . .

They sat back and waited for it all to take place . . .
With its new leadership, new voices, new plans, they cried—
oh, the neighborhood is out of our hands! . . .
And so, they got busy and made new plans to determine
the target—back in their hands. (Figure 4.2a)[15]

Jones also critiqued the "professional" antipoverty workers, who had seldom paid attention to the ghettos in the past but suddenly became "professional" workers in the War on Poverty:

Passed us each day with her head in the air.
Lived near us and never seemed to care . . .
So, finally the war on poverty came here . . .
The neighbor became an expert in health and disease,
the ghetto's problems and the ghetto's needs . . .
To be an authority in health, law, and crime, but tell us,
dear lady, where have you been all this time? (Figure 4.2b)[16]

Jones was concerned about the absence of dedication on the part of antipoverty workers. Jones was surely intent on critiquing "white middle-class experts" here, yet she also directed her critique at her own professional practices as well. Having worked as a professional settlement worker, Jones had always been interested in the relationship between the "experts" and people served by the programs. Jones emphasized that in order to ensure the participation of the poor in the antipoverty programs, the "experts" or "professional" antipoverty workers, including herself, had to change. She wrote in another pamphlet that "we must listen more and talk less, we must ask more and tell less, we must learn more and teach less, we must release control of some of the ideas that we have held as the 'only way to fly.'" Jones stressed that if NAPP workers were content with the status quo and would not become "agents of change," then all the programs and every project would be "the same old soup warmed over."[17]

Los Angeles mayor Yorty and EYOA executive director Joe Maldonado saw Opal C. Jones and NAPP as a political threat. Mayor Yorty was especially concerned with Jones's close affiliation with Hawkins, who had been in a running battle with the mayor over the establishment of the antipoverty agency. As early as the summer of 1965, Maldonado ordered Jones to stay away from the community and civil rights meeting, as Jones and

Figure 4.2. Opal C. Jones's critique of the "professional" antipoverty workers. Courtesy of California Social Welfare Archives, Special Collections, University of Southern California.

other NAPP workers struggled to have a part in the formation of an antipoverty group in Los Angeles.[18]

The Yorty-EYOA coalition and Jones came into direct conflict when in December 1965 the EYOA required that all but five community aides be pulled out of each outpost to work in public and private agencies. This ran contrary to Jones's view that NAPP should be a vehicle for the participation of the poor in local antipoverty programs. Jones opposed the idea of pulling NAPP aides out of community development and placing them in agencies, contending that it would force the program to move "people out of the community" and leave aides "brainwashed into the power structure."[19]

African American leaders like Hawkins and Bradley had complained that Yorty was trying to take over NAPP. Hawkins regarded NAPP as an arena for building more "indigenous leadership" in poor neighborhoods.[20] Bradley, who thought of NAPP as "one of the successful anti-poverty programs" in Los Angeles, contended that NAPP should have been taken away from the EYOA. Bradley asked Samuel F. Yette of the OEO to send some "responsible" OEO persons to visit Los Angeles and investigate the EYOA's involvement in NAPP.[21] These black leaders were concerned that Yorty was preventing NAPP from mobilizing the poor.

In February 1966, there was a rumor that the EYOA would fire Opal C. Jones. One of the core newspapers for African American residents in Los Angeles, the *Los Angeles Sentinel*, reported that Maldonado had allegedly said at the meeting that someone was causing confusion in the city's poverty program and Robert Goe, Mayor Yorty's representative on the EYOA board, had advised Maldonado to fire Jones. The *Sentinel* stated that this was because Jones and the successful operation of NAPP had become a "threat to the power structure of EYOA."[22] Bill Riviera, public affairs director of the EYOA, argued that "an anti-Yorty bias [was] transferred to our organization" through NAPP. Mayor Yorty and the EYOA regarded Jones's NAPP as a stumbling block precisely because it had become a significant arena for building political organizations against the government officials.[23]

The conflict reached its climax in March 1966. Jones expressed her opinion that NAPP should be separated from the EYOA and operated for the benefit of the community. Maldonado contended that NAPP should work through the EYOA to help produce jobs. When Jones proceeded with a public meeting in March intended to clarify the role of NAPP in the

Los Angeles War on Poverty and improve the relationship between Mexican workers and African American workers, the EYOA ordered Jones to cancel it. The four hundred NAPP workers staged a protest march to the EYOA headquarters in support of Jones's leadership on March 28. Jones refused to cancel the meeting. Subsequently, Maldonado fired Jones at the end of March.[24]

There were two grounds for the dismissal of Jones, according to the EYOA. First, Jones was fired for "insubordination" after she refused to cancel the meeting. Maldonado explained that the decision to fire Jones was the result of the "unanimous agreement of the EYOA board members in attendance."[25] However, the *Sentinel* reported that this was not quite true. Rather, the seven representatives of the poor expressed as much surprise and shock at the dismissal of Jones as the rest of the community, with one representative, Samuel Anderson, saying that they were all "disturbed and concerned about the dismissal of Opal C. Jones." Second, Maldonado accused Jones of having solicited funds from her aides for an unauthorized trip to Washington, DC, in September 1965. Yet Ursula Gutierrez, another poverty representative, explained that the EYOA board had no evidence of any wrongdoing by Jones. Gutierrez questioned Maldonado's claim that he did not learn about the trip until February and had not brought the matter to the attention of the board "because of vacations and the time required to gather evidence." Jones told the *Sentinel* that she had gone to Washington during her own vacation time in October and at her own expense to plead with the OEO to make NAPP a separate agency from the EYOA. The *Sentinel* concluded that the real and recurring issue between Jones and the EYOA was the "philosophy behind the operation of her NAPP program."[26] The *Sentinel* suggested that the EYOA dismissed Jones because she tried to recast the antipoverty programs to incorporate the voices of the poor.

In addition to these charges against Jones, some media represented the firing of Jones as a "black-Latino conflict." The editor of the *Herald-Dispatch*, for example, contended that the "battle between Mrs. Jones and the Maldonado office" would become a "threat to the peace and unity presently existing between Negroes and Mexican-Americans." The underrepresentation of Latinos was attracting increasing attention. Some Latino activists pointed a finger at NAPP because predominantly African American residential areas held ten out of the thirteen NAPP posts.[27]

There were criticisms from Mexican American residents that they had not been adequately served by the OEO. As some scholars have pointed out, the Watts uprising, which led to the organization of the Los Angeles War on Poverty task force, brought about a reallocation of antipoverty funds to the predominantly black neighborhood of Los Angeles, South Central. Latino leaders such as member of Congress Edward Roybal demanded equal opportunities for Mexican Americans. Roybal, who graduated from Roosevelt High School in East Los Angeles and became the first Mexican American elected to the U.S. Congress in 1962, charged that the Mexican American community received "only token attention" in antipoverty programs even though "Spanish-speaking Americans face the same economic problems and have suffered the ravage of discrimination" as did African American residents.[28] Ernesto Galarza, the Mexican American EYOA program developer, also noted that black residents had a greater voice in making their demands heard.[29] These Latino leaders argued that East Los Angeles had not received their fair share of the funding from antipoverty programs.

What the media did not reveal, however, was that Jones was in the middle of responding to Mexican American residents' criticisms against the Los Angeles War on Poverty when she got fired. The meeting the EYOA ordered her to cancel was, in fact, a "community relations conference" in order to improve the relationship between black and Latino Angelenos. When Jones was dismissed, several Mexican American leaders, such as Tony Rios, the NAPP outpost director, and Al Romo, a Mexican American poverty area representative, sided with her. Jones argued that the press and politicians were "fanning the flames" of racial conflict between the two groups.[30]

African American leaders quickly took action and demanded that Jones be rehired. When about 350 people rallied in support of Jones on April 3, Hawkins, the principal speaker at the demonstration, demanded her reinstatement. Bradley, chairperson of the Conference of Negro Elected Officials (which consisted of all twenty-two elected African Americans in the Los Angeles County area), also took the initiative and called for Jones's reinstatement. Hawkins and Bradley filed a protest against the dismissal of Jones, the director of one of the most popular and influential antipoverty programs in Los Angeles.[31]

Jones also received support from other African American activists involved in the local antipoverty efforts. Mary Henry, member of the OEO

National Citizens Advisory Committee and one of Jones's colleagues at the Avalon-Carver Community Center, requested the EYOA board to reconsider the firing of Jones. Maulana Karenga and Tommy Jacquette, leaders of Black Nationalist groups who organized the Watts Summer Festival, also joined the demonstration. Furthermore, when the EYOA board voted its confidence in its executive director, Joe Maldonado, five of the seven poverty area representatives abstained. Objecting to the EYOA's handling of Jones as well as the representatives of the poor constantly being outvoted by members of government and private agencies, they left the meeting in protest. One participant in the walkout, Evelyne Copeland, stated that "evidently something has come up that is not 'maximum feasible participation'" and that people in poor neighborhoods "should have the opportunity to do something for themselves." Jones was not the only black female activist who forcefully challenged a local antipoverty agency under the control of local government officials.[32]

Jones did not hold her tongue. She was fully aware that she was so easily dismissed because she was one of the very few female directors. She told the *Sentinel*, "I will fight for my own right and reputation as a social worker and for NAPP to become an independent, vital, community action program." She continued by saying that Maldonado should treat her "not only as a woman, but as a staff member."[33] Jones thus demanded that Maldonado and the EYOA change their perceptions of "appropriate women's roles."

On the day she was fired, Jones wrote a pamphlet titled "I Wonder Why Some People Don't Like Me?" and sent it to Maldonado. In it she wrote,

> You will remember that our neighbors began to read the Community Action Guidelines and they discovered all about that "feasible participation." But, although you always talked about your belief in the idea, I never really felt or thought you really meant it. Why? Because from time to time you expressed your lack of high expectation of neighborhood people; you expressed your doubts and you always seemed to shy away from conflict, criticism and "unsanded down" or real opinions. You always seemed to be on the side of the powerful, and you always seemed to protect the "powerful" more than you seemed to "look out" for the "powerless."[34]

Jones asked Maldonado, who was once a social worker like Jones, a very fundamental question: "How much do you really care?" Jones knew that she was dismissed because she challenged the "powerful" and had done her best to bring the antipoverty programs closer to the poor people.[35]

The story did not end there. Jones actually succeeded in recovering her position as the director of NAPP. She even achieved her goal of wresting control of NAPP from the EYOA. As more and more of the media in Los Angeles covered the controversy over the Jones dismissal, the OEO, afraid of the negative impact on the War on Poverty programs, took action in order to settle the dispute. Sargent Shriver, the director of the OEO, got Mayor Yorty and Maldonado to agree to rehire Jones as long as NAPP was divested from the EYOA. On April 7, Daniel Luevano, regional director of the OEO, issued a directive divesting the EYOA from direct control over NAPP. On April 25, Jones was rehired as interim director of NAPP in a temporary truce until the EYOA could turn over control of NAPP to the Los Angeles Federation of Settlement and Neighborhood Centers in July 1966.[36]

The controversy over the dismissal of Jones had a significant impact on the organization of the EYOA itself as well as its control over NAPP. Luevano also issued a directive stripping the EYOA of its sole control over the Community Action Program, although he declined to link his directive to the uproar over the battle for control of NAPP. The EYOA was directed to reorganize and decentralize its operation. Four new agencies were created in late 1966 and early 1967 in Los Angeles County.[37] Jones's critique of the EYOA led to the reorganization of the EYOA in the end.

While local activists welcomed the new directive to decentralize the Los Angeles Community Action Agency, Mayor Yorty was filled with anger. Reverend H. H. Brookins, chairperson of the United Civil Rights Committee, for instance, thought highly of the directive, contending that it would be a "first step in bringing the poverty program back to the people."[38] Yorty, on the other hand, argued that the War on Poverty was "in danger of collapsing" because of "ill-considered actions taken by the Office of Economic Opportunity and because there has been a deliberate attempt to sabotage the program on the part of some federal officials." Yorty especially cast blame on Hawkins for "continuously misleading the community by stating that I run the program and that I am preventing the poor from realizing its benefits."[39]

Placed in a political predicament, Yorty came up with another plan to prevent Hawkins's side from taking control of the War on Poverty. When city council member Billy G. Mills, who served as a representative of the City of Los Angeles on the EYOA board, resigned his seat in protest against the new directive issued by Luevano, Yorty announced that Edward Hawkins, older brother of Augustus Hawkins, would be the new city representative. Ed Hawkins, who Yorty claimed to have a $15,240-a-year job on the Board of Public Works, had been at odds with his brother over the antipoverty program. Once again pursuing his "divide and conquer" strategy, Yorty challenged, "Now let's see if he [Augustus Hawkins] wants to fight with his brother."[40] Augustus Hawkins countered that Yorty's appointment was "nothing more than an attempt to confuse the issues" and that "Yorty is just playing games."[41] The Augustus Hawkins group and the Yorty followers collided once again as the controversy over the dismissal of Jones resulted in the reorganization of the EYOA.

Jones, in spite of all these difficulties, succeeded in keeping NAPP moving forward. In 1971, she was recognized for her achievements in NAPP by being elected president of the Los Angeles Federation of Settlements and Neighborhood Centers. The Los Angeles Federation of Settlements and Neighborhood Centers was one of the most important delegate agencies of the Los Angeles War on Poverty. Jones regarded this promotion as "an honor and a privilege" and made efforts to make the organization a vital instrument for attacking poverty. By 1976, NAPP had become one of the largest and oldest poverty programs in Los Angeles.[42]

Whereas the OEO did not specify racial or class differences among women working in the War on Poverty, Jones saw these workers as a diverse group made up of people of varied social and economic status and race. Jones repeatedly referred to the relationship between racial discrimination, especially residential segregation, and poverty. She also paid close attention to the class differences between people who were served by the programs and the "experts" involved in poverty programs. By criticizing "professional" antipoverty workers, whom she believed lacked dedication, Jones provided a significant critique of the local welfare system that prevented the people being served from playing an active role. Attacking racial discrimination, critiquing middle-class "experts" for ignoring the voices of the poor, and contesting the EYOA's notions of "appropriate women's roles" were inseparable commitments in Jones's political career.

Furthermore, Jones was not passive in her response to the dominant discourse constructed by the local antipoverty agency, EYOA. As historian Deborah G. White has argued, local welfare activists involved in the Los Angeles War on Poverty such as Opal C. Jones certainly refused to "internalize" the official discourse. What was equally significant was that Jones vigorously challenged and recast the official discourse by writing various kinds of pamphlets and documents herself. Opal C. Jones was not a powerless victim but a historical actor who provided an alternative way of understanding the meaning of welfare through the eyes of the people who were served by the programs.

From "Maximum Feasible Participation" to Welfare Rights: The Watts Labor Community Action Committee and ANC Mothers Anonymous

Watts as a National Model: The WLCAC

The Watts Labor Community Action Committee was organized early in 1965 by labor union members living in the Watts area with financial support from the OEO, the American Federation of Labor and Congress of Industrial Organizations (AFL-CIO), and the Department of Labor. Ted Watkins became its first chairperson in March 1965. Watkins was born in Mississippi in 1912 and moved to Los Angeles in the late 1920s. Originally working for the Ford Motor Company, he joined the local chapter of the UAW and later became its international representative. With his organizing skills and experiences, Watkins was chosen as the first chairperson of the WLCAC.[43]

A WLCAC pamphlet explained that the purpose of WLCAC projects was to "transform the community into a place where anyone of any background or life style would want to live" and "to kindle the fire of pride and self-respect in its people." It emphasized that economic power was the first step toward bringing community stability. The WLCAC acted for improvement in such areas as health and hospital facilities, jobs, housing, transportation, education, consumer protection, welfare rights, voter registration and participation, street maintenance and lighting, and trash collection.[44]

While the WLCAC took responsibility for administering the War on Poverty programs such as the Neighborhood Youth Corps, it also created its own original programs. One of the most successful programs was a three-month Community Conservation Corps project that provided recreational, educational, and community service activities and jobs for approximately 2,100 youths between the ages of seven and twenty-one. It was funded in July 1966 by the Department of Labor and by labor unions with about $375,000. One of the most popular activities in the Community Conservation Corps project was the neighborhood cleanup and park development in the Watts area. In the neighborhood cleanup, Community Conservation Corps crews planted flower beds and trees around the WLCAC buildings. They also cleaned up the street, distributing the following memo: "To: Watts Community Residents . . . We are seeking to build an understanding among our young people of the fact that this is their community also and that they have a responsibility to it as well as reasons for being proud of it." In its park development activities, the Community Conservation Corps leased neglected and unused properties from public and private owners, cleaned them up, and developed them into "vest-pocket"-sized parks and recreational playgrounds. As a result of these efforts, as many as twelve parks were built through June 1967 in the Watts area. The *Sentinel* praised the program's efforts, reporting, for example, that the WLCAC turned the "U.S. upside down for kids." According to the *Sentinel*, the WLCAC effort was "one of the most phenomenal programs ever attempted."[45]

The WLCAC pointed out that its major accomplishment had been to bring union organizational skills back into Watts and to change the image of labor among the youth. One of the enrollees in the Community Conservation Corps chanted as follows: "Lift your heads and hold them high: CCC is marching by! . . . We're from Watts: mighty, mighty Watts!" WLCAC emphasized that many Community Conservation Corps enrollees were beginning to feel and demonstrate "a sense of community" and that this "sense of community" would become a tool for "the treatment and cure of . . . widespread human alienation and despair."[46]

A "sense of community" for the members of the Community Conservation Corps did not necessarily exclude nonblack residents. Although a majority of the enrollees and staff of the Community Conservation Corps were African Americans, there were substantial Mexican American enrollees and staff members as well as a number of white staff. In addition to remedial English and mathematics, Community Conservation Corps classes taught Mexican American cultural heritage and conversational Spanish as well as black cultural heritage. The most important criteria in choosing the staff of the Community Conservation Corps were whether they were residents of the areas or residents of adjacent and similar communities and whether they had grown up under conditions similar to those common to the youth in the program. Although these activists stressed "community control," they remained open to people of other racial/ethnic groups.

The Community Conservation Corps was certainly a male-oriented project, reinforcing the notion that fathers should be the primary breadwinners and leaders. The *1967 Report*, for example, stressed that by bringing men out of union shops to work with the boys and girls in the program, the committee was able to "break down the status quo relationship of mothers as the major influence over young men and to reestablish the role of men as their leaders and models."[47] The WLCAC endorsed gender conservatism, which regarded the matriarchal family structure as a causal factor of poverty.

It is significant, however, to understand the complexities of WLCAC programs. Some women played crucial roles in the organization. For example, Delores McCoy served as a financial secretary, Josephine Whitfield as a corresponding secretary, Rosa Smith as an assistant treasurer, and Wilma Barnes as a Neighborhood Youth Corps liaison. One of the female WLCAC members, Carolee Gardner, emphasized that it became a major site for fostering new black leadership in Watts. Gardner explained as follows: "In the past, 'leadership' in poor communities had come from outsiders. Professionals working in poverty areas have been middle class intellectuals whose role was seen by their clients as one of 'telling poor people what was wrong with them.' The organization of a community by its residents, under the independent leadership of members of that community, is a new kind of urban poverty area development which the WLCAC exemplifies." Ted Watkins agreed. He stated, "The only way people can be proud of their community is if they have a part in building it and a part of owning it."[48]

The WLCAC designed a wide range of projects. First, it established a WLCAC credit union using the OEO grant and provided free check cashing for every credit union member, emphasizing the importance of consumer savings. It also developed a WLCAC nursery for general community beautification and planted more than a hundred thousand dollars' worth of plants and trees. Community Conservation Corps enrollees prepared vacant lots for an agricultural project to grow vegetables and fruits. Furthermore, the WLCAC leased a newly constructed Mobil Oil service station. It was "the first new economic facility built in Watts" since the 1965 revolts and became a job-training center for residents. Finally, the WLCAC acted as a liaison between Watts youth and people living in other areas of

Los Angeles so that they could send Watts youths to families who were interested in WLCAC programs.[49]

The WLCAC facilities also became a site for the Watts Summer Festival, which was initiated by local activists, such as Maulana Karenga and Tommy Jacquette, to honor those who died during the Watts revolts and to remember the uprising as a positive event. Karenga was born in Maryland in 1941 and had a master's degree in political science from UCLA. He taught Swahili and African history at the Westminster Neighborhood Association, a program initiated by the United Presbyterian Church, and started programs with a grant from the EYOA and the OEO to improve health, housing, education, and employment as well as to eradicate poverty in Watts. Karenga stated that one of the problems in Watts was that established organizations such as the National Urban League and the NAACP had not paid sufficient attention to the "cultural" means to solve problems after the Watts uprising. He established the organization Us on September 7, 1965.[50] Jacquette worked at the Westminster Association as a coordinator, introducing the programs there to the Watts youth. He helped organize the Watts Summer Festival in 1966. In October of that same year, he organized Self Leadership for All Nationalities Today (SLANT) to attack unemployment problems among black youth and to promote "political empowerment." SLANT had three hundred members and became the city's "largest Black Nationalist group" by 1970.[51] The WLCAC provided a unique social space for these Black Nationalists in Watts.

With assistance from the Los Angeles County Human Relations Commission, Karenga, Jacquette, and other activists organized the Watts Summer Festival. The first festival was held in August 1966 in Will Rogers Park, and it was estimated that around 130,000 people attended. The Jordan High School Alumni Association served as the official sponsor of the festival. Opal C. Jones expressed her approval for the festival, writing a pamphlet titled "Pride and Progress, Watts Festival." OEO director Sargent Shriver led the parade.[52]

The festival was a great success and had various activities such as concerts, plays, films, social and artistic discussions, and even an exhibition of paintings and sculptures by Watts artists. An editorial in the *Sentinel* reported that the festival was designed to bring to the area "a brighter new look and an escalated feeling of pride" and that it was "symbolic of progress, interracial cooperation, and hope for a better

Figure 4.3. Watts Summer Festival parade on Central Avenue and 103rd Street (August 11, 1967). Courtesy of Herald-Examiner Collection, Los Angeles Public Library.

future." The *Los Angeles Times* declared that the festival gave "drive to the new spirit of the community."[53]

It did not mean, however, that all the Black Nationalist groups supported the Watts Summer Festival. Some regarded it as a pacification program. Bruce M. Tyler criticized the County Human Relations Commission for cultivating "a group of cooperative anti-riot Black Nationalists to repress pro-riot advocates . . . The bargain was sealed with money and jobs."[54] For the critics of the WLCAC and the Watts Summer Festival, its programs were nothing but a well-designed project by the federal government for the purpose of "counter-insurgency and pacification" after the 1965 uprising.[55] In fact, as Gerald Horne has argued, the festival was designed by the Human Relations Commission and other entities to draw youth militancy from "political nationalists" who belonged to the Black Panther Party.[56]

Karenga and Jacquette, however, did not simply follow the OEO, nor were they always supportive of the War on Poverty. Karenga stated that he was aware that the War on Poverty officials intended to cool down the uprising and co-opt efforts by the Black Nationalists, but he also claimed that he used antipoverty programs "in another way." Jacquette later criticized the OEO for giving up their antipoverty efforts too soon. He acknowledged that the War on Poverty had empowered African Americans in Watts and developed their skills. He argued, however, that it stopped its efforts halfway and did not finish the job.[57] Even after the War on Poverty was gone, Jacquette and Karenga managed to continue to hold the festivals so that younger generations would remember what happened in 1965.[58]

WLCAC projects' high reputation led to the transformation of the representation of Watts. Antipoverty activists heralded the WLCAC as a national model for Community Action Agencies. The projects of the WLCAC caught the attention of antipoverty activists in other cities. Eighty project directors and administrators from all the Neighborhood Youth Corps projects in Southern California and Arizona visited WLCAC centers. Watkins also convinced senators (including Robert F. Kennedy of New York) to visit WLCAC facilities.[59] As Olympic gold medalist and WLCAC project leader Ulis Williams described, WLCAC programs like the Community Conservation Corps became "stepping stones" to reformulate the negative images promulgated by the mass media after the Watts revolt.[60] Moreover, after the funding of the WLCAC, the East Los Angles Community Union was established by local unionists in February 1968 with the aid of the EYOA, the OEO, and the UAW. Inspired by the WLCAC's efforts to bring the War on Poverty to the grassroots level, Latino activists created this organization in East Los Angeles to suit their needs.[61] The WLCAC transformed Watts into a "model community" for other localities.

Although the WLCAC made a formidable contribution, one might wonder whether these programs were inside the purview of what poverty warriors envisioned. While Watkins and the WLCAC turned Watts into a national model, Watkins was not simply a tool of the OEO. He sharply questioned one of the most neglected features of the War on Poverty: the lack of accessible jobs. The War on Poverty originally targeted youth as its major focus in the attack on poverty by emphasizing the need to "prevent entry into poverty." In Los Angeles, almost half of the funds went to educational programs. The funding for job training and other employment programs was only 22 percent of the overall grant, and most of this money was aimed at youth, except in the Neighborhood Adult Participation Project. While the EYOA created 48,797 temporary and permanent jobs for poor people, the number of jobs was far from sufficient for the poor residents.[62]

In addition to the OEO's lack of attention to job access, employment opportunities for African American workers were increasingly narrowed due to deindustrialization. Manufacturing firms started leaving South Central Los Angeles in the 1960s. Ever since the 1960s, Los Angeles had gradually shifted from being a highly specialized industrial center focused on aircraft production to a more diversified and decentralized industrial/financial metropolis. While Los Angeles experienced a characteristically "Sunbelt" expansion of high-technology industry and associated services centered on electronics and aerospace, there was an almost Detroit-like decline of traditional, highly unionized work in heavy industry. There occurred a deindustrialization of a huge industrial zone stretching from downtown Los Angeles to the twin ports of San Pedro and Long Beach. When the plants in the automotive, tire, and civilian aircraft sectors disappeared, the highly unionized and relatively high-paying jobs employing large numbers of people of color also followed suit.[63]

It was precisely this beginning process of deindustrialization that Watkins brought into question. According to Watkins, with the old railroad lines gone, the "vital connection" between Watts and the rest of the Los Angeles area was also severed. At the May 1967 Los Angeles hearing on the examination of the War on Poverty, Watkins argued that the War on Poverty had to first focus on job opportunities and transportation needs so that residents would be given a "chance to at least get out to jobs that might become available in other areas."[64]

Watkins and the WLCAC also sought to create job opportunities for residents through the use of antipoverty funds. The campaign to have a "Watts hospital" led to the establishment of Los Angeles County Southeast General Hospital (Martin Luther King Jr. General Hospital) in 1968, which provided not only health-care services but also job opportunities for the residents.[65] Yet the more the WLCAC came to shoulder responsibility for creating accessible jobs for residents, the more it started taking on the form of a business corporation. Historian Horne, for example, has acknowledged that the WLCAC left a significant legacy for residents in Watts. Nevertheless, he denounced the WLCAC for remaining within the hegemonic discourse of private enterprise and free markets, pointing out the irony in the WLCAC's apparent separation from its labor movement roots.[66] With all the problems left unresolved, however, the WLCAC did endeavor to suit the needs of residents in South Central Los Angeles. It is vital to situate Watkins and other unionists' struggles in the context of the War on Poverty, which failed to provide enough job opportunities for poor residents when the processes of white flight and deindustrialization were already under way.

"Jobs or Income Now!": ANC Mothers Anonymous

When Watkins and the WLCAC launched a campaign to bring a hospital to South Central Los Angeles, Johnnie Tillmon and her organization, ANC Mothers Anonymous, insisted that a child care center be built at the hospital site. They argued that even if there were plenty of job opportunities, it would be impossible for poor women with dependent children to work at the newly established hospital without child care.[67]

Tillmon was born in Scott, Arkansas, in 1926. A migrant sharecropper's daughter, she moved to Southern California in 1959 to join her brothers and worked as a union shop steward in a Compton laundry. Tillmon developed her organizing skills there and became involved in a community association called the Nickerson Garden Planning Organization, which was established to improve living conditions in that particular housing project. Tillmon became ill in 1963 and was advised to seek welfare. She was hesitant at first but decided to apply for assistance in order to take care of her children. She immediately learned how caseworkers harassed welfare recipients by investigating their apartments for evidence of extra support and controlled how the recipients should spend money. Tillmon later explained that she thought she had to do something for herself and her neighbors in the housing project: "I felt it was part of my responsibility for people not to get run around. I was seeing the women around me—their experience and hardship—not having a person to call, not having an organization to offer support, that gave an idea."[68] In order to fight against harassment and to assist herself as well as her neighbors, Tillmon organized women on welfare, and in 1963 she founded one of the nation's oldest grassroots organizations: ANC Mothers Anonymous.[69]

Tillmon and her allies used the term "anonymous" in their organization name to show the dehumanizing effects of welfare. She explained, "We understood that what people thought about welfare recipients and women on welfare was that they had no rights, they didn't exist, they was a statistic and not a human being."[70] On establishing ANC Mothers Anonymous, Tillmon interviewed women on welfare in the Watts housing project to see what urgent issues they had. She found out that most of the women wanted to go into training and find jobs rather than receive welfare. As a result, ANC Mothers Anonymous called not only for an adequate amount of Aid to Families with Dependent Children (AFDC) payments but also for decent jobs and training for women on welfare. Tillmon and her allies enumerated the following objectives for their organization: "to obtain decent jobs with adequate pay for those who can work, and to obtain an adequate income for those who cannot work—an annual income to properly include the poor in our democratic society." Under this banner, the organization provided "information, legislative, and action service for the welfare recipients of Watts."[71]

Given that the lack of child care provision was a major obstacle for women on welfare who wished to participate in job training, establishing child care centers in Watts was one of their first priorities. When the Martin Luther King Jr. General Hospital was being established as a response to the need for health resources, ANC Mothers Anonymous persuaded the Federal Department of Health, Education, and Welfare (HEW) to construct a child care center at the hospital site. Within the hospital service district, 26 percent of residents (approximately 83,000) were under ten years of age, yet only 1,480 children were provided with day care. Furthermore, there were no facilities to care for children under two and half, and no child care facilities within the district were available twenty-four hours a day to meet emergencies.[72] The ANC Mothers Anonymous played a key role in establishing a center. They developed an original proposal. In June 1972, they held a child care seminar at the WLCAC to develop interest among local residents. The pamphlet for the seminar explained as follows:

> Rarely has the Black Community been deeply involved at the point of conception of any ideas and plans for the satisfaction of it's [*sic*] needs. The Child Care Center, to be built at the Martin Luther King Jr. Hospital site, was conceived of and the original proposal written by ANC Mothers Anonymous, the forerunners of National Welfare Rights Organization. ANC Mothers Anonymous and other members of the community from various walks of life have been continually involved in all phases of the procedure which brought us to the point of organizing this seminar, for now our committee recognizes the need to stimulate massive community awareness and involvement in the balance of the planning along with the entire future of the Child Care Centers in Our Community.[73]

For Tillmon, a child care center at the MLK Hospital was a touchstone for the "maximum feasible participation" clause. It was imperative for local residents, especially women with dependent children, to get involved in the whole process and make their voices heard. Tillmon noted, "Community Action Agencies across the country seem to be under attack now from without and within, that's all a part of 'Community Action.' Our primary concern is to have full participation in the planning of the Child Care Center."[74] In 1974, their tireless efforts bore fruit. A child care center was finally opened. Tillmon and her allies in ANC Mothers Anonymous maintained that day care should be one of the antipoverty effort's highest priorities. By insisting on their rights to child care, they brought to the forefront the concept of "maximum feasible participation," sharply questioning what this really meant for the poor.

Tillmon joined Jones's Neighborhood Adult Participation Project, and NAPP became a stepping stone to her career as a prominent activist for welfare rights. Impressed by Tillmon's remarkable capacity to organize her neighbors in Watts, Jones urged her to attend a meeting of the Citizens' Crusade against Poverty (CCAP) in Washington, DC, April 13–14, 1966. The CCAP, founded in October 1964, organized individuals dedicated to fighting poverty. It also aimed to combine the civil rights movement with the antipoverty struggle under the leadership of Walter P. Reuther, the president of the United Auto Workers.[75] In order to promote the exchange of ideas among local activists involved in the War on Poverty, the CCAP invited sixty activists, including Tillmon, to its national convention. This convention was a watershed, both in the history of the War on Poverty and in the movement for welfare rights, since it vividly revealed an unbridgeable divide between the OEO, which claimed to be the closest ally of the poor, and delegates from poor neighborhoods, who were ready to denounce the OEO for its inadequate funding and lack of impact.[76]

The vast gap between the two parties came to the surface when Sargent Shriver, OEO director, gave a keynote address to the frustrated audience. While Shriver presented the delegates with the remarkable "accomplishments" of his agency, he was heckled and bombarded with questions by the audience.[77] Dismayed, he walked out right after his speech despite requests for him to remain for questions. This confrontation was widely covered in the national media and interpreted differently by the activists and officials. For those who sympathized greatly with the delegates of the poor, the fault lay with Shriver and the OEO. Richard Boone, the executive director of Citizens' Crusade against Poverty, criticized Shriver for delivering a meaningless list of "success stories" to the very audience who knew that to be incorrect. Boone noted that the great majority of people came from areas where the poor were "disenchanted" with the federal antipoverty program. He continued by saying, "I do not believe that under these circumstances it was well advised to speak of the basic successes of the Federal Anti-Poverty Program."[78] Preston R. Wilcox, an assistant professor at the Columbia University School of Social Work, agreed with Boone and turned a critical eye toward Shriver. He wrote, "Sargeant [*sic*] Shriver owes an apology to all present for his 'political public relations statement' to the very audience who knows more than anyone else of the weaknesses of the War on Poverty . . . Shriver missed a golden opportunity to tap into a viable, nation-wide movement."[79] On the other hand, those who were critical of the idea of "maximum feasible participation" of the poor condemned the delegates' audacity and insolence. Frank P. Graham, chairperson of the National Sharecroppers Fund, consoled Shriver by stating that "we deplore the rudeness of a handful of persons who caused a commotion and disrupted our very important meeting."[80] Daniel Moynihan later noted that "a final irony, and in its many ramifications a fateful one, is that the Federal antipoverty warriors, for all their desperately good intentions, got precious little thanks . . . Shriver appeared, but far from receiving support, he was hooted, booed, jostled, and verbally attacked."[81]

For Tillmon, the CCAP convention turned out to be a crucial space in which to directly confront the OEO and make her voice heard. She protested that the antipoverty funds were far from adequate, and the money did not necessarily reach the poor. Tillmon noted, "We're concerned over the big salaries paid to the people to survey our needs . . . the money isn't getting to the poor . . . the rich are getting richer . . . we are staying poor." She also did not forget to make an appeal to the audience to reinstate Opal C. Jones, declaring that "our program director got fired last week because she wanted poor people on the board."[82] What Tillmon sought to draw attention to was that, in spite of its mighty pronouncements, the War on Poverty was woefully inadequate both in its appropriations and in the ways in which the programs were operated. She emphasized that it failed to help most people out of poverty and that "maximum feasible participation" of the poor had yet to materialize as a reality.[83]

The Washington, DC, meeting of CCAP proved to be a pivotal event for both federal antipoverty warriors and local activists. The OEO began to restrict the power of the poverty district representatives by deciding not to fund any more elections that would give the poor membership on antipoverty boards unless city officials approved it. At the same time, delegates began to steer themselves toward a movement for welfare rights under the leadership of George Wiley.[84] In fact, two and a half months after the Washington convention, Wiley, a former associate national director of the Congress of Racial Equality and a member of CCAP, helped to establish the National Welfare Rights Organization (NWRO). With the formation of the NWRO, local struggles were linked to each other, and individual activists across the nation were able to fight for their rights in collaboration.

The convention also brought to the forefront not only the economic deprivation of the poor but also the question of inequality and particularly the lack of representation of the poor in the War on Poverty. A report prepared by Pamela Roby of CCAP reflected on this aspect of the event. "CCAP was talking about poverty while the real question which appeared indirectly time and again was one of inequality," she said. She continued, "The question of inequality or relative deprivation goes deeper than raising people above a given income level." She also noted that it seemed that "although the poor were to speak, they were to second the voice presented by the leaders of national organizations represented by CCAP."[85] Her hunch was right, and at the convention, the delegates proposed the elimination of the ambiguous word "feasible" from the phrase "maximum feasible participation" in order to extend the involvement of the poor to the utmost. It should also be emphasized that the Washington meeting shed light on Tillmon's ingenuity in organizing the poor and sharply questioning the antipoverty "experts." Tillmon would be appointed as a chairperson of NWRO in August 1967 and would soon become a representative voice for the welfare recipients of the NWRO.

Even after Tillmon moved her base from ANC Mothers Anonymous in Watts to the national office of the NWRO in Washington, DC, she and her allies continued pursuing the same goals and struggled for "decent jobs with adequate pay for those who [could] work, and adequate income for those who [could] not." For critics of "welfare dependency," such as California governor Ronald Reagan, "welfare" meant public assistance only. He regarded this narrow definition of "welfare" either as a gift or as a favor, thus justifying welfare cuts and workfare. In September 1967, Reagan contended that welfare should no longer be considered an "inalienable right" of the poor. He argued that welfare was "something of a gift granted by people who earn their own way to those who can not, or in some cases even to those who will not? . . . it is one government program whose success can only be measured by a decline in the necessity for continuing it."[86] For Tillmon and the women of the NWRO, "welfare" included the right to work, and it was not a charity but a right—a prerequisite for citizenship. Tillmon and the NWRO argued that decent jobs with adequate pay and social security for those unable to work were part of their rights as "Americans to a fair share in the good things of our national life."[87] For them, "welfare rights" did not simply mean a right to public assistance. It embodied a set of rights as American citizens—adequate income, dignity, justice, and democratic participation.

While the NWRO was officially run by welfare recipients, the middle-class staff managed the finances and administered the national office under the direction of Wiley, thereby wielding great influence over the organization. Tillmon and her allies strongly raised objections against Wiley and the middle-class staff (generally made up of white males paid through CAP or VISTA programs), who dismissed the child care issue and tended to give priority for securing jobs to unemployed males rather than to mothers who received AFDC. They criticized the (implicit) goals of "welfare for women" and "jobs for men" pursued by Wiley and his followers. Tillmon later explained the disagreements she had with Wiley regarding the goals of the NWRO. According to Tillmon, what mattered to Wiley was not to offer women jobs but to secure money in their checks and a respectful treatment for them. For Tillmon, however, welfare payments were something that "you used . . . for whatever you needed it for, until you could do better."[88] As Guida West has suggested, NWRO women fought for the "freedom of choice to determine whether to work in the home caring for their children or to work in the labor market or to do both."[89] Tillmon forcefully argued that child rearing and housework constituted real work, yet poor women on welfare were always classified as "unproductive." She emphasized the necessity to expand the definition of "work" and "welfare."

Under the banner of "Jobs or Income Now!," Tillmon fought for both decent jobs with adequate pay for those able to work and adequate income for those unable to work. When the Work Incentive Program (WIN)—designed to provide services to move AFDC recipients from "dependency" to stable employment—was added to the social security amendments in 1967, Tillmon and the NWRO argued that it would force women into low-paid jobs with no future.[90] The 1967 amendments enabled residents to retain the first $30 of their monthly earnings and one-third of the remainder. Yet the criterion of success for WIN was the amount of reduction in AFDC expenditures, not the extent to which it would bring the recipients and their families out of poverty. While the Department of Labor stressed that people would be placed in "good full-time jobs—where there is a chance for advancement and a chance to get ahead in life," the average wage was $2.29 an hour, and 48 percent of the women on welfare made less than $2 an hour. In thirty states, WIN participants earned less than what they had received as AFDC recipients. The reports concluded that they would actually have "little incentive . . . for leaving welfare to work."[91] Whereas the Department of Labor also argued that WIN would provide the education and work experience needed, WIN's emphasis was placed on job training and immediate job placement, and this was strengthened in 1971.[92] Finally, day-care arrangements were far from sufficient, leaving WIN participants to cover the costs after training and the first three to six months of employment.[93] Tillmon and the NWRO argued that without sufficient day-care arrangements, WIN would force mothers to accept dead-end jobs and inadequate training or else be cut off from welfare entirely.

President Nixon proposed the Family Assistance Plan on August 8, 1969, which would guarantee $1,600 a year for a family of four with no working members. It also promised that a family of four with an employed household head would receive benefits combined with annual earnings up to a total income of $3,920. The NWRO contended that most AFDC families would get less money under this plan and proposed that a family needed at least $5,500 in 1969 ($6,500 in 1971) to get out of poverty. Using the same expressions that Jones employed, Tillmon said that the Nixon plan was "nothing but the same old soup warmed over."[94]

When the number of recipients rapidly increased and the NWRO was under fierce attack, the internal conflict between the staff members and welfare recipients came to the forefront. While Wiley and his advisers attempted to mobilize and integrate the working poor—especially white blue-collar workers—into the welfare rights movement, welfare mothers led by Tillmon came to believe that such a direction would marginalize the needs of women and children as well as weaken their own influence within the national office.[95]

Figure 4.4. Johnnie Tillmon addressing a Mother's Day march on Washington (May 12, 1968). Courtesy of Wisconsin Historical Society. WHS-8771.

As a result, Tillmon sought instead to align with the women's movement and gain support from feminist organizations such as the National Organization for Women (NOW). In 1972 Tillmon published an article in *Ms.* magazine titled "Welfare Is a Women's Issue," which articulated how the welfare system controlled the lives of women on welfare and constantly placed them under the scrutiny of government authorities. She also contended that NWRO women were the frontline troops in the struggle for women's freedom. Tillmon raised three questions in her article. First, she argued once again that mother work was a full-time job. Tillmon commented, "If I were president . . . I'd just issue a proclamation that women's work is real work. In other words, I'd start paying women a living wage for doing the work we are already doing—child-raising and housekeeping. Housewives would be getting wages—a legally determined percentage of their husband's salary—instead of having to ask for and account for money they've already earned."[96] AFDC recipients, however, were classified as unproductive, and their child raising and housework were considered to have no value. Tillmon called for expanding this narrow definition of "work." She tried to broaden the horizon of the feminist movement by redefining poverty as a "women's issue" and, by so doing, win the feminists over to her side.[97]

Second, she demonstrated how race, class, and gender were intertwined in producing discourses of "welfare dependency." Tillmon argued that the notion of the American "work ethic" possessed a double standard. It did not apply to all women. Tillmon said, "If you're a society lady from Scarsdale and you spend all your time sitting on your prosperity paring your nails, that's O.K. Women aren't supposed to work. They're supposed to be married."[98] She pointed out that affluent white women were free from the assumed "work ethic." The poor women of color were the main targets for it, and they were charged with "being unproductive."

Finally, Tillmon drew attention to the fact that AFDC women were the nation's source of cheap labor. Tillmon noted, "The president keeps repeating the 'dignity of work' idea. What dignity? . . . There is no dignity in starvation. The problem is that our economic policies deny the dignity and satisfaction of self-sufficiency to millions of people—the millions who suffer in underpaid dirty jobs and still don't have enough to survive."[99] She emphasized that the fundamental problem was that there were no jobs, and if some of the welfare recipients were lucky enough to find an occupation, it was usually an intermittent low-paying dead-end job. They would never be able to lift themselves out of poverty. While the critics regarded "welfare" as a notion diametrically opposed to "work," for Tillmon, "to obtain decent jobs with adequate pay for those who can work" did not contradict "to obtain an adequate income for those who cannot work"—they were simply different sides of the same coin of life with dignity.

Local activists in South Central Los Angeles appropriated the antipoverty programs and transformed them into vehicles for social change. Opal C. Jones, a female welfare activist of color in Los Angeles, carried on the struggle against the official antipoverty agency, the EYOA. Like the female CAP workers in Philadelphia and New York depicted by Nancy A. Naples, Jones did not passively accept the subordinate role in the antipoverty programs that the OEO originally expected women to play. Jones was neither the tool of the OEO nor of the EYOA. Rather, Jones vigorously encouraged the participation of the poor and succeeded in bringing the antipoverty programs closer to the neighborhood residents. Jones constituted a challenge to the OEO's official representation of women. Moreover, she also challenged the EYOA's vision of the programs as being dominated by the local antipoverty agency rather than local people.

By appropriating the funds granted by the War on Poverty and constituting multiple forms of resistance, the activists in the WLCAC carved out a unique social space for Watts residents. They used the War on Poverty funds not just for economic programs but also for the development and elaboration of community control. These activists' struggles were crucial to broadening the scope of the Los Angeles Community Action Program. These activists refashioned the meanings of the antipoverty programs and sent back a new programmatic model that stressed "community control."

The OEO was abolished in 1974, and the EYOA was replaced by an organization called the Greater Los Angeles Community Action Agency in 1973. It was terminated in 1978. Nonetheless, the abolition of the OEO and EYOA did not mean that the WLCAC had no further impact on the residents in South Central Los Angeles. The WLCAC continues to carry on projects such as Manpower Training and General Watts Transportation to this day. These programs continue to have a significant impact on the everyday struggles waged by residents in Watts and beyond.[100]

Finally, Johnnie Tillmon, through her struggles in ANC Mothers Anonymous and the NWRO, contested the narrow definitions of "welfare" endorsed by the critics of AFDC. First, Tillmon contended that welfare recipients should get either "decent jobs with adequate pay" or adequate income to live decent lives. She insisted on the right of individuals to obtain jobs with wages adequate enough to lift them out of poverty, if they were willing and able to work outside the home. Then Tillmon argued that child rearing and housework were full-time jobs and insisted that mothers (and fathers) had the right to receive financial aid. By so doing, she contested what the dominant society assumed to be "work"—the presumption that enabled critics to cast welfare recipients as "lazy" mothers unworthy of support. Tillmon sought to construct a system in which women on welfare could make a choice whether they preferred working outside the home or remaining at home and devoting themselves to child rearing and housework. Through her struggles in ANC Mothers Anonymous and the NWRO, Tillmon contested the narrow definitions of "work" and "welfare," the very premises on which the American welfare state had been built.

5

Translating Black Theology into Korean Activism

The Hitachi Employment Discrimination Trial

In chapters 5 and 6, I shed light on the struggles of the new generation of *zainichi* Koreans in the 1970s and early 1980s and the impact of their activism on the reorganization of citizenship. Through this examination of Kawasaki, with a special focus on the movement led by Korean churches and the Seikyusha organization, I investigate how Korean residents challenged discriminatory employment practices, redefined themselves in the Japanese welfare state, and created an alternative model of "community." I demonstrate how they succeeded in transforming Kawasaki into a bastion of equal rights, forging the so-called Kawasaki system, whereby a city government preceded the central government in abolishing the nationality clause.

Regarding the Seikyusha movement, a few books and dissertations have been written in Japanese in the fields of linguistics and education, and some monographs have been published by city government officials recently.[1] Most of the extant literature today, however, tends to put primary emphasis on the post-1982 period and delineates the birth and development of the Kawasaki Fureaikan ("Fureai hall"—*fureai* means "having contact with others"), an innovative community center for cultural exchange between Korean and Japanese residents.[2] The struggle of Korean activists for welfare rights, which started at a much earlier stage, has received inadequate scholarly attention and remains understudied. In chapter 5 I document the growth of Korean neighborhoods in the coastal areas of Kawasaki City, the role of the Korean church in laying the groundwork for later activism, the emergence of a "progressive" local government (*kakushin jichitai*) and its influence on *zainichi* livelihood, and the implications of the Hitachi Employment Discrimination Trial, which was a watershed in the history of the Korean struggle in Japan during the postwar period. These chapters combine a local story with national debates, demonstrating how notions of welfare were contested on the ground as well as how a subjugated people's local struggles became a major issue on the public agenda.

This chapter also places the global within the local. It examines the interconnections between black church leaders in the United States and *zainichi* Koreans' pursuit of extended citizenship. I examine how Korean activists in the Kawasaki Korean Christian Church embraced black theology and invested it with new meaning, how they encountered African and African American leaders through worldwide organizations such as the World Council of Churches and searched for common ground, and how black church leaders helped Koreans in Kawasaki and other parts of Japan win a victory in the Hitachi Employment Discrimination Trial. Transnational networks with global church leaders, especially with African American leaders, offered a significant framework for Korean leaders in Japan to contest a narrow definition of citizenship.

Revisiting Korean Kawasaki in the 1960s

The Sakuramoto, Ikegami, and Hamachō districts, located along the coastal industrial areas in the southern part of Kawasaki City, housed almost half of the entire Korean population in the city. These Korean laborers were enlisted by the Japanese government to establish military factories and were mobilized into the war effort during World War II. The Sakuramoto, Ikegami, and Hamachō districts quickly became a hub for the military industry when Nihon Kōkan Kabushikigaisha (NKK, currently operated as part of the JFE group), one of the major steel companies, undertook the building of a factory in a portion of reclaimed land in 1913. Other factories followed NKK, and the districts witnessed a rapid increase in their Korean population. In addition, when the Tamagawa ballast railway (presently Japan Railway's Nanbu line) was constructed in 1919, many Koreans took on ballast collection work along the railroad. Between 1923 and 1939, the Korean population in Kawasaki City grew from 569 to 5,343 and from 0.58 percent of city's total population to 2 percent. Many of them lived near the military factories. With a rapid rise in the number of Korean workers, the Sakuramoto, Ikegami, and Hamachō districts gradually turned into one multiethnic neighborhood.[3] When the Japanese war effort escalated in the 1930s, the state coercively recruited more Korean workers. According to historian Pak Kyŏng-sik, as many as 1,113,000 Koreans were conscripted to work in mining, construction, and other branches of manual labor throughout the nation. With a limited command of the Japanese language and only a few skills, most of them were engaged in manual work and lived together in ethnic neighborhoods like the Sakuramoto, Ikegami, and Hamachō districts. When the state enlisted Koreans, first under the name of *boshū* ("contract workers"), then as *kan assen* ("officially set-up workers"), and finally as *chōyō* ("conscripted laborers"), the NKK purchased the present Ikegami district and built a military factory. Several hundred Koreans found their homes in this district, living in temporary quarters close to their workplace. It has been said that these Korean laborers, who took on demanding and dangerous manual labor, created the following rhyme: "Working for NKK is to sacrifice one's life for the company" (*Nihon kōkan wa inochi no kōkan*). And even though they were mobilized into the war effort as Japanese nationals, they were differentiated from those of Japanese ancestry through the *koseki* system (the family register—*koseki* is different from *jūminhyō*, which registers current addresses), experiencing inequality and discrimination.[4]

After the war, Korean workers living in transitory quarters or factory dormitories quickly filled the void left by the Japanese employees who retreated to their homes in the countryside. Kawasaki City, especially the coastal part of Kawasaki comprising the Sakuramoto, Ikegami, and Hamachō districts, became a center for Korean laborers and a port of entry for new migrants. Together with Korean workers who had been conscripted during the war, new arrivals crowded Kawasaki City and found shelter there. In 1955, the Korean population stood at 6,969, making up 1.56 percent of the total population of the city (Table 5.1). With limited access to other types of jobs and increasing competition with Japanese laborers, many of them were self-employed in such occupations as running restaurants or selling copper and iron to big companies like NKK (Table 5.2).[5]

While Kawasaki experienced tremendous growth as the center of the Keihin industrial belt, and even though workers benefited from the postwar boom, poverty remained pervasive in the Sakuramoto, Ikegami, and Hamachō districts. In Japan, between 1955 and 1973, the real GNP expanded at an annual rate of 10 percent, increasing more rapidly than in any other industrial economy in the world. In Kawasaki, real economic growth remained high in the late 1960s, rising at an annual rate of 12–13 percent. During this era of the so-called economic miracle, wages and

Table 5.1. Korean Population of Kawasaki City, 1955–85

	TOTAL POPULATION OF KAWASAKI CITY	KOREAN POPULATION	KOREAN SHARE OF THE OVERALL POPULATION (%)
1955	445,520	6,969	1.56
1970	973,486	9,371	0.96
1985	1,088,624	8,964	0.82

Sources: Kawasaki shi Sōmukyoku Sōmubu Tōkeika, *Kawasaki shi tōkeisho* (Kawasaki: Kawasaki City, 1958–70); Kawasaki City, *Kawasaki: Sūji de miru hanseiki* (Kawasaki: Kawasaki City, 2001), 1.

Table 5.2.Type of Business of Korean Merchants in Kawasaki City, 1957

TYPE OF BUSINESS	NUMBER	% OF TOTAL
Restaurant	143	45.3
Copper and iron	74	23.4
Saccharin	24	7.6
Pachinko (and other amusement services)	17	5.3
Hospital and pharmacy	5	1.5
Organization	6	1.9
Real estate and hotel	5	1.5
Factory	5	1.5
Others	40	12.0

Source: Higuchi Yuichi, "Kawasaki shi Ōhin chiku Chōsenjin no seikatsu jōkyō: 1955 nen zengo o chūshin ni," *Kaikyō* 20 (2000): 62–63.

personal income rose at a surprisingly rapid rate. However, poverty persisted in places like the Ikegami district. In 1969 in Ikegami, about 28.3 percent of the total residents (604 residents out of 2,129 in total—281 were Japanese and 323 were Korean) were on public assistance. Yet only 1 percent of the population received welfare in the entire city.[6]

Furthermore, residents were continuously exposed to environmental pollution. With the rapid expansion of the huge petrochemical complex along the coastal industrial areas, that part of Kawasaki witnessed a rise in pollution. Sooty smoke, smog, and exhaust fumes darkened the skies along the industrial belt. A study by a social welfare organization described the Ikegami district in the 1960s: "Like flurries of snow, black smoke coming out of as many as three thousand factory chimneys fell on the laundry dried under the eaves and piled up on tatami mats and furniture. Iron powder and cement dust fluttered in the air. Black smoke has been in decline since 1963, yet with the replacement of coal with heavy oil, the town is now facing a new devil called sulfur dioxide." Sociologist

Tashiro Kunijiro called the Ikegami and Sakuramoto areas "slums . . . not suitable for the survival of human beings." Sakuramoto, Iketgami, and Hamachō residents were forced to face social contradictions produced by rapid economic growth.[7]

There was, however, a sign of change for *zainichi* workers in Kawasaki. Unlike in Los Angeles where African American activists involved in CAP worked with the federal government to launch an attack on the conservative mayor Samuel Yorty, in cities like Kawasaki, *zainichi* activists gained the support of the newly elected left-wing mayors and challenged the Liberal Democratic Party (LDP)–dominated central government. Korean activists used left-wing mayors' "progressive" narratives to extend citizenship rights.

Environmental pollution caught the public's attention in the 1960s. Voters voiced discontent with the LDP, which prioritized economic growth and neglected issues of public health and environment. While the LDP continued to dominate the central government, voters started to brush off LDP candidates at the local government level. As I discussed in chapter 2, backed by the Socialist Party and the Japan Communist Party, left-wing mayors and governors were elected in major urban centers such as Tokyo, Osaka, and Kanagawa. Minobe Ryokichi, a Tokyo university professor, for instance, won the governorship in Tokyo in 1967 with a slogan that called for "blue skies over Tokyo." Passing antipollution regulations and regarding the welfare of local residents as the most pressing matter, these left-wing governors and mayors criticized the national government's fixation on economic growth.[8]

Kawasaki was no exception to this trend in the ascendancy of progressive local governments. Located in the middle of the Keihin industrial belt, Kawasaki served as a major working-class town and a hub for labor activism near Tokyo. City hall, however, had been dominated by a conservative mayor, Kanazashi Fujitaro, since the end of World War II. A major breakthrough came in 1971. Supported by the Japan Socialist Party and the Japan Communist Party, Ito Saburo, who was a city employee and a chairperson of the city officials' labor union, won the mayorship with a promise to bring back "blue skies and white clouds" to a "polluted city." Ito served as Kawasaki's mayor for eighteen years until his resignation in October 1989.[9]

Calling for the "creation of a humanitarian city" (*Ningen toshi no sōzō*), Ito enacted several antipollution measures and placed great emphasis on welfare. He took a number of steps: the expansion of the Bureau of

Pollution in order to regulate contaminating firms, the legislation of a rigid city regulation against pollution in 1972, the compensation of pollution-related victims by establishing special funds provided by forty-three contaminating firms and the city government in 1973 and 1974, and the creation of special schools for asthmatic children. Ito was also determined to expand social welfare programs by increasing the number of nursery schools, schools for disabled children and adults, and cultural centers for the elderly. The Ito administration not only launched an attack on polluting firms but also vigorously promoted redistribution policies.

Furthermore, in response to the *zainichi* activists' demands for equal rights, Ito's slogan that promised the "creation of [a] humanitarian city" would eventually encompass the provision of aid to the dependent children of Korean residents and the abolition of a nationality clause for applicants for city public housing. In the mid-1980s, when *zainichi* activists struggled to amend the foreign registration law and abolish the fingerprinting requirement for permanent residents, Ito sided with Koreans and refused to denounce those who declined to be fingerprinted. Ito, in fact, was the first mayor who officially expressed sympathy for the antifingerprinting movement. During his mayorship, Kawasaki became a bastion of Korean residents' struggle for equal rights.[10]

Interactions, Exchanges, and Translations: Black Theology and Korean Activism in Kawasaki

For Korean laborers and their descendants in these areas, the church became the vehicle for social change. The Korean Christian Church in Japan functioned not only as a house of worship but also as an advocate for the advance of education and welfare rights. While ethnic organizations such as Mindan and Chongryun were divided along national lines—reflecting the division of Korea itself—and continued to regard Korean residents (even second- and third-generation Koreans) as sojourners, the church and its welfare organization afforded them an arena in which to contest the narrow definition of citizenship. It also became a site of interracial cooperation.[11]

The Korean church in Kawasaki has its roots in a Presbyterian church called the Hamachō kyōkai, established for Korean laborers in August 1936. Due to suppression by the Japanese police, it operated without a leader until a Japanese minister, Kuramochi Yoshio, was inducted in

February 1941. While most of the members were Korean, the church had some Japanese followers, functioning as a site of interracial companionship. Despite being destroyed by a U.S. air raid in April 1945, the church building reopened in November 1947. It then became part of the Korean Christian Church in Japan (KCCJ, or Zainichi Daikan Kirisuto Kyōkai) in 1951, and a year later, a new chapel was established in the Sakuramoto district, which became a hub for extending citizenship rights in the 1970s.[12]

One cannot tell the story of the Kawasaki Korean Christian Church's welfare struggles without mentioning the role played by Reverend Lee In Ha. Born in Korea's North Kyongsang Province in 1925, Lee moved to Kyoto in 1941, married a Japanese woman named Sakai Sachiko, and completed work at the Nihon Kirisutokyō Shingaku Senmon Gakkō (today's Tokyo Union Theological Seminary) in 1952. After spending two years at Knox College in Toronto, Reverend Lee became the first minister assigned to the Kawasaki Korean Christian Church in March 1959, serving there for thirty-seven years.[13] He quickly became a key figure both in the Korean Christian Church in Japan and in the National Christian Council in Japan. The latter group held a central role in organizing Protestant churches in Japan and establishing relationships with other churches throughout the world.

Under the leadership of Reverend Lee, the Kawasaki Korean Christian Church opened a nursery school inside the chapel for double-income families in April 1969. This endeavor was executed under the guidance of the Korean Christian Church in Japan, which adopted a resolution in 1968 that it would pay more attention to the plight of Korean residents and their day-to-day difficulties. According to Reverend Lee, the Sakuramoto nursery school also owed its existence to his personal experience. When he tried to enroll his daughter in a public nursery school in Kawasaki, he was denied access because, according to the public official, "he was from the other side of the world." (It is also interesting to note that his daughter was later given special treatment and was allowed to enter the public nursery school because "she was a daughter of a minister.") Because of this disheartening experience, he came to realize that it was vital to establish a nursery school for Korean families who were placed in a similar situation.[14]

The Sakuramoto nursery school promoted the concept of the "ethnic nursery" (*minzoku hoiku*), which was designed to advance minority group members' political consciousness to fight against discrimination, although it remained open to any child regardless of nationality, ethnicity, religion, or faith. It provided service for families in the neighborhood, serving seven Korean children and twenty-seven Japanese children during the first year.[15] As the next chapter discusses, the concept of an "ethnic nursery" became the basis for demanding educational rights. The Sakuramoto nursery school would evolve into a welfare organization called Seikyusha, which would become a unique vehicle for the battles fought by Korean residents against the discriminatory welfare system.

Korean activists in the Kawasaki Korean Christian Church, like Reverend Lee, were strongly influenced by African American church leaders committed to black liberation struggles. They embraced what they learned from black ministers and reshaped these lessons to suit their needs. When Martin Luther King Jr. organized the monumental Montgomery Bus Boycott in 1955, Reverend Lee was in Toronto, "feeling black people's pursuit for liberty keenly." In fact, when a Japanese minister by the name of Kajiawara Hisashi organized a study group on King in August 1976 and decided to hold a workshop every summer in Karuizawa, Nagano Prefecture, Lee did not hesitate in participating.[16]

Reverend Lee and other members of the Kawasaki Korean Christian Church were also inspired by a black theologian by the name of James H. Cone, who was then teaching at Union Theological Seminary in New York City. Cone, one of "the most creative and pace-setting contemporary black theologians," brought together Christianity and black power.[17] He was influenced both by Martin Luther King Jr.'s demand for the church to be a vanguard for black liberation struggles and by Malcolm X's affirmation of the African origin and blackness of African Americans. Cone was not the only theologian who formulated such a black theology. In fact, his ideas evolved in dialogue with other black theologians including J. Deotis Roberts, Gayraud S. Wilmore, Charles H. Long, and Jaramogi Abebe Agyeman (the former Albert Cleage).[18] Most interestingly, for Kawasaki Koreans, Cone's work in particular became a source of inspiration and thus worthy of attention.

Born in Fordyce, Arkansas, in 1938 and raised in Bearden, about fourteen miles away from his birthplace, Cone spent his early years living in the Jim Crow South where black residents were constantly dehumanized. Cone was profoundly influenced by his father, who was committed to the struggle for freedom and had filed a lawsuit against the Bearden School Board on the grounds that the segregated white and black schools were not equal. Cone's mother, who was a firm believer in the Macedonia

African Methodist Episcopal (AME) Church, was also a great influence. Cone entered the AME Church's two-year college in North Little Rock, Arkansas, and transferred to Philander Smith College, a Methodist college in Little Rock, where he started reading about King and "experienced first-hand the 1957 integration crisis at Central High School."[19] Cone then moved to Evanston, Illinois, to attend Garret Biblical Institute, where he earned his PhD. There Cone realized that neither the black Evanstonians nor the African American students at Garret were actually free and that blacks were dehumanized even "up North." In the midst of widespread black liberation struggles, Cone started formulating the "theological meaning of black people's commitment to political and social injustice."[20]

Cone's black theology was crafted in the context of black liberation struggles, particularly for the sake of ghetto residents. Shocked by the urban uprisings that occurred in Detroit and many other cities during the summer of 1967, and more so by white preachers' condemnation of black violence despite their silence on the matter of what Cone called "structural white violence," he wrote a brief "manifesto" in order to bring to the forefront the question of racism in the field of theology.[21] Cone later explained, "A theology created for comfortable white suburbia could not answer questions that blacks were asking in their struggle for dignity in the wretched conditions of the riot-torn ghettoes of U.S. cities. Black church leaders had to create their own theological perspective from within the context of the ghetto, using whatever resources they knew from black history and culture."[22]

Cone published his first book, *Black Theology and Black Power*, in 1969, forcefully arguing that Christianity was not alien to black power but rather black power was "Christ's central message to twentieth-century America."[23] *Black Theology and Black Power* was an eye-opener for many black Christian leaders, especially those caught between Black Nationalists, who condemned the black church as not activist enough, and white church leaders, who urged them to follow King's nonviolent Christian love and denounce black power advocates. Cone was not necessarily the first black Christian who embraced black power. The National Committee of Negro Churchmen (NCNC; later the NCBC, the National Committee of Black Churchmen, and then the National Conference of Black Christians) published their "Black Power Statement" in the *New York Times* on July 31, 1966, which served as an inspiration for Cone.[24] Yet according to Gayraud S. Wilmore, the first chairperson of NCNC, with the publication of *Black Theology and Black Power*, Wilmore and other black church leaders finally found "an authentic voice—a platform upon which to stand."[25] Cone reconciled Christianity and black power, thus creating the groundwork for black Christians in the struggle for liberation.

Cone developed his ideas and published his second book, *A Black Theology of Liberation*, in 1970. He constructed a new perspective in viewing the discipline of theology, arguing that Christianity was basically a theology of liberation. He maintained that "American white theology" gave religious sanction to the "genocide of Amerindians and the enslavement of Africans." The task of black theology, then, was to analyze the nature of the Christian gospel in the light of subjugated blacks so that they would see the gospel as "bestowing on them the necessary power to break the chains of oppression."[26]

Korean church leaders were exposed to black theology through the works of a Japanese minister, Kajiwara Hisashi, who was a key figure in introducing the lives and struggles of Martin Luther King Jr. and James H. Cone to a Japanese audience. He established the study group on King that Reverend Lee attended; he translated into Japanese Cone's major works, such as *A Black Theology of Liberation*, *God of the Oppressed*, and *Martin and Malcolm and America*. Kajiwara argued that Cone had "successfully resystematized Christian theology from the perspective of the oppressed black community."[27] Cone's works afforded ministers in Japan like Kajiwara an opportunity to critically examine the current practice of the church organizations and engage in battles for the subjugated people in Japan. According to Kajiwara, Japanese Christians tended to be individualistic under the totalitarian oppression of the *tennō* ("emperor") system. They only concerned themselves with the "salvation of their own souls," not the conditions of the marginalized people. He argued that Cone's theology gave Japanese Christians "a light to overcome [their] individualistic constitution of faith" and made it possible for them to see the "problems of suffering and discriminated minority groups in this society like Ainu, koreans [*sic*], Mikaiho Buraku [the former outcast group], etc."[28] Through Kajiwara's works, Korean activists in Kawasaki came to embrace black theology.

Two themes in Cone's black theology particularly caught the attention of Christian leaders in Japan. First, Cone stressed the relevance of Christianity to black liberation. According to Cone, there was a tendency to argue that "Christianity has nothing to do with black self-determination" in view of its misuse in the interests of slavery and white supremacy. Cone, however, maintained that black theology should be built on the foundation laid by Martin Luther King Jr., who preached black liberation in the light of Christianity.[29] This emphasis on the role of the church in the struggle for freedom appealed to ministers in Japan, who sought to engage in a movement geared toward social change.[30]

Cone also argued that the focus on blackness did not mean that only blacks suffered as victims of racial discrimination. Rather, he stressed that blackness symbolized oppression and liberty in any society and also stood for all victims of oppression: "The focus on blackness does not mean that only blacks suffer as victims in a racist society, but that blackness is an ontological symbol and a visible reality which best describes what oppression means in America."[31]

This emphasis on black theology as the "theology of the oppressed" inspired Christian leaders in various parts of the world, especially in Latin America and Asia. Pablo Richard contends that *A Black Theology of Liberation* has served as "a fount from which living water keeps on running," enabling the poor to interpret their struggles at home by relating them to African Americans' fight for freedom.[32] In addition, according to K. C. Abraham, Cone's statements struck a "sympathetic chord in the minds and hearts of many oppressed groups in India."[33] To *zainichi* Koreans struggling in Kawasaki, it offered them a ray of hope and a framework through which they could contest discriminatory practices in Japan.[34]

Members of the Kawasaki Korean Christian Church not only read Cone's books on black theology but also invited him to lecture in Japan. At the WCC meeting held in Berlin, Reverend Lee asked Cone to visit Japan and give lectures for the *zainichi* Koreans. Cone first declined the invitation, saying, "I do not know very much about *zainichi* Koreans or Japan." Then Lee told him, "You developed a theology that was useful to Koreans in Japan. So tell us how the church serves as a force for liberation—just tell your story, and we will adjust it and reinterpret it." Thus persuaded, Cone decided to deliver lectures on the civil rights movement, the life of Martin Luther King Jr., and black theology.[35] In May 1975, the Korean Christian Church in Japan invited Cone to lead a three-week workshop titled "The Church Struggling for the Liberation of the People" in Tokyo, Nagoya, Osaka, and Fukuoka.[36]

Through interactions with *zainichi* Christians, Cone came to realize that what black people had gone through in the United States was actually quite similar to what *zainichi* Koreans had endured. While many *zainichi*

Figure 5.1. James H. Cone (left) with Lee In Ha (middle) and Sakai Sachiko (right), 1975. Source: Lee In Ha, Rekishi no hazama o ikiru *(Tokyo: Nihon Kirisuto Kyōdan Shuppankyoku, 2006), 95. Courtesy of Nihon Kirisuto Kyōdan Shuppankyoku.*

Christians welcomed Cone and embraced black theology, some Japanese religious leaders simply refused his interpretation. For instance, according to Kajiwara, one Japanese preacher pressed Cone for an explanation, asking him, "Who in the world did you think was the oppressor, and who could not be the oppressor?"[37] Cone noted that some Japanese preachers were reluctant to listen to his lectures, and their distant and unwelcoming attitude toward black theology reminded him of the white religious leaders in his homeland. Cone thus understood that, in spite of their differences, what he wrote about African Americans and the Christian gospel had many parallels to the situation surrounding Koreans in Japan and the Korean church. He also noticed similarities between white American church leaders and Japanese Christians, based on their response and opposition to black theology.[38] He later noted that his encounter with *zainichi* Christians, especially with Reverend Lee, enlarged his perspective, helping him situate black theology among other theologies of liberation.[39] Lee and Cone helped unite *zainichi* theology (*kiryūno tami no shingaku*, or sojourner theology) and black theology, as well as *zainichi* Christians and black Christians, in a common antiracist cause.

Breaking the Ice: The Hitachi Employment Discrimination Trial and Its Repercussions

The Hitachi Employment Discrimination Trial, which started in 1970, represented a watershed in the history of the *zainichi* Korean struggle for extending citizenship rights in postwar Japan. Lee later recalled that the struggle against Hitachi could be compared to the Montgomery Bus Boycott in Alabama in terms of its impact on subsequent movements. He noted, "I regard this [the Hitachi Employment Discrimination Trial] as an event equivalent to the [Montgomery] Bus Boycott, which led to their victory in the courtroom and marked the beginning of an epoch in the black Americans' civil rights movement."[40] Neither Mindan nor Chongryun, which continued to regard *zainichi* Koreans as sojourners (people who were supposed to belong to their divided "home" countries, whether it be North or South Korea), supported this alternative movement. The Hitachi trial generated a new type of movement that focused on resident Koreans' political rights in Japan, creating a unique coalition among young Japanese-born Koreans, Japanese activists, and Christian leaders of the world who were committed to antidiscrimination struggles.[41]

There are several reasons why this new type of movement took place in the early 1970s. First, crucial shifts in resident Korean political consciousness had occurred as a result of the generation shift. By the mid-1970s, over three-fourths of *zainichi* Koreans were Japanese born. In Kawasaki City, for instance, 78 percent were second or third generation. These young Koreans struggled to find who they were and where they belonged in the places where they grew up, not just in North or South Korea. Second, as Bae Joong Do, who became the first director of Fureaikan in the late 1980s, suggested, these Japanese-educated young Koreans were strongly influenced by the Japanese student revolt and antiwar movement in the late 1960s. They worked together with members of *Zenkyōto* (All Student Joint Struggle Councils), the radical student organization, and also the popular *Beheiren* (Japan "Peace for Vietnam!" Committee). As a result, they gained support from these student organizations. Finally, as I explain later, a transnational network was forged among Christian leaders representing subjugated people. This alliance played a significant role in supporting the *zainichi* Korean battles for equality. All of these factors, along with the emergence of progressive local governments, led to Korean activists' successful fight against the Hitachi company and eventually the transformation of exclusionary welfare programs at the local level.[42]

Park Jong Seok was born in Nishio, Aichi Prefecture. As a Japanese-educated second-generation Korean, he was raised as Arai Shoji (his Japanese alias) and did not even know how to pronounce his own Korean name. After he graduated from a local public high school in 1970, he worked in a small company—his high school teacher recommended that he seek employment in this company because "it would hire even Koreans." One day he saw a classified ad for a clerical job at the Hitachi software firm in Totsuka in Kanagawa Prefecture. Aspiring to work at Hitachi, one of the biggest consumer electronics companies in Japan and in the world, he applied for this position in August 1970, hiding his Korean identity by using his Japanese alias and reporting his birthplace as his *koseki*. Park passed the entrance exam and was offered a job as one of seven successful candidates out of thirty-two applicants.[43]

The Hitachi company ordered him to turn in his *koseki tōhon* (a full copy of one's family register that includes the names of relations beyond one's parents) on September 4. Park could not get a copy because his *koseki* was in Korea, so he called the Hitachi company on September 15. Learning of his Korean identity, the Hitachi company panicked and told him that they would suspend his employment notice and call him the next day. Park waited but got no reply, so he called the company again. Then Toma Takeshi, the manager of the labor division, gave a curt answer that the company would not hire "foreigners in general" (*ippan gaikokujin*) and that if Park had given his true identity in his application, he would have never been offered a job in the first place. Park, who was dismissed without formal explanation, asked for help from his high school teacher and the Labor Standard Supervision Office. Under pressure from Hitachi, his high school teacher attempted to persuade him to give up his efforts, giving a coldhearted answer that it was unfortunate that he was born as a Korean and that "he had to accept his fate."[44]

Angered by Hitachi's unfair treatment, Park went to visit the firm in Totsuka with his sister and young Japanese supporters. Japanese followers later helped to form a group called "*Park-kun o Kakomu Kai* (Association surrounding Mr. Park, or the Legal Defense Committee for Mr. Park)." Toma, once again, replied that the company would not hire "foreigners in general." While Hitachi repeatedly made an excuse that they would not hire "*ippan gaikokujin*," it later changed its position and justified itself by explaining that Park was dismissed because he turned in a deceitful work record (using his Japanese alias). Waiting two months, Park did not get a satisfactory reply from Hitachi. Therefore, he decided to file a suit against the company.[45]

What Park had experienced was far from exceptional. It was "commonplace" in Japan for Korean youths to be denied employment at large companies on the basis of their ethnic origin. According to Ozawa Yusaku, who at the time was an associate professor of education at Tokyo Municipal College, among the 106 large industries with a capital of more than ¥3,000,000,000, 42 percent replied that it would matter whether a job applicant was *zainichi* or not; 38 percent answered that it would matter but it was up to each individual.[46] The Hitachi case was significant because Park was the first to challenge these ongoing discriminatory employment practices against Koreans in Japan. The Hitachi trial brought to public attention the past and present discrimination against *zainichi* Koreans and would be a turning point in their struggles for justice.

The trial also created a unique coalition between young Korean activists and Japanese students/intellectuals. Park asked for help from Keio University students who were involved in *Beheiren* at the Yokohama station in October 1970. Soon, a young leader of the Kawasaki Korean Christian Church, Choi Seungkoo, joined their group, and other members of the Kawasaki church followed him. Reverend Lee and other Christian leaders, activists, and professors—both Korean and Japanese—established the Association surrounding Mr. Park in April 1971.[47] The association claimed that what Park went through was only "the tip of the iceberg" and that even this "tip" was forgotten and hushed up because of ignorance and indifference among the Japanese.[48] The association was a "forerunner of a unique citizens' movement" that created a partnership between Korean and Japanese youth.[49]

The traditional ethnic organizations, Mindan and Chongryun, found the Hitachi case to be problematic precisely because it questioned employment discrimination against *zainichi* youth for the first time and because it created a rare interethnic coalition. For members of these two organizations, employment in a major Japanese company was simply another step toward assimilation. There was a powerful backlash against *zainichi* Koreans who were involved in the anti-Hitachi struggles. Choi Seungkoo of the Kawasaki Korean Christian Church, for instance, was forced to resign from his position as a youth representative because he was branded "as a traitor, as an assimilationist."[50] For Mindan and Chongryun members, *zainichi* Koreans who supposedly belonged to North or South Korea should be concerned with their status in their "home" countries rather than their citizenship rights in Japan.

From the time when Park filed his lawsuit on December 8, 1970, twenty-two trials were held before the verdict was announced. In addition to some members of the Association surrounding Mr. Park, historians Pak Kyŏng-sik and Kajimura Hideki appeared as witnesses for the prosecution. There were two issues of law: first, in terms of labor contract, whether it was the cancellation of an informal appointment or a dismissal, and second, whether or not it was an unfair discharge based on Park's ethnic background.[51]

Zainichi Korean activists linked their battle against Hitachi to antidiscrimination struggles worldwide. The bonds of solidarity created among Christian activists in Korea, the United States, and the rest of the world had enabled Korean equal rights advocates to challenge one of the world's leading electronics companies on a global scale.

The Hitachi Employment Discrimination Trial was closely linked to the democratization movements in South Korea. Reverend Lee, along with other Koreans in Japan, the United States, and the world, actively supported religious leaders in South Korea who resisted Park Chung Hee's dictatorship.[52] In turn, Christians in South Korea gave strength to the Hitachi struggle. Choi Seungkoo played a significant role in winning support from them and fashioning a transnational activism. After being forced to resign from his position as a representative of the Korean youth in the KCCJ, Choi left for Korea to study at Seoul University. There, he became acquainted with Korean students and women in church organizations. Together they launched a campaign against Hitachi. The Korean Student Christian Federation (KSCF), for example, made a statement in early 1974 that the Japanese government should abolish discrimination against *zainichi* Koreans immediately. Church Women United denounced employment discrimination against Park and called for a boycott of Hitachi goods in April 1974. Through Choi's networking efforts, Christian activists in South Korea joined the *zainichi* Koreans' battle against the Hitachi company.[53]

Reverend Lee also played a significant role in translating Park's struggles into battles for racial and ethnic equality on a supranational scale. Crucial shifts in the stance of Japanese church organizations concerning World War II had occurred during the late 1960s, which strengthened

Reverend Lee's leading position. Church organizations in Japan sought to respond to the ecumenical movement that aimed to bring various religious organizations together as one group under the World Council of Churches. In the name of its moderator, Suzuki Masahisa, the United Church of Christ in Japan (Nihon Kirisuto Kyōdan), in March 1967, made a confession of responsibility during World War II. The confession openly acknowledged that the United Church of Christ in Japan "neglected to perform its mission as a 'watch man'" when Japan committed war crimes and sought for the "forgiveness of the people of all nations, particularly in Asia." It actively endeavored to cooperate with church organizations in Asia, especially in Korea.[54] Influenced by the United Church of Christ in Japan's official statement, the National Council of Churches (NCC) established the Committee on Ethnic Minority Issues, and Lee was chosen as its member. Through this position, he was not only selected as one of four representatives from Asia to the WCC's Program to Combat Racism (PCR) but also named as its vice chairperson. Through the PCR, Reverend Lee encountered African American leaders like Andrew J. Young Jr., who would ultimately be mayor of Atlanta and U.S. ambassador to the United Nations, and black leaders from various African countries. Serving as a vice chairperson of the PCR not only helped him establish connections with black church leaders but also enabled him to understand racism in a transnational perspective and to compare Koreans' experiences in Japan with what was going on in the United States and Africa.[55]

Reverend Lee played an active part in worldwide ecumenical antidiscrimination struggles and helped the Hitachi case win both moral and financial support. Under the leadership of Lee, the Association surrounding Mr. Park appealed for and received a $5,000 donation from the World Council of Churches' Program to Combat Racism on October 11, 1971, and another grant of $10,000 on March 1, 1974.[56] At a conference held in the Netherlands in April and May of 1974, the PCR also made a resolution to boycott Hitachi company goods. Through the PCR, Lee and the Association surrounding Mr. Park organized antidiscrimination struggles across borders, linking the specific case of the Hitachi Employment Discrimination Trial to a transnational fight against racism.[57]

Through exchange with Reverend Lee, African American church leaders also gained a new perspective on racism. While much of the PCR's attention was focused on Africa and black liberation struggles in the United States, Reverend Lee explained how former colonial subjects, mostly Koreans and Taiwanese, experienced discrimination on the basis of their ethnic origin in Japan. According to Lee, his speech seemed to have an influence on the black leaders of the PCR. He wrote,

> African Americans and African representatives tended to view racial discrimination as a black and white issue. I wonder if that understanding came from their shared historical experience, where they underwent systemic discrimination that had been continuously perpetuated by the controlling white majority in Europe and the United States. That was why they translated "racism" into "white supremacy." I introduced the case of a *zainichi* Korean youth who was dismissed by a Japanese company due to his ethnic origin. Then, the black representatives, one after another, said that it sounded very much like the type of discrimination that black people experienced every day. They expressed feelings of solidarity and support for *zainichi* Koreans and their struggles against ethnic discrimination.[58]

It is worth mentioning here that Lee cast Hitachi's discriminatory practice against Park as the archetype of "racism." If one regards "racism" not simply as a matter of color but also as a system for protecting the privileges of people who hold more power by denying the subjugated people "opportunities for asset accumulation and upward mobility" and pushing them outside the borders of citizenship, Hitachi's dismissal of Park would be a prime example of racism.[59] By connecting the Koreans' fight for extending citizenship rights to black liberation struggles and Africa's battle for independence, Reverend Lee sought to create a common language among subjugated people, thereby revealing the interconnectedness of oppression.[60]

The Yokohama district court finally announced the verdict on June 19, 1974, upholding Park's claim almost entirely. It ruled that Park was under labor contract to the Hitachi company, therefore his dismissal was a breach of contract. It also held that Hitachi owed Park the payment of his wages in arrears and that Hitachi should pay financial reparations to Park.[61]

It was an epoch-making verdict for several reasons. First, the court officially found evidence of discrimination against Koreans and admitted that what Hitachi had done was emblematic of Japanese companies that had constantly discriminated on the grounds of ethnicity. The verdict became a weapon in a battle over equal rights and abolition of the nationality

Figure 5.2. Zainichi *activist Park Jong Seok at the Hitachi Trial Victory Rally (September 1, 1974). Source: Minzoku Sabetsu to Tatakau Renraku Kyōgikai,* Minzoku sabetsu to no tatakai: Hitachi shūshoku sabetsu kyūdan, *1975, DVD-ROM, ed. Kawasaki Renraku Kaigi (Kawasaki: Kawasaki Renraku Kaigi, 2008). Courtesy of Park Jong Seok.*

clause. Second, it was a life-changing experience for Japanese supporters who opposed the discriminatory Alien Registration Law but who seldom had had firsthand experience of discrimination. The Hitachi Employment Discrimination Trial generated a unique alliance between young Korean activists and Japanese students/intellectuals and eventually led to the establishment of the organization Mintōren (Minzoku Sabetsu to Tatakau Renraku Kyōgikai, or the National Council for Combating Discrimination against Ethnic Peoples). Finally, for Park himself, the result was much more than a legal victory over Hitachi. At first, he contended that he was no different than a Japanese applicant and, therefore, that Hitachi should have treated him the same. Gradually, however, he emerged with a clearer sense of his Korean identity. During the testimony, he made a statement that whatever the verdict turned out to be, he had won because he had finally become Park Jong Seok, not Arai Shoji: "For me, the biggest change was that I have decided to live as a Korean using my Korean name, even if it means experiencing discrimination because of that change . . . Hitachi gave me an opportunity to spend the rest of my days as a Korean, thereby humanizing my life. As such, I believe that I have already won the case. I would have no regrets, even if I lost."[62]

Staging a battle against Hitachi was a life-changing event for Park and his *zainichi* supporters, because it gave them a chance to question the way they lived and, in Park's words, to "make themselves more human."[63] After the trial, he took up residence in Kawasaki and established community programs for Korean children with other members of the Kawasaki Korean Christian Church. Kawasaki would ultimately evolve into a laboratory for *zainichi* Koreans' struggle for welfare rights.[64]

Furthermore, even after the verdict was announced, the Association surrounding Mr. Park established bonds of solidarity with African American church leaders and succeeded in persuading Hitachi to change its policy. Black leaders put pressure on Hitachi, demanding fair treatment of Korean employees like Park. When the Korean Christian Church in Japan held a meeting called a "Strategic Missionary Meeting on Minority People," Christian leaders representing subjugated people in America and Asia joined them. From the United States, African American, Native American, and Mexican American leaders attended the meeting. At the meeting, W. Sterling Cary, an African American minister who served as the president of the National Council of Churches (NCC), USA, promised to support the association's battle against the Hitachi company.[65] He kept his word. When Hitachi refused to accept the association's suggestion to establish a consultative committee regarding the employment of non-Japanese workers, he sought to persuade the company with other Christian leaders representing NCC and the Japan-North American Commission on Cooperative Mission. They visited Hitachi's New York branch in August 1974 and handed the company a letter saying that they were interested in Park Jong Seok, who was subjected to unfair treatment, and that church leaders in the United States would continue to monitor discrimination by the company. It was reported that the president of Hitachi's New York branch hurriedly went to visit the head office of Hitachi in Tokyo on August 15. As a result, Hitachi bowed to the pressure and agreed to establish a consultative committee.[66]

Transnational activist networks and transborder activities, forged among Korean students and women, the World Council of Churches' Program to Combat Racism, and American church leaders under the direction of Cary, helped Park win a victory over one of the largest electronics companies in Japan and in the world. By so doing, it challenged the hegemonic ideology of big Japanese companies that had excluded former colonial subjects from job opportunities and had relegated them to the margins.

* * *

In this chapter I have examined how Kawasaki City, located in the heart of the "Keihin kogyōchitai"—one of the largest arsenals of the prewar period and gigantic industrial belt of postwar Japan—emerged as a major *zainichi* Korean district near Tokyo. For Korean residents in the coastal areas of Kawasaki, the church functioned as an advocate for the advancement of their citizenship rights. Reverend Lee In Ha and the members of the Kawasaki Korean church became key figures in promoting Korean residents' citizenship.

When the Hitachi Employment Discrimination Trial started in 1970, the Kawasaki Korean Christian Church and the Sakuramoto nursery school became the hub of *zainichi* activism. There, Reverend Lee and young *zainichi* activists were immersed in the works of African American church leaders committed to black liberation struggles, such as Martin Luther King Jr. and James Cone. Transnational networks of global Christian leaders, including those with black church leaders in the United States, offered a significant framework through which Korean activists in Japan could eventually challenge the narrow definitions of citizenship under which they lived. With help from these leaders who committed themselves to antiracist struggles, *zainichi* Koreans won an epoch-making victory at the Hitachi Employment Discrimination Trial, which represented a watershed in the history of the Korean struggle in Japan during the postwar period. As I explore in the next chapter, armed with their victory over Hitachi, Korean activists in Kawasaki would go on to challenge the city and nation's exclusionary local and national welfare policies, asserting their welfare rights and voicing alternative visions of citizenship.

6

Voicing Alternative Visions of Citizenship

The "Kawasaki System" of Welfare

The Kawasaki Koreans' struggles over citizenship signaled a new phase after the Hitachi Employment Discrimination Trial. Kawasaki Koreans expanded their activism by establishing a welfare foundation named Seikyusha (*Seikyu* refers to the Korean Peninsula) and developing the Sakuramoto School (Sakuramoto Gakuen), which supported its graduates. Through Seikyusha and the Sakuramoto School, they sought to abolish the nationality clause, thereby challenging the narrow definition of Japanese citizenship. First they took aim at specific city welfare and education programs that had historically excluded Koreans, such as an allowance for dependent children, the right to public housing, a bulletin of elementary schools, and the right to apply for scholarships. In so doing, they turned Kawasaki City into a bastion of equal rights. They then established the Kawasaki Association for Promoting Zainichi Koreans' Education (Zainichi Kankoku Chōsenjin Kyōiku o Susumeru Kai) and worked to transform the city's education policies. The Association of Mothers Watching Out for Children (Kodomo o Mimamoru Omoni no Kai), led by a second-generation Korean, Song Puja, became a vanguard for challenging the city's board of education. They eventually succeeded in persuading the city to enact a policy toward resident non-nationals—a landmark for the educational rights of *zainichi* Koreans and other non-nationals. In addition, they successfully pressured the city into creating a youth community center, Fureaikan. The *burakumin* (people from historically discriminated communities) became a source of inspiration to them. "Living together" became the slogan for their activism, although it was challenged by some original members who left the Seikyusha organization in the early 1980s. The enactment of an education policy geared for resident non-nationals and the establishment of the Fureaikan came to represent the "Kawasaki system" of welfare, a different community vision from the one pursued by the Ministry of Home Affairs.

Contestations over Welfare, Housing, and Education

The Hitachi Employment Discrimination Trial offered a framework for voicing alternative visions of citizenship. Under the influence of the Hitachi trial, *zainichi* teachers and activists of the Sakuramoto Nursery School initiated a movement geared toward letting children use their Korean names as opposed to their Japanese aliases. They promoted what they called an "ethnic nursery" (*minzoku hoiku*) so that children would respect their ethnic backgrounds without succumbing to discrimination.[1] In order to extend their efforts in supporting *zainichi* children, they reorganized the nursery school. First, the school separated from the Kawasaki Korean Christian Church and developed into a welfare organization called Seikyusha in October 1973. It was authorized as a Kawasaki City welfare agency in February 1974. With seventy students and fifteen staff members, it started organizing several educational programs. Seikyusha eventually became a crucial political space for challenging exclusive social security programs and fighting for Korean children's rights to education.[2] Furthermore, the nursery school itself was expanded. In April 1975, the Sakuramoto Nursery School expanded to become the Sakuramoto School, which provided education all the way through high school. The nursery school teachers and parents thought that it was imperative to expand the nursery school so that *zainichi* children could continue to receive support after graduating from it and so that they would continue to be able to assert themselves as *zainichi* Koreans without hesitation. With the establishment of the Sakuramoto School, the "ethnic nursery" became an "ethnic education."[3] The Sakuramoto School afforded *zainichi* Korean children and their parents a social space from which they could launch a challenge against the city and the central government. Armed with the Sakuramoto School and its "ethnic education," they came to assert more control over the education of Korean children.

Supporters of Park initiated new programs for *zainichi* Korean children in Kawasaki, transforming the monumental victory over Hitachi into a weapon in the fight for welfare and educational rights. Korean activists created several organizations in the midst of the Hitachi Employment Discrimination Trial. Mothers at the Sakuramoto nursery, for instance, established the Association of Mothers Watching Out for Children in April 1975. Later they would play a critical role in advancing Korean students' rights in Kawasaki public schools. In November 1974, the Association surrounding Mr. Park evolved into an organization called the National Council for Combating Discrimination against Ethnic Peoples (Minzoku Sabetsu to Tatakau Renraku Kyōgikai, or Mintōren), a network created by Korean and Japanese activists united against ethnic discrimination. The Korean branch of the association, in particular, established the Association to Protect Zainichi Koreans in Kawasaki (Kawasaki Zainichi Dōhō no Jinken o Mamorukai) under Park's leadership. In order to maintain the spirit of the anti-Hitachi struggles, the Association to Protect Zainichi Koreans in Kawasaki initiated educational and recreational programs for children in the Ikegami district, one of the poorest neighborhoods in coastal Kawasaki.[4] In explaining their reasons for launching children's programs in the coastal parts of Kawasaki, its leaders declared,

> The employment discrimination against Park was only the tip of the iceberg—a well-known, common experience for *zainichi* Koreans in Kawasaki. Weren't we used to accepting discrimination as something inescapable? . . . We have been watching Mr. Park for three years. After floundering and writhing, he sometimes looked as if he were crushed sometimes, but he grew and eventually emerged with a stronger sense of ethnic identity, and openly made a testimony that he regained his confidence through the trial . . . He did that by fighting against discrimination, which was so common to Koreans that many of them felt hopeless about it . . . The roots of the problems are deep, and that is why we need to look at the concrete realities that Korean residents are facing at the local level.[5]

Park, too, wrote a message to his supporters in Korea:

> We, the youth section of the Kawasaki church held a meeting for children in the Ikegami district, a place located in the middle of Kawasaki's industrial zone in Kawasaki, where our fellow Korean citizens live. People lead their lives without any kind of support from the Japanese society . . . Now, after continuously holding meetings for the children, they have started calling themselves by their Korean names and have begun talking to the older generation

> in the neighborhood. We want them to have confidence in themselves as Koreans. We will continue to make efforts until the day our fellow citizens become free.[6]

What these different organizations had in common was that they wanted young Koreans to be able to stand up against discrimination and poverty, just as Park Jong Seok had done. The basic principles of their activism lay in the Hitachi Employment Discrimination Struggle. Their day-to-day activities were conducted at the Kawasaki Korean Christian Church, especially at the Sakuramoto School.[7] These *zainichi* Korean activists would soon demand equal treatment in welfare programs from the city government, crafting a tradition of political activism known as the "Kawasaki system."

The struggles over the Hitachi trial became the cornerstone for addressing alternative visions of citizenship for Koreans in Kawasaki. In addition to developing educational programs for Korean children, Park's supporters launched campaigns for an allowance for dependent children and the right to public housing. When they held a meeting in Kawasaki in April 1974, two months before the Yokohama district court announced the final verdict, some of the attendees brought up the question of why *zainichi* residents were not covered by the city government's allowances for dependent children and public housing programs.[8] At that moment, they began to set their sights on the issues of child welfare and public housing (Figure 6.1).

Figure 6.1. Kawasaki activists gathered to demand an allowance for dependent children and the right to public housing. Courtesy of Kawasaki Zainichi Korean Seikatsu Bunka Shiryōkan.

The Japanese government had used the nationality clause as a justification for excluding *zainichi* Koreans from financial aid (in the form of allowances) for dependent children and public housing programs. Allowances for dependent children had begun in January 1972, providing assistance to families with three or more children under eighteen (with one or more under fifteen). In addition to the income restriction, the Child Allowance Law, which was enacted in May 1971, held the condition that applicants must be *Japanese nationals* who currently resided in Japan.[9] Due to this nationality clause, Koreans in Japan were denied access to the child allowances.

As for public housing, there were two types: those administered by the Japan Housing Public Corporation (Nihon Jūtaku Kōdan) and those operated by local governments. The Japan Housing Public Corporation functioned under the nationality clause and excluded resident non-nationals. Those operated by local governments were dependent on the local authorities' discretion, yet the infamous bulletin titled "Regarding the Treatment of Foreign Applicants for Public Housing" sent by the Housing Bureau of the Ministry of Construction was used as an excuse for limiting public housing access to Japanese nationals only. It declared, "The aim of public housing is . . . to provide low-income families who have difficulties finding affordable housing with apartments and inexpensive rent, to secure the lives of Japanese nationals (*Nihon kokumin*), and to contribute to the expansion of social welfare. The Constitution of Japan guarantees this right to Japanese nationals only, therefore non-nationals cannot make demands for this as their entitlement . . . However, under special circumstances, such as the removal of housing units for the renovation of deteriorated areas, it is appropriate that even non-nationals are given the right to apply."[10] In October 1972, the Ministry of Construction revised their bulletin, once again making clear that, except "under special circumstances," "non-nationals" were not allowed to apply for public housing.[11] Similar to the way that financial aid for dependent children was used to reaffirm boundaries between "non-nationals" (especially former colonial subjects) and "Japanese nationals," public housing was utilized to demarcate the former from the latter.

In July 1974, *zainichi* activists sent an open letter to the mayor of Kawasaki and the head of the bureau of social work, demanding that "resident non-nationals in Japan" (*zainichi gaikokujin*) be given the right to receive allowances for dependent children and public housing. Much to their surprise, city hall was quick to respond and accepted their demands on July 30. The Ito administration replied that, from 1975 on, non-nationals living in Kawasaki would be entitled to an allowance for dependent children and public housing.[12] Park's supporters then pressed the city to revise its ordinances so that *zainichi* residents would be formally included in the city's social security programs. They also petitioned the city council to put pressure on the central government to revise its national social security laws so that not only residents of Kawasaki but also those of other cities would be able to enjoy these rights. They sent the following letter to the council in February 1975: "To the city council . . . we urge Kawasaki City to strongly recommend that the central government amend the law on allowances for dependent children, and repeal the nationality clause with regard to the occupation of public housing. If that happens, the Kawasaki City government would be the nation's first city to achieve this epoch-making accomplishment."[13]

The city council agreed to meet these demands. It asked the central government to change its policy regarding the status of non-nationals living in Japan, issuing the following statement: "To the Prime Minister, the Ministers of Justice, Finance, Health, Labor, & Welfare, and Home Affairs . . . So many non-nationals live in our country, yet they are entitled to almost no protection under the laws that govern their lives. While they are obligated to pay taxes just like Japanese citizens, they are not granted the right to receive an allowance for dependent children . . . it is an extremely unfair system against these foreign residents."[14] There was a reason the Ito administration raised no objection to the *zainichi* activists' demands. Providing welfare services to Korean residents would enhance the image of the Ito administration's "progressiveness" in a form of propaganda that demonstrated the progressive local government's moral superiority to the LDP-dominated central government. Korean activists knew this, and that was why they stressed that Kawasaki should seize the initiative in guaranteeing resident non-nationals' welfare rights. It would also bolster the image of Ito as an advocate of welfare and human rights, and they were well aware that the Ito administration was willing to take such risks. Equally significant was the fact that providing these welfare services to Korean residents in Kawasaki did not cast a heavy financial burden on city hall. As Yamada Takao pointed out in an interview, an allowance for dependent children was granted only to families with three or more children, and protecting the *zainichi* Koreans' rights to public housing was not costly since their number was relatively small.[15] The Kawasaki government in turn adopted a pro-*zainichi* policy as part of its progressive agenda, as *zainichi* activists used the local government's progressive rhetoric surrounding welfare and human rights to contest the narrow definitions of citizenship.

Once Kawasaki Koreans succeeded in breaking a hole in the wall that barricaded them from the full rights of citizenship, *zainichi* Koreans in other cities followed their strategy. In places like Osaka, Amagasaki, Kobe, Kyoto, Nagoya, and Kitakyushu, *zainichi* Koreans initiated struggles to eliminate the nationality clause in their city's child welfare and public housing policies. While Kawasaki was not the first city to provide resident non-nationals with financial aid for dependent children and the right to move into public housing (Tokyo had already granted both and Yokohama granted the former only), Kawasaki was a remarkable case because Koreans achieved these rights through their own efforts. Kawasaki Koreans took the lead in abolishing the nationality clause in welfare. Their activism held the spotlight and became known as the "Kawasaki system."[16]

Armed with their victory at achieving allowances for dependent children and public housing, *zainichi* mothers, nursery school teachers, and activists affiliated with the Korean Christian Church now turned their attention to *zainichi* children's rights to education. As many of them were involved in the Sakuramoto School, devoting themselves to protecting Korean children's educational rights on a day-to-day basis, this was no surprise. They held a meeting with the Kawasaki Board of Education on November 24, 1976, urging it to send a bulletin listing elementary schools for *zainichi* preschoolers. To Japanese families with preschool-aged children, city hall usually sent out bulletins in early January listing the names of the schools, the dates for the beginning of the school year, and the dates for physical checkups. *Zainichi* families, however, received no information because, according to the city officials, they were "non-nationals" and therefore not subject to compulsory education. *Zainichi* Korean families with preschoolers had to ask their Japanese neighbors in order to gain detailed information about schools.[17]

It hadn't been so long prior that government officials had created the excuse that Koreans were not covered by Japan's compulsory education policy because of their status as "non-nationals." During the prewar period, it was mandatory for Korean children to attend the Japanese schools as "Japanese imperial subjects," although the law was not strictly enforced due to the fact that many Korean children were working to support their families. When World War II was over and Japan was under the control of the Supreme Commander for the Allied Powers, the question of citizenship of Koreans remaining in Japan was left ambiguous. In a directive issued in November 1945, SCAP stated that Koreans were to be treated as "liberated nationals" as long as they did not become a matter of military security. In some cases, however, they would be regarded as "enemies" given that they had also been Japanese imperial subjects. SCAP and the Japanese government continued to take this ambiguous and dual position on the legal status of Koreans.[18]

On the one hand, Koreans in Japan were regarded as "aliens." When the Alien Registration Ordinance was enacted in May 1947, they were required to carry registration cards. They were "aliens" belonging to *Chōsen*, meaning Korea, although neither the Republic of Korea nor the Democratic People's Republic of Korea existed back then, so *Chōsen* signified not a nationality but rather an ethnicity.[19]

On the other hand, Koreans were ordered to abide by Japanese education laws as "Japanese nationals." Koreans remaining in the nation established the League of Koreans in Japan in order to protect their rights and worked to construct ethnic schools for Korean children. When they began teaching Korean history and language with their own textbooks, SCAP, worried about the Koreans' becoming a security problem, declared that Koreans should be treated as Japanese nationals in November 1946. Accordingly, the Japanese Ministry of Education declared that Koreans in Japan had to submit to compulsory education. SCAP tightened its policies, and as a result, the Ministry of Education issued an official statement that all Korean schools should abide by Japanese education laws. This meant that Korean schools had to give up both their own curriculum and the Korean language education program or they would not be counted as official schools. The League of Koreans in Japan fought vigorously against this order, urging the government to take into consideration their special needs. The minister of education, however, asserted that if unregistered Korean schools failed to close by April—the time when the new school year officially began—the government would not rule out using force against them. Tensions between Korean activists and SCAP / the Ministry of Education escalated. With police and government officials enforcing the expulsion of Korean children from schools, and Korean activists and Japanese supporters holding mass demonstrations, violent conflict finally erupted in Kobe and Osaka. The U.S. military commander of the Kobe area declared a state of emergency and started randomly arresting the protestors. More than 1,700 people were taken into custody. In Osaka, a U.S. military officer allowed the governor to use firearms against the protestors. A teenage Korean boy was shot to death, and nine were severely wounded. Most of the media, censored by SCAP, put the blame on the League of Koreans in Japan, not the U.S. military officer or the Japanese police. The league was ordered to dissolve, along with their "ethnic schools."[20] Many remembered the Kobe and Osaka conflict as brutal incidents, suppressing Koreans' rights to education by both the United States and Japanese governments. SCAP and the Japanese government increasingly regarded the existence of Koreans in Japan as a security issue and sought to solve the "problem" of former colonial subjects through forced assimilation policies.

With the conclusion of the 1952 San Francisco Peace Treaty, however, the government of Japan officially declared its Korean residents to be "aliens." In 1952, Koreans lost their citizenship, and as "non-nationals in general," they were no longer covered by the mandate of compulsory education. While Korean schools were reconstructed by the pro–North Korea organization Chongryun (General Association of Korean Residents in Japan), they were classified as "miscellaneous schools" by the Ministry of Education, losing financial assistance from the Japanese government.[21]

On February 11, 1953, the Ministry of Education sent the following bulletin to each local government: "If Korean children apply for Japanese schools, they will be allowed to attend just as it had been before 1952. The government, however, will not urge them to enter school and finish compulsory education. The principle of free and compulsory education will not be applied to them."[22] In 1965, when the Republic of Korea–Japan Normalization Treaty was signed, only people with South Korean nationality who had lived in Japan prior to the end of World War II and had turned in their applications within five years from the effective date of the treaty were entitled to the right of permanent residence. The Japanese Ministry of Education changed its policy, and now only children affiliated with South Korea would receive school bulletins if they applied, and they would be covered under the policy of free and compulsory education.[23] Many researchers argued that this change in policy only intensified the tension between residents affiliated with North Korea and those affiliated with South Korea. The question of *zainichi* Koreans' educational rights—once again—had been left ambiguous for authorities to enforce at their own discretion.

After holding several meetings with the Kawasaki City Board of Education, *zainichi* mothers, nursery school teachers, and activists affiliated with Seikyusha won a string of government concessions. While the city government replied that they would not be able to send a bulletin to every *zainichi* family that year due to a "lack of time," they agreed to make an announcement of the same information for *zainichi* preschoolers on the city news report and promised to get rid of the notorious statement concerning the applications for non-Japanese preschoolers. Several local governments, including Kawasaki, forced matriculating *zainichi* children to sign a statement saying, "I will obey Japanese laws while attending school," before entering the public elementary school system. They were coerced to do this in spite of strong opposition from Korean parents, who considered this treatment humiliating. Brandishing their victories over the school bulletin and statement issues, *zainichi* activists in coastal Kawasaki became frontline troops in the struggle for educational rights for non-Japanese children in Japan.[24]

They also demanded the right to apply for scholarships. *Zainichi* activists affiliated with Seikyusha turned their attention to the issue of scholarships and loans for low-income families with dependent children. In January 1977, they sent a letter to Mayor Ito and the director of the Social Work Bureau questioning the exclusion of Korean residents from being able to apply for scholarships and loans for families on welfare. They held several meetings with officials in charge, yet their negotiations broke off because of irreconcilable differences. In order to break the ice, they visited families in coastal Kawasaki (Ikegami, Sakuramoto, and Hamachō), asking them to sign a petition against the exclusion of low-income Korean families from the fellowship and loan programs. With help from Kawasaki City's teachers' union, they collected as many as 3,700 signatures. Their continuous efforts bore fruit: the Social Work Bureau finally abolished the nationality clause for its fellowship and loan programs.[25] Since that time, regardless of their nationality, all children qualified to receive public assistance are able to apply for fellowships and loans. Through their struggles for welfare, housing, and educational rights, *zainichi* mothers, teachers, and activists affiliated with Seikyusha began to make significant steps toward eliminating the nationality clause, thereby gradually changing the city and nation's definition of citizenship.

Kawasaki as an Alternative Model: Establishing the Kawasaki Association for Promoting Zainichi Koreans' Education and the Fureaikan

The year 1982 was a watershed in the *zainichi* Korean struggle in Kawasaki. The Kawasaki Association for Promoting Zainichi Koreans' Education emerged. *Zainichi* activists also made a request to city hall for a community center, which would become a symbol of the "Kawasaki system" of welfare. Through these efforts, Korean activists turned Kawasaki into a bulwark of citizenship rights. The early 1980s marked another transition point as some of the original members, including Park, split away from Seikyusha at the beginning of the decade, voicing other critical visions of citizenship.

Zainichi activists in coastal Kawasaki now strived for a fundamental change in education for their children—that is, for transforming Japanese public schools. There were several reasons why they targeted public schools. Through the Sakuramoto Nursery School and later the Sakuramoto School, they sought to establish an environment where Korean children in Kawasaki would not hesitate to assert themselves as *zainichi*. Using Korean names and not Japanese aliases was a significant symbolic gesture. Yet even though these activists supported the children in their fight against everyday acts of discrimination, they knew that Korean children would be continuously harassed unless they attacked the Japanese public school system itself.[26]

Zainichi activists discovered that Korean children and Japanese pupils in the coastal areas of Kawasaki were experiencing similar difficulties, such as poverty, lack of educational opportunities, environmental pollution, and the breakup of families due to divorce. Schoolteachers tended to leave "troubled" schools in coastal Kawasaki because of the low level of scholastic achievement and the high rate of juvenile delinquency to search for "better" schools in northern Kawasaki. In cases where teachers decided to stay, they were so busy giving supplementary lessons, visiting families, and supporting students that, save for a handful of outstanding teachers, they did not have time to go beyond maintaining the status quo. Korean activists in Seikyusha, Japanese supporters, and school teachers recognized the necessity of fighting for educational rights at the "community" level and changing public schools for both Korean and Japanese children in coastal Kawasaki.[27]

In June 1982, they organized the Kawasaki Association for Promoting Zainichi Koreans' Education (hereafter referred to as the Association). It worked to build a coalition among parents, teachers, and activists; encouraged Kawasaki citizens to learn *zainichi* Koreans' history; and transformed the city's education policies. One of the goals of the Association was to make the Kawasaki City Board of Education acknowledge that within the public school system, Korean children suffered discrimination due to their ethnicity and nationality and that it was the board's responsibility to stop it. They argued that unless the board of education understood what was going on with Korean children and dedicated itself to cracking down on discrimination based on ethnicity, things would remain the same—it would be the same soup warmed over again.[28] The city board of education, however, insisted that no cases of discrimination were reported and that *zainichi* students were getting along with Japanese children. The Association's strategy was to present officials in charge with concrete evidence about what was actually happening in these schools.[29]

Whose "Human Rights"? Song Puja and the Association of Mothers

Zainichi mothers took the lead in confronting the Kawasaki City Board of Education, fighting for the right to education and welfare. Here, I focus on one of these *zainichi* mothers, Song Puja, who became the president of the parents' association of the Sakuramoto Nursery School and who also served as the president of the Association of Mothers Watching Out for Children for six years, thereby becoming a representative voice for Korean mothers in coastal Kawasaki (Figure 6.2).[30]

Song was one of the *zainichi* Koreans who came to assert her Koreanness through her involvement in the Hitachi employment discrimination struggles and the Seikyusha movement that followed. Song was a second-generation Korean born in a *buraku* neighborhood in Nara Prefecture in 1941. She moved to coastal Kawasaki in 1961 to get married. While her Korean husband helped with his father's ironwork, Song prepared meals for the employees in her father-in-law's factory. She gave birth to four children and raised them in Kawasaki. She used to go by her Japanese alias, Iwai Tomiko. "Iwai" was her husband's Japanese alias, and "Tomiko" (meaning "rich girl," pronounced as "puja" in Korean) was a nickname that her father gave her with hopes that she would marry a rich man and be happy. She did not even know how to pronounce her name in Korean until she became involved with the Sakuramoto Nursery School, which her children attended. There she met Reverend Lee and other Christian

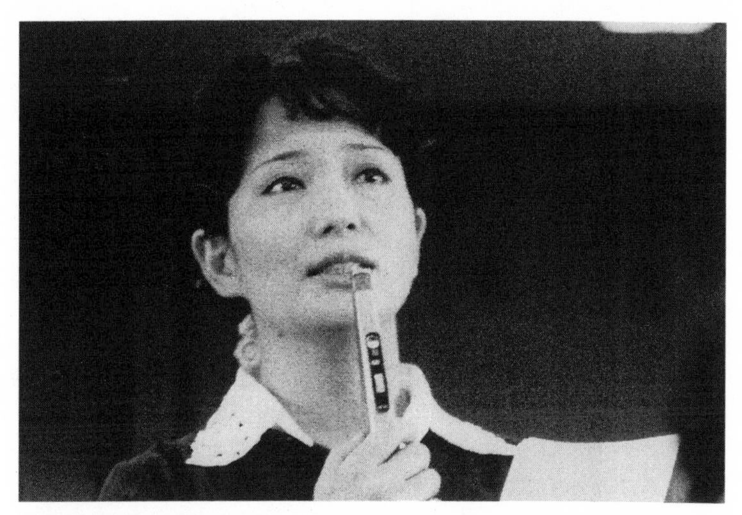

Figure 6.2. Song Puja making remarks at the open forum "Thinking about Tomorrow's Youth" in 1979. Photography by Maekawa Keiji; courtesy of Song Puja.

activists, both Korean and Japanese, who struggled for Korean children's educational and welfare rights. As she learned about *zainichi* Korean history (which was taught at the Kawasaki Korean Christian Church) and got involved in demonstrations related to the Hitachi Employment Discrimination Trial, she started questioning why she had to call herself by her Japanese name, even though she was a second-generation Korean. She regarded her Japanese name as a "*slave* name." She believed that discarding her Japanese alias and using her real name should be the first step toward accepting and asserting her Korean identity. Song not only began to call herself Song (her maiden surname) Puja instead of Iwai Tomiko but also suggested that her children use Korean names despite her husband's opposition.[31]

She also saw her children being continuously harassed by Japanese schoolmates. Her daughter would return home crying, saying that her classmates told her that "Koreans should go back to their own country." Song later wrote that having her children use Korean names in a Japanese public school was like "sending them out as sheep in the midst of wolves." She gradually learned how ignorance of *zainichi* history had led to insults and prejudice against Korean children. She also came to realize that if the Japanese public schools did not change, her children and other *zainichi* children would be "squashed" by the school system.[32]

Through the parents' association as well as the flower arranging lessons she offered at the Sakuramoto Nursery School, Song gradually made connections with other mothers. She urged them to use their Korean names as an affirmation of *zainichi* identity. She also became the president of the Association of Mothers, asking school teachers to pay more attention to *zainichi* children's needs and bringing awareness to why students used Korean names. For instance, when her friend's son was harassed by his classmates, Song visited the principal's office and said, "Aren't teachers supposed to embrace each student's heart, and help all the students grow? . . . Everyday, Korean children are oppressed and bullied at Japanese schools. In order to correct the Japanese children's twisted sense of superiority and disdainful attitudes, and in order to take away that sense of inferiority that Korean children are forced to have, aren't schools and teachers supposed to teach what actually happened in the past, setting up an environment where Korean children are able to live, accept and even be proud of who they are?"[33] Yet most of the teachers simply ignored these mothers' voices. All these experiences, once again, made Song recognize that the public school system itself should be transformed.

In September 1979, Song attended an open forum on the theme "Thinking about Tomorrow's Youth." The forum had been initiated by Nagasu Kazuji, governor of Kanagawa Prefecture, along with Reverend Lee and other members of the Association of Mothers. None of the other attendees raised questions relating to *zainichi* children's educational rights, but Song stepped forward and broke the ice. She suggested that because many Japanese teachers possessed only a limited knowledge of *zainichi* history, Korean children in Japan developed a sense of inferiority and were forced to hide their Korean identities. Song then read aloud essays written by Korean children about their lives at school, explaining how they were teased by Japanese peers, how they internalized the stigma attached to Koreans in Japan, and how they aspired to remain true to themselves. Reverend Lee and other members of the Association of Mothers followed her and made remarks. Their testimonies led to the development of People-to-People Diplomacy from Within (*Uchinaru Minsai Gaikō*) in Kanagawa Prefecture, and the publication of a special handbook on this theme in 1982.[34]

Song played a critical role in organizing the Kawasaki Association for Promoting Zainichi Koreans' Education. During negotiations with the city administration, Song used Mayor Ito's progressive narratives—the vision of creating a "humanitarian city"—to challenge current education policies and to assert *zainichi* children's educational rights.[35] Song asked whose "human rights" Kawasaki City promised to protect. Song later recalled, "Usually about ten members from the Association of Mothers attended the negotiations. They took front seats and appealed to the city board of education. They explained what was happening to Korean children at Japanese schools, sometimes in tearful voices. They knew that Korean children's lives were dependent on these meetings."[36] Song and the Association of Mothers claimed that Kawasaki should be a humanitarian city, not only for Japanese residents, but for Korean residents as well. She and the Association of Mothers appropriated leverage—"human rights"—supplied by the progressive Kawasaki City government and transformed it into a vehicle for social change.

While Song used motherhood to boost her group's moral authority and to enlarge *zainichi* Korean citizenship rights, her activism was not simply based on a vision of women as mothers. She also contested perceptions of what constituted "appropriate women's roles," which were held by the male church leaders. In the mid-1980s, when Song was denied the right to apply for a position as a minister, she quit the Kawasaki church in protest. In addition to the requirement that an applicant have a high school diploma, the church's rules specified that if a female applicant was married, she must have a Christian husband in order to apply. Although she eventually reconciled with the leaders of the Kawasaki Korean Christian Church, she argued that she could not stand the way the church leaders assigned women to secondary roles and that turning down female applications for the position of minister was only the tip of the iceberg. In fact, she was not the only woman who brought up the issue of sexism to the Seikyusha movement. A group of members held a meeting to discuss how *zainichi* women had been affected by the fetters of double oppression—ethnic *and* sexual discrimination.[37] These Korean women problematized both ethnic and gender subjugation, opposing them as a whole.

Korean mothers led by Song, some Japanese schoolteachers, and local activists brought pressure on the city government to enact a policy to protect *zainichi* children's educational rights through the Kawasaki Association for Promoting *Zainichi* Koreans' Education. They sought to recast education for Korean children "not as a charity but as a right" and as a prerequisite for citizenship.[38]

In March 1986, Korean activists successfully convinced the city to enact an epoch-making policy called the Basic Education Policy toward

Resident Non-Nationals (*Zainichi-gaikokujin kyōiku kihon hōshin*). It represented a watershed in the history of *zainichi* Koreans and non-Japanese residents and an alternative "model community"—a different vision of "community" from the one pursued by the Ministry of Home Affairs. It promised to (1) secure educational rights for all children, regardless of their nationality or ethnicity; (2) respect different cultures and support non-national residents' participation in various fields; and (3) strive toward the realization of a "humanitarian city," overcoming its past assimilation and exclusionary policies.[39] It became a cornerstone of Kawasaki City's policies toward non-national residents. Using the progressive government's human rights narratives, Korean activists in Kawasaki rebuilt the city into a pioneer in the field of educational policies geared toward *zainichi* and other resident non-nationals in Japan.

Establishing the Fureaikan: From the Buraku Liberation Movement to Korean Activism in Kawasaki

In addition to organizing the Kawasaki Association for Promoting *Zainichi* Koreans' Education, in September 1982 Korean activists in Kawasaki requested that the city establish a community center for the youth, the Fureaikan in Sakuramoto, the heart of *zainichi* activism in Kawasaki. The center's purpose was to promote cultural exchange between Korean and Japanese young people as well as improve their living and working conditions.[40]

The establishment of a community center was the culmination of years of efforts in assisting children and their families, both Korean and Japanese, at the local level. There were several reasons why activists associated with Seikyusha pressured the city to create a community center in their district. The Sakuramoto Nursery School had expanded into an educational institution that covered the elementary, junior high, and high school levels. The Kawasaki Korean Christian Church chapel and the spare room in the nursery were by no means large enough to manage all these school activities. In addition, the school was burdened by a lack of financial support as well as neighbors' complaints about noise. In order to continue with their battle over the right to education and welfare, the school was in urgent need of a larger space.[41]

Mayor Ito's progressive policies also buttressed their efforts to establish a community center. The Ito administration was in the middle of creating a children's hall (*jidōkan*) in every junior high school district. In Sakura-moto, however, no public facility for that purpose existed, except for the schools themselves. The city administration was willing to help them set up a center for children.[42]

However, besides special problems and the city's progressive policies, another factor helped Kawasaki Koreans achieve a community center. Just as Korean activists forged a network with African American leaders—people with "similar but nonidentical experiences"—challenging the narrow definition of citizenship with their help, they forged networks with another subjugated people, the *burakumin* of Japan. The Buraku liberation movement became a source of inspiration for Korean activists in coastal Kawasaki.

The liberation movement led by a former group of outcasts in Japan, known as the *burakumin*, or *hisabetsusha* (the discriminated), provided a radical critique of postwar Japanese society and offered a framework in which Korean activists in Kawasaki could challenge the narrow definition of citizenship. Although the *burakumin* became "free new commoners" (*shin heimin*) through the 1871 Emancipation Decree, they were still differentiated from "commoners" (*heimin*) through the family registry system. Also, because of residential segregation, they were forced to live in "special communities" (*tokushu buraku*) with inferior infrastructures. Poverty persisted in these areas, and they were excluded from major companies and marriages with "mainstream" Japanese. In 1922, an organization for protecting the rights of the *burakumin*, called Suiheisha (Leveling Society), was founded. After the war, Suiheisha expanded into what came to be known as the Buraku Kaihō Domei (Buraku Liberation League), which included the more moderate supporters of the Japanese government's assimilation policy. Learning from worldwide struggles against racism and imperialism, including black liberation struggles in the United States, they succeeded in winning concessions from the Japanese government in the 1960s and 1970s. In 1969, the government passed the Law on Special Measures for Dōwa Projects and launched programs to improve *burakumin* welfare, education, and living conditions, spending about ¥6 billion between 1969 and 1981.[43] While former colonial subjects had been pushed outside the boundaries of citizenship and denied the right to welfare since 1952, the *burakumin*, who also were deprived of their social and welfare rights, started breaking down the doors to citizenship in the 1970s.[44]

In the mid-1970s the Buraku liberation movement started paying attention to the discrimination suffered by their Korean neighbors. For instance, *Buraku kaihō* (liberation) magazine, published by Buraku Kaihō Kenkyūjo, covered "Koreans in *Buraku*" in February and March 1974. *Burakumin* activists acknowledged that Koreans in Japan were forced to live at the bottom of Japanese society, facing discrimination based on ethnicity *and* poverty and that the Japanese government had set up legal barriers to "drive the *zainichi* to despair," leaving them with no social security or jobs. *Buraku kaihō* regarded attacking discrimination against Koreans as part of the "total liberation of *buraku*."[45] For activists involved in the Buraku liberation movement, fighting prejudice against Koreans came to be recognized as a constituting element of their quest for equality.

Korean activists in Kawasaki, for their part, looked to the Buraku liberation movement for inspiration and guidance. In 1978, four nursery school teachers from the Sakuramoto School attended their first national convention on the "social integration of child care." On learning how *burakumin* nursery school teachers educated children to fight against discrimination, they formed a study group on "ethnic education" after returning to Kawasaki.[46] Other Korean activists in Kawasaki also visited the *buraku* districts in west Japan, exchanging ideas with activists there and learning from their struggles. Bae Joong Do, a key figure in the National Council for Combating Discrimination against Ethnic Peoples (*Mintōren*) and Seikyusha and the first *zainichi* director of the Kawasaki Fureaikan in 1990, later noted, "Whenever we visited the *buraku*, we found a center for the youth . . . we thought we should have this type of center in Sakuramoto."[47] Reverend Lee In Ha of the Kawasaki Korean Christian Church also explained, "As the Buraku liberation movement succeeded in making the government establish day nurseries, *burakumin* activists found *zainichi* children outside the gate of their nursery schools, chewing at their fingernails and gazing at *burakumin*-children . . . The *burakumin* leaders raised the issue of *zainichi* Koreans who lived close to their neighborhoods, and argued that if the *burakumin* neglected the problems that the *zainichi* Koreans faced, their liberation movement would be nothing but hypocritical and deceitful . . . Inspired by this Buraku liberation movement, we struggled for freedom, searching for a new type of local community."[48] Korean activists affiliated with Seikyusha learned how *burakumin* activists created community centers and child care centers in the neighborhoods. They took their cue from the *burakumin* struggle for welfare and education rights and sought to reshape these activities to suit their needs in coastal Kawasaki.

The Banner of "Living Together" and Critical Voices from Within

The Buraku liberation movement regarded the fight against the prejudice inflicting their Korean neighbors as part of the "total liberation of *burakumin*."[49] Along those same lines, activists affiliated with Seikyusha interpreted improving the living conditions of their Japanese neighbors as part of the liberation of *zainichi* Koreans. Under the banner of "living together" (*kyōsei*, or symbiosis), they sought to create a common ground with their Japanese neighbors. For instance, they paid attention to issues of environmental pollution in coastal Kawasaki and supported children in their struggle to overcome asthma. They also held classes for the disabled children in their neighborhood. They argued that the deeper they dug into the *particular* problems of *zainichi* Koreans, the more they would be open to the issues that troubled both Korean and Japanese residents in coastal Kawasaki, such as the poor living and working conditions and the lack of cultural facilities for disabled and nondisabled children.[50]

While the opening of the Fureaikan did not go smoothly due to the opposition of local Japanese residents, it was their principle of *kyōsei* that broke the ice. It took Seikyusha four years to negotiate with city officials and one more year to persuade Japanese neighbors to establish the community center. Neighborhood associations (*chōnaikai*) and children's associations of Japanese residents in and around Sakuramoto took the lead in opposing the establishment of Fureaikan, arguing that Korean residents had not been discriminated against in their neighborhoods and that the city, not Seikyusha, should run the center. One of the representatives of the neighborhood associations, however, later noted that when he visited Sakuramoto School and attended one of their programs for disabled children, he decided to retract his opposition to the establishment of the Fureaikan. After a year of intense conversation, activists affiliated with Seikyusha, the city, and local Japanese residents finally reached an agreement. The city opened the Fureaikan community center and the Children's Culture Center as a joint facility in June 1988; their management would eventually be entrusted to Seikyusha. Along with the Basic Education Policy toward Resident Non-Nationals, Fureaikan became a symbol of the "Kawasaki system" of welfare.[51]

The legacy of their struggles has continued far beyond the 1970s and early 1980s. The Basic Education Policy toward Resident Non-Nationals led to the establishment of the Kawasaki City Representative Assembly for Foreign Residents in 1996 and the enactment of the Multicultural Society Promotion Guide in 2005.[52] The Fureaikan continues to serve local residents—Korean, Japanese, and other resident non-nationals—with a variety of educational and cultural programs and has become a reservoir of information for scholars and activists who are interested in *zainichi* Korean history as well as the fight against prejudice based on race, nationality, and disability in postwar Kawasaki. The Fureaikan currently provides a wide range of programs for local residents of all ages. Those programs include after-school activities for children, social clubs for Korean students, support for disabled children, literacy education programs for older first-generation Koreans, classes in Korean language and culture, and public lectures on Korean and *zainichi* history. The Fureaikan also maintains *zainichi* historical archives, which have helped many researchers, including myself, to study the lives of Koreans in Japan. In recent years, the Fureaikan began to offer support to a diverse spectrum of newcomers, including Filipinos, *Nikkei* Brazilians, Chinese, and newly arrived South Koreans. It has become a hub for local residents, both Korean and Japanese; newcomers; activists; and scholars pursuing their interest in *zainichi* history and East Asian relations.[53] The Basic Education Policy toward Resident Non-Nationals and the Fureaikan provide an alternative community vision that values the welfare and education rights of resident non-nationals.

The Kawasaki Koreans' fight for citizenship, led by Seikyusha, was not entirely free from criticism. Seikyusha's efforts were put under close scrutiny within Korean Kawasaki. Ethnic organizations, especially the pro–North Korean organization Chongryun, which created Korean schools after the League of Koreans in Japan was dissolved, resisted the idea of pressuring the local government into guaranteeing *zainichi* children the right to attend Japanese public schools. Chongryun regarded this as a step toward assimilation into Japanese society, reversing the trend of promoting ethnic education (*minzoku kyōiku*).[54] Activists affiliated with Seikyusha contended that established ethnic organizations like Chongryun and the pro–South Korean organization Mindan failed to address issues that were significant for *zainichi* residents in the realm of their daily lives, such as discrimination in Japanese public schools and workplaces in addition to education and welfare rights for Korean children in Japan. The Seikyusha symbolized the coming age of second- and third-generation Korean activists, who primarily saw themselves as *zainichi*—that is, Koreans in Japan—rather than North Koreans or South Koreans.[55]

Also, some members within the movement criticized Seikyusha for its banner of "living together." In the early 1980s, a few original members, second-generation Koreans, left the organization. Among them was Choi Seungkoo, who was a representative of Korean youth in the Kawasaki Korean Christian Church and who played a critical role in building networks with church organizations in Korea during the Hitachi trial; Cho Kyong-hi, former Sakuramoto Nursery School teacher and Choi's partner; and Park Jong Seok himself. While the conflict between the two groups has been dismissed as an internal power struggle and a personal conflict, it did symbolize the diverging paths. Whereas Seikyusha stressed the importance of uniting as one organization to confront the city government, these members argued that Seikyusha should pay more attention to different opinions coming from within, including those of the Korean and Japanese mothers who sent their children to nurseries. This group was also critical of Seikyusha paying more and more attention to its negotiations with the local government rather than day-to-day activities. They criticized the organization for "leaning too much on the government."[56]

Once the activists affiliated with Seikyusha achieved major victories, such as the Basic Education Policy toward Resident Non-Nationals and the establishment of the Fureaikan in the late 1980s, and became an increasing presence in the media, Choi, Cho, and Park formulated their challenge against it. They especially regarded Seikyusha's emphasis on "living together" as a problem, given that "living together" and the rhetoric of multiculturalism had become the official slogan of many localities in the 1990s and even the national government in the 2000s. Choi contended that Seikyusha had become a part of the establishment—manifesting itself as the "most powerful partner" of Kawasaki, a city that came to boast about its multicultural postures.[57]

In addition to his day-to-day challenges at Hitachi, Park also carried on his struggle in a different form. After entering Hitachi as a computer software engineer at the Totsuka factory branch, he engaged in what he called "a sequel to the Hitachi struggle" (*zoku Hitachi tōsō*).[58] He turned his attention to "the workplace right at his feet," where laborers were not allowed to express themselves and would be left out in the cold when they did. Park argued that in a place based on the principle of maximum profit and efficiency, workers could not afford to think about the people surrounding them, let alone issues of citizenship rights for resident non-nationals. Hitachi's trade unions failed to provide a social space for workers to challenge the company's business goals; rather, they sought to muffle the laborers' voices on behalf of management. Park contended that the discrimination against Koreans in Japan and the alienation of workers were different sides of the same coin.[59]

Seikyusha activists in Kawasaki had questioned the city's seemingly progressive position as a "humanitarian city" and successfully redrew the boundaries of citizenship through their local struggles over welfare, housing, and education. However, as the activists achieved the power to transform the city's policies—having by then a vested interest in them—some of the original members, such as Choi and Park, criticized that they had been co-opted by the city government. The critical voices of the people who left the organization, however, would not reverse the accomplishments that Koreans in coastal Kawasaki—including themselves—had made since the establishment of the Sakuramoto Nursery School and the Hitachi employment discrimination struggles. Rather, they posed significant questions that persist to this day: In what capacity can the "living together" banner continue to have meaning when inclusionary multiculturalism has become an official government policy? And in what way can a city continue to be a bastion of equal rights?

Korean activists in Kawasaki crafted a tradition of activism that challenged the narrow definition of citizenship in postwar Japan. After the Hitachi Employment Discrimination Trial, the small nursery school established inside the Kawasaki Korean Christian Church evolved into a social welfare organization called Seikyusha. Korean activists successfully pressured the city into eliminating the nationality clause, which formerly required a person to be a Japanese national to be eligible to receive an allowance for dependent children, the right to public housing, the elementary school bulletin, and the right to apply for scholarships. They then convinced the city to enact an epoch-making education policy toward resident non-nationals and to establish a community center for young people. As they expanded their efforts into new areas, putting emphasis on banding together in their struggles against local and central governments, they also confronted criticisms from within. While they succeeded in transforming government policies, they were accused of having become part of the establishment itself and of losing their original fighting spirit through use of their "living together" slogan. Nevertheless, these critical voices strengthened rather than weakened the position of Korean Kawasaki as a very special site for citizenship and welfare rights. They helped deconstruct the postwar myth of Japan as a "homogeneous" nation and provided an alternative vision of "community," one in which ethnicity and nationality were not the basis for citizenship.[60] Together with these voices, they changed not only the city but also the nation's education and welfare policies toward *zainichi* Koreans and other resident non-nationals.

Conclusion

The Interconnectedness of Oppression and Freedom

Despite the divergent directions, strategies, and outcomes of discourses on community and citizenship in the Community Action Program and the Model Community Program, comparable frameworks have offered an opportunity to see some parallels. Both CAP and the MCP were political responses to perceived national "crises" brought about by social movements in the 1960s. Transforming dissenters into active and participatory citizens was the main answer to those crises. Policy makers and scholars introduced this tactic of participation and used it as a main strategy for the construction of community programs.[1] Consequently, these community programs reconstituted what Etienne Balibar once named the "imaginary singularity of national forms"—the incorporation of individuals into the "weft of a collective narrative."[2]

Both CAP and the MCP produced gendered notions of citizenship and community. In both cases, residents were divided into those "worthy" of state-sponsored security and those considered "unworthy." And the "deserving" recipients of government support were made up of male heads of households and their families. While they regarded women as playing prominent roles in each of the programs, this standing was based on a vision of women as volunteers and aides, not as paid workers and main agents. They assigned women to a secondary citizenship based on their roles as family members and dependents.[3]

Furthermore, in this book I have not only compared CAP with the MCP and found some parallels but also explored points of intersection between American and Japanese policy making. Japanese scholars affiliated with the Ministry of Home Affairs introduced the "technology of citizenship," but they changed it to suit different political needs—to counter the ascendancy of residents' movements and oppositional left-wing power. Some of them were quite aware that CAP generated a conflict between local residents and the city government, so they sought to transform it into a moderate community project.

CAP and the MCP, however, produced different meanings of citizenship and yielded different results for black Angelenos and Kawasaki Koreans. In the Community Action Program, the idea of CAP as a vehicle for fostering the participation of the poor and African Americans coexisted with the notion that "maximum feasible participation" would simply be a symbolic gesture. Policy makers' approaches toward CAP reflected the uncertain attitudes they displayed regarding how to incorporate the poor and people of color into the American welfare state. CAP's working rhetoric was suspended between the languages of inclusion and exclusion. As I have shown, African American activists in Los Angeles took advantage of this ambiguous aspect of CAP. Once the programs were initiated, they fought to realize their visions of CAP by transforming the concept of "maximum feasible participation" into a pathway through which new political opportunities could be pursued. In the 1960s, they addressed the inadequacies in the welfare system and sought to reconstitute citizenship from "inside" the American welfare state.

The MCP, on the other hand, became another apparatus in recreating a racialized national orthodoxy. The MCP reinforced the traditional boundaries of citizenship through the simultaneous inclusion of Japanese nationals and exclusion of former colonial subjects. Whereas the Japanese government utilized nationality as an excuse to deny former colonial subjects access to the expanding welfare state in the 1960s and 1970s, Kawasaki Koreans contested this limited notion of citizenship. Armed with their victory in the Hitachi Employment Discrimination Trial, they problematized the demarcation between citizens and noncitizens in the fields of welfare and education. They mobilized alternative visions of citizenship from outside the Japanese welfare state.

Black Angelenos and Kawasaki Koreans developed different strategies in dealing with their city and the federal/national governments. With support from the Office of Economic Opportunity, the federal antipoverty agency, African American activists in Los Angeles such as Opal C. Jones, Johnnie Tillmon, Augustus Hawkins, and Thomas Bradley staged a protest against the local Community Action Agency, the Economic and Youth Opportunities Agency of Greater Los Angeles. They questioned the EYOA's vision of the programs as being dominated by the local antipoverty agency rather than local people. They mounted an attack on city hall and carved out a political path for African Americans and the poor.

In contrast to black Angelenos who struggled against city hall with the assistance of the federal government, *zainichi* activists won over the left-wing Kawasaki City government itself. In order to extend their education and welfare rights, they appropriated Mayor Ito Saburo's progressive agenda, such as his declaration of the creation of a "humanitarian city." They challenged the narrow interpretations of citizenship adopted by the central government by eliciting support from the progressive local government, which claimed to be an advocate of human rights.

The different strategies developed by black Angelenos and Kawasaki Koreans reached beyond the era of massive welfare expansion and continued to shape the political landscape in Los Angeles and Kawasaki City through the 1970s. It was certainly the case that poverty persisted long after CAP had either disappeared or become part of regular local welfare activities. The War on Poverty, which focused on education and training, did not itself create enough accessible jobs for the poor; consequently, people who were trained during the War on Poverty were still forced to engage in a struggle over meager resources.[4] Furthermore, African American leaders witnessed, as soon as they acquired meaningful political power, a rapid increase in poverty and inequality based on divisions of race, ethnicity, nativity, and gender. As a result of the dramatic decline in industrial employment, especially the loss of unionized, skilled and semiskilled, well-paid jobs, poverty became concentrated in South Central Los Angeles in the 1970s. While there was an increasing demand for services geared toward the poor, the tax base was narrowed due to the outward migration of middle-class families from the central city.[5] Reflecting on all these challenges for newly elected black leaders, one could argue that their actual impact on unemployment and poverty may indeed have been modest.

Nor did alternative discourses of welfare and citizenship remain powerful after the 1970s. The black Angelenos' struggles for ensuring the participation of the poor, African Americans, and women exemplified an effort to revise the New Deal legacy that reinforced racial and gender inequality.[6] Their activism in the 1960s and early 1970s was a struggle to constitute what sociologist Jill Quadagno has termed an "equal-opportunity welfare state."[7] Yet these black activists pushed even further and transformed the contours of liberalism, moving beyond simply providing equal economic opportunity, and fighting to secure appropriate resources *and* power for the poor and people of color. That is why they were met with intense criticism, not only from politicians and scholars who vigorously opposed the idea of big government and expansions of federal program expansions, but also from white male laborers, the chief beneficiaries of the New Deal welfare state, who felt increasingly left out in a newly emerging liberalism.[8] It was precisely black leaders' success in bringing to the forefront the question of racial, class, and gender inequality that undermined the support for the welfare state in the later period. Their ingenuity in appropriating CAP and its antipoverty efforts—in addition to providing alternative visions of welfare and citizenship—became the prime source of the backlash against "welfare" from the 1960s onward.[9]

However, the advancement of black leadership was indeed a significant turning point in opening up new possibilities for black Angelenos. The struggles over CAP set the stage for the emergence of formal black political leadership in Los Angeles, exemplified by the victory of Tom Bradley as mayor in 1973. African American leaders insisted on the right to realize the participation of the poor in the Los Angeles War on Poverty and used the antipoverty program as a way to politically confront Mayor Samuel Yorty and other government officials who sought to secure control of the antipoverty programs at the expense of poor people themselves. They appropriated and reshaped the principle of "maximum feasible participation" that had been the foundation of the Community Action Program. "Urban decline," an idea that casts the inner cities in an unrelentingly negative light, does not allow us to adequately appreciate how a metropolis like Los Angeles could become an arena of struggle over the meaning of the poor's and people of color's participation in the welfare programs of the 1960s. Rather than dismissing the metropolis as a deserted, poverty-stricken inner city, historians of postwar urban America need to interrogate how African American leaders gained political control over contested terrain during the 1960s.

Whereas the EYOA and its successors came to a halt by 1978, many of the War on Poverty programs, including Head Start, Upward Bound, Job Corps, VISTA, Foster Grandparents, and legal services, have remained and continue to offer support for low-income Angelenos. Also, some of the organizations that grew out of the War on Poverty survived. For instance, the Watts Labor Community Action Committee carried on its wide range of programs, serving everyone from infants to senior citizens.

It provided, to name a few of its achievements, a housing complex for low-income and homeless families, job training and placement, postemployment programs, education and cultural programs, and support for the Watts Summer Festival in an area with an increasingly Latino population.[10] As historian Annelise Orleck has observed, even though the War on Poverty came to an end, many of its programs survived with revisions, supplying "some of the most enduring and unassailable strands of the national safety net."[11] The simple labels of "failure" or "success," so common in the extant literature on the subject of CAP, are not able to capture the complexity of this history.

Tillmon transformed the notion of "maximum feasible participation" into a weapon in the battle for welfare rights. In March 1975, the National Welfare Rights Organization went bankrupt and the organization came to an end.[12] Its legacy—along with that of Tillmon's struggles—however, continued. Tillmon argued that welfare recipients should be given either "decent jobs with adequate pay" or adequate income to live decent lives. What mattered most was that women on welfare could choose from viable options, whether it be working outside, remaining at home for parenting and housework, or both. Through her struggles in ANC Mothers Anonymous, the War on Poverty, and the NWRO, Tillmon challenged a cornerstone of the U.S. welfare state by problematizing its race-, class-, and gender-based exclusionary policies. She accomplished this by contesting its narrow interpretation of "work" and "welfare" and also by asserting the right of recipients to control their own lives and live with genuine dignity. Tillmon and her NWRO allies were able to develop a distinct perspective based on their status as AFDC recipients, offering a path to the creation of black feminist thought that would come into full bloom in later decades.[13]

Unlike black Angelenos who wielded significant political power in the 1960s, *zainichi* Korean political influence was severely restricted, as they were denied the right to vote at both the local and national levels.[14] Kawasaki Koreans, however, also became the vanguard for refashioning the concept of citizenship in postwar Japan. They successfully transformed Kawasaki into a bastion of equal rights, especially in the fields of education and the political participation of resident non-nationals. They helped constitute the "Kawasaki system" of welfare and turned the city into a model for eliminating the nationality requirement in child welfare, public housing, and compulsory education. In fact, the struggles of the local Korean population—along with Japan's ratification in 1979 of the International

Covenant on Civil and Political Rights and the International Convention on the Status of Refugees in 1981—resulted in the abolition of the nationality clause in major social welfare programs at the national level.

These *zainichi* Koreans advanced their rights as Kawasaki *residents* and *citizens* without necessarily becoming Japanese *nationals*. In other words, they could be North Korean, South Korean, Japanese, or other *nationals*, but they insisted on their rights as Kawasaki *residents* and *citizens*. The 1996 establishment of the Kawasaki City Representative Assembly for Foreign Residents (*Kawasakishi Gaikokujin Shimin Daihyōsha Kaigi*), for instance, was a major breakthrough in guaranteeing resident non-nationals the right to participate in the local government's policies. The very name of the assembly highlights their unique political status in Kawasaki. The term *gaikokujin shimin* basically combines two denominations into one, meaning "foreigners (non-nationals) and citizens."[15] The struggles of the Kawasaki Koreans problematized the citizenship and nationality equation and produced an alternative, postnational vision of citizenship.[16]

Furthermore, as the catchword of *kyōsei* ("living together" or "symbiosis") became an official agenda, pursued not only by the progressive local government but also by the conservative local and national governments, some of the original activists contended that it had become a mere cosmetic slogan that hid the government's racism and unequal practices. They argued that *kyōsei* became what historian Tessa Morris-Suzuki called "cosmetic multiculturalism," a gesture whereby multicultural discourses are adopted by the government not to extend citizenship but to disclaim everyday acts of prejudice and discrimination against Koreans and other resident non-nationals in Japan and incorporate them into the status quo.[17] For instance, Kawasaki took the lead in abolishing the nationality clause in the hiring of city hall staff and began to employ resident non-nationals in 1996. It once again became a model, and other cities followed its lead. Yet it continued to exclude resident non-nationals from jobs related to the "exercise of public authority," such as the collection of taxes and the selection of welfare assistance for the poor, and positions related to "involvement in the formation of public opinion," thereby creating a glass ceiling that limited their prospects for promotion.[18] These *zainichi* activists contended that, in the name of multicultural symbiosis, the city built a two-track system, pushing *zainichi* and other resident non-nationals into a position of secondary citizenship once again. They questioned the meaning of the city's "living together" slogan and continued to challenge the city government for denying them full membership.

African Americans and *zainichi* Koreans stood at the center of debates about citizenship and welfare during an era of massive welfare expansion. As such, they were well positioned to display the inadequacies in the welfare systems and assert alternative visions of welfare and citizenship.[19] These subjugated individuals were not passive in their responses to the dominant discourse. Scholarship on the welfare state must not only address the question of race and gender but also register the agency of these subordinated individuals and locate them as historical actors in the formation of welfare programs and policy.[20]

The agency of African Americans and *zainichi* Koreans cannot be fully explored without investigating their day-to-day experiences as well as the oppositional discourses they developed at the local level. Local activists in South Central Los Angeles and coastal Kawasaki appropriated official "community" programs and developed them according to their own political visions and aspirations. African American and *zainichi* women, particularly, played critical roles in advancing their citizenship rights. Neither group won a once-and-for-all victory. However, they succeeded in exploiting the contradictions among policy makers, creating limited coalitions, securing limited concessions, and transforming the welfare programs into a struggle for racial, class, and gender equality. These subjugated people redrew what Margaret R. Somers has called the "internal borders of exclusion within the nation state."[21] They changed Los Angeles and Kawasaki into arenas of struggle over the definitions of welfare and citizenship.

Furthermore, interactions, exchanges, and translations took place at the level of grassroots activism. Black liberation struggles and the *zainichi* pursuit of citizenship were not only parallel movements from which a comparison could be drawn, but they were also linked with each other. *Zainichi* activists in Kawasaki connected their own cause to the causes of African American Christian leaders, and together they formed "antiracist alliances."[22] Transborder networking among church leaders empowered Kawasaki Koreans to challenge the racialized ways of differentiation by Hitachi, one of the largest electronics corporations in the world, and laid the groundwork for the Korean struggle for welfare and educational rights in the 1970s and 1980s. The stories of both African American and *zainichi* Korean mobilization in the 1960s and the 1970s powerfully show why it is imperative for historians, as well as American studies and Japanese studies scholars, to go beyond the nation-centered approach and explore comparative and relational histories of antiracist alliances. These activists' visions make it possible for one to see the interconnectedness of oppression and freedom and to chronicle a new transnational history.

Acknowledgments

During the course of this project, so many people have nurtured both me and my work. I would like to begin by expressing my deepest gratitude to those who generously offered me the opportunity to talk to them despite their busy schedules. Bae Joong Do, Choi Seungkoo, James H. Cone the late Mary B. Henry, I Son Jon, the late Tommy Jacquette, Kajiwara Hisashi, Maulana Karenga, Kimura Hitoshi, the late Lee In Ha, Nishio Masaru, Omori Wataru, Park Jong Seok, Song Puja, and Yamada Takao shared their experiences with me and introduced me to the history of black Los Angeles, Korean Kawasaki, and the world of community programs and activism. It is my hope that I have presented some of their stories and visions with the attentiveness they deserve. I also thank the archivists and the staff who kindly and patiently assisted me in my research, especially Joellen P. Elbashir at Howard University's Moorland-Spingarn Research Center; Allen Fisher at the Lyndon Baines Johnson Library; Todd Gaydowski at the Los Angeles City Records Center; Lawrence H. McDonald at the National Archives at College Park, Maryland; Dace Taube at the Department of Special Collections, University of Southern California; Kadoyama Yasuaki of Japan's Ministry of Internal Affairs and Communications; and the generous staffs at the New York Public Library's Schomburg Center, the Sophia Smith Collection at Smith College, the Southern California Library, the Department of Special Collections at the University of California in Los Angeles, the Walter P. Reuther Library at Wayne State University, the Wisconsin Historical Society, the Kawasaki City Archives, and the Kawasaki City Fureaikan.

I feel incredibly lucky to have had the opportunity to learn from a remarkable group of professors at the University of California, San Diego.

It would be difficult to overstate my gratitude to Michael A. Bernstein and Takashi Fujitani. I would not have completed this manuscript without Michael Bernstein's generous guidance and his eagerness to offer his time and ideas. He provided me with incisive and helpful suggestions, not to mention abundant encouragement. I would like to express my deepest appreciation to Takashi Fujitani for his invaluable words of advice as he shared his vast knowledge of Japanese history. He made me aware of the significance of overcoming a nation-centered approach to history and making connections between American and Japanese histories. George Lipsitz's wisdom, integrity, and continuous commitment to social justice have always been a source of inspiration and admiration. He guided me through this manuscript from beginning to end, helping me to locate individual stories within a broader social and historical context. I will always cherish the heartfelt words of encouragement he has given me. I would also like to thank Rebecca Jo Plant for sharing her knowledge in the field of welfare states studies and women's history and for her many insightful suggestions. I am deeply grateful to Daniel Widener for his helpful comments on the history of black Los Angeles. I have greatly benefited from Becky M. Nicolaides's insightful suggestions. I owe special thanks to Nancy Kwak for her friendship throughout the years and for sharing her knowledge in the field of urban history.

I am also enormously indebted to the faculty of the Program in American Studies at the University of Tokyo. One of my greatest acknowledgments goes to Yui Daizaburo for his heartfelt advice and guidance, for it was he who, at Tokyo Woman's Christian University and the University of Tokyo, set me on my present path. The Yui Seminar has given me the opportunity to discuss my work with extraordinary friends and colleagues in the field of American, Asian, and European history over the past decade. I would like to thank Notoji Masako for her suggestions and encouragement. I greatly benefited from my conversations with Endo Yasuo in his inspiring seminars. I owe a special thanks to Yaguchi Yujin for welcoming me to his writing groups and for providing friendship and career guidance over many years. I am grateful to Sheila Hones for her invaluable advice. I express my deepest gratitude to Furuya Jun, Hashikawa Kenryu, Iwabuchi Sachiko, and others at the Center for Pacific and American Studies, University of Tokyo. The CPAS gave me the opportunity to meet scholars from Japan, the United States, Australia, and beyond, and it was a real honor to be able to work there as a postdoctoral research associate in such a stimulating intellectual environment. In addition, I would like to thank Sakuma Kosei for his continuing advice on the theme of race and ethnicity, Yazawa Sumiko for her valuable suggestions on the Model Community Program in Japan, and the late Tsujiuchi Makoto for offering me the chance to join his unforgettable seminars.

My colleagues in the Faculty of Foreign Languages at Kanagawa University provided a supportive place while I completed this book. I would like to express my sincere gratitude to Yamaguchi Yoshiko for her guidance and generous encouragement. I also would like to thank two chairs, Murai Mayako and Takahashi Kazuyuki, and other colleagues in the English department for their support for the past four years. I am grateful to Yoon Keun Cha, Isaka Seishi, Goto Masako, Kumagai Kensuke, and the members of three research groups in Kanagawa University's Institute for Humanities Research: Representations of the Modern City, organized by Torigoe Teruaki; the Comparative Study of Colonial Modernity, organized by Nagano Yoshiko; and the Body and Gender, organized by Komatsubara Yuri. I would also like to thank Watanabe Miki and Yuri for their support and friendship on and off campus.

I am also indebted to the scholars who have inspired me and shared their knowledge with me over the years. I would like to thank the chairpersons, commentators, and organizers at the conferences and meetings where I presented my work in progress who shared their knowledge and pointed me in new directions. I am grateful to Akutsu Yoichi, Ruth Bloch, Mark Brilliant, Izeki Tadahisa, Kenneth T. Jackson, Minagawa Masaki, Murata Katsuyuki, Noda Shogo, Onozawa Akane, Otsuji Chieko, Martin Joseph Ponce, Sato Chitose, Robert Self, Shoji Keiichi, Takenaka Koji, Tobe Hideaki, Todayama Tasuku, Quintard Taylor, and Yoneyama Hiroshi for their helpful suggestions. I have also benefited greatly from two research groups: On the Transborder Sixties, organized by Yui Daizaburo, and African American Communities in Flux, organized by Higuchi Hayumi. I would like to thank the members for their comments and sharing their expertise with me.

Many colleagues helped me throughout my coursework, research, and writing. They were sources of ideas, intellectual challenge, and most of all, warm friendship that have been indispensable to my academic life in San Diego, Tokyo, and Yokohama. Among them, I would especially like to thank Abe Kosuzu, Araki Wakako, Asai Rieko, Daniella Ashburn-Kreijen, Jeremy Brown, Minsoo Chong, Lauren E. Cole, Michael Cronin,

Choi Deokhyo, Jennifer Eusebio, Fujinaga Yasumasa, Fukagawa Mina, Goto Chiori, Hosoya Noriko, Julietta Hua, Itatsu Yuko, Volker Janssen, Ji Hee Jung, Kamimura Yasuhiro, Kato Koichi, Kawaguchi Yuko, Denise Khor, Jinah Kim, Su Yun Kim, Kitawaki Michiyo, Kurihara Ryoko, Lee Rika, Lorena V. Marquez, Matsubara Hiroyuki, Matsuda Haruka, Minamikawa Fuminori, Miyata Ichiro, Nakamura Rika, Nakano Yumiko, Nakashima Tomoko, Nishiyama Takayuki, Nomura-Ichimasa Shiori, Numajiri Akinobu, Ogido Yuji, Omori Kazuteru, Oyagi Go, David Pye, Nicolas Rosenthal, Sasaki Tomoyuki, George Solt, Sunada Erika, Tachi Mikiko, Tada Mikiko, Takei Hiroshi, Toyoda Maho, and Yonemura Rika. I am especially indebted to Jennifer Eusebio, Katy Meigs, and Daniel Constantino for their careful reading of and invaluable comments on the book in manuscript form.

Several institutions were critical to the completion of this project. I am grateful to the Department of History and the Japanese Studies Program at the University of California, San Diego; the Fulbright Commission; the Japan Scholarship Foundation; the Japan Society for the Promotion of Science; the Center for Pacific and American Studies, University of Tokyo; and Kanagawa University.

I thank the anonymous reader at the University of Minnesota Press (UMP), whose advice helped me reshape my ideas and enlarge my perspective. I owe much to Richard Morrison, Erin Warholm-Wohlenhaus, and other members of the UMP for their steadfast guidance and assistance.

This book could not have been written without the earnest support of my family. My parents, Tsuchiya Hideo and Shizuko, have given me material and emotional assistance throughout my academic career. My parents-in-law, Umezaki Satoshi and Kazuko, welcomed me into their family and offered me generous support. All have provided loving and dedicated care to my son, Joe, who was born in the middle of writing the dissertation upon which this book is based and who has brought immense pleasure and joy to my life. Finally, I would like to thank my partner, Umezaki Toru, who, in addition to helping care for Joe, has provided many fresh ideas, sharp but constructive criticism, numerous dinners, and constant encouragement. His love, integrity, and good humor have sustained me in ways that words can never express. I dedicate this book to my parents and Toru, with love and gratitude.

Notes

Introduction

1. Memo, Paul Weeks to Edgar May, April 3, 1966, File "Los Angeles (EYOA), April 1966–May 1966," Box 8, Entry 74, RG 381, National Archives (hereafter EYOA-NA); Memo, Paul Weeks to Marvin R. Fullmer, April 7, 1966, File "Los Angeles (EYOA), April 1966–May 1966," EYOA-NA; Memo, Paul Weeks to Edgar May, April 25, 1966, File "Los Angeles (EYOA), April 1966–May 1966," EYOA-NA; Memo, Dick Fullmer and C. B. Patrick to Edgar May, April 27, 1966, File "Los Angeles (EYOA), April 1966–May 1966," EYOA-NA; "Negro Elected Officials Want Opal Jones Back," *Los Angeles Sentinel*, April 28, 1966.

2. Los Angeles Report Based on Trip, February 26–27, undated (1965), File "Los Angeles (EYOA), January 1965–March 1965," EYOA-NA.

3. Iwabuchi Hideyuki, "Kawasaki shi ni okeru *zainichi* gaikokujin kyōiku to Seikyusha," in *Tomoni ikiru: Seikyusha sōritsu 20 shūnen kinen*, ed. Seikyusha, 29; Kanagawa Shinbunsha Shakaibu, *Nihon no naka no gaikokujin*, 183–84. I have translated Japanese words based on the standard Japanese Romanization system, except for those people or organizations that have opted for their own style. For Japanese and *zainichi* Korean names, I have put surnames first, followed by given names.

4. *Zainichi* means "resident in Japan." As Erin Aeran Chung suggests, there are several ways of naming Koreans in Japan, reflecting divisions among Koreans by national identities (Japanese/North Korean/South Korean), regional ties (the Kansai and Kanto regions in Japan and the Kyongsang, Cholla, and Cheju regions in Korea), class, and generations. Some Koreans prefer calling themselves according to their nationalities, *zainichi Kankokujin* (South Korean) or *zainichi Chōsenjin* (North Korean). Others just use the abbreviation *zainichi* or *zainichi Koreans* because of its neutrality and reference to Koreans as an ethnic group. In this book, I use *zainichi* or "(resident) Koreans in Japan." Following Fukuoka Yasunori's study, I define *zainichi* as (1) ethnic Koreans who came to Japan before or during World War II and have lived in Japan ever since and (2) their offspring who have been born and raised in Japan and regard Japan as their permanent place of residence.

See Chung, "Exercising Citizenship," 163–64; Fukuoka, *Lives of Young Koreans in Japan*, 271.

5. My book covers two decades of welfare state expansion in the United States and Japan. In the United States, the Great Society programs launched by the Johnson administration greatly expanded the preexistent welfare state. While the Social Security Act and other New Deal programs laid the groundwork for American welfare policies in the 1930s, the Great Society programs not only extended social services and increased government social spending but also linked the welfare state with the pursuit of racial equality during the 1960s and early 1970s. Michael B. Katz has summarized the impact this "improvement and extension of social welfare" had on the poor and African Americans: "New or expanded government programs, much more than economic growth, reduced poverty, hunger, malnutrition, and disease; increased the access of the poor to important social services; and lowered barriers to political participation; employment, housing, and education for black Americans." Katz, *In the Shadow of the Poorhouse*, 262–63. In a similar fashion to the United States, the 1960s and early 1970s were times of massive welfare expansion in Japan. By the mid-1960s, the Japanese government established both national health insurance and a national pension system. In addition, it enacted three new laws: the Intellectually-Disabled Welfare Law (1960); the Elderly Law (1963); and the Maternal, Child, and Widow Welfare Law (1964). Along with three pieces of legislation from the 1940s and 1950s (the Living Protection Law, which was originally enacted in 1946 and revised in 1950; the Child Welfare Law of 1947; and the Physically-Disabled Welfare Law of 1949), it established the "six welfare acts" regime. As I explain in chapter 2, with pressure from residents' movements and "progressive" mayors and governors, government social spending continued to increase. Yet when the oil shock hit the economy and the time of high economic growth came to a halt in 1973, the administration headed by Tanaka Kakuei reversed its position, emphasizing the importance of "people's individual efforts, families, and communities," rather than government spending, in social welfare. Furukawa Koujun, "Shakai fukushi no kakudai to dōyō: 70 nendai no dōkō sobyō," in *Shakai fukushi no gendaiteki tenkai,* ed. Nihon shakai jigyō daigaku, 19–36; Shimoebisu Miyuki, "Kazoku seisaku no rekishiteki tenkai: Ikuji ni taisuru seisaku taiō no hensen," in *Gendai kazoku to shakai hoshō,* ed. Shakai Hoshō Kenkyūjo, 257; Jimi Kim, *Fukushi kokka taisei kakuritsuki ni okeru jichitai fukushi seisaku katei*, 59.

6. I interviewed several activists and community workers in South Central Los Angeles and southern Kawasaki. Oral histories are helpful in order to capture what motivated and sustained these local activists' struggles to recast "community" programs. The use of oral historical evidence, however, requires special caution. As Nancy A. Naples has pointed out, scholars who consult oral histories need to think about how they are able to counter their privileged position as storytellers.

Furthermore, it is imperative to contextualize the interviewees' narratives. I will attempt to locate local activists' stories in other published and unpublished sources in order to historicize and verify their narratives. Naples, *Grassroots Warriors*, 8–11.

7. I follow those who critique the idea of American exceptionalism and incorporate a transnational perspective into the scholarship of American Studies, American history, and the history profession. See Kelley, "But a Local Phase of a World Problem," 1045–77; Thelen, "The Nation and Beyond," 965–75; Noble, *Death of a Nation*; Bender, *Rethinking American History in a Global Age*; Pease and Wiegman, *The Future of American Studies*; Kelley, *Freedom Dreams*; Singh, *Black Is a Country*; Bender, *A Nation among Nations*; Gaines, *American Africans in Ghana*; Tyrrell, *Transnational Nation*; Johnson and Graybill, *Bridging National Borders in North America*.

8. 78 Stat. 508; Office of Economic Opportunity, *Community Action Program Guide*, 7. In 1966 the Economic Opportunity Act was amended to specify the role of the poor in the programs. It required that the poor should make up at least a third of the Community Action Agency board's membership, and representatives of the poor should live in the area they represented and be selected by the residents in areas of concentration of poverty. 80 Stat. 1457. The 1967 Green Amendment gave control of CAP to public officials by stating that local governments had the responsibility of establishing Community Action Agencies and that a third of the board members were to be public officials. 81 Stat. 691 and 693.

9. Daniel P. Moynihan, former assistant secretary of the Department of Labor, contended that the inclusion of the phrase "maximum feasible participation" in CAP was nothing but an accident and a misunderstanding. He subsequently argued that it was a small number of idealistic social reformers who gave CAP a structure that "neither those who drafted it, those who sponsored it, nor those who enacted it ever in any way intended." Moynihan stressed that the "maximum feasible participation" phrase was designed simply to "ensure [that] persons excluded from the political process in the South and elsewhere would nonetheless participate in the *benefits*." In his view it was not meant to mobilize the poor as agents in making social policy. Moynihan, *Maximum Feasible Misunderstanding*, 86–87, 98. Frances Fox Piven and Richard Cloward, along with David Zarefsky, have challenged Moynihan's view and claimed that CAP was a political strategy developed by the Democratic Party. They have argued that leading Democratic Party officials created CAP in order to deal with "the political problems created by a new and unstable electoral constituency, namely blacks." These Democratic leaders believed that CAP could offer a way to "prod the local Democratic party machinery to cultivate the allegiance of urban black voters" by providing a greater share of services to them and "to do this without alienating urban white voters." In other words, Piven and Cloward understood the War on Poverty programs

administered through CAP as an apparatus designed to conceal the Democrats' political goal of appealing to an urban African American constituency. Piven and Cloward, *Regulating the Poor*, 249, 254–56. Zarefsky emphasized the importance of urban African American voters for the Democratic Party as well. He argued that the Democrats attempted to solidify the loyalty of urban African Americans by making them "the beneficiaries of federal largesse." Far from arguing that CAP came to embrace a characteristic that nobody in the task force originally intended, Piven and Cloward, along with Zarefsky, stressed that the Democratic party leaders created CAP and the War on Poverty in order to accumulate urban African American votes. Zarefsky, *President Johnson's War on Poverty*, 27–28.

10. Cruikshank, *The Will to Empower*, 1–5, 69.

11. Quadagno, *The Color of Welfare*; Quadagno, "Promoting Civil Rights through the Welfare State," 68–89; Naples, *Grassroots Warriors*; Williams, *The Politics of Public Housing*; Greene, *Our Separate Ways*; Orleck, *Storming Caesars Palace*; Cazenave, *Impossible Democracy*; Ashmore, *Carry It On*; Bauman, *Race and the War on Poverty*; Levenstein, *A Movement without Marches;* Goldstein, *Poverty in Common.* See also Greenstone and Peterson, *Race and Authority in Urban Politics*; Orleck and Hazirjian, *The War on Poverty.*

12. Annelise Orleck, "Introduction: The War on Poverty from the Grass Roots Up," in *The War on Poverty,* ed. Orleck and Hazirjian, 8–9.

13. Gwendolyn Mink and Molly Ladd-Taylor, for example, pay closer attention to racial and class aspects of middle-class women's activities in the early twentieth century. Instead of emphasizing the "universal" interests that women shared across race and class, Mink and Ladd-Taylor argue that its appeal cannot be understood apart from the white Protestant alarm over "race suicide" in the late nineteenth and early twentieth century. They contend that early twentieth-century "maternalist" legislation cannot be separated from the racial and class anxieties of reformers. See Mink, *The Wages of Motherhood*; and Ladd-Taylor, *Mother-Work.* Jill Quadagno analyzes why the United States failed to develop a more generous welfare state, compared to European countries. She contends that the core issue is "how working-class politics have been weakened by racial divisions, both in the workplace and in the community." Quadagno, *The Color of Welfare,* 7–9. Kenneth J. Neubeck and Noel A. Cazenave emphasize the role of "welfare racism" in the U.S. welfare state. They criticize scholars of U.S. welfare policies for concluding that racism does not play a significant role in the formation and implementation of welfare policy in the United States. They assert that a "racism-centered approach" enables one to understand how nation-states, along with other institutions such as mass media, have historically supported white racial hegemony through welfare policy. Neubeck and Cazenave, *Welfare Racism*, vi, vii, 12, 17–18; Neubeck, *When Welfare Disappears.* See also Abramovitz, *Regulating the Lives of Women*;

Gordon, *Women, the State, and Welfare*; Lieberman, *Shifting the Color Line*; Ward, *The White Welfare State.*

14. Bernstein, *A Perilous Progress*, 248. See also Dudziak, *Cold War Civil Rights*; Goldstein, *Poverty in Common*, 6–11.

15. O'Connor, *Poverty Knowledge*, 203–10.

16. Furukawa Kojun discussed several reasons for the government's interest in them, including the increasing attention to "new social welfare needs" (the elderly, disabled people, mothers, and children) along with the decreasing need for services for the unemployed during the boom years of Japan's "Economic Miracle"; the collapse of traditional family and local networks brought about by a rapid increase in urban populations and the necessity of re-creating the "community" from above; and the increase in welfare programs led by left-wing local government leaders who became influential in the 1960s. Furukawa explained that conservative politicians created these "community" programs in order to counteract locally initiated programs developed by left-wing governors and mayors. Furukawa Koujun, "Sengo Nihon ni okeru shakai fukushi sābisu no tenkai," in *Fukushi kokka 6*, ed. Tokyo Daigaku Shakai Kagaku Kenkyūjo, 218–29. Kawai Katsuyoshi and other scholars emphasized this third aspect of "dealing with the left-wing governors and mayors" by arguing that these "community" policies had particular political intentions—for instance, absorbing social movements that had succeeded in electing left-wing mayors and governors. In fact, so-called left-wing local governments rapidly increased in number from only ten in 1960 to more than one hundred in 1971. Kawai, "Chiiki fukushi no seisaku tenkai," 82–83. See also Hayase, "Fukushi to iu sōchi," 199–221.

17. Yamaguchi Yasushi, "Shimin sanka ni okeru kakushin to hoshu," in *Gendai toshi seisaku II: Shimin sanka*, ed. Shinohara et al., 187–212; Shimada, "Chihō jichi to jūmin no shutai keisei," 686–702.

18. O'Connor, *Poverty Knowledge*, 164.

19. Etienne Balibar develops Benedict Anderson's concept of the "imagined community" and explores the role played by the state in constructing the "imaginary singularity of national forms." Balibar contends that the creation of the imagined community is based on the "projection of individual existence into the weft of a collective narrative, on the recognition of a common name and on traditions lived as the trace of an immemorial past." According to Balibar, the fundamental question one needs to ask is what makes the people produce themselves continually as a "national community." Balibar calls these state projects of creating imagined community the "delayed nationalization of society." Anderson, *Imagined Communities*; Étienne Balibar, "The Nation Form: History and Ideology," in *Race, Nation, Class*, ed. Balibar and Wallerstein, 92–93; Balibar, *We, the People of Europe?*, 61.

20. Regarding the history of black Los Angeles, see De Graaf, "The City of Black Angeles," 323–52; Sears and McConahay, *The Politics of Violence*; Lonnie G. Bunch,

"A Past Not Necessarily Prologue: The Afro-American in Los Angeles," in *20th Century Los Angeles*, ed. Klein and Schiesl, 101–30; George, *No Crystal Stair*; Horne, *Fire This Time*; Susan Anderson, "A City Called Heaven: Black Enchantment and Despair in Los Angeles," in *The City*, ed. Scott and Soja, 336–64; De Graaf and Taylor, *Seeking Eldorado*; Taylor, *In Search of the Racial Frontier*, 222–50; Sides, *L.A. City Limits*; Freer, "L.A. Race Woman," 607–32; Flamming, *Bound for Freedom*; Vargas, *Catching Hell in the City of Angeles*; Kurashige, *The Shifting Grounds of Race*; Widener, *Black Arts West*; Hunt and Ramōn, *Black Los Angeles*; Sides, *Post-Ghetto*. See also Leonard, *The Battle for Los Angeles*; Kurashige, *The Shifting Grounds of Race*; Brilliant, *The Color of America Has Changed*; Bernstein, *Bridges of Reform*.

21. Studies of the Los Angeles War on Poverty through CAP have produced two interpretations. First, Dale Rogers Marshall participated on the board of the Economic and Youth Opportunities Agency of Greater Los Angeles in 1968 and conducted interviews with the thirty-two board members. Marshall's work is valuable since there are not many sources available today that focus on EYOA board members. But her work concentrated on the impact of the participation of the poor on the EYOA board. Therefore, she did not examine how activists outside the EYOA challenged the local and federal welfare agencies. Second, Robert Alan Bauman examined the history of the implementation of the War on Poverty in Los Angeles. He focused not only on the EYOA but also on local struggles in Watts and East Los Angeles. Marshall, *The Politics of Participation in Poverty*; Bauman, *Race and the War on Poverty*.

22. Honey, *Southern Labor and Black Civil Rights*, 8.

23. Regarding the NWRO, see Bailis, *Bread or Justice*; Kotz and Kotz, *A Passion for Equality*; Piven and Cloward, *Poor People's Movements*; West, *The National Welfare Rights Movement*; Davis, *Brutal Need*; Melnick, *Between the Lines*; Davis, "Welfare Rights and Women's Rights in the 1960s," 144–65; Kornbluh, "To Fulfill Their 'Rightly Needs,'" 76–113; White, *Too Heavy a Load*, 212–42; Valk, "Mother Power," 34–58; Nadasen, *Welfare Warriors*; Kornbluh, *The Battle for Welfare Rights*; Valk, *Radical Sisters*; Chappell, *The War on Welfare*; Tsuchiya, "Tillmon, Johnnie"; Tsuchiya, "Wiley, George Alvin"; Tsuchiya, "National Welfare Rights Organization, 1966–1975."

24. Thompson, *Whose Detroit?*, 5, 219. See also Pritchett, *Brownsville, Brooklyn*, 7.

25. Joseph, *Against the Romance of Community*, vii.

26. Kashiwazaki Chikako, "The Politics of Legal Status: The Equation of Nationality with Ethnonational Identity," in *Koreans in Japan*, ed. Ryang, 13–31.

27. Onuma Yasuaki delved into the implications of the San Francisco Peace Treaty in 1952. He argued that it was an "illegal action to deprive as many as five hundred thousand Koreans of their citizenship" based on the *koseki* system (family register), which was employed to demarcate those of Japanese ancestry from nationals of colonial origin in the prewar period. According to Onuma, the real

intention of the 1952 treaty was to "disavow the Japanese invasion of Asia." Onuma, *Zainichi Kankoku/Chōsenjin no kokuseki to jinken*, vi–vii, 3–13.

28. "Kakushin 10 nen: Ito Kawasaki shisei no kiseki," *Kanagawa shinbun,* May 26, 1981; "Kakushin 10 nen: Ito Kawasaki shisei no kiseki," *Kanagawa shinbun,* May 27, 1981; Kawasaki shigikai, *Kawasaki shigikai shi,* 271–73; "Zassō no 18 nen: Ito Kawasaki shisei o furikaeru," *Kanagawa shinbun,* September 26, 1989; Kawasaki chihō jichi kenkyū sentā, *Kawasaki shimin jichi no jikken 1971–2001,* 7–9. See also Tsuchiyama Kimie, "Kawasaki 'Senku jichitai' no rekishi teki ichi," in *Kawasaki shisei no kenkyū,* ed. Uchikoshi and Uchiumi, 43–108.

29. Tonomura, *Zainichi Chōsenjin shakai no rekishigakuteki kenkyū*, 4–15.

30. For example, scholars have demonstrated how the Supreme Commander for the Allied Powers (SCAP) participated in the marginalization of Koreans during the U.S. occupation by failing to protect former colonial subjects' civil rights. Others examined the ways in which Koreans, who once had rendered service to Imperial Japan, were deprived of legal rights and how the Japanese government used foreign citizenship as an excuse to exclude them from social security programs. Mitchell, *The Korean Minority in Japan,* 100–18; Kim Il-Wha, "*Zainichi* Chōsenjin no hōteki chii," in *Zainichi Chōsenjin: Rekishi, genjō, tenbō,* ed. Park, 175–212; Yoshioka, *Zainichi Chōsenjin to shakai hoshō*, 15; see also Yoshioka, *Zainichi Chōsenjin to jūmin undō*; Yoshioka, *Zainichi gaikokujin to shakai hoshō*; Changsoo Lee, "The Legal Status of Koreans in Japan," in *Koreans in Japan*, ed. Lee and De Vos.

31. Kim Chan-jung, *Zainichi Korian hyakunenshi*, 10–14; Fukuoka, *Lives of Young Koreans in Japan*; Tonomura, *Zainichi Chōsenjin shakai no rekishigakuteki kenkyū*, 10–11, 469–75. See also Fujiwara Shoten Henshūbu, *Rekishi no naka no "zainichi."*

32. Fujitani, *Race for Empire*, 8, 16.

33. Oguma, *Tanitsu minzoku shinwa no kigen*, 299, 316; see also his *A Genealogy of "Japanese" Self-Images* and *Nihonjin no kyōkai.*

34. Yoon, *Nihon kokumin ron*, 121–22; Yoon, *Shisō taiken no kōsaku*, vi; Kang, *Orientarizumu no kanata e*, 229; Morris-Suzuki, *Exodus to North Korea*; Kashiwazaki Chikako, "The Politics of Legal Status: The Equation of Nationality with Ethnonational Identity," in *Koreans in Japan*, ed. Ryang, 13-31.; Lie, *Multiethnic Japan*; Lie, *Zainichi (Koreans in Japan)*; Hyun, "Mikkō, Ōmura shūyōjo, Saishūtō," 163; Ryang and Lie, *Diaspora without Homeland*; Chung, *Immigration and Citizenship in Japan.*

35. Ryang, "Inscribed (Men's) Bodies, Silent (Women's) Words," 3–15; Ryang, *Korian diasupora*; Jung, *Tamigayo seishō*; Song Eoun-ok, "'Zainichi' josei no sengoshi," in *Rekishi no naka no "Zainichi,"* ed. Fujiwara Shoten Henshūbu, 131–52; Kim, *Keizoku suru shokuminchishugi to jendā.*

36. Lipsitz, *A Life in the Struggle*, 135–40; Kelley, *Race Rebels*, 7, 36; Kelley, *Freedom Dreams*, 8; Levenstein, *A Movement without Marches*, 6; Masur, *An Example for All the Land*, 7.

37. Lipsitz, *American Studies in a Moment of Danger*, 118–22, 132.

1. Between Inclusion and Exclusion

1. The Economic Opportunity Act consisted of six titles: Youth Programs (Title I); Urban and Rural Community Action Programs (Title II); Special Programs to Combat Poverty in Rural Areas (Title III); Employment and Investment Incentives (Title IV); Work Experience Programs (Title V); and Administration and Coordination (Title VI). 78 Stat. 508. As for the Economic Opportunity Act, see Blumenthal, "The Bureaucracy," 169–72; Sundquist, "Origins of the War on Poverty," 6–33; Piven and Cloward, *Regulating the Poor*, 248–84; Katz, *The Undeserving Poor*, 79–123; Patterson, *America's Struggle against Poverty 1900–1994*, 99–115; Quadagno, *The Color of Welfare*; Gillette, *Launching the War on Poverty*; U.S. Office of Economic Opportunity, *Catalog of Federal Programs for Individual and Community Improvement*; U.S. Office of Economic Opportunity, *Community Action Program Guide*, 7.

2. Kessler-Harris, *In Pursuit of Equity*, 12.

3. Levitan, *The Great Society's Poor Law*, 11–12; Sundquist, "Origins of the War on Poverty," 6.

4. Galbraith, *The Affluent Society*, 325–33; O'Connor, *Poverty Knowledge*, 146–53.

5. Charles L. Schultze, interview by Davide G. McComb, in *Launching the War on Poverty*, ed. Gillette, 3.

6. Harrington, *The Other America*, 10, 21–24. Here, Harrington was quoting anthropologist Oscar Lewis's theory of the "culture of poverty." See O'Connor, *Poverty Knowledge*, 150–51.

7. Cruikshank, *The Will to Empower*, 77.

8. MacDonald, "Our Invisible Poor," 82–132.

9. Jule Sugarman, interview by Stephen Goodell, in *Launching the War on Poverty*, ed. Gillette, 19; Sundquist, "Origins of the War on Poverty," 9–13; Blumenthal, "The Bureaucracy," 133–35.

10. Cloward and Ohlin, *Delinquency and Opportunity*. Yet there were significant differences between Cloward and Ohlin's understanding of antipoverty efforts and Ylvisaker and Hackett's opinion of what constituted appropriate antipoverty programs. According to Richard Blumenthal, the critical division between these investigators was the question of "conflict versus consensus." Whereas Hackett and Ylvisaker saw "community action" as a means of nurturing more effective cooperation and alliances between the establishment and "the poor," Cloward and Ohlin valued disruption and conflict as ends in themselves. Furthermore, they advocated creating new and separate institutions so that the poor would be able to express dissent and challenge local officials. Although these different understandings about the nature of antipoverty programs were still under the surface at this

time, they became significant once the creation of community action programs in the War on Poverty began. See Blumenthal, "The Bureaucracy," 137–42.

11. See O'Connor's discussion of Charles S. Johnson, E. Franklin Frazier, Gunnar Myrdal, Oscar Lewis, Michael Harrington, and Daniel Patrick Moynihan in chapters 3 and 4 and pages 203–10 in her book, *Poverty Knowledge.*

12. O'Connor, *Poverty Knowledge*; Katz, *In the Shadow of the Poorhouse*, 264. See also Feldstein, *Motherhood in Black and White.*

13. Charles L. Schultze, interview by Davide G. McComb, in *Launching the War on Poverty,* ed. Gillette, 3; Piven and Cloward, *Regulating the Poor*, 250–56.

14. Piven and Cloward, *Regulating the Poor*, 250–56; Zarefsky, *President Johnson's War on Poverty*, 27–28.

15. William M. Capron, in *Launching the War on Poverty,* ed. Gillette, 9; Robert J. Lampman, interview by Michael L. Gillette, May 24, 1983, Oral History Collection, Lyndon B. Johnson Library, Austin (hereafter LBJ Library); Robert Lampman, in *Launching the War on Poverty,* ed. Gillette, 5; Blumenthal, "The Bureaucracy," 143; Levitan, *The Great Society's Poor Law*, 14; O'Connor, *Poverty Knowledge*, 139–46.

16. Robert J. Lampman, interview by Michael L. Gillette, May 24, 1983, Oral History Collection, LBJ Library; Lampman, in *Launching the War on Poverty,* ed. Gillette, 6.

17. Capron, in *Launching the War on Poverty*, ed. Gillette, 10.

18. Robert J. Lampman, interview by Michael L. Gillette, May 24, 1983, Oral History Collection, LBJ Library; Lampman, in *Launching the War on Poverty,* ed. Gillette, 6.

19. Lampman, in *Launching the War on Poverty,* ed. Gillette, 6; Blumenthal, "The Bureaucracy," 144; Levitan, *The Great Society's Poor Law*, 16. Lampman recalled that the political interests turned around the question of "which parts of the nonpoor would be attracted." The Kennedy administration attempted to obtain support from women, especially "church women and League of Women Voters people." In fact, these women's organizations did become the main targets of what later became the War on Poverty.

20. This memorandum, tentatively titled "Widening Participation in Prosperity," had three objectives: minimizing "handouts" and maximizing "self-help"; emphasizing the prevention of poverty, particularly among the young; and concentrating on relatively few groups and areas where "problems" were most severe and "solutions" most feasible. Heller and other members were preoccupied with achieving maximum effects at minimal costs even at this early stage. James L. Sundquist, interview by Stephen Goodell, April 7, 1969, Oral History Collection, LBJ Library; James L. Sundquist, interview by Stephen Goodell, in *Launching the War on Poverty,* ed. Gillette, 13; Sundquist, "Origins of the War on Poverty," 20–21; Blumenthal, "The Bureaucracy," 145–46.

21. "How the Poverty Program Might Work in an Urban Slum and a Poor Rural Area," December 28, 1963, Executive File, WE 9, Box 25, LBJ Library.

22. William M. Capron, in *Launching the War on Poverty,* ed. Gillette, 12–13.

23. William B. Cannon, interview by Michael L. Gillette, May 21, 1982, Oral History Collection, LBJ Library; William B. Cannon, interview by Michael L. Gillette, in *Launching the War on Poverty,* ed. Gillette, 20; Blumenthal, "The Bureaucracy," 146–49. For example, James Sundquist, then deputy undersecretary of agriculture, wrote that an outline of staff thinking as of January 21 specified "only that a community should have, preferably, a single or official with authority to coordinate public and private efforts." Sundquist argued that "it made no mention of organizing the poor for self-assertion." See Sundquist, "Origins of the War on Poverty," 24.

24. Walter Heller, in *Launching the War on Poverty,* ed. Gillette, 16.

25. Ibid.

26. Blumenthal, "The Bureaucracy," 150–53; Zarefsky, *President Johnson's War on Poverty*, 22–24.

27. Memo, Lyndon B. Johnson to Robert L. Mallatt Jr., mayor of Keene, January 23, 1964, Executive File, WE 9, Box 25, LBJ Library; Memo, Kermit Gordon to Lyndon B. Johnson, January 22, 1964, Subject File, FG11–15, Box 124, LBJ Library; Capron, in *Launching the War on Poverty,* ed. Gillette, 22; Blumenthal, "The Bureaucracy," 152–53.

28. For example, spokesmen for the U.S. Department of Health, Education, and Welfare (HEW) worried that the Community Action Program would absorb or substitute for their existing programs. At the same time, the Department of Labor opposed the inclusion of a youth work component in CAP.

29. Capron, in *Launching the War on Poverty,* ed. Gillette, 23; Memo, Walter W. Heller to Theodore Sorensen, January 6, 1964, Executive File, WE 9, Box 25, LBJ Library; Levitan, *The Great Society's Poor Law*, 21–29.

30. Memo, Kermit Gordon and Walter W. Heller to Secretary of Agriculture, Commerce, Labor, HEW, Interior, and Administrator of the Housing and Home Finance Agency, January 6, 1964, Executive File, WE 9, Box 25, LBJ Library; Levitan, *The Great Society's Poor Law*, 21–29.

31. Blumenthal, "The Bureaucracy," 162–63.

32. James L. Sundquist, interview by Stephen Goodell, April 7, 1969, Oral History Collection, LBJ Library; Sundquist, in *Launching the War on Poverty,* ed. Gillette, 24.

33. Letter, Lyndon B. Johnson to Sargent Shriver, February 12, 1964, Subject File, FG11–15, Box 124, LBJ Library; R. Sargent Shriver, in *Launching the War on Poverty,* ed. Gillette, 31; Levitan, *The Great Society's Poor Law*, 28. Shriver later recalled that he was appointed because Johnson thought "it was going to be difficult to get it through Congress and he thought I could help get it through." The War on Poverty Task Force, headed by Shriver, included a variety of members such as Richard Boone (from PCJD), Wilbur Cohen (from HEW), Michael Harrington (author

of *The Other America*), Walter Heller (from the CEA), Daniel P. Moynihan (from the Department of Labor), Norbert A. Schlei (from the Office of Legal Counsel), Charles Schultze (from the Bureau of the Budget), James Sundquist (from the Department of Agriculture), W. Williard Wirtz (from the Department of Labor), Adam Yarmolinsky (then special assistant to the secretary of defense), and Paul N. Ylvisaker (from the Ford Foundation). Moynihan, *Maximum Feasible Misunderstanding*, 82–86; Sundquist, "Origins of the War on Poverty," 25.

34. Shriver contended that the fledging federal unit would not survive without the direct, personal backing of the president. John Baker, then assistant secretary of agriculture, shared his opinion. He later noted that "if you really wanted to put it upstairs instead of being buried down in the hierarchy somewhere, the thing you had to do was to put it in the White House." Consequently, the Office of Economic Opportunity was given a special location in the Executive Office. On the other hand, Kermit Gordon, the director of the Bureau of the Budget, recommended to the president that the OEO be established as an independent agency outside the Executive Office. He argued that if it were established in the Executive Office, such a location would bring the day-to-day decisions of the office so close to the president "as to risk involving him directly in the occasional errors and failures." Memo, Kermit Gordon to Lyndon B. Johnson, March 7, 1964, Subject File, FG11-15, Box 124, LBJ Library; John Baker, in *Launching the War on Poverty*, ed. Gillette, 54.

35. Adam Yarmolinsky, interview by Paige Mulhollan, July 13, 1970, Oral History Collection, LBJ Library; Adam Yarmolinsky, interview by Michael L. Gillette, October 21 and 22, 1980, Oral History Collection, LBJ Library; Adam Yarmolinsky, in *Launching the War on Poverty*, ed. Gillette, 32.

36. Cannon, in *Launching the War on Poverty*, ed. Gillette, 31–32.

37. Shriver later noted that "I just wasn't of the opinion that the U.S. government could spend $500 million intelligently in one year in that way or according to that formula . . . Of course, I still think that decision was correct, to make community action an essential part but not the whole of the War on Poverty." R. Sargent Shriver, in *Launching the War on Poverty*, ed. Gillette, 34–36; Blumenthal, "The Bureaucracy," 163–66; Sundquist, "Origins of the War on Poverty," 25–29.

38. John M. Steadman, interviewed by Stephen Goodell, April 5, 1985, Oral History Collection, LBJ Library; John M. Steadman, in *Launching the War on Poverty*, ed. Gillette, 56–57.

39. Sundquist, "Origins of the War on Poverty," 27.

40. The actual drafters of Title II (CAP) were Harold Horowitz, associate general counsel at HEW, and Norbert Schlei, assistant attorney general. William B. Cannon, interview by Michael L. Gillette, May 21, 1982, Oral History Collection, LBJ Library; Cannon, in *Launching the War on Poverty*, ed. Gillette, 79; Norbert A. Schlei, interview by Michael Gillette, May 15, 1980, Oral History Collection, LBJ Library;

Schlei, in *Launching the War on Poverty,* ed. Gillette, 82; Harold W. Horowitz, interview by Michael L. Gillette, February 23, 1983, Oral History Collection, LBJ Library, 81; Blumenthal, "The Bureaucracy," 167.

41. Boone, "Reflections on Citizen Participation and the Economic Opportunity Act," 445.

42. Frank Mankiewicz, interviews by Stephen Goodell, April 18, 1969, May 1, 1969, May 5, 1969, Oral History Collection, LBJ Library.

43. Ibid.; Mankiewicz, in *Launching the War on Poverty,* ed. Gillette, 75–76.

44. Frederick O'R. Hayes, interview by Michael L. Gillette, in *Launching the War on Poverty,* ed. Gillette, 70–71, 74–75, 86–87.

45. Norbert A. Schlei, interview by Michael Gillette, May 15, 1980, Oral History Collection, LBJ Library; Norbert A. Schlei, interview by Michael Gillette, in *Launching the War on Poverty,* ed. Gillette, 72–73, 76, 82.

46. Adam Yarmolinsky, interview by Paige Mulhollan, July 13, 1970, Oral History Collection, LBJ Library; Adam Yarmolinsky, interviews by Michael L. Gillette, October 21 and 22, 1980, Oral History Collection, LBJ Library; Yarmolinsky, in *Launching the War on Poverty,* ed. Gillette, 73–74, 77–78.

47. According to McKee, Johnson eventually became bluntly hostile to the program. On August 18, 1965, right after the Watts uprising, for example, Johnson remarked, "I think somebody ought to veto these damn fool community action [programs]." See Guian A. McKee, "'This Government Is with Us': Lyndon Johnson and the Grassroots War on Poverty," in *The War on Poverty,* ed. Orleck and Hazirjian, 31–62.

48. Boone, "Reflections on Citizen Participation and the Economic Opportunity Act," 446–47.

49. William B. Cannon, interview by Michael L. Gillette, May 21, 1982, Oral History Collection, LBJ Library; Cannon, in *Launching the War on Poverty,* ed. Gillette, 81.

50. Zarefsky, *President Johnson's War on Poverty*, 27; O'Connor, *Poverty Knowledge*, 154–55.

51. William P. Kelly Jr., who later became the acting director of CAP as well as the director of the Job Corps, noted that the task force members were always "optimistic" about the bill. Kelly pointed out that there was "an excellent esprit de corps" in the task force. Shriver gave the following testimony before the House Education and Labor Committee on March 17: "This country, with its enormous productivity, its advanced technology, the mobility of its people, and the speed of its communications has both the resources and the know-how to eliminate poverty" since "we now have a far greater understanding of the complex causes of poverty." Shriver and other task force members were sure of their rapid victory in Congress. Statement by Sargent Shriver, March 17, 1964, Subject File, FG11–15,

Box 124, LBJ Library; William P. Kelly Jr., interview by Stephen Goodell, in *Launching the War on Poverty,* ed. Gillette, 61.

52. Furer, *Lyndon B. Johnson, 1908*, 87.

53. One of the major questions about CAP in the House was the issue of aid to parochial schools. The House Education and Labor Committee agreed to allow aid to private schools for special remedial education programs and other noncurricular activities open to all children in a neighborhood. Another question was on the development of plans. Edith Green persuaded the committee to remove any phrases that suggested the development of comprehensive plans before funding. See Blumenthal, "The Bureaucracy," 169–71. Adam Yarmolinsky, interview by Paige Mulhollan, July 13, 1970, Oral History Collection, LBJ Library; Adam Yarmolinsky, interviews by Michael L. Gillette, October 21 and 22, 1980, Oral History Collection, LBJ Library; Yarmolinsky, in *Launching the War on Poverty,* ed. Gillette, 116; Memo, Sargent Shriver to Lyndon B. Johnson, June 29, 1964, Subject File, FG11–15, Box 124, LBJ Library; Senate Committee on Labor and Public Welfare, Economic Opportunity Act of 1964, S. Rept. 88–1218, 88th Cong., 2nd sess., 1964, 69–79; Sundquist, "Origins of the War on Poverty," 28; Levitan, *The Great Society's Poor Law*, 46–47.

54. Donald M. Baker, interview by Stephen Goodell, February 24, 1969, March 5, 1969, Oral History Collection, LBJ Library; Baker, in *Launching the War on Poverty,* ed. Gillette, 124; Sundquist, "Origins of the War on Poverty," 29; Moynihan, *Maximum Feasible Misunderstanding*, 89–91.

55. C. Robert Perrin, interview by Stephen Goodell, in *Launching the War on Poverty,* ed. Gillette, 128–29.

56. For instance, when he sent the special War on Poverty message to Congress on March 16, he made following remarks: "On similar occasions in the past we have often been called upon to wage war against foreign enemies which threatened our freedom . . . today we are asked to declare war on a domestic enemy which threatens the strength of our Nation and the welfare of our people." Furer, *Lyndon B. Johnson, 1908–*, 84.

57. Memo, W. Willard Wirtz to Lyndon B. Johnson, January 1, 1964, Office Files of Harry McPherson, Box 21, LBJ Library; President's Taskforce on Manpower Conservation, "One-Third of a Nation: A Report on Young Men Found Unqualified for Military Service," January 1, 1964, Office Files of Harry McPherson, Box 21, LBJ Library; "Statement by President Johnson on Report 'One-Third of a Nation,'" January 5, 1964, Office Files of H. McPherson, Box 21, LBJ Library.

58. Robert J. Lampman, interview by Michael L. Gillette, May 24, 1983, Oral History Collection, LBJ Library; Lampman, in *Launching the War on Poverty,* ed. Gillette, 8.

59. William B. Cannon, interview by Michael L. Gillette, May 21, 1982, Oral History Collection, LBJ Library.

60. Memo, Daniel Patrick Moynihan to Harry McPherson, July 16, 1965, Office Files of Harry McPherson, Box 21, LBJ Library; Lampman, in *Launching the War on Poverty,* ed. Gillette, 8; Zarefsky, *President Johnson's War on Poverty*, 28–44.

61. "Why Should Conservatives Support the War on Poverty?," memo, Bill Moyers to President Johnson, Jenkins, Valenti, O'Brien, Wilson, and Manatos, January 6, 1964, Executive File, WE 9, Box 25, LBJ Library; memo, U.S. Information Agency to All USIS Posts, October 6, 1965, Confidential File, WE9, Box 98, LBJ Library; Dudziak, *Cold War Civil Rights*; Bernstein, *A Perilous Progress*, 248.

62. Table Ea698–703, "Federal Government Expenditure, by Major Function: 1934–1999," in *Historical Statistics of the United States,* ed. Carter et al.

63. National Strategy Information Center, May 1, 1967, Confidential File, WE9, Box 98, LBJ Library; memo, Morris I. Leibman to Joseph A. Califano Jr., June 20, 1967, Confidential File, WE9, Box 98, LBJ Library.

64. U.S. Department of Labor, Office of Policy Planning and Research, *The Negro Family.*

65. Pearce, "The Feminization of Poverty," 28–36.

66. Quadagno and Fobes, "The Welfare State and the Cultural Reproduction of Gender," 172.

67. Office of Economic Opportunity, *Conference Proceedings*, 4–6, 52.

68. Memo, Sargent Shriver to President Johnson, April 20, 1967, Confidential File, Box 129 (Reel 13), in *The Presidential Documents Series, the War on Poverty*, microfilm; Office of Economic Opportunity, *Conference Proceedings*, 57.

69. Office of Economic Opportunity, *Women in the War on Poverty*, 1–2.

70. Office of Economic Opportunity, *Conference Proceedings*, 1–2, 20–21, 40–41.

71. Office of Economic Opportunity, *Women in the War on Poverty*, 3; Naples, *Grassroots Warriors*, 5–6.

72. Memo, Orville L. Freeman, secretary of agriculture, to the president, August 19, 1968, Executive File, WE 9, Box 32, LBJ Library; memo, to President Johnson, August 23, 1968, Subject File, Box 32 (Reel 6), in *The Presidential Documents Series, the War on Poverty.*

73. Kessler-Harris, *In Pursuit of Equity,* 12.

74. Neubeck and Cazenave, *Welfare Racism,* 120–21.

75. Jack T. Conway, interview by Michael L. Gillette, in *Launching the War on Poverty,* ed. Gillette, 86; Blumenthal, "The Bureaucracy," 173–74. The CAP guide, published in February 1965 under the leadership of Conway, officially declared that "a vital feature of every community action program is the involvement of the poor themselves." Office of Economic Opportunity, *Community Action Program Guide*, 7.

76. Office of Economic Opportunity, *Community Action Program Guide*, 16; Blumenthal, "The Bureaucracy," 174.

77. Memo, Buford Ellington, Office of Emergency Planning, Executive Office of the President, to the president, August 2, 1965, Executive File, WE 9, Box 98, LBJ

Library; memo, Charles L. Schultze, director of the Bureau of the Budget, to the president, September 18, 1965, Executive File, WE 9, Box 98, LBJ Library; Office of Economic Opportunity, *The Quiet Revolution*, 9; Office of Economic Opportunity, *The Tide of Progress*, 7; Haider, "Governors and Mayors View the Poverty Program," 277; Gunther, *Federal-City Relations in the United States*, 223–25.

78. James Button compared postriot expenditure increases in a sample of forty riot cities with the overall OEO budget outlay increase over the same period. According to Button, urban uprisings had a "greater direct, positive impact" than any other independent variable (such as the size of a city, the number of African Americans, the percentage of the poor, the crime rate, etc.) on total OEO expenditure increases in the latter 1960s, as well as on most individual poverty program increases. The War on Poverty became more and more an urban ghettos-oriented program. Button, *Black Violence*, 9–12, 27–37; J. David Greenstone and Paul E. Peterson, "Reformers, Machines, and the War on Poverty," in *City Politics and Public Policy*, ed. Wilson, 288; Bullock, *Watts*, 51–54.

79. Democrat senator Robert C. Byrd stated furiously that it was the time to avert "incidents such as had wracked Detroit, Newark, and New York." He contended that "we must not let firebrands go uncontested or uninvestigated, especially when those same firebrands draw their salaries from moneys provided by the taxpayers who bear the costs of repairing and rebuilding the damage left behind by those who inspire and cause trouble and mass civil unrest." U.S. Congress, Senate, Senator Byrd speaking on "Antipoverty Officials and the Riots," 90th Cong., 1st sess., *Congressional Record* 113, pt. 15 (July 27, 1967): 20410–11.

80. Addonizio, "The Mayors Speak," 7–8; U.S. Congress, Senate, Senator Thurmond speaking on "L.B.J. on Toleration of Riots," 90th Cong., 1st sess., *Congressional Record* 113, pt. 15 (July 27, 1967): 20468–69; Moynihan, *Maximum Feasible Misunderstanding*, 150.

81. For instance, against the charge that "the recent riots prove that the anti-poverty program has been a failure," the OEO stressed that "there is hard evidence that job training and educational programs, aimed at taking people out of poverty, build peaceful alternatives to disorder"; it also rejected the charge that "Detroit got all the money they wanted to eliminate the sources of poverty and they still had a riot," arguing that Detroit received only 14 percent of what it requested from OEO. Memo, Sargent Shriver to Lyndon B. Johnson, July 27, 1967, Confidential File, Box 129, LBJ Library; memo, Sargent Shriver to Lyndon B. Johnson, September 7, 1967, Confidential File, Box 129, LBJ Library; memo, Sargent Shriver to Lyndon B. Johnson, September 12, 1967, Subject File, FG11-15, Box 125, LBJ Library; memo, Sargent Shriver to Lyndon B. Johnson, March 7, 1968, Confidential File, Box 129, LBJ Library; Office of Economic Opportunity, "OEO and the Riots—A Summary," Confidential File, Box 129, in *The Presidential*

Documents Series, the War on Poverty; "Myths and Facts about OEO," Confidential File, Box 129, in *The Presidential Documents Series, the War on Poverty*; Button, *Black Violence*, 42–44.

82. Robert B. Semple Jr., "Mayors to Fight U.S. Fund Cutback," *New York Times*, January 28, 1967; Bertrand M. Harding, interviews by Stephen Goodell, November 20 and 25, 1968, Oral History Collection, LBJ Library; Gillette, *Launching the War on Poverty*, 329–30; Haider, "Governors and Mayors View the Poverty Program," 278, 302–3; Levitan, *The Great Society's Poor Law*, 101–3.

2. Fostering Community and Nationhood

1. Matsubara, *Jūmin sanka to jichi no kakushin*; Shimada, "Chihō jichi to jūmin no shutai keisei," 686–702; Fōramu 90s kenkyū iinkai, *20 seiki no seiji shisō to shakai undo*; Iwasaki et al., *Sengo Nihon sutadīzu*.

2. Kimura Hitoshi, "Komyunitī taisaku ni tsuite," in *Komyunitī dokuhon*, ed. Chihō Jichi Seido Kenkyukai, 120; Matsubara, *Komyunitī no riron to jissen*; Matsubara, "Komyunitī shisaku o hitsuyō to shita haikei," in *Komyunitī kenkyū hōkoku*, ed. Jichishō Komyunitī Kenkyūkai.

3. Johnson, *MITI and the Japanese Miracle*, 3–6; Duus, *Modern Japan*, 291–96, 303–7.

4. Ochiai Emiko, *21 seiki kazoku e*; Ochiai Emiko, "Sekai no naka no sengo nihon kazoku," in *Nihonshi kōza*, ed. Rekishigaku Kenkyūkai, Nihonshi Kenkyūkai, 162; Ueno Chizuko, "Kōdo seichōki to seikatsu kakumei," in *Sengo Nihon sutadīzu*, ed. Iwasaki et al., 169–71.

5. It was only after 1975 that the number of working women began to rise. Ochiai, *21 seiki kazoku e*, 22; Shimoebisu Miyuki, "Kazoku seisaku no rekishiteki tenkai," in *Gendai kazoku to shakai hoshō*, ed. Shakai Hoshō Kenkyūjo, 264; Nishikawa Yuko, "Otoko no ie, onna no ie, seibetsu no nai heya: Zoku sumai no hensen to 'katei' no seiritsu," in *Jendā no Nihon shi*, ed. Wakita and Hanley, 609–44.

6. Aside from "Minamata disease," the Big Four Pollution Diseases included Niigata Minamata disease (mercury-filled effluents from the Shōwa Denkō Corporation in Niigata Prefecture), Ita-itai (meaning "it hurts, it hurts") disease (cadmium-filled effluents from a Mitsubishi Mining Corporation refinery in Toyama Prefecture), and Yokkaichi asthma (asthma caused by air pollution near the petrochemical industrial complex in Yokkaichi City, Mie Prefecture). Kamioka, *Nihon no kōgaishi*; Frank K. Upham, "Unplaced Persons and Movements for Peace," in *Postwar Japan as History*, ed. Gordon, 325–46.

7. Muto Ichiyou, "Shakai undō to bunsuirei to shite no 68nen," in *20 seiki no seiji shisō to shakai undō*, ed. Fōramu 90s kenkyū iinkai, 81; Shirakawa Masumi, "Chiiki jyūmin undo," in *20 seiki no seiji shisō to shakai undō*, ed. Fōramu 90s

kenkyū iinkai, 124; Yasuda, "Gendaishi ni okeru jichi to kōkyōsei ni kansuru oboegaki," 367–68; Michiba Chikanobu, "Chiiki tōsō: Sanrizuka, Minamata," in *Sengo Nihon sutadīzu*, ed. Iwasaki et al., 104–5.

8. Goto Michio, "Nihongata shakaihoshō no kōzō: Sono keisei to tankan," in *Kōdo seichō to kigyō shakai,* ed. Watanabe, 211.

9. Shindo Hyo, "Kakushin jichitai," in *Kōdo seichō to kigyō shakai,* ed. Watanabe, 224–25. See also Abe, "Jūmin undō to chiiki seiji," 56–69; Nakamura, "Jūmin undō no soshiki to kōzō," 22–32; Omori, "Jūmin undō no tenkai katei," 13–21; Sato, "Jūmin undō to jichitai gyōsei," 43–55; Yamamoto, "Jūmin undō no hassei yōin," 2–12; Yasuhara, "Jūmin undō ni okeru rīdā sō no seikaku," 33–42.

10. Tanaka Kakuei, "Jimintō no hansei," 284–93; Shinohara, *Shimin sanka*, 3.

11. Yamaguchi, "Shimin sanka ni okeru kakushin to hoshu," in *Gendai toshi seisaku II: Shimin sanka,* ed. Shinohara et al., 187–212. While the LDP failed to win a majority of the vote, it managed to control the cabinet through the electoral districting system, whose boundaries had not been redrawn since the early postwar period when half of the population still lived in the countryside. See Duus, *Modern Japan,* 315–18.

12. Tokyoto Minseikyoku, *Komyunitī kea no suishin ni tsuite.*

13. Professors in such fields as sociology, law, education, and engineering constituted the subcommittee of community problems in the National Life Council. Along with the Community Study Group later established by the Ministry of Home Affairs, it became the main task force for the Model Community Program. Kokumin Seikatsu Shingikai, *Komyunitī*; memo, "Koremade no komyunitī o meguru ugoki," n.d., Gyōseika, Sōmushō.

14. Kokumin Seikatsu Shingikai, *Komyunitī,* 2.

15. Ibid., vi, 13–14.

16. Omori, "Gendai gyōsei ni okeru 'jūmin sanka' no tenkai," 267–325; Nishio, *Kenryoku to sanka.*

17. Omori, "Gendai gyōsei ni okeru 'jūmin sanka' no tenkai," 311–15.

18. Nishio, *Kenryoku to sanka,* iii, v, 69. Nishio acknowledged that what was going on in Japan, such as the prevalence of residents' movements, the concept of citizens' participation, and the development of communities, had influenced his book, although he had accomplished a significant amount of research by the time the MCP was initiated by the Ministry of Home Affairs.

19. Musashino City, *Musashino shi no komyunitī,* 13–20.

20. Okuda Michihiro, "Komyunitī keisei o meguru gyōsei to jūmin," in *Jūmin sanka to jichi no kakushin,* ed. Matsubara, 201–3.

21. Majima, "Komyunitī to jichitai nai bunken: Jūmin jichi no kiso tani no saikouchiku," in *Kōiki to kyōiki no gyōsei seido,* ed. Ito, 356.

22. Okuda Michihiro, "Shimin undō to shimin sanka," in *Gendai toshi seisaku II: Shimin sanka,* ed. Shinohara et al., 103–5.

23. Omori Wataru, interview by author, December 23, 2005, Tokyo.

24. "Komyunitī (kinrinshakai) ni kansuru taisaku yōkō," Jichishō jimu jikan (administrative vice-minister of the Ministry of Home Affairs) to governors, April 3, 1971, in *Komyunitī dokuhon,* 241–44; Matsubara, *Komyunitī no riron to jissen*; Morimura, *Komyunitī no keikaku gihō*, 25; Jichi Sōgō Sentā, *Komyunitī kankei yōkō tou shiryōshū*; memo, "Koremade no komyunitī o meguru ugoki," n.d., Gyōseika, Sōmushō.

25. Jichishō Komyunitī Kenkyūkai, *Komyunitī kenkyūkai chūkan hōkoku*; Jichishō Komyunitī Kenkyūkai, *Komyunitī kenkyūkai hōkoku*; memo, "Koremade no komyunitī o meguru ugoki," n.d., Gyōseika, Sōmushō. The following scholars joined the Community Study Group: Higasa Tadashi (professor at Department of Engineering, University of Tokyo), Ishida Yorifusa (associate professor at Department of Engineering, Tokyo Metropolitan University), Ito Shigeru (associate professor at Department of Engineering, University of Tokyo), Kurasawa Susumu (associate professor at Department of Humanities, Tokyo Metropolitan University), Matsubara Haruo (associate professor at Department of Education, University of Tokyo), Morimura Michiyoshi (associate professor at Department of Engineering, University of Tokyo), and Sato Atsushi (professor at Department of Law, Seikei University).

26. Shimizu Keihachiro, "Komyunitī hōkoku ni tsuite," in *Komyunitī,* ed. Komyunitī Mondai Shōiinkai, iv–v.

27. Matsubara, "Komyunitī shisaku o hitsuyō to shita haikei," in *Komyunitī kenkyū hōkoku,* ed. Jichishō Komyunitī Kenkyūkai, 7; Sato, "Gyōsei shisaku to shite no komyunitī," in *Komyunitī kenkyū hōkoku,* ed. Jichishō Komyunitī Kenkyūkai, 15–17.

28. Miyazawa, "Komyunitī ni tsuite," 4–5.

29. Kurasawa Susumu, "Jūmin katsudō kara mita komyunitī," in *Komyunitī kenkyū hōkoku,* ed. Jichishō Komyunitī Kenkyūkai, 104–5.

30. Matsubara, "Komyunitī shisaku o hitsuyō to shita haikei," in *Komyunitī kenkyū hōkoku,* ed. Jichishō Komyunitī Kenkyūkai, 5; Matsubara, "Komyunitī shisaku no tenbō—shakai keikaku no tachibakara," in *Komyunitī kenkyū hōkoku,* ed. Jichishō Komyunitī Kenkyūkai, 139, 141. See also Matsubara, *Komyunitī no riron to jissen, 77–79.*

31. Garon, *Molding Japanese Minds.* See also Smethurst, *A Social Basis for Prewar Japanese Militarism*; Hastings, *Neighborhood and Nation in Tokyo, 1905–1937.*

32. Garon, *Molding Japanese Minds,* 8, 17–18.

33. Shimada, "Chihō jichi to jūmin no shutai keisei," 692–93.

34. Sato, "Jūmin undō to jichitai gyōsei," 43–55.

35. The Ministry of Health and Welfare established the Central Social Welfare Council in December 1971 and published a document titled "Community

Formation and Social Welfare." The Ministry of Education started improving the conditions of public halls (*kōminkan*), which were created in 1949 to encourage educational and cultural activities. The National Land Agency had granted a subsidy to local governments in such places as depopulated areas, isolated islands, and heavy snowfall areas for the purpose of establishing "community centers" since 1971. The Ministry of Agriculture, Forestry, and Fisheries created a variety of centers (mountain village development centers, centers for the environmental improvement of rural villages/work opportunities) since 1970. Finally the Ministry of Labor improved the conditions of the Centers for Working Women and Homes for Working Young People. Matsubara, "Jichishō moderu komyunitī shisaku," 22–33.

36. Memo, "Koremade no komyunitī o meguru ugoki," n.d., Gyōseika, Sōmushō.

37. Kokumin Seikatsu Shingikai, *Komyunitī,* vi; Chuō Shakai Fukushi Shingikai, *Komyunitī keisei to shakai fukushi (Tōben)*, 8, 19; Miyazawa, "Komyunitī ni tsuite," 2–9.

38. Kimura, "Komyunitī taisaku ni tsuite," 119.

39. Kurasawa, "Komyunitī to wa nani ka," in *Komyunitī dokuhon,* ed. Chihō Jichi Seido Kenkyukai, 23.

40. Yoshihara, *Sengo kaikaku to chiiki jūmin soshiki*, 48–50; Kurasawa and Akimoto, *Chōnaikai to chiiki shūdan*; Kwon, "Chōnaikai no sengo kaikaku (1)," 45–67; Kwon, "Chōnaikai no sengo kaikaku (2)," 67–89.

41. Omori Wataru, interview by author, December 23, 2005; Nishio Masaru, interview by author, August 26, 2010.

42. Kimura, "Komyunitī taisaku ni tsuite (1)," 119. See also Kimura, "Komyunitī taisaku," 12; Kimura, "Komyunitī taisaku no mondaiten," 31; Kimura, "Komyunitī taisaku no kinkyō to kadai," 28–29; Kimura, "Shōwa 47 nendo no komyunitī taisaku ni tsuite," 59.

43. Kurasawa, "Komyunitī to wa nani ka," in *Komyunitī dokuhon,* ed. Chihō Jichi Seido Kenkyukai, 19.

44. Higasa Tadashi, "Komyunitī shisetsu no keikaku ni atatte no kihon jōken," in *Zoku komyunitī dokuhon,* ed. Chihō Jichi Seido Kenkyūkai, 6.

45. Omori Wataru, interview by author, December 23, 2005.

46. For more information on the role of the *chōnaikai* and *burakukai* in the MCP, see Sato, *Komyunitī o meguru mondai jirei*, 60, 171.

47. Kokumin Seikatsu Shingikai, *Komyunitī,* 16.

48. Matsubara, "Komyunitī no seikaku to igi," in *Zoku komyunitī dokuhon,* ed. Chihō Jichi Seido Kenkyūkai, 31; Matsubara, *Komyunitī no riron to jissen,* 35.

49. Washimi Takeshi, "Komyunitī taisaku no genjō to kadai," in *Zoku komyunitī dokuhon,* ed. Chihō Jichi Seido Kenkyūkai, 119.

50. When the so-called oil shock hit the economy and the era of the "economic miracle" came to an end, the LDP-dominated central government shifted the responsibility of social security onto "people's self efforts, families, and communities," calling this a "Japanese style of welfare society." In Shimoebisu's words, now families were assumed to support social security, instead of vice versa. Shimoebisu, "Kazoku seisaku no rekishiteki tenkai," in *Gendai kazoku to shakai hoshō,* ed. Shakai Hoshō Kenkyūjo, 257.

51. Omori Wataru, interview by author, December 23, 2005; Kimura Hitoshi, interview by author, January 27, 2006. Even though the Model Community Program reinforced women's marginal position in the wage labor market, housewives were assigned a political significance as the guardian of "communities." Local women asserted their rights in public spaces, with a special emphasis on environmental issues, education, and welfare.

52. Ochiai, "Sekai no naka no sengo nihon kazoku," 189.

53. Kokumin Seikatsu Shingikai, *Komyunitī,* 3.

54. Ibid., 3, 16.

55. Park Chong-Myong and Kim Young-Ja, "Sabetsu kokufuku ni mukete," in *Zainichi Chōsenjin: Rekishi, genjō, tembō*, ed. Park, 17.

56. These discriminatory practices continued up until 1981, when the International Convention on the Status of Refugees was ratified by the Japanese government. This agreement required ratifiers to provide noncitizens social security on equal terms with citizens. The Japanese government therefore abolished the provisions that denied foreign citizens' access to social security programs. See Kim Il-Wha, "*Zainichi* Chōsenjin no hōteki chii," in *Zainichi Chōsenjin: Rekishi, genjō, tembō*, ed. Park, 184–93; Shin Yong-Hong, "*Zainichi* Chōsenjin to shakai hoshō," in *Zainichi Chōsenjin: Rekishi, genjō, tembō*, ed. Park, 265–71; Yoshioka, *Zainichi gaikokujin to shakai hoshō*; Tanaka, *Zainichi gaikokujin*, 66–76, 160–66.

57. Omori Wataru, interview by author, December 23, 2005, Arcadia Ichigaya Shigakukaikan, Tokyo; Kimura Hitoshi, interview by author, January 27, 2006.

58. Miyazawa, "Komyunitī ni tsuite," 9.

59. Endo, "Chiikiteki rentai ishiki to komyunitī," 2–14.

3. Struggling for Political Voice

1. An earlier version of this chapter was presented to the Kyoto American Studies Summer Seminar in 2005. I wish to thank participants for their comments and suggestions.

2. Lonnie G. Bunch, "A Past Not Necessarily Prologue: The Afro-American in Los Angeles," in *20th Century Los Angeles,* ed. Klein and Schiesl, 101–30.

3. Flamming, *Bound for Freedom*, 3.

4. *The Crisis*, August 1913, 192.

5. Susan Anderson, "A City Called Heaven: Black Enchantment and Despair in Los Angeles," in *The City*, ed. Scott and Soja, 336–64; Taylor, *In Search of the Racial Frontier*, 222–50; Sides, *L.A. City Limits*, 11–35.

6. Los Angeles County Commission on Human Relations, *Population and Housing in Los Angeles County*, 1–5; Los Angeles County Commission on Human Relations, *Patterns of Social Change*; Lonnie G. Bunch, "A Past Not Necessarily Prologue: The African American in Los Angeles," in *20th Century Los Angeles*, ed. Klein and Schiesl, 115–20; David M. Grant, Melvin L. Oliver, and Angela D. James, "African Americans: Social and Economic Bifurcation," in *Ethnic Los Angeles*, ed. Waldinger and Bozorgmehar, 381–82; Sides, *L.A. City Limits*, 176–81.

7. Casstevens, "California's Rumford Act and Proposition 14," 237–84; Wolfinger and Greenstein, "The Repeal of Fair Housing in California," 753–69.

8. The Rumford Fair Housing Act declared that "discrimination because of race, color, religion, national origin, or ancestry" in housing accommodation was against public policy in California. The principal innovation in the Rumford Act was "the assignment to FEPC of responsibility for administrative enforcement and for conducting a program of education and affirmative action to eliminate discrimination in housing." The FEPC operated four offices including seven commissioners, associate legal counsels, assistant education offices, consultants, and clerical employees. The commission performed a quasi-judicial function by hearing the consultant's presentation of the evidence of discrimination and homeowner's evidence to the contrary and then rendering a decision. The FEPC dealt with 192 cases during the first year. State of California, Division of Fair Employment Practices, *Questions and Answers about the California Fair Housing Law*, 1; "First-Year Case Experience under Rumford Fair Housing Act," in *Materials on Proposition 14,* comp. University of California, Los Angeles (UCLA), School of Law.

9. The formal name of Proposition 14 was "Sales and Rentals of Residential Real Property Initiative Constitutional Amendment." It prohibited "state, subdivision, or agency thereof from denying, limiting, or abridging, rights of any person to decline to sell, lease, or rent residential real property to any person as he chooses." The California Real Estate Association advised as follows: "State appointed bureaucrats may force you, over your objections, to deal concerning your own property with the person they choose . . . Fair Employment Practices Commission becomes investigator, prosecutor, jury, and judge." "Excerpts from Spike Wilson's Speech of June 27, 1964, to the California Real Estate Association," in *Materials on Proposition 14,* comp. UCLA, School of Law; *The California State Employee,* September 4, 1964.

10. Other than civil rights organizations and the AFL-CIO, "Californians against Proposition 14" included the following organizations: Japanese-American Citizens League, Chinese-American Citizens Alliance, Mexican-American Political Association, State Bar of California, Catholic Social Justice Committee, Democratic

Party organizations, and Los Angeles County Human Relations Commission, among others. The pamphlet "Californians against Proposition 14" advised the following: "The most important issue on your November 3 ballot is Proposition 14, the scheme by multi-billion dollar real estate interests to write hate and bigotry into our California Constitution . . . you must have to combat effectively this attempt to turn California into another Mississippi or Alabama." Total votes on Proposition 14 were cast by 6,922,207 (84.6 percent) of the state's 8,184,143 registered voters. There were 4,526,460 "Yes" votes (65.4 percent) and 2,395,747 "No" votes (34.6 percent) on Proposition 14. "Vital Questions and Answers on Proposition 14," in *Materials on Proposition 14,* comp. UCLA, School of Law; *Crisis: A Record of the Darker Races* 71, no. 1 (1964): 25; Casstevens, "California's Rumford Act and Proposition 14," 264–69; "ELA Realtors Group to Oppose Prop. 14," *Eastside Sun,* September 24, 1964; Horne, *Fire This Time*, 224; Nicolaides, *My Blue Heaven*, 306–15.

11. "South Los Angeles" includes Watts, Central, Avalon, Florence, Green Meadows, Exposition, and Willowbrook. U.S. Senate Committee on Labor and Public Welfare, Subcommittee on Employment, Manpower, and Poverty, *Examination of the War on Poverty,* 3778–93; Soja and Scott, "Introduction to Los Angeles," in *The City,* ed. Scott and Soja, 11–17; Sides, *L.A. City Limits*, 176–81.

12. U.S. Senate Committee on Labor and Public Welfare, Subcommittee on Employment, Manpower, and Poverty, *Examination of the War on Poverty,* 3783, 3785–87.

13. According to Diane Pearce, the "feminization of poverty" took place in the 1960s and the early 1970s even though other trends, such as the increase in women's labor force participation, the mandating of affirmative action, and the increasing employment of better-educated women, would suggest the potential for improving women's economic status. In 1976, nearly two out of three of the fifteen million poor persons over sixteen were women. While Pearce is among the first scholars to employ the term "feminization of poverty" and deserves wide reading, her analysis of poverty does not explore racial inequalities in poverty. Although Pearce acknowledges that "disadvantages suffered by poor women are exacerbated by race and prejudice for minority women," she maintains that "for a woman race is a relatively unimportant consideration in determining economic status." Pearce, "The Feminization of Poverty," 28–36; Gertrude Schaffner Goldberg and Eleanor Kremen, "The Feminization of Poverty: Discovered in America," in *The Feminization of Poverty,* ed. Goldberg and Kremen, 5.

14. Horne, *Fire This Time*, 7–16, 171–76.

15. Davis, *City of Quartz*, 126.

16. Yorty was also a staunch anti-Communist. When the Watts uprising occurred, Yorty blamed "outside agitators" and Communists for causing it. Yorty supported President Johnson's policies in Vietnam even when "some of the other

people were backing off." Samuel Yorty, interview by Joe B. Frantz, February 7, 1970, LBJ Library; memo, Bill Haddad to Sargent Shriver, June 15, 1965, File "Los Angeles (EYOA), April 1965–July 1965," EYOA-NA; Bollens and Geyer, *Yorty*; Bauman, "Race, Class, and Political Power," 118–20; Widener, "Perhaps the Japanese Are to Be Thanked?," 92–94.

17. "Positions Taken by Councilman Thomas Bradley," n.d., File 27, Box 4727, Thomas Bradley Administrative Papers, 1963–1993, Department of Special Collections, University of California, Los Angeles; "Augustus Hawkins," in Ragsdale and Treese, *Black Americans in Congress, 1870–1989*; Payne and Ratzan, *Tom Bradley*; Sonenshein, *Politics in Black and White*, 40–46; Bauman, "Race, Class, and Political Power," 124–28.

18. "Los Angeles Report Based on Trip, February 26–27," undated (1965), File "Los Angeles (EYOA), January 1965–March 1965," EYOA-NA; Greenstone and Peterson, *Race and Authority in Urban Politics*, 275–78; Sonenshein, *Politics in Black and White*, 56–58; Horne, *Fire This Time*, 295–98.

19. Memo, Samuel Yorty to Council of the City of Los Angeles, October 22, 1962, File "Youth Opportunities Board: 1962 (1 of 2)," Box C-1007, Samuel Yorty Collection, Records Management Division, Office of the City Clerk, City of Los Angeles (hereafter Yorty-LA); "Informational Statement Number 1—Youth Opportunities Board of Greater Los Angeles," December 1962, File "Youth Opportunities Board: 1962 (1 of 2)," Yorty-LA; Youth Opportunities Board of Greater Los Angeles, *The Los Angeles "War against Poverty,"* 1–10; Marshall, *The Politics of Participation in Poverty*, 13–15; Bauman, "Race, Class, and Political Power," 128–34.

20. Memo, Samuel Yorty to Council of the City of Los Angeles, April 3, 1962, File "Youth Opportunities Board: 1962 (2 of 2)," Yorty-LA.

21. "Informational Statement Number 1—Youth Opportunities Board of Greater Los Angeles," December 1962, File "Youth Opportunities Board: 1962 (1 of 2)," Yorty-LA.

22. Memo, Bill Haddad to Sargent Shriver, June 15, 1965, File "Los Angeles (EYOA), April 1965–July 1965," EYOA-NA.

23. "Poverty Fight Mapped at Community Level," *Los Angeles Times*, April 7, 1964; "Bradley Initiates Anti-Poverty Move," *Los Angeles Sentinel*, August 27, 1964.

24. "Poverty War," *Los Angeles Sentinel*, August 27, 1964.

25. "Los Angeles Report Based on Trip, February 26–27," undated (1965), File "Los Angeles (EYOA), January 1965–March 1965," EYOA-NA; Bauman, "Race, Class, and Political Power," 136.

26. Memo, James E. Ludlam to Mayor S. Yorty, September 3, 1964, File "Los Angeles (EYOA), August 1965–September 1965," EYOA-NA.

27. As for the competition between the YOB and the EOF, see Marshall, *The Politics of Participation in Poverty*, 15–16; Greenstone and Peterson, *Race and Authority in Urban Politics*, 30–34, 140–42; Bauman, "Race, Class, and Political

Power," 135–48; Kazuyo Tsuchiya, "Race, Class, and Gender in America's 'War on Poverty,'" 213–36.

28. Memo, Samuel Yorty to James E. Ludlam, September 8, 1964, File "Los Angeles (EYOA), August 1965–September 1965," EYOA-NA.

29. Memo, Samuel Yorty to Walter Jenkins, September 25, 1964, Ex LG/Los Angeles, LBJ Library; Youth Opportunities Board of Greater Los Angeles, *The Los Angeles "War against Poverty."*

30. Memo, Sam Hamerman, chairperson of YOB, and Joseph L. Wyatt, president of EOF, to L. E. Timberlake, president of Los Angeles City Council, February 11, 1965, File #122706, Box A-1888, City Council File, Records Management Division, Office of the City Clerk, City of Los Angeles.

31. Ibid.; memo, Roger Arnebergh to Thomas Bradley, March 3, 1965, File #122706, Box A-1888, City Council File, Records Management Division, Office of the City Clerk, City of Los Angeles; memo, C. Erwin Piper to Mayor S. Yorty and State, County and Federal Affairs Committee of the City Council, March 26, 1965, File #122706, Box A-1888, City Council File, Records Management Division, Office of the City Clerk, City of Los Angeles; "Anti-Poverty Meet Set for Feb. 28," *Los Angeles Sentinel,* February 28, 1965; Gus Hawkins, "What Are the Answers to Poverty," *Los Angeles Sentinel,* March 18, 1965; Bauman, "Race, Class, and Political Power," 138–39.

32. Memo, Samuel Yorty to Council of the City of Los Angeles, April 23, 1965, File #122706, Box A-1888, City Council File, Records Management Division, Office of the City Clerk, City of Los Angeles; Bauman, "Race, Class, and Political Power," 139–40.

33. "Yorty Claims Leadership in Poverty Fight," *Los Angeles Sentinel,* February 25, 1965.

34. Horne, *Fire This Time*, 51–52.

35. Memo, Bill Haddad to Sargent Shriver, June 15, 1965, File "Los Angeles (EYOA), April 1965–July 1965," EYOA-NA.

36. Memo, Bill Haddad to Sargent Shriver, May 7, 1965, File "Los Angeles (EYOA), April 1965–July 1965," EYOA-NA; "'Uneasiness' Noted in Poverty War Support," *Los Angeles Times,* April 28, 1965; "Brown to Back Merger of Anti-Poverty Boards," April 27, 1965, File "Los Angeles (EYOA), April 1965–July 1965," EYOA-NA; memo, Augustus F. Hawkins to president, Los Angeles City Council, May 28, 1965, File "Anti-Poverty Programs. Misc.," Box 91, Augustus F. Hawkins Papers, 1935–1990, Department of Special Collections, University of California, Los Angeles; memo, H. Hartford Brookins, Community War on Poverty Committee, Los Angeles County, to Samuel W. Yorty, June 7, 1965, File "Anti-Poverty Programs. Misc.," Box 91, Augustus F. Hawkins Papers, 1935–1990, Department of Special Collections, University of California, Los Angeles; memo, Augustus F. Hawkins to Sargent Shriver, June 25, 1965, File "Anti-Poverty Programs.

Misc.," Box 91, Augustus F. Hawkins Papers, 1935–1990, Department of Special Collections, University of California, Los Angeles; "U.S. Blocks Poverty Funds in Personnel Row," *Los Angeles Times,* May 25, 1965; "Anti-Poverty Pitfalls," *Los Angeles Sentinel,* May 27, 1965; "Outsiders Running War on Poverty," *Los Angeles Sentinel,* May 27, 1965; Payne and Ratzan, *Tom Bradley,* 70; Marshall, *The Politics of Participation in Poverty,* 15; Bauman, "Race, Class, and Political Power," 140–41.

37. "Yorty: Poverty Fund Won't Be a 'Pork Barrel,'" n.d., File "Los Angeles (EYOA), April 1965–July 1965," EYOA-NA.

38. Memo, Jesse M. Unruh to Jack Valenti, special assistant to the president, August 18, 1965, File "HU2/ST5 10/12/65–4/14/66," General HU2/ST5, 6–11, LBJ Library.

39. "Yorty Compromise Rejected, Peters May Be Named to YOB," *Los Angeles Sentinel,* June 24, 1965; "No Solution Seen for Poverty Program Bog," *Los Angeles Sentinel,* July 1, 1965; "Yorty Forces Come Up with New Poverty Plan," *Los Angeles Times,* July 17, 1965; "Mills Backed on Poverty by Pastors: Debate Recall," *Los Angeles Sentinel,* July 22, 1965; Greenstone and Peterson, *Race and Authority in Urban Politics,* 276–77; Bauman, "Race, Class, and Political Power," 143–44.

40. "Know Your Congressman: Crisis in the War on Poverty," *Los Angeles Sentinel,* June 10, 1965.

41. "Hawkins Asks Letters on Poverty Goal," *Los Angeles Sentinel,* July 22, 1965.

42. "OEO—For Release," June 10, 1965, File "Los Angeles (EYOA), April 1965–July 1965," EYOA-NA; memo, Augustus F. Hawkins to Mr. William Bassett, Los Angeles County Federation of Labor, June 7, 1965, File "Anti-Poverty Programs. Misc.," Box 91, Augustus F. Hawkins Papers, 1935–1990, Department of Special Collections, University of California, Los Angeles; "L.A. Area Warned It May Lose Poverty Funds," *Los Angeles Times,* May 26, 1965; "Poverty Unity Needed," *Los Angeles Sentinel,* June 10, 1965; "Poverty Grant Given Directly to City Schools," *Los Angeles Times,* June 11, 1965; "Mass Poverty Demonstrations," *Los Angeles Sentinel,* July 15, 1965; "32-Member Poverty Bd. Backed by King," *Los Angeles Sentinel,* July 15, 1965; Bauman, "Race, Class, and Political Power," 144–48.

43. The Governor's Commission on the Los Angeles Riots [McCone Commission], "Violence in the City: An End or a Beginning?," in *The Los Angeles Riots,* comp. Fogelson; Robert M. Fogelson, "White on Black: A Critique of the McCone Commission Report on the Los Angeles Riots," in *The Los Angeles Riots,* comp. Fogelson, 113; Nathan E. Cohen, "The Context of the Curfew Area," in *The Los Angeles Riots,* ed. Cohen, 41; Horne, *Fire This Time,* 3; Bauman, "Race, Class, and Political Power," 150.

44. McCone Commission, "Violence in the City," 1–25.

45. Ibid.; Fogelson, "White on Black," 115–16.

46. "L.A. Lacks Leadership on Rights, King Says," *Los Angeles Times,* August 21, 1965.

47. "King Assailed by Yorty after Stormy Meeting," *Los Angeles Times,* August 20, 1965; memo, Lee White to President Johnson, August 20, 1965, Office Files of Lee White, LBJ Library.

48. Horne, *Fire This Time*, 183. See also "James Farmer to Amsterdam News," August 28, 1965, vol. 15 (Reel 18), Congress of Racial Equality Papers: Addendum, 1944–1968.

49. Maulana Karenga, interview by author, September 25, 2000; Horne, *Fire This Time*, 185–212; Tyler, "Black Radicalism in Southern California, 1950–1982"; Bullock, *Watts*.

50. Richard T. Morris and Vincent Jeffries, "The White Reaction Study," in *The Los Angeles Riots*, ed. Cohen, 480–601. Morriss and Jeffries chose a sample of six hundred whites in six selected areas (Baldwin Hills, Pacific Palisades, Leimert Park, Reseda, Central Long Beach, and Bell) in Los Angeles, with one hundred white residents drawn from each place. The areas were chosen on the basis of socioeconomic status, indexed by occupation, education, income, and the degree of integration, using 1960 census figures.

51. Memo, Jesse M. Unruh to Jack Valenti, August 18, 1965, Gen HU2/ST5, LBJ Library.

52. Bollens and Geyer, *Yorty*, 154.

53. Memo, Louis Martin to John Bailey and Cliff Carter, August 23, 1965, Office Files of Lee White, LBJ Library; Bollens and Geyer, *Yorty*, 149–62.

54. Bollens and Geyer, *Yorty*, 149–62.

55. Gary Orfield, "Race and the Liberal Agenda: The Loss of the Integrationist Dream, 1965–1974," in *The Politics of Social Policy in the United States*, ed. Weir, Orloff, and Skocpol, 327–30; Horne, *Fire This Time*, 280–82, 290–92, 301–2; Nicolaides, *My Blue Heaven*, 322–26.

56. Horne, *Fire This Time*, 281.

57. James W. Button, *Black Violence*, 30–31.

58. Memo, Ernest C. Friesen Jr. to Lawrence E. Levinson, October 4, 1965, Ex HU2/ST5, LBJ Library; Horne, *Fire This Time*, 281–87.

59. Cohen, *The Los Angeles Riots*.

60. Memo, Dick Fullmer to Bob Clampitt, September 27, 1965, File "Los Angeles (EYOA), October 1965–December 1965," EYOA-NA.

61. "Poor Wait Outside in Poverty War," *Los Angeles Times*, August 11, 1965.

62. "The Poverty Issue," *Los Angeles Sentinel*, August 12, 1965; "Why—the Rioting?," *Los Angeles Sentinel*, August 19, 1965; Bauman, "Race, Class, and Political Power," 154–62.

63. Sonenshein, *Politics in Black and White*, 83; Payne and Ratzan, *Tom Bradley*, 74.

64. Memo, Louis Martin to John Bailey and Cliff Carter, August 23, 1965, Office Files of Lee White, LBJ Library.

65. Memo, Augustus F. Hawkins to President Johnson, August 23, 1965, File "Anti-Poverty Programs. Misc.," Box 91, Augustus F. Hawkins Papers, 1935–1990,

Department of Special Collections, University of California, Los Angeles; memo, Augustus F. Hawkins to William J. Williams, August 31, 1965, File "Anti-Poverty Programs. Misc.," Box 91, Augustus F. Hawkins Papers, 1935–1990, Department of Special Collections, University of California, Los Angeles. Attorney General Ramsey Clark, who investigated the causes of the uprising, also found that unemployment was one of the most severely felt concerns for black residents. Lipsitz, *The Possessive Investment in Whiteness*, 40.

66. Memo, Senator George Murphy to Sargent Shriver, August 17, 1965, File "General: United States Gov., Economic Opportunity, 1965," Box D-25, Yorty-LA.

67. "Yorty Raps Shriver over Poverty Funds," *Los Angeles Times,* August 19, 1965; Bollens and Geyer, *Yorty*, 152; Horne, *Fire This Time*, 290.

68. Horne, *Fire This Time*, 284.

69. Memo, Joseph A. Califano Jr. to the president, September 11, 1965, Ex LG/Los Angeles, LBJ Library.

70. Memo, LeRoy Collins to Sargent Shriver, August 23, 1965, Ex HU2/ST5, LBJ Library; memo, Sargent Shriver to Joseph Califano Jr., August 23, 1965, EX HU2/ST5, LBJ Library; "Los Angeles: Help from U.S. Task Force," *Los Angeles Times,* August 29, 1965; Button, *Black Violence*, 30–31; Horne, *Fire This Time*, 281–85; Bauman, "Race, Class, and Political Power," 168–77.

71. "Collins' Proposal Rejected," *Los Angeles Sentinel,* August 26, 1965.

72. Memo, Augustus F. Hawkins to Sargent Shriver, September 2, 1965, File "Los Angeles (EYOA), August 1965–September 1965," EYOA-NA; memo, Dick Fullmer to Bob Clampitt, September 27, 1965, File "Los Angeles (EYOA), August 1965–September 1965," EYOA-NA; memo, Augustus F. Hawkins to William J. Williams, August 31, 1965, File "Anti-Poverty Programs. Misc.," Box 91, Augustus F. Hawkins Papers, 1935–1990, Department of Special Collections, University of California, Los Angeles; memo, Augustus F. Hawkins to Louis J. Ambler Jr., September 13, 1965, File "Anti-Poverty Programs. Misc.," Box 91, Augustus F. Hawkins Papers, 1935–1990, Department of Special Collections, University of California, Los Angeles; "Hawkins Attacks Anti-Poverty Pact," *Los Angeles Times,* August 26, 1965; "Causes of Riot Still Prevail, Hawkins Says," *Los Angeles Times,* September 21, 1965; Bauman, "Race, Class, and Political Power," 172–77.

73. Memo, Senator George Murphy to R. Sargent Shriver, August 17, 1965, File "General: United States Gov., Economic Opportunity, 1965," Box D-25, Yorty-LA.

74. Memo, Sargent Shriver to Augustus F. Hawkins, n.d., File "Los Angeles (EYOA), August 1965–September 1965," EYOA-NA.

4. Recasting the Community Action Program

1. At first, the EYOA was the only Community Action Agency in Los Angeles County. Four new agencies were created in late 1966 and early 1967 in Los Angeles County. U.S. General Accounting Office, *Review of the Community Action Program in the Los Angeles Area under the Economic Opportunity Act*, 5–6; Kaye, *Distribution of Poor Youths in Los Angeles County*, v; U.S. Senate Committee on Labor and Public Welfare, Subcommittee on Employment, Manpower, and Poverty, *Examination of the War on Poverty*, 3844.

2. Marshall, *The Politics of Participation in Poverty*, 135–36.

3. U.S. General Accounting Office, *Review of the Community Action Program in the Los Angeles Area under the Economic Opportunity Act*, 1–23; Patterson, *America's Struggle against Poverty 1900–1994*, 136. In addition to the educational and employment programs, Teen Post, which consisted of 150 recreational and cultural programs for teenagers in "poverty" areas, was one of the most popular programs in the Los Angeles "War on Poverty."

4. U.S. General Accounting Office, *Review of the Community Action Program in the Los Angeles Area under the Economic Opportunity Act*, 8–10; memo, Robert L. Goe to Irvin Walder, January 10, 1966, File #126307, Box A-1938, City Council File, Records Management Division, Office of the City Clerk, City of Los Angeles; U.S. Senate Committee on Labor and Public Welfare, Subcommittee on Employment, Manpower, and Poverty, *Examination of the War on Poverty*, 3845.

5. Some people questioned this point during the hearing on *Examination of the War on Poverty in Los Angeles* in May 1967. For example, George Knox Roth, a research director at General Research Consultants in Pasadena, stated that "the Negro and Mexican-American poor have been favored both with jobs and assistance with an almost total disregard for the other segments of the poor equally in need of assistance." U.S. Senate Committee on Labor and Public Welfare, Subcommittee on Employment, Manpower, and Poverty, *Examination of the War on Poverty*, 3986.

6. Ibid., 3895–98.

7. Ibid., 3979–80, 3986.

8. Mary Henry, interview by author, September 30, 2002.

9. Neighborhood Adult Participation Project, *This Is N.A.P.P.!: A Little Reader about the Neighborhood Adult Participation Project*, in Box 1, NAPP, California Social Welfare Archives, Special Collections, University of Southern California (USC); NAPP, *NAPP Now: An Explanation of the Neighborhood Adult Participation Project Incorporated*, in Box 1, NAPP, California Social Welfare Archives, Special Collections, USC; NAPP, *This Is the Neighborhood Adult Participation Project Story in a Capsule*, in Box 2, NAPP, California Social Welfare Archives, Special Collections, USC.

10. NAPP, *This Is the Neighborhood Adult Participation Project Story in a Capsule.*

11. Although the pamphlets written by Jones are valuable sources, readers should note that there is a methodological problem concerning the use of her pamphlets. These pamphlets are important since they would help readers understand the character of NAPP and Jones's viewpoints toward the antipoverty programs. Also, these pamphlets are significant because there are not many resources available today about a specific program funded by the OEO through the EYOA. Many of the pamphlets, however, do not have specific dates, so it is difficult to put them in chronological order and examine how her views changed after 1965.

12. U.S. Senate Committee on Labor and Public Welfare, Subcommittee on Employment, Manpower, and Poverty, *Examination of the War on Poverty,* 3949–53.

13. Opal C. Jones, *Strategy and Strategists,* May 28, 1968, in Box 3, NAPP, California Social Welfare Archives, Special Collections, USC; Opal C. Jones, *How to Work with People of All Ethnic Groups,* in Box 4, NAPP, California Social Welfare Archives, Special Collections, USC.

14. Opal C. Jones, *A New Look in Community Service,* in Box 4, NAPP, California Social Welfare Archives, Special Collections, USC; Opal C. Jones, *I Wish My Child's Teacher Would . . . ,* in Box 4, NAPP, California Social Welfare Archives, Special Collections, USC.

15. Opal C. Jones, *Guess Who's Coming to the Ghettos?,* in Box 2, NAPP, California Social Welfare Archives, Special Collections, USC, 2–11.

16. Ibid., 14–21.

17. Opal C. Jones, "It's the Same Old Soup Warmed Over—Unless—," n.d., in Box 2, NAPP, California Social Welfare Archives, Special Collections, USC.

18. Opal C. Jones, *I Wonder Why Some People Don't Like Me?,* April 1, 1966, in Box 2, NAPP, California Social Welfare Archives, Special Collections, USC; memo, Dick Fullmer to Bob Clampitt, September 27, 1965, File "Los Angeles (EYOA), August 1965–September 1965," EYOA-NA; Bauman, "Race, Class, and Political Power," 195. Jones reacted to Maldonado's orders by writing a picture book titled *New Committee in the Zoo.* Jones compared the power politics in Los Angeles "War on Poverty" to a zoo containing big mean animals (the "powerful" who tried to dominate antipoverty programs for themselves); big, kind animals (the "powerful" who tried to bring the programs closer to the people); small, mean animals (the "powerless" who collaborated with big mean animals); and small, kind animals (the "powerless" who tried to recast the antipoverty programs based on the experiences of poor people). Opal C. Jones, *The New Committee in the Zoo,* in Box 2, NAPP, California Social Welfare Archives, Special Collections, USC.

19. Memo, Paul R. Weeks to Dick Fullmer, February 2, 1966, File "Los Angeles (EYOA), January 1966–February 1966," EYOA-NA; memo, Paul R. Weeks to Edgar May, March 30, 1966, File "Los Angeles (EYOA), March 1966," EYOA-NA.

20. Memo, Augustus Hawkins to Sargent Shriver, September 2, 1965, File "Los Angeles (EYOA), August 1965–September 1965," EYOA-NA.

21. Memo, Paul R. Weeks to Marvin R. Fullmer, January 13, 1966, File "Los Angeles (EYOA), January 1966–February 1966," EYOA-NA; memo, Samuel F. Yette to Sargent Shriver and Bernard Boutin, January 14, 1966, File "Los Angeles (EYOA), January 1966–February 1966," EYOA-NA.

22. "Opal Jones Remains in Poverty Position, but Job Still in Doubt," *Los Angeles Sentinel,* February 17, 1966; Bauman, "Race, Class, and Political Power," 195–96.

23. Memo, Paul R. Weeks to Dick Fullmer, February 2, 1966, File "Los Angeles (EYOA), January 1966–February 1966," EYOA-NA; memo, Edgar May to Sargent Shriver, February 13, 1966, File "Los Angeles (EYOA), January 1966–February 1966," EYOA-NA.

24. Memo, Edgar May to Sargent Shriver, February 13, 1966, File "Los Angeles (EYOA), January 1966–February 1966," EYOA-NA; "Poverty War Flares over Bill Nicholas," *Los Angeles Sentinel,* March 31, 1966.

25. "For Immediate Release," Information Services Dept., EYOA, March 31, 1966, File "Los Angeles (EYOA), March 1966," EYOA-NA.

26. "Hearing on Dismissal Set Wednesday," *Los Angeles Sentinel,* April 7, 1966.

27. *Herald-Dispatch,* March 31, 1966.

28. Memo, Dick Fullmer to Edgar May, May 14, 1966, File "Los Angeles (EYOA), March 1966," EYOA-NA; "Economic Hardships Faced by ELA Neighborhoods," *Eastside Sun,* August 26, 1965; "Equal Opportunities Demanded by Rep. Roybal in House," *Eastside Sun,* September 23, 1965; "Neglect of Mexican-American Group," *Los Angeles Times,* August 1, 1966; Ambrecht, *Politicizing the Poor*; Acuña, *A Community under Siege,* 107–77; Bauman, "Race, Class, and Political Power," 208.

29. Memo, Nick Kostopulos to Dick Fullmer, February 4, 1966, File "Los Angeles (EYOA), January 1966–February 1966," EYOA-NA.

30. Jones would be caught in a difficult situation when she fired Gabrile Yanez, a Mexican American outpost director, for not attending meetings called by Jones and contributing to the split between Latino and black residents. Jones was criticized by Latino residents, and she thus rehired Yanez and promised to plan more outposts in Mexican American areas. Memo, Dick Fullmer to Edgar May, March 16, 1966, File "Los Angeles (EYOA), March 1966," EYOA-NA; memo, Paul Weeks to Edgar May, May 30, 1966, File "Los Angeles (EYOA), March 1966," EYOA-NA; memo, Paul Weeks to Marvin R. Fullmer, April 7, 1966, File "Los Angeles (EYOA), April 1966–May 1966," EYOA-NA; "March or Be Fired, NAPP Workers Told," *Herald-Dispatch,* March 31, 1966; "Opal Jones Fires Aide for 'Ineffectiveness,'" *Los Angeles Sentinel,* October 6, 1966. For a detailed analysis of the relationship between African American and Latino residents in the Los Angeles "War on Poverty," see Bauman, "Race, Class, and Political Power," 206–15.

31. Memo, Paul Weeks to Edgar May, April 3, 1966, File "Los Angeles (EYOA), April 1966–May 1966," EYOA-NA; "Negro Elected Officials Want Opal Jones Back," *Los Angeles Sentinel,* April 28, 1966.

32. Memo, Paul Weeks to Marvin R. Fullmer, April 7, 1966, File "Los Angeles (EYOA), April 1966–May 1966," EYOA-NA; memo, Paul Weeks to Edgar May, April 25, 1966, File "Los Angeles (EYOA), April 1966–May 1966," EYOA-NA; memo, Dick Fullmer and C. B. Patrick to Edgar May, April 27, 1966, File "Los Angeles (EYOA), April 1966–May 1966," EYOA-NA.

33. "Hearing on Dismissal Set Wednesday," *Los Angeles Sentinel,* April 7, 1966.

34. Opal C. Jones, *I Wonder Why Some People Don't Like Me?,* April 1, 1966, in Box 2, NAPP, California Social Welfare Archives, Special Collections, USC, 2.

35. Ibid.

36. "Rights Official Hails Poverty War Shake-Up," *Los Angeles Times,* April 9, 1966; "Ousted Poverty Aide Rehired in Stormy Session," *Los Angeles Times,* April 26, 1966; "EYOA Reinstates Mrs. Opal Jones," *Los Angeles Sentinel,* April 28, 1966; Bauman, "Race, Class, and Political Power," 197–98.

37. "Los Angeles CAP to Be Reorganized, De-Centered," Office of Economic Opportunity, April 8, 1966, File "Los Angeles (EYOA), April 1966–May 1966," EYOA-NA; "Legal Fight Seen in Poverty War," *Los Angeles Sentinel,* April 14, 1966; "Clarified Rules Sought in Poverty War Here," *Los Angeles Times,* May 3, 1966.

38. "Rights Official Hails Poverty War Shake-Up," *Los Angeles Times,* April 9, 1966.

39. Memo, Samuel Yorty to President Lyndon B. Johnson, April 25, 1966, Ex LG/Los Angeles, LBJ Library; "Yorty Attacks Hawkins Again, to Ask Probe," *Los Angeles Sentinel,* April 28, 1966; "Yorty Warns Johnson of Antipoverty Collapse," *Los Angeles Times,* April 28, 1966.

40. Memo, Edward A. Hawkins to Augustus F. Hawkins, August 6, 1965, File "Edward A. Hawkins," Box D-27, Yorty-LA.; "Angry Mills Quits Poverty War Post," *Los Angeles Times,* April 19, 1966; "Mills Exits EYOA, Charges Poverty Program Patronage," *Los Angeles Sentinel,* April 21, 1966; "Yorty Appoints Brother of Bitter Critics to Poverty Post," *Los Angeles Times,* April 21, 1966; Bauman, "Race, Class, and Political Power," 182–87.

41. "Hawkins Hits at Yorty over Poverty Post," *Los Angeles Times,* April 26, 1966; "Congressman Hits Ed's Appointment," *Los Angeles Sentinel,* April 28, 1966.

42. Mary Henry, interview by author, September 30, 2002; Opal C. Jones, "President's Report, 1971–1972," January 24, 1973, in Minutes (70s), Los Angeles Federation of Settlements and Neighborhood Centers Inc., California Social Welfare Archives, Special Collections, USC.

43. "The Watts Labor Community Action Committee," in the Watts 65 Project Collection, Southern California Library, Los Angeles (SCL); Watts Labor Community Action Committee (WLCAC), "To Serve the Present Age—Youth Parade,"

in the Watts 65 Project Collection, SCL; Malaika Brown, "WLCAC's Ted Watkins Leaves Valuable Living Legacy," *Los Angeles Sentinel*, November 11, 1993; WLCAC, *1967 Report*.

44. WLCAC, *1967 Report*; WLCAC, *Community Conservation Corps*; WLCAC, *WLCAC: Changing . . . Moving . . . the Lives of a People*; WLCAC, *Community Conservation Corps*, ix–7, 41–44; "Saluting CCC," *Los Angeles Sentinel*, September 8, 1966; "Watts Labor Community Action Committee Get Praise, $260,806 Grant from OEO," *Los Angeles Sentinel*, July 13, 1967; "Watts Labor Leader Turns U.S. Upside Down for Kids," *Los Angeles Sentinel*, August 17, 1967.

45. "The Watts Labor Community Action Committee," in the Watts 65 Project Collection, SCL; WLCAC, *Community Conservation Corps*, ix–7, 41–44; "Saluting CCC," *Los Angeles Sentinel*, September 8, 1966; "Watts Labor Community Action Committee Get Praise, $260,806 Grant from OEO," *Los Angeles Sentinel*, July 13, 1967; "Watts Labor Leader Turns U.S. Upside Down for Kids," *Los Angeles Sentinel*, August 17, 1967.

46. WLCAC, *1967 Report*, 15; WLCAC, *Community Conservation Corps*, xii–xiii.

47. WLCAC, *Community Conservation Corps*, 5. See also Feldstein, *Motherhood in Black and White*.

48. WLCAC, *1967 Report*, 24–25.

49. Ibid., 8–9, 48.

50. Maulana Karenga, interview by author, September 25, 2000; Bullock, *Watts*; Tyler, "Black Radicalism in Southern California, 1950–1982," 225; Horne, *Fire This Time*, 181, 200.

51. "Westminster Reports on Watts," *Los Angeles Sentinel*, November 3, 10, 24, 1966. Tommy Jacquette, interview by author by phone, September 27, 2000; Tommy Jacquette, interview by author, August 9, 2002.

52. Karenga, interview by author, September 25, 2000; Jacquette, interview by author, August 9, 2002; Neighborhood Adult Participation Project, "Featuring NAPP and What Is It All About? Pride and Progress, Watts Festival," in Box 1, NAPP, California Social Welfare Archives, Special Collections, USC; Tyler, "Black Radicalism in Southern California, 1950–1982," 226, 229–30.

53. "The Watts Festival," *Los Angeles Sentinel*, August 11, 1966; "Watts Festival Opens Mon.: Thousands Look for Surprise," *Los Angeles Sentinel*, August 11, 1968; "Watts: The Second and Greater Festival," *Los Angeles Times*, August 13, 1967; Tyler, "Black Radicalism in Southern California, 1950–1982," 232; Horne, *Fire This Time*, 204.

54. Tyler, "Black Radicalism in Southern California, 1950–1982," 225.

55. Black Committee of Inquiry, *The Truth about the Watts Summer Festival*, 18.

56. Horne, *Fire This Time*, 203–4.

57. Bullock, *Watts*, 66–67; Taylor, *In Search of the Racial Frontier*, 309; Karenga, interview by author, September 25, 2000; Jacquette, interview by author, August 9, 2002.

58. "After Absence, Festival Comes Back to Watts, Where It Began," *Wave,* October 4, 1993.

59. "Laudable Approach in Poverty War," *Los Angeles Times,* December 19, 1966; "Kennedy, Murphy, Clark Visit Watts Project," *Star Review,* May 18, 1967; WLCAC, *Community Conservation Corps,* 85–88.

60. "Watts Kids Accept Robert's Rule," *San Luis Obispo County Telegram-Tribune,* August 26, 1967. An editorial in the *Los Angeles Times* acknowledged that the Community Conservation Corps program deserved to be and would become a "model for use across the nation." The Los Angeles City Council also raised their voices in praise of the WLCAC and Ted Watkins for the development of a "self-help program." Los Angeles City Council Resolution, February 21, 1968, Los Angeles City Council File #138000, Box A2102, Records Management Division, Los Angeles City Archives.

61. After the funding of the WLCAC, Glenn O'Loane, a local member of the UAW in East Los Angeles, pressed for similar aid. Esteban Torres, a native of East Los Angeles and the first executive director of the East Los Angeles Community Union, explained that they had also been systematically excluded from social, economic, educational, and political advancement and that drawing economic resources into the area was indispensable in changing the situation in East Los Angeles. *El Alambre* (the newspaper of the East Los Angeles Community Union) 1, no. 1 (1972): 1, 2; *El Alambre* 2, no. 1 (1973): 1; "New Name for E. L. A. Labor Action Committee," *Eastside Sun,* April 3, 1969; Martin, *Social Protest in an Urban Barrio,* 171–99; Chavez, *Eastside Landmark,* 77–92.

62. U.S. General Accounting Office, *Review of the Community Action Program in the Los Angeles Area under the Economic Opportunity Act,* 1–23; Patterson, *America's Struggle against Poverty 1900–1994,* 136; Self, *American Babylon,* 233–42.

63. Soja, Morales, and Wolff, "Urban Restructuring," 195–230; Soja, *Postmodern Geographers*; Nicolaides, *My Blue Heaven,* 227, 329–30; Sides, *L.A. City Limits,* 176–89.

64. Statement of Ted Watkins, in U.S. Senate Committee on Labor and Public Welfare, Subcommittee on Employment, Manpower, and Poverty, *Examination of the War on Poverty,* 3935–38.

65. "New Watts Hospital Named in Honor of Dr. M. L. King, Jr.," *Los Angeles Sentinel,* April 18, 1968; WLCAC, *Community Conservation Corps,* 77–83; "The Watts Labor Community Action Committee," in the Watts 65 Project Collection, SCL.

66. Horne, *Fire This Time,* 278; Chavez, *Eastside Landmark,* 29–30.

67. "Preliminary Proposal for Child Care and Development Center at Los Angeles County-Martin Luther King, Jr., General Hospital," n.d., Records of the National Welfare Rights Organization [the collection is unprocessed, November 1, 2004], Manuscript Department, Moorland-Spingarn Research Center, Howard University, Washington, DC (hereafter NWRO Papers).

68. Johnnie Tillmon, interview by Sherna Berger Gluck, February 1984 and Spring 1991, Special Collections, California State University, Long Beach.

69. "Biography of Mrs. Johnnie Tillmon," n.d., NWRO Papers. See also West, *The National Welfare Rights Movement,* 92; Sherna Berger Gluck in collaboration with Maylei Blackwell, Sharon Cotrell, and Karen S. Harper, "Whose Feminism, Whose History?: Reflections on Excavating the History of (the) U.S. Women's Movement(s)," in *Community Activism and Feminist Policies,* ed. Naples, 31–56; White, *Too Heavy a Load,* 19–20, 224–26; Nadasen, *Welfare Warriors,* 19–20; Kornbluh, *The Battle for Welfare Rights,* 28; Tsuchiya, "National Welfare Rights Organization, 1966–1975," "Tillmon, Johnnie."

70. White, *Too Heavy a Load,* 224.

71. "ANC-Mothers Anonymous, Fact Sheet," n.d., NWRO Papers.

72. "Preliminary Proposal for Child Care and Development Center at Los Angeles County-Martin Luther King, Jr., General Hospital," n.d., NWRO Papers; West, *The National Welfare Rights Movement,* 92.

73. "Program: ANC Mother's Annonymous [*sic*] Child Care Seminar," June 17, 1972, NWRO Papers.

74. Memo, Johnnie L. Tillmon to Barbara L. Jacquette, April 20, 1972, NWRO Papers.

75. Kornbluh, *The Battle for Welfare Rights,* 36; Boyle, *The UAW and the Heyday of American Liberalism 1945–1968,* 190; Lichtenstein, *The Most Dangerous Man in Detroit,* 389–90.

76. Nan Robertson, "Shriver Defends Program to the Poor, but He Is Booed," *New York Times,* April 15, 1966, 1, 21; Nan Robertson, "Shriver Explains Convention Boos," *New York Times,* April 19, 1966, 44; Penn Kemble, "Report on CCAP Conference: Problems of Anti-Poverty Coalition," *New America,* April 22, 1966, 3; Kotz and Kotz, *A Passion for Equality,* 185, 187; Cazenave, *Impossible Democracy,* 157–58, 176.

77. Memo, "What Happened at the Convention," Folder "Annual Meeting CCAP, April 13–14," Box 1, Citizens' Crusade against Poverty Papers, 1964–1970, Walter P. Reuther Library, Wayne State University, Detroit, Mich. (hereafter Reuther Library).

78. Memo, Richard W. Boone to Harry Fleischman, Race Relations Coordinator of the American Jewish Committee, May 16, 1966, Folder "Annual Meeting CCAP, April 13–14," Box 1, Citizens' Crusade against Poverty Papers, 1964–1970, Reuther Library; Nan Robertson, "Shriver Explains Convention Boos," *New York Times,* April 19, 1966, 44.

79. Preston R. Wilcox, "The Two-Day Fiasco in Washington—April 13 and 14, 1966," Folder "Annual Meeting CCAP, April 13–14," Box 1, Citizens' Crusade against Poverty Papers, 1964–1970, Reuther Library.

80. Memo, Frank P. Graham, the chairperson of the National Sharecroppers Fund, to Sargent Shriver, April 19, 1966, Box 6, Folder "CCAP Corres., May–July 1966," Citizens' Crusade against Poverty Papers, 1964–1970, Reuther Library.

81. Moynihan, *Maximum Feasible Misunderstanding*, 140–41.

82. Pamela Roby, "Citizen's Crusade against Poverty, Second Annual Meeting, April, 1966, Report I," Folder "Annual Meeting CCAP, April 13–14," Box 1, Citizens' Crusade against Poverty Papers, 1964–1970, Reuther Library.

83. Penn Kemble, "Report on CCAP Conference: Problems of Anti-Poverty Coalition," *New America*, April 22, 1966, 3; Memo, "What Happened at the Convention," Folder "Annual Meeting CCAP, April 13–14," Box 1, Citizens' Crusade against Poverty Papers, 1964–1970, Reuther Library.

84. Kemble, "Report on CCAP Conference: Problems of Anti-Poverty Coalition," 3.

85. Pamela Roby, "CCAP, Comments—I Maximum Feasible Participation?," Folder "Annual Meeting CCAP, April 13–14," Box 1, Citizens' Crusade against Poverty Papers, 1964–1970, Reuther Library.

86. "Public Welfare System a Failure, Reagan Says," *Washington Post*, September 20, 1967.

87. NWRO in cooperation with United Church Board for Homeland Ministries, "Six Myths about Welfare," n.d., NWRO Papers, 14; "Goals of the National Welfare Rights Organization," *NOW!: Publication of the National Welfare Rights Organization*, August 21, 1968.

88. Johnnie Tillmon, interview by Sherna Berger Gluck, February 1984 and Spring 1991, Special Collections, California State University, Long Beach.

89. West, *The National Welfare Rights Movement*, 86–92. See also White, *Too Heavy a Load*, 237–39; Nadasen, *Welfare Warriors*, 125–55.

90. U.S. Department of Labor and U.S. Department of Health, Education, and Welfare (HEW), "Reports on the Work Incentive Program," 1; "Introduction," n.d., NWRO Papers, 1–8; "The 1967 Anti-Welfare Social Security Amendments Law: A Summary," *NOW!: Publication of the National Welfare Rights Organization*; Johnnie Tillmon, "Where We've Come From . . . ," *Welfare Fighter* 1, no. 1 (September 1969); West, *The National Welfare Rights Movement*, 87.

91. U.S. Dept. of Labor, Manpower Administration, "Work Incentive Program: From Welfare to Wages," July 1969, U.S. Government Printing Office, Box 2237, NWRO Papers; U.S. Department of Labor and HEW, "Reports on the Work Incentive Program," 34.

92. U.S. Dept. of Labor, Manpower Administration, "Work Incentive Program: From Welfare to Wages," July 1969, U.S. Government Printing Office, Box 2237, NWRO Papers; U.S. House of Representatives, Committee on Ways and Means, "The Work Incentive Program, Second Annual Report of the Department of Labor on Training and Employment under Title IV of the Social Security Act,"

21–22; U.S. House of Representatives, Committee on Ways and Means, "The Work Incentive Program, Fourth Annual Report to the Congress on Training and Employment under Title IV of the Social Security Act" (January 21, 1974), 10.

93. U.S. Department of Labor and HEW, "Reports on the Work Incentive Program," 36.

94. "Hard Hitting Speeches from Chairman and Director," *Welfare Fighter* 2, no. 2 (November 1970). See also "NWRO Raps on Nixon Plan (Family Assistance Plan)," *Welfare Fighter* 1, no. 1 (September 1969); "NWRO Adequate Income Plan," *Welfare Fighter* 2, no. 5 (February 1971).

95. "Power to Recipients," n.d., NWRO Papers; West, *The National Welfare Rights Movement,* 93, 115–17; Nadasen, *Welfare Warriors*, 126–30.

96. Johnnie Tillmon, "Welfare Is a Women's Issue," 55.

97. West, *The National Welfare Rights Movement,* 89–92; Tsuchiya, "Tillmon, Johnnie."

98. Tillmon, "Welfare Is a Women's Issue," 52.

99. Ibid.

100. "After Absence, Festival Comes Back to Watts, Where It Began," *Wave,* October 4, 1993, in the Los Angeles Subject File/Watts File, SCL; Button, *Black Violence,* 52–53; Gillette, *Launching the War on Poverty,* 359–60; U.S. House Committee on Government Operations, *26th Report: The Demise of the Greater Los Angeles Community Action Agency,* 1–7; *La Causa* 1, no. 1 (1993).

5. Translating Black Theology into Korean Activism

1. Saruhashi, "Tagengo kyōseigata gengo keikaku to sono hattendankai shosō no shakai gengogakuteki kenkyū"; Hoshino, *Jichitai no henkaku to zainichi Korian*; Kim, "*Zainichi* Kankoku Chōsenjin no aidentitī keisei to tabunka kyōsei kyōiku ni kansuru kenkyū"; Kim, *Tabunka kyōsei to aidentitī.*

2. "Shi Fureaikan ōpun: 'Rinjin' kōryū no kyoten ni," *Yomiuri shinbun,* June 15, 1988; "Minzoku sabetsu kaishō no yakata," *Kanagawa shinbun,* February 21, 1988. See Kawasaki City Fureaikan, *Daremoga chikara ippai ikiteiku tameni.*

3. The Japanese annexation of Korea in 1910 led to a rapid rise in the number of tenant farmers who lost their land, thus creating a large landless class in Korea. These tenant farmers left their homes, searching for better economic opportunities in the metropole. Seikyusha, *Kawasaki shi Sakuramoto chiku seishōnen mondai chōsa kenkyu hōkoku,* 24–29, 32–37; Kanagawa Shinbunsha Shakaibu, *Nihon no naka no gaikokujin*, 103–29; Kawasaki City Tajima Fukushi Jimusho, *Tajima no kurashi* (Kawasaki City: Tajima Fukushi Jimusho, 1985), file "Kawasaki jittai chōsa hōkoku," Kawasaki City Fureaikan; Kanagawa to Chōsen no Kankeishi

Chōsaiinkai, *Kanagawa to Chōsen*, 157–69; Mitchell, *The Korean Minority in Japan*, 27–28; Chung, "Exercising Citizenship," 173; Lie, *Multiethnic Japan*, 106–7.

4. Nihon kōkan, *Nihon kōkan kabushiki gaisha yonjūnenshi*; Pak, *Nihon teikokushugi no Chōsen shihai*; Seikyusha, *Kawasaki shi Sakuramoto chiku seishōnen mondai chōsa kenkyū hōkoku*, 27–29; Kanagawa Shinbunsha Shakaibu, *Nihon no naka no gaikokujin*.

5. Seikyusha, *Kawasaki shi Sakuramoto chiku seishōnen mondai chōsa kenkyū hōkoku*, 29–31; Pamphlet, Kanagawaken Daini Aisen Hōmu, "Kawasakishi Ikegamichō ni okeru jūmin to hōmu no fukushi kankei," 1968, File "Kawasaki jittai chōsa hōkoku," Kawasaki City Fureaikan; Higuchi, "Kawasaki shi Ōhin chiku Chōsenjin no seikatsu jōkyō," 62–71.

6. Seikyusha, *Kawasaki shi Sakuramoto chiku seishōnen mondai chōsa kenkyū hōkoku*, 29–31; Kawasaki City, *Kawasaki shi shi: Tsūshi hen*, 293–304; Duus, *Modern Japan*, 291–300.

7. Kawasaki shi Eiseikyoku, *Kawasaki shi ni okeru taiki osen*; Tashiro, "Toshi no fukushi mondai (2)," 2–34; Pamphlet, Kanagawaken Daini Aisen Hōmu, "Kawasakishi Ikegamichō ni okeru jūmin to hōmu no fukushi kankei," 1968, File "Kawasaki jittai chōsa hōkoku," Kawasaki City Fureaikan; Serizawa and Machii, *Ningen toshi e no fukken*, 75–76; Duus, *Modern Japan*, 318.

8. Frank K. Upham, "Unplaced Persons and Movements for Peace," in *Postwar Japan as History*, ed. Gordon, 325–46; Duus, *Modern Japan*, 322–23; Watanabe, *Kōdo seichō to kigyō shakai*.

9. "Kakushin 10 nen: Ito Kawasaki shisei no kiseki," *Kanagawa shinbun*, May 26 and 27, 1981; Kawasaki Shigikai, *Kawasaki shigikai shi*, 271–73; "Zassō no 18 nen: Ito Kawasaki shisei o furikaeru," *Kanagawa shinbun*, September 26, 1989; Kawasaki Chihō Jichi Kenkyū Sentā, *Kawasaki shimin jichi no jikken 1971–2001*, 7–9. See also Tsuchiyama Kimie, "Kawasaki 'Senku jichitai' no rekishi teki ichi," in *Kawasaki shisei no kenkyū*, ed. Uchikoshi and Uchiumi, 43–108.

10. "Kakushin 10 nen: Ito Kawasaki shisei no kiseki," *Kanagawa shinbun*, May 28 and 29, 1981; Ito Saburō, *Nomi to kanaduchi*, 247; Kawasaki shigikai, *Kawasaki shigikai shi*, 339–60, 396–403; "Zassō no 18 nen: Ito Kawasaki shisei o furikaeru," *Kanagawa shinbun*, September 27 and October 2, 1989.

11. Pak, *Kaihōgo zainichi Chōsenjin undōshi*, 4–5, 36–39; Yamada, "Kawasaki ni okeru gaikokujin tono kyōsei no machi zukuri no taidō," 55.

12. Seikyusha, *Tomoni ikiru: Seikyusha sōritsu 10 shūnen kinen*, 14–18; Kawasaki Kyōkai, *Kawasaki kyōkai 50 nenshi*, 45–60; Zainichi Daikan Kirisuto Kyōkai, *Senkyō 90 shūnen kinenshi, 1908–1998*, 44–49.

13. Kawasaki Kyōkai, *Kawasaki kyōkai 50 nenshi*, 45–60; Lee, *Kiryū no tami no sakebi*; Lee, *Asuni ikiru kiryū no tami*; Lee, *Rekishi no hazama o ikiru*.

14. Lee In Ha, interview by author, Song Kwon, and Tonomura Masaru, September 4, 2005; Kawasaki kyōkai, *Kawasaki kyōkai 50 nenshi,* 60–64; Seikyusha, *Tomoni ikiru: Seikyusha sōritsu 10 shūnen kinen,* 14–18.

15. Kawasaki kyōkai, *Kawasaki kyōkai 50 nenshi,* 60–64; Seikyusha, *Tomoni ikiru: Seikyusha sōritsu 20 shūnen kinen*, 17–20.

16. Lee, *Rekishi no hazama o ikiru,* 190, 198; Kajiwara Hisashi, interview by author, September 20, 2009.

17. Burrow, *James H. Cone and Black Liberation Theology*, xvii. See also Kubic, "Between Malcolm and Martin," 448–67.

18. Cleage, *The Black Messiah*; Roberts, *Liberation and Reconciliation*; Long, "Perspectives for a Study of Afro-American Religion in the United States," 54–66; Wilmore, *Black Religion and Black Radicalism*; Cone, *The Spirituals and the Blues*; Cone, *My Soul Looks Back.*

19. Cone, *My Soul Looks Back*, 25.

20. Ibid., 42.

21. Ibid., 44–45.

22. Cone, *For My People*, 14.

23. Cone, *Black Theology and Black Power*, 38.

24. "Statement by the National Committee of Negro Churchmen," *New York Times,* July 31, 1966; Mance Jackson, "The National Conference of Black Churchmen: A Historical Survey," File 25 "NCBC," Box 6, Records of the Black Theology Project, Schomburg Center, New York Public Library.

25. Gayraud S. Wilmore, "Black Theology: Review and Assessment," 9, File 15, Box 5, Records of the Black Theology Project, Schomburg Center, New York Public Library.

26. Cone, *A Black Theology of Liberation,* 1, 4, 5; Cone, *God of the Oppressed.*

27. Cone, *A Black Theology of Liberation,* 35–36.

28. Kajiwara, "The Meaning of Heaven in Cone's Theology," 134–35.

29. Cone, *A Black Theology of Liberation,* 37.

30. Kajiwara, "Saikin no burakku seorojī rikai eno ichi shiron," 59–60; Kajiwara, "The Meaning of Heaven in Cone's Theology," 127.

31. Cone, *A Black Theology of Liberation,* 7. Cone later noted that his encounters with Christian leaders in Asia, Africa, and Latin America had a profound impact on his intellectual and spiritual development. In his biography, he once again stressed that "we must never absolutize a particular struggle (whether black, African, Asian, or Latin) to the exclusion of others." Then he asked, "How could I say that the black liberation struggle in the U.S. is a more valid expression of the gospel than the Korean liberation struggle in Japan? Or the struggles of the poor in Latin America? Or the Native American struggle in the U.S.?" Cone, *My Soul Looks Back,* 12, 99.

32. Pablo Richard, "Black Theology: A Liberating Theology in Lain America," in *A Black Theology of Liberation,* 20th anniversary ed., 171–72.

33. K. C. Abraham, "Black Theology: A Reflection from Asia," in *A Black Theology of Liberation,* 20th anniversary ed., 185.

34. Kajiwara, "Saikin no burakku seorojī rikai eno ichi shiron," 55; Kajiwara, *Kaihō no shingaku,* 20.

35. James H. Cone, interview by author, September 7, 2010.

36. Lee In Ha, interview by author, Song Kwon, and Tonomura Masaru, September 4, 2005; Kajiwara Hisashi, interview by author, September 20, 2009; James H. Cone, e-mail message to author, June 12, 2009; Lee, *Rekishi no hazama o ikiru,* 216–17; Kajiwara, *Kaihō no shingaku,* 203.

37. Kajiwara Hisashi, interview by author, September 20, 2009.

38. James H. Cone, "Nihongo ban e no jobun" (preface to the Japanese edition), in *Yokuatsu sareta mono no kami,* trans. Kajiwara Hisashi, 7. See also Kajiwara, "Daisan sekai to kaihō no shingaku," 23–42; Kajiwara, "On the Social Responsibility of Christians," 59–70; Kajiwara, "Jeimuzu Kōn no 'kokujin shingaku' ni okeru monogatari no koō ni tsuite," 64–74; Kajiwara, "Kaihō no shingaku ni okeru kunan no igi," 97–110; Kajiwara, *Kaihō no shingaku*; Cone, *My Soul Looks Back,* 111.

39. James H. Cone, interview by author, September 7, 2010.

40. Lee, *Kiryū no tami no sakebi,* 114.

41. Kato, "1970 nendai Nihon no 'minzoku sabetsu' o meguru undō," 22.

42. Kawasaki City Fureaikan, *Daremoga chikara ippai ikiteiku tameni,* 44; Lie, *Multiethnic Japan,* 108–9. With regard to the Hitachi Employment Discrimination Trial, see also Takenoshita, "Hitachi shūshoku sabetsu jiken o meguru *zainichi* Kankoku Chōsenjin no shakai undo"; Katsuyama, "Hitachi shūshoku sabetsu saiban shien katsudō ni okeru Nihonjin seinen no kenkyū." For a brief discussion of the Hitachi Trial in English, see Fukuoka, *Lives of Young Koreans in Japan,* 296–97; Chung, "Exercising Citizenship," 169–70.

43. Park Jong Seok, "Minzokuteki jikaku eno michi: Shūshoku sabetsu saiban jōshinsho," in *Minzoku sabetsu,* ed. Park-kun o Kakomu Kai, 237–60; Wada, "Park kun no 'shūshoku sabetsu saiban' no keika to mondaiten," 18–29; Wada Jun, "Saiban no keika to hanketsu no imi," in *Minzoku sabetsu,* ed. Park-kun o Kakomu Kai, 129–31.

44. Wada Jun, "Saiban no keika to hanketsu no imi," in *Minzoku sabetsu,* ed. Park-kun o Kakomu Kai, 129–31.

45. Wada Jun, "Saiban no keika to hanketsu no imi," in *Minzoku sabetsu,* ed. Park-kun o Kakomu Kai, 129–31; Park-kun o Kakomu Kai, *Park Jong Seok shūshoku sabetsu saiban shiryōshū, no. 6.*

46. Ozawa Yusaku, "*Zainichi* Chōsenjin no shūshoku: Sabetsu, haijo no atsui kabe," *Asahi shinbun,* April 24, 1972.

47. "Warera shūshoku sabetsu o seotte," *Asahi shinbun,* January 13, 1971; Takanami Tetsuo, "Park-kun o Kakomu Kai kono 3 nen," in *Minzoku sabetsu,* ed. Park-kun o Kakomu Kai, 59–63; Choi Seungkoo, "Hitachi tōsō 30 shūnen o hete miete kita chihei," in *Hitachi shūshoku sabetsu saiban 30 shūnen kinen no tsudoi: Hōkokushū,* ed. Hitachi Shūshoku Sabetsu Saiban 30shūnen Kinen Shūkai Jikkō Iinkai, 30. Originally, Japanese supporters regarded the Hitachi case simply as a "labor issue"—a matter of dismissing a job applicant even though he had been hired on the basis of successfully passing the employment entrance exam. Choi and other *zainichi* members urged them to recognize that it was not just a matter of labor contracts but a matter of ongoing discrimination against Koreans in Japan. Choi Seungkoo, "Jinken no jitsugen ni tsuite," 97.

48. The following seven people called for support for the Association surrounding Mr. Park: Ozawa Yusaku (associate professor, Tokyo Metropolitan University), Osawa Shinichiro (journalist), Sato Katsumi (the management director of *Nihon Chōsen Kenkyūjo*), Lee In Chok (novelist), Lee In Ha (the minister of the Korean Christian Church in Japan), Yamashita Masanobu (the minister of the United Church of Christ in Japan), and Tagawa Kenzo (lecturer of Wakayama University). "Park-kun o Kakomu Kai eno yobikake," *Genkainada,* no. 1 (April 1973): 10.

49. Kawasaki kyōkai, *Kawasaki kyōkai 50 nenshi,* 64.

50. Choi, "Yugamerareta minzokukan," 2–8; Choi, "Hitachi tōsō 30 shūnen o hete miete kita chihei," 30–31; Lee, *Kiryū no tami no sakebi,* 116, 125–26, 150; Lee In Ha, "Seikyusha: Minzoku sabetsu to tatakai ningen shutai no kakuritsu o mezashite," 60; Kobayashi, *Kawasaki minshū no ayumi,* 313.

51. Wada Jun, "Saiban no keika to hanketsu no imi," in *Minzoku sabetsu,* ed. Park-kun o Kakomu Kai, 132–44; "Iinogare o danjite yurusuna," *Genkainada* 8 (November 1973): 4.

52. Chi, *Kyōkaisen o koeru tabi*; Yoon, *Shisō taiken no kōsaku,* 309; Lee, *Rekishi no hazama o ikiru,* 205–26.

53. "Hitachi o utsu: Sokoku to no rentai ni atatte," *Genkainada* 12 (March 1973): 5; "Hitachi seihin fubai o tettei saseru ketsugi," *Asahi shinbun,* May 9, 1974; "Kankoku no Hitachi fubai undō ni kotae shōri ni mukete zenshin shiyō," *Genkainada* 15 (June 1974): 1; Lee, *Kiryū no tami no sakebi,* 128.

54. Suzuki, "Kyōdan no sensō sekinin kokuhaku o ninatte" and "Dainiji taisenka ni okeru Nihon kirisuto kyōdan no sensō sekinin ni tsuiteno kokuhaku," 1–8; Nakadaira, "*Zainichi* Kankokujin mondai to kirisutosha no sekinin," 43–52. Regarding the United Church of Christ in Japan's confession of responsibility during World War II, see http://www.kohara.ac/church/kyodan/schuldbekenntnis.html.

55. Lee, "Jinshu sabetsu to tatakau kyōkai," 41–46; Lee, *Rekishi no hazama o ikiru,* 179–87; Lee In Ha, interview by author, Song Kwon, and Tonomura Masaru, September 4, 2005, Kawasaki City Fureaikan; World Council of Churches Archives, "Special Fund, Box 5 Grants 1970–80 LI: Organizations Combating

Discrimination in Japan, 1971–1979" (Reels 46–47), *Programme to Combat Racism, 1939–1996, World Council of Churches Archives*, microfilm (hereafter cited as *Programme to Combat Racism*); Programme to Combat Racism, World Council of Churches, Ans J. van der Bent, ed., *Breaking Down the Walls.*

56. "Authority to Pay, WCC to National Christian Council of Japan," October 11, 1971, "Special Fund, Box 5 Grants 1970–80 LI: Organizations Combating Discrimination in Japan, 1971–1979" (Reel 46), *Programme to Combat Racism*; "Authority to Pay, WCC to Legal Defense Committee for Mr. Park," March 1, 1974, "Special Fund, Box 5 Grants 1970–80 LI" (Reel 46), *Programme to Combat Racism.*

57. The World Council of Churches Archives, "Special Fund, Box 5 Grants 1970–80 LI: Organizations Combating Discrimination in Japan, 1971–1979" (Reels 46–47), *Programme to Combat Racism*; Lee In Ha, "Jinshu sabetsu to tatakau kyōkai," 41–55; Lee, *Kiryū no tami no sakebi*, 121, 128–29; Lee In Ha, *Rekishi no hazama o ikiru,* 179–86. See also Bock, *In Search of a Responsible World Society*, 177.

58. Lee, *Rekishi no hazama o ikiru,* 184–85.

59. Lipsitz, *The Possessive Investment in Whiteness*, viii; Komagome, "Nihon no shokuminchi shihai to kindai: Orikasanaru bōryoku," 180.

60. Lee, "Jinshu sabetsu to tatakau kyōkai," 41–46.

61. Wada, "Saiban no keika to hanketsu no imi," in *Minzoku sabetsu,* ed. Park-kun o Kakomu Kai, 144–47; "Sabetsu naki shakai eno tegakari: Shūshoku sabetsu saiban hanketsu (riyū bubun)," in *Minzoku sabetsu,* ed. Park-kun o Kakomu Kai, 261–80; "*Zainichi* Chōsenjin kaiko wa futō: Yokohama chisai hanketsu," *Yomiuri shinbun,* June 19, 1974.

62. Park-kun o Kakomu Kai, *Park Jong Seok shūshoku sabetsu saiban shiryōshū, no.* 6, 96–97.

63. "Park soshō, Hitachi ga haiso," *Asahi shinbun*, June 19, 1974; "'Hitachi shūshoku sabetsu saiban 30 shūnen kinen shūkai' jikkō iinkai kenkai" in *Hitachi shūshoku sabetsu saiban 30 shūnen kinen no tsudoi: Hōkokushū*, ed. Hitachi Shūshoku Sabetsu Saiban 30shūnen Kinen Shūkai Jikkō Iinkai, 5.

64. Lee, *Kiryū no tami no sakebi,* 114, 123; Wada Jun, "Park kun no 'shūshoku sabetsu saiban' no keika to mondaiten," 18–29; Lee, *Rekishi no hazama o ikiru,* 198–99; Yamada Takao, interview by author, April 28, 2006.

65. *Arirang* (published by the Korean Christian Church in Japan) 6 (Fall 1974): 3–4.

66. Park-kun o Kakomu Kai, *Minzoku sabetsu*, 281; Lee, *Kiryū no tami no sakebi,* 129–30; Kawasaki kyōkai, *Kawasaki kyōkai 50 nenshi,* 66.

6. Voicing Alternative Visions of Citizenship

1. Seikyusha Katsudōsha Kaigi, ed., "Minzoku sabetsu to tatakau chiiki katsudō o mezashite," 2–5, file "Minzoku hoikuen kankei shiryō (3) 1981-Sakuramoto hoikuen," Kawasaki City Fureaikan; Lee In Ha, "Seikyusha no ayumi o kaerimite," in *Tomoni ikiru: Seikyusha sōritsu 10 shūnen kinen*, ed. Seikyusha, 14–18.

2. Seikyusha, *Tomoni ikiru: Seikyusha sōritsu 10 shūnen kinen*, 16; Seikyusha, *Tomoni ikiru: Seikyusha sōritsu 20 shūnen kinen*, 17–20; Kawasaki Kyōkai, *Kawasaki kyōkai 50 nenshi*, 62–63; Kim Yun-jeong, "*Zainichi* Kankoku Chōsenjin no aidentitī keisei to tabunka kyōsei kyōiku ni kansuru kenkyū," 50–52.

3. Kawasaki Zainichi Dōhō no Jinken o Mamorukai, *Minzoku undō toshite no chiiki katsudō 3*, 7, file "Minzoku undō toshite no chiiki katsudō," Kawasaki City Fureaikan; Seikyusha Unei Iinkai Kōhōbu, ed., "Chiiki ni micchaku shita kyōiku jissen o mezashite—Seikyusha undō no kiroku," November 1978, 8–9, file "Minzoku undō toshite no chiiki katsudō," Kawasaki City Fureaikan, 6–7.

4. *Genkainada* 17 (October 1974); Kawasaki Zainichi Dōhō no Jinken o Mamorukai, *Minzoku undō toshite no chiiki katsudō 3*, file "Minzoku undō toshite no chiiki katsudō," Kawasaki City Fureaikan, 3–4; Fukuoka, *Lives of Young Koreans in Japan*, 50–51, 272; Kim Yun-jeong, "*Zainichi* Kankoku Chōsenjin no aidentitī keisei to tabunka kyōsei kyōiku ni kansuru kenkyū," 52–54.

5. "4.28 Hitachi to chiiki o kangaeru Kawasaki shūkai hōkoku," *Genkainada* 15 (June 1974): 3.

6. "Hongoku no omoni tachi e," *Genkainada* 17 (October 1974): 7.

7. Seikyusha, *Tomoni ikiru: Seikyusha sōritsu 10 shūnen kinen*, 17; Seikyusha, *Tomoni ikiru: Seikyusha sōritsu 20 shūnen kinen*, 28–29; Seikyusha Katsudōsha Kaigi, ed., "Minzoku sabetsu to tatakau chiiki katsudō o mezashite," file "Minzoku hoikuen kankei shiryō (3) 1981-Sakuramoto hoikuen," Kawasaki City Fureaikan, 2–5; Seikyusha Unei Iinkai Kōhōbu, ed., "Chiiki ni micchaku shita kyōiku jissen o mezashite—Seikyusha undō no kiroku," November 1978, 8–9, file "Minzoku undō toshite no chiiki katsudō," Kawasaki City Fureaikan, 4–5.

8. Iwabuchi Hideyuki, "Kawasaki shi ni okeru *zainichi* gaikokujin kyōiku to Seikyusha," in *Tomoni ikiru: Seikyusha sōritsu 20 shūnen kinen*, ed. Seikyusha, 29; Kanagawa Shinbunsha Shakaibu, *Nihon no naka no gaikokujin*, 183–84.

9. RAIK, *Jidō teate no shikyū, kōei jūtaku nyūkyo tō no seikatsuken yōgo undō no kiroku*, 1.

10. Ibid., 2–3.

11. Ibid., 4.

12. Ibid., 10; "Zeikin onaji, kenri wa sabetsu," *Mainichi shinbun*, July 16, 1974; "Jidō teate ya shiei nyūkyo Kawasakishi mo mitomeru," *Mainichi shinbun*, July 31, 1974; "Jidō teate, raishunkara," *Yomiuri shinbun* (Kawasaki), July 31, 1974; "Gaikokujin nimo sabetsu senu," *Asahi shinbun*, July 31, 1974.

13. "Kawasaki shi no keneki undō ato hitooshi 'jidō teate,'" *Tōyō keizai nippō,* February 14, 1975; RAIK, *Jidō teate no shikyū, kōei jūtaku nyūkyo tō no seikatsuken yōgo undō no kiroku,* 15–16.

14. RAIK, *Jidō teate no shikyū, kōei jūtaku nyūkyo tō no seikatsuken yōgo undō no kiroku,* 17–18; "Jidō teate tsuini kakutoku!," *Tōyō keizai nippō,* April 4, 1975.

15. Yamada Takao, interview by author, April 28, 2006.

16. "Zeikin wa onaji kenri wa sabetsu 'Kawasaki hōshiki' de kakutoku e," *Tōyō keizai nippō,* October 4, 1974.

17. "Nyūgaku annai o dashite," *Yomiuri shinbun,* November 25, 1976; "Shūgaku tsūchi o dashite," *Tōyō keizai nippō,* December 3, 1976.

18. Bae Joong Do, "'Shūgaku annai' yōkyū undō ni tsuite no sankō iken," File "Kawasaki shūgaku tsūchi (annai) yōkyū undō 1976 11.24," Kawasaki City Fureaikan; Kim Il-Wha, "*Zainichi-Chōsenjin* no Hōteki Chii," in *Zainichi-Chōsenjin: Rekishi, Genjō, Tenbō,* ed. Park, 188; Kim T'ae-gi, *Sengo Nihon seiji to zainichi Chōsenjin mondai,* 159–62; Inokuchi Hiromitsu, "Korean Ethnic Schools in Occupied Japan, 1945–52," in *Koreans in Japan,* ed. Ryang, 145; Chung, "Exercising Citizenship," 165–66.

19. Kim Il-Wha, "*Zainichi-Chōsenjin* no Hōteki Chii," in *Zainichi-Chōsenjin: Rekishi, Genjō, Tenbō,* ed. Park; Chung, "Exercising Citizenship," 165–66; Kim T'ae-gi, *Sengo Nihon seiji to zainichi Chōsenjin mondai.*

20. Inokuchi, "Korean Ethnic Schools in Occupied Japan, 1945–52," in *Koreans in Japan,* ed. Ryang, 146–54; Yi Wol-sun, "*Zainichi* Chōsenjin no minzoku kyōiku," in *Zainichi Chōsenjin,* ed. Park, 146; Pak, *Kaihōgo zainichi Chōsenjin undōshi,* 183–208.

21. Bae Joong Do, "'Shūgaku annai' yōkyū undō ni tsuite no sankō iken," file "Kawasaki shūgaku tsūchi (annai) yōkyū undō 1976 11.24-," Kawasaki City Fureaikan, 1–5; Inokuchi, "Korean Ethnic Schools in Occupied Japan, 1945–52," in *Koreans in Japan,* ed. Ryang, 154–55; Mun, *Zainichi Chōsenjin mondai no kigen,* 31.

22. Monbushō shochū kyokuchō (tsūtatsu), "Chōsenjin no gimu kyōiku shōgakkō e no shūgaku ni tsuite," February 11, 1953, in *Gaikokujin shitei no kyōiku ni tsuiteno shomondai,* ed. RAIK, 1.

23. Monbu jimu jikan (tsūtatsu), "Nihon koku ni kyojū suru Daikanminkoku kokumin no hōteki chii oyobi taigū ni kansuru Nihon koku to Daikanminkoku to no aida no kyōtei ni okeru kyōiku kankei jikō no jisshi ni tsuite," December 28, 1965, in *Gaikokujin shitei no kyōiku ni tsuiteno shomondai,* ed. RAIK, 4–7.

24. "Shisei dayori de nyūgaku annai o," *Yomiuri shinbun,* December 19, 1976; "Raishū e ketsuron enki," *Tōyō keizai nippō,* December 12, 1976.

25. Seikyusha Unei Iinkai Kōhōbu, ed., "Chiiki ni micchaku shita kyōiku jissen o mezashite—Seikyusha undō no kiroku," November 1978, 8–9, File "Minzoku undō toshite no chiiki katsudō," Kawasaki City Fureaikan; Kawasaki City Fureaikan, *Daremoga chikara ippai ikiteiku tameni,* 96.

26. Choi Seungkoo, "Honmei o nanoraseru kyōiku jissen no kadai to seika," December 26, 1978, File "Zainichi Kankoku Chōsenjin Kyōiku o Susumeru Kai (jun) 82.1–6," Kawasaki City Fureaikan; "Kawasaki shi kyōi (kyōiku iinkai) kōshō ni mukete," October 1, 1981, File "Zainichi Kankoku Chōsenjin Kyōiku o Susumeru Kai (jun) 82.1–6," Kawasaki City Fureaikan; "Kawasaki shi kyōi (kyōiku iinkai) kōshō ni mukete," November 5, 1981, File "Zainichi Kankoku Chōsenjin Kyōiku o Susumeru Kai (jun) 82.1–6," Kawasaki City Fureaikan.

27. "Kawasaki shi kyōi (kyōiku iinkai) kōshō ni mukete," October 1, 1981, File "Zainichi Kankoku Chōsenjin Kyōiku o Susumeru Kai (jun) 82.1–6," Kawasaki City Fureaikan; "Kawasaki shi kyōi (kyōiku iinkai) kōshō ni mukete," November 5, 1981, File "Zainichi Kankoku Chōsenjin Kyōiku o Susumeru Kai (jun) 82.1–6," Kawasaki City Fureaikan.

28. "'Zainichi Kankoku Chōsenjin Kyōiku o Susumeru Kai' junbikai," May 20, 1982, File "Zainichi Kankoku Chōsenjin Kyōiku o Susumeru Kai (jun) 82.6–12," Kawasaki City Fureaikan; "Susumeru kai kessei shushibun," June 20, 1982, File "Zainichi Kankoku Chōsenjin Kyōiku o Susumeru Kai (jun) 82.6–12," Kawasaki City Fureaikan; "Kawasaki Zainichi Kankoku Chōsenjin Kyōiku o Susumeru Kai kessei shūkai ni sanka o!," June 26, 1982, File "Zainichi Kankoku Chōsenjin Kyōiku o Susumeru Kai (jun) 82.6–12," Kawasaki City Fureaikan; "'*Zainichi* dōhō kyōiku o susumeru kai' o kessei," *Tōitsu nippō,* June 20, 1982; Kawasaki City Fureaikan, *Daremoga chikara ippai ikiteiku tameni,* 82–86.

29. "Nihon no gakkō ni zaiseki suru *zainichi* Kankoku Chōsenjin seito no kyōiku ni kansuru yōbōsho (an)," File "Zainichi Kankoku Chōsenjin Kyōiku o Susumeru Kai (jun) 82.6–12," Kawasaki City Fureaikan; "'Nihon no gakkō ni zaiseki suru *zainichi* Kankoku Chōsenjin seito no kyōiku ni kansuru yōbōsho' o shi kyōi (kyōiku iinkai) ni teishutsu," File "Zainichi Kankoku Chōsenjin Kyōiku o Susumeru Kai (jun) 82.6–12," Kawasaki City Fureaikan; "Nihon no gakkō ni zaiseki suru *zainichi* Kankoku Chōsenjin seito no kyōiku ni kansuru yōbōsho," File "Zainichi Kankoku Chōsenjin Kyōiku o Susumeru Kai (jun) 82.6–12," Kawasaki City Fureaikan.

30. Song, *Aisuru toki kiseki wa tsukurareru*; Lee, "Seikūsha: Minzoku sabetsu to tatakai, ningen shutai no kakuritsu o mezashite," 58–60; Lee In Ha, "Seikūsha no nijūnen o kaerimite," in *Tomoni ikiru: Seikyusha sōritsu 20 shūnen kinen,* ed. Seikyusha, 22–23; Osami, *Jichitai no henkaku to zainichi Korian.*

31. Lǔ Xùn, one of the major Chinese novelists of the twentieth century, said that slaves become slaves when they do not know that they are slaves. When Song came across this author, she came to strongly believe that her Japanese alias was a "slave name" and that using real names would be the first step at fighting against inequality. Song, *Aisuru toki kiseki wa tsukurareru,* 204.

32. Ibid., 168, 210.

33. Ibid., 206–7.

34. Kanagawaken Kōshōbu Kokusaikōryūka, *Uchinaru minsai gaikō*; Song, *Aisuru toki kiseki wa tsukurareru*, 214–17; Song Puja, interview by author, August 14, 2012.

35. "Kyōi (kyōiku iinkai) chō tono mendan," July 24, 1982, File "Zainichi Kankoku Chōsenjin Kyōiku o Susumeru Kai (jun) 82.6–12," Kawasaki City Fureaikan; "Shi kyōi (kyōiku iinkai) kōshō," September 24, 1982, File "Zainichi Kankoku Chōsenjin Kyōiku o Susumeru Kai (jun) 82.6–12," Kawasaki City Fureaikan; "Shi kyōi (kyōiku iinkai) kōshō," November 9, 1982, File "Zainichi Kankoku Chōsenjin Kyōiku o Susumeru Kai (jun) 82.6–12," Kawasaki City Fureaikan.

36. Song, *Aisuru toki kiseki wa tsukurareru*, 218.

37. Ibid., 242; "'Josei no kai' ima made no hōkoku," n.d., 1978, File "Josei no kai," Kawasaki City Fureaikan.

38. "'Susumeru kai' jimukyoku-Shi kyōi (kyōiku iinkai) kōshō ni mukete," October 15, 1982, File "Zainichi Kankoku Chōsenjin Kyōiku o Susumeru Kai (jun) 82.6–12," Kawasaki City Fureaikan; "Shi kyōi (kyōiku iinkai) jimu sesshō," December 15, 1982, File "Zainichi Kankoku Chōsenjin Kyōiku o Susumeru Kai (jun) 82.6–12," Kawasaki City Fureaikan. Song helped to establish the Korea Museum (Korai Hakubutsukan) in Okubo, Tokyo, in December 2001 and served as its first director.

39. Kawasaki City, *Kawasaki shi tabunka kyōsei shakai suishin shishin*, 37–39; Iwabuchi Hideyuki, "Kawasaki shi ni okeru *zainichi* gaikokujin kyōiku to Seikyusha," in *Tomoni ikiru: Seikyusha sōritsu 20 shūnen kinen*, ed. Seikyusha; Kim, "Zainichi Kankoku Chōsenjin no aidentitī keisei to tabunka kyōsei kyōiku ni kansuru kenkyū," 74–75.

40. Seikyusha, *Kawasaki shi Sakuramoto chiku seishōnen mondai chōsa kenkyu hōkoku*; Kawasaki City Fureaikan, "To Let Everyone Live up to Their Potential—'Fureai' Hall"; Iwabuchi Hideyuki, "Kawasaki shi ni okeru *zainichi* gaikokujin kyōiku to Seikyusha," in *Tomoni ikiru: Seikyusha sōritsu 20 shūnen kinen*, ed. Seikyusha, 30–34; Kanagawa Shinbunsha Shakaibu, *Nihon no naka no gaikokujin*, 6, 21–27, 30–36, 44, 76; Kawasaki City Fureaikan, *Daremoga chikara ippai ikiteiku tameni;* Kim, "*Zainichi* Kankoku Chōsenjin no aidentitī keisei to tabunka kyōsei kyōiku ni kansuru kenkyū," 77–94.

41. Kawasaki City Fureaikan, *Daremoga chikara ippai ikiteiku tameni*, 86–87; Kim, "*Zainichi* Kankoku Chōsenjin no aidentitī keisei to tabunka kyōsei kyōiku ni kansuru kenkyū," 78.

42. Kim, "*Zainichi* Kankoku Chōsenjin no aidentitī keisei to tabunka kyōsei kyōiku ni kansuru kenkyū," 78.

43. Lie, *Multiethnic Japan*, 88.

44. Watanabe, *Burakushi ga wakaru*, 102; Kurokawa, *Ika to dōka no aida*, 305–13; Koshiro, "Beyond an Alliance of Color," 203; Yoon, *Shisō taiken no kōsaku*, 353.

See also Akisada, *Buraku no rekishi*; Teraki and Noguchi, *Buraku mondai ron eno shōtai*; Kurokawa Midori, *Kindai burakushi*.

45. Buraku Kaihō Kenkyūjo, "'Buraku kaihō o zen jānarisuto ni' ni tsuite: Jiko hihan to ketsui," 14–17; see also other articles in *Buraku kaihō* 51 (February 1974); *Buraku kaihō* 52 (March 1974).

46. Seikyusha Katsudōsha Kaigi, ed., "Minzoku sabetsu to tatakau chiiki katsudō o mezashite," 31, File "Minzoku hoikuen kankei shiryō (3) 1981-Sakuramoto hoikuen," Kawasaki City Fureaikan.

47. Bae Joong Do, interviews by author, September 24, October 1, and November 2, 2005.

48. Lee, "Seikūsha: Minzoku sabetsu to tatakai, ningen shutai no kakuritsu o mezashite," 58–60.

49. Buraku Kaihō Kenkyūjo, "'Buraku kaihō o zen jānarisuto ni' ni tsuite," 17.

50. Kawasaki Zainichi Dōhō no Jinken o Mamorukai, *Kawasaki ni okeru chiiki undō*, 6, 27; Kawasaki shi no Shōgakukin Seido ni okeru Minzoku Sabetsu o Tadasu Iinkai Jimukyoku, ed., "Minzoku sabetsu to wa nani ka: *Zainichi* Kankoku Chōsenjin no tatakai no keishō hatten ni sokushite," February 1977, 15, File "Kawasaki shōgakukin tōsō naibu tōgi shryō," Kawasaki City Fureaikan; Bae Joong Do, interviews by author, September 24, October 1, and November 2, 2005.

51. Kawasaki City Fureaikan, *Daremoga chikara ippai ikiteiku tameni,* 87–94.

52. Kim, "*Zainichi* Kankoku Chōsenjin no aidentitī keisei to tabunka kyōsei kyōiku ni kansuru kenkyū," 103–12.

53. Chung, *Immigration and Citizenship in Japan,* 127–28.

54. Bae Joong Do, "'Shūgaku annai' yōkyū undō ni tsuite no sankō iken," file "Kawasaki shūgaku tsūchi (annai) yōkyū undō 1976 11.24-," Kawasaki City Fureaikan, 4.

55. Kawasaki shi no Shōgakukin Seido ni okeru Minzoku Sabetsu o Tadasu Iinkai Jimukyoku, ed., "Minzoku sabetsu to wa nani ka: *Zainichi* Kankoku Chōsenjin no tatakai no keishō hatten ni sokushite," February 1977, 6, File "Kawasaki shōgakukin tōsō naibu tōgi shryō," Kawasaki City Fureaikan; Lee In Ha, interview by author, Song Kwon, and Tonomura Masaru, September 4, 2005; Bae Joong Do, interviews by author, September 24, October 1, and November 2, 2005; Mun, *Zainichi Chōsenjin mondai no kigen,* 191–92.

56. Choi Seungkoo, "Hitachi tōsō to wa nan datta no ka," in *Nihon ni okeru tabunka kyōsei to wa nanika*, ed. Choi and Kato, 64–73; Cho Kyong-hi, "'Minzoku hoiku' no jissen to mondai," in *Nihon ni okeru tabunka kyōsei to wa nanika*, ed. Choi and Kato, 126–50.

57. "'Hitachi shūshoku sabetsu saiban 30 shūnen kinen shūkai' jikkō iinkai kenkai," in *Hitachi shūshoku sabetsu saiban 30 shūnen kinen no tsudoi: Hōkokushū*, ed. Hitachi Shūshoku Sabetsu Saiban 30shūnen Kinen Shūkai Jikkō Iinkai, 13–14, 39–40; Choi, "Kyōsei no machi Kawasaki o tou," in *Hitachi shūshoku sabetsu saiban 30 shūnen kinen no tsudoi: Hōkokushū*, ed. Hitachi Shūshoku Sabetsu Saiban

30shūnen Kinen Shūkai Jikkō Iinkai, 169; Choi, *Gaikokujin sanseiken ni tsuite,* 16–17.

58. Park Jong Seok, "Zoku 'Hitachi tōsō': Shokuba kankyō no nakade," in *Nihon ni okeru tabunka kyōsei to wa nanika,* ed. Choi and Kato, 74–119.

59. Ibid.; Park Jong Seok, "Zoku Hitachi tōsō no imi," June 8, 2011, notes from lecture, Nakahara shimin kaikan, Kawasaki City; "Kōron: Hiyameshi o kuu," *Asahi shinbun,* May 12, 2012.

60. Bae Joong Do, interviews by author, September 24, October 1, and November 2, 2005; Kashiwazaki Chikako, "The Politics of Legal Status: The Equation of Nationality with Ethnonational Identity," in *Koreans in Japan,* ed. Ryang, 13–31.

Conclusion

1. Cruikshank, *The Will to Empower.*

2. Étienne Balibar, "The Nation Form: History and Ideology," in *Race, Nation, Class,* ed. Balibar and Wallerstein, 92–93; Balibar, *We, the People of Europe?*

3. Kessler-Harris, *In Pursuit of Equity,* 12.

4. Greenstone and Peterson, *Race and Authority in Urban Politics,* xv; Self, *American Babylon,* 237.

5. Ong et al., *The Widening Divide*; Soja and Scott, "Introduction to Los Angeles," in *The City,* ed. Scott and Soja, 11–17; Jeffrey S. Adler, "Introduction," in *African-American Mayors,* ed. Colburn and Adler, 1–22. See also Sides, *Post-Ghetto.*

6. Many scholars have discussed how the New Deal welfare state reinforced racial inequality by excluding agricultural workers and domestic servants—most of whom were African Americans in the South—from both old-age insurance and unemployment compensation. Instead, they were pushed toward public assistance programs, where local officials set up benefit levels and eligibility rules. Quadagno, *The Color of Welfare,* 20–21; Neubeck and Cazenave, *Welfare Racism,* 46–59.

7. Quadagno, *The Color of Welfare,* 9. See also Quadagno, "Promoting Civil Rights through the Welfare State," 68–89.

8. Davis, *From Opportunity to Entitlement*; Orleck, "Conclusion: The War on the War on Poverty and American Politics since the 1960s," in *The War on Poverty,* ed. Orleck and Hazirjian, 452.

9. Martin Gilens explores how support for the poor and the War on Poverty shrank as popular images of the poor came to focus on African Americans, reinforcing the racialization of welfare and poverty in the mid-1960s. Gilens, *Why Americans Hate Welfare.*

10. Bauman, *Race and the War on Poverty,* 89.

11. Orleck, "Conclusion: The War on the War on Poverty and American Politics since the 1960s," in *The War on Poverty,* ed. Orleck and Hazirjian, 438.

12. When Wiley resigned in December 1972, Tillmon was chosen as the new executive director of the NWRO. The funding for the organization, however, had become depleted by the time she became director. After the NWRO folded in 1975, Tillmon returned to Los Angeles and continued her struggle for welfare rights at the local and state levels. In 1995 Tillmon died at the age of sixty-nine. "Welfare Rights Pioneer Tillmon-Blackston Dies," *Los Angeles Times,* October 25, 1995.

13. White, *Too Heavy a Load,* 223, 230; Nadasen, *Welfare Warriors,* 229–30. For a discussion of black feminism, see, for instance, James and Sharpley-Whiting, *The Black Feminist Reader.*

14. The 1995 Japanese Supreme Court landmark decision held that voting rights for foreign residents were not granted by the constitution but granting local voting rights was not unconstitutional. While the New Komeito Party, the Democratic Party of Japan, and the Japan Communist Party have taken the lead in introducing a bill to endow local voting rights for resident non-nationals, due to strong opposition in the National Diet (Parliament) in Japan, it is still under discussion as of this publication. See Kondo, *Gaikokujin sanseiken to kokuseki*; Chung, *Immigration and Citizenship in Japan*, 110–11.

15. In June 2008, following recommendations put forward by the Kawasaki City Representative Assembly for Foreign Residents, the City of Kawasaki granted resident non-nationals voting rights in referendums. This was a significant victory for Koreans and other non-nationals who were fighting for the right to vote. See Jūmin tōhyō seido kentō iinkai, "Jūmin tōhyō seido o sōsetsu shimashita," http://www.city.kawasaki.jp/20/20bunken/home/site/jichi/touhyou/report/committee/juumintouhyou_ index.htm; "Seiji sanka tsuzuku tesaguri," *Asahi shinbun,* September 21, 2008.

16. See Kashiwazaki Chikako, "The Politics of Legal Status: The Equation of Nationality with Ethnonational Identity," in *Koreans in Japan,* ed. Ryang, 14.

17. See Morris-Suzuki, *Hihanteki sōzōryoku no tameni,* 154–56; Song, "'Koria kei Nihonjin'ka purojekuto no isō o saguru," 225–39. See also Takashi Fujitani's discussion on "polite racism" in Japan: Fujitani, "Right to Kill, Right to Make Live," 17; Fujitani, *Race for Empire.*

18. "Kawasaki hōshiki wa sabetsu seitōka: Kokuseki jōkō teppai de *zainichi* Kankokujin ga kōgibun/Kanagawa," *Asahi shinbun* (Kanagawa), May 25, 1996; "Kokuseki jōkō, 'Kawasaki hōshiki' ni izen mondai: Shiminra 200 nin, kanzen teppai motome shūkai/Kanagawa," *Mainichi shinbun* (Kanagawa), January 27, 1997; Choi Seungkoo, "'Kyōsei no machi' Kawasaki o tou," in *Nihon ni okeru tabunka kyōsei to wa nanika*, ed. Choi and Kato, 155–56.

19. Kate Masur discusses how, during Reconstruction, black Washingtonians struggled over equality and insisted on their rights as constituting members of the civic body. Masur, *An Example for All the Land.*

20. Linda Gordon, "The New Feminist Scholarship on the Welfare State," in *Women, the State, and Welfare*, ed. Gordon, 28; Gordon, "Who Deserves Help? Who Must Provide?," 12–25.

21. Somers, *Genealogies of Citizenship*, 20.

22. Lipsitz, *American Studies in a Moment of Danger*, 118–22.

Bibliography

Manuscript Collections

Los Angeles/The United States

California Social Welfare Archives.

- Economic and Youth Opportunities Agency of Greater Los Angeles.
- Neighborhood Adult Participation Project Inc.

City of Los Angeles. Office of the City Clerk. Records Management Division, Los Angeles.

- City Council File.
- Economic and Youth Opportunities Agency of Greater Los Angeles.
- Samuel Yorty Collection.

Congress of Racial Equality Papers: Addendum, 1944–1968. Glen Rock, N.J.: Microfilming Corporation of America, 1981. Microfilm.

Department of Special Collections, University of California, Los Angeles.

- Augustus F. Hawkins Papers, 1935–1990.
- Thomas Bradley Administrative Papers, 1963–1993.

Gelfand, Mark I, ed. *The Presidential Documents Series, the War on Poverty, 1964–1968: Part 1: The White House Central Files. Selections from the Holdings of the Lyndon B. Johnson Library.* Frederick, Md.: University Publications of America, 1986. Microfilm.

Lyndon B. Johnson Library, Austin.

- Confidential File, WE 9 (Welfare-Poverty Program).
- Executive File, WE 9 (Welfare-Poverty Program).
- Ex LG/Los Angeles.
- General HU2/ST5.
- Interviews.
- Office Files of Harry McPherson.
- Office Files of Lee White.
- Subject File, FG11–15 (Federal Government, Office of Economic Opportunity).

Moorland-Springarn Library, Howard University, Washington, DC.

- Records of National Welfare Rights Organization.

National Archives, College Park.

- Record Group 381 (Office of Economic Opportunity).

Schomburg Center, New York Public Library, New York.

- Records of the Black Theology Project.

Sophia Smith Collection, Smith College, Northampton.

- Frances Fox Piven Papers, 1957–1999.

Southern California Library (SCL), Los Angeles.

- Watts 65 Project Collection.

Special Collections, University of Southern California, Los Angeles.

State Historical Society of Wisconsin, Madison.

- George A. Wiley Papers.

Walter P. Reuther Library, Wayne State University, Detroit.

- Papers of Citizens' Crusade against Poverty.

Kawasaki/Japan

Kawasaki City Archives, Kawasaki.

Manuscript collections, Kawasaki City Fureaikan, Kawasaki.

- "Kawasaki jittai chōsa hōkoku."
- "Kawasaki shōgakukin tōsō naibu tōgi shiryō."
- "Kawasaki shūgaku tsūchi (annai) yōkyū undō 1976 11.24."
- "Minzoku hoikuen kankei shiryō (3) 1981-Sakuramoto hoikuen."
- "Minzoku undō toshite no chiiki katsudō."
- "Zainichi Kankoku Chōsenjin Kyōiku o Susumeru Kai (jun) 82.1–6."
- "Zainichi Kankoku Chōsenjin Kyōiku o Susumeru Kai (jun) 82.6–12."

Unpublished documents, Gyōseika, Sōmushō (Japan's Ministry of Internal Affairs and Communications).

The World Council of Churches Archives. *Programme to Combat Racism, 1939–1996.* Leiden: IDC Publishers, 2005. Microfilm.

Government Publications

Los Angeles/The United States

California. Governor's Commission on the Los Angeles Riots [McCone Commission]. "Violence in the City: An End or Beginning?" In *The Los Angeles Riots: Mass Violence in America*, composed by Robert M. Fogelson. New York: Arno Press and *New York Times*, 1969.

Congressional Records

Los Angeles County Commission on Human Relations. *Patterns of Social Change: Los Angeles County, 1960–73: A Statistical Review*. Los Angeles: Los Angeles County Commission on Human Relations, 1974.

———. *Population and Housing in Los Angeles County: A Study in the Growth of Residential Segregation*. Los Angeles: Los Angeles County Commission on Human Relations, 1963.

State of California. Division of Fair Employment Practices (FEPC). *Questions and Answers about the California Fair Housing Law*. San Francisco: FEPC, 1963.

U.S. Congress. House of Representatives. Committee on Education and Labor. *Antipoverty Programs in New York City and Los Angeles: Hearings before the Subcommittee on the War on Poverty Programs*. 89th Cong., 1st sess., 1965.

———. *Economic Opportunity Act of 1964*. 88th Cong., 2nd sess., 1964.

———. *Examination of the War on Poverty Program: Hearings before the Subcommittee on Poverty Programs*. 89th Cong., 1st sess., 1965.

U.S. Congress. House of Representatives. Committee on Government Operations. *26th Report: The Demise of the Greater Los Angeles Community Action Agency*. Report prepared by Committee on Governmental Operations. 96th Cong., 2nd sess., 1980.

U.S. Congress. House of Representatives. Committee on Ways and Means. *The Work Incentive Program, Fourth Annual Report to the Congress on Training and Employment under Title IV of the Social Security Act*. January 21, 1974.

———. *The Work Incentive Program, Second Annual Report of the Department of Labor on Training and Employment under Title IV of the Social Security Act*. 92nd Cong., 1st sess., 1971.

U.S. Congress. Senate. Committee on Labor and Public Welfare. Subcommittee on Employment, Manpower, and Poverty. *Economic Opportunity Act of 1964*. 88th Cong., 2nd sess., 1964.

———. *Examination of the War on Poverty*. 90th Cong., 1st sess., 1967.

U.S. Department of Labor. Office of Policy Planning and Research. *The Negro Family: The Case for National Action*. Washington, DC: U.S. Government Printing Office, 1965.

U.S. Department of Labor and U.S. Department of Health, Education, and Welfare (HEW). *Reports on the Work Incentive Program*. 91st Cong., 2nd sess., 1970.

U.S. General Accounting Office. *Review of the Community Action Program in the Los Angeles Area under the Economic Opportunity Act: Report to the Congress on the Office of Economic Opportunity*. Washington, DC: U.S. Government Printing Office, 1968.

U.S. Office of Economic Opportunity. *Catalog of Federal Programs for Individual and Community Improvement: A Description of Governmental Programs to*

Help Individuals and Communities Meet Their Own Goals for Economic and Social Development. Washington, DC: U.S. Government Printing Office, 1965.
———. *Community Action Program Guide: Instructions for Developing, Conducting, and Administering a Community Action Program, as Authorized by Sections 204 and 205 of Title II-A, Economic Opportunity Act of 1964*. Washington, DC: U.S. Government Printing Office, 1965.
———. *Conference Proceedings: Second Annual Conference on Women in the War on Poverty*. Washington, DC: U.S. Government Printing Office, 1968.
———. *Conference Proceedings: Women in the War on Poverty*. Washington, DC: U.S. Government Printing Office, 1967.
———. *A Nation Aroused: 1st Annual Report*. Washington, DC: Office of Economic Opportunity, 1965.
———. *The Quiet Revolution: 2nd Annual Report*. Washington, DC: Office of Economic Opportunity, 1967.
———. *The Tide of Progress: 3rd Annual Report*. Washington, DC: Office of Economic Opportunity, 1968.
———. *Women in the War on Poverty*. Washington, DC: U.S. Government Printing Office, 1969.
U.S. Office of the Federal Register, National Archives and Records Service, General Services Administration. *Public Papers of the Presidents of the United States, Lyndon B. Johnson: Containing the Public Messages, Speeches, and Statements of the President, November 22, 1963, to January 20, 1953, to January 20, 1969*. Washington, DC: U.S. Government Printing Office, 1965–1970.

Kawasaki/Japan

Chihō Jichi Seido Kenkyūkai, ed. *Komyunitī dokuhon*. Tokyo: Gyōsei, 1973.
———. *Zoku komyunitī dokuhon*. Tokyo: Gyōsei, 1975.
Chuō Shakai Fukushi Shingikai. *Komyunitī keisei to shakai fukushi (Tōben)*. Tokyo: Chuō Shakai Fukushi Shingikai, 1971.
Jichishō Gyōseikyoku Gyōseika. *Chihō kōkyō dantai ni okeru komyunitī shisaku no jōkyō*. Tokyo: Jichishō Gyōseikyoku Gyōseika, 1983.
———. *Komyunitī suishin chiku ni okeru komyunitī katsudō no jōkyō*. Tokyo: Jichishō Gyōseikyoku Gyōseika, 1987.
Jichishō Komyunitī Kenkyūkai, ed. *Chihō kōkyō dantai ni okeru komyunitī seisaku no jōkyō*. Tokyo: Jichishō Komyunitī Kenkyūkai, 1978.
———. *Komyunitī kenkyū hōkoku*. Tokyo: Jichishō Komyunitī Kenkyūkai, 1977.
———. *Komyunitī kenkyūkai chūkan hōkoku*. Tokyo: Jichishō Komyunitī Kenkyūkai, 1973.
Jichi Sōgō Sentā. *Chihō kōkyō dantai no komyunitī shisaku*. Tokyo: Zaidan Hōjin Jichi Sōgō Sentā, 1984.
———. *Komyunitī kankei yōkō tou shiryōshū*. Tokyo: Jichi Sōgō Sentā, 1979.

———. *Moderu komyunitī chiku ni okeru komyunitī katsudō nado no jōkyō*. Tokyo: Zaidan Hōjin Jichi Sōgō Sentā, 1983.

Kawasaki City. *Kawasaki shi shi: Tsūshi hen*. Vol. 4, no. 2. Kawasaki: Kawasaki City, 1997.

———. *Kawasaki shi tabunka kyōsei shakai suishin shishin*. Kawasaki: Kawasaki City, 2005.

Kawasaki shi Eiseikyoku. *Kawasaki shi ni okeru taiki osen*. Kawasaki: Kawasaki shi Eiseikyoku, 1965.

Kawasaki shigikai. *Kawasaki shigikai shi*. Vol. 3. Tokyo: Daiichi Hōki Shuppan, 1985.

Kokumin Seikatsu Shingikai. *Komyunitī: Seikatsu no ba ni okeru ningensei no kaifuku* [Community: The Recovery of Humanity in Everyday Life]. Tokyo: Ōkurashō insatsukyoku, 1969.

Musashino City. *Komyunitī hakusho*. Tokyo: Musashino City, 1985.

———. *Komyunitī sentā gaiyō*. Tokyo: Musashino City, 1998.

———. *Musashino shi no komyunitī: Komyunitī no kihon gensoku*. Tokyo: Musashino City, 1998.

Musashino shi Shokuin Komyunitī Kenkyūkai. *Seijuku shakai ni okeru komyunitī no arikata*. Tokyo: Musashino City, 1998.

Tokyoto Minseikyoku. *Komyunitī kea no suishin ni tsuite: Dai ikkai hōkoku* [On the Development of Community Care in Tokyo: First Report]. Tokyo: Tokyoto Minseikyoku, 1977.

Unpublished Documents

Los Angeles/The United States

Black Committee of Inquiry. *The Truth about the Watts Summer Festival*. Los Angeles: Black Committee of Inquiry, 1972.

Kaye, Mary. *Distribution of Poor Youths in Los Angeles County: By Census Tract and Community Action Agencies Area*. Los Angeles: Economic and Youth Opportunities Agency, 1967.

———. *Ethnic Composition of the Population of Los Angeles County, April 1970: An Estimate Based upon School Enrollment Data: Summary Results for Los Angeles County, Its Community Action Agencies, and EYOA's 10 Poverty Planning Areas*. Los Angeles: Economic and Youth Opportunities Agency, 1970.

———. *Selected Health District Characteristics of Los Angeles County: Statistical Report, August, 1966*. Los Angeles: Economic and Youth Opportunities Agency, 1967.

University of California, Los Angeles, School of Law, comp. *Materials on Proposition 14, the Initiative Constitutional Amendment Relating to Sales and Rentals of Residential Real Property, Including Positions Pro and Con, which Was Submitted to the Voters of California on Nov. 3, 1964*. Los Angeles: UCLA, School of Law, 1964.

Watts Labor Community Action Committee (WLCAC). *Community Conservation Corps*. Los Angeles: WLCAC, 1967.

———. *1967 Report*. Los Angeles: WLCAC, 1967.

———. *WLCAC: Changing . . . Moving . . . the Lives of a People*. Los Angeles: WLCAC, 1969.

Welfare Planning Council, Los Angeles Region. *Social Profiles: Los Angeles County*. Los Angeles: Welfare Planning Council, 1965.

Youth Opportunities Board of Greater Los Angeles. *The Los Angeles "War against Poverty": A Proposal Submitted for Funding . . . the Office of Economic Opportunity*. Los Angeles: Youth Opportunities Board of Greater Los Angeles, 1964.

Kawasaki/Japan

Bae, Joong Do. "Sengo no zainichi Kankoku Chōsenjin no hōteki chii oyobi taigū no suii." Unpublished typewritten manuscript.

———. "Zainichi Kankoku Chōsenjin no shokenri tōsō no hensen kara miru 'ikikata' ron no tenkai." Unpublished typewritten manuscript.

———. "Zainichi Kankoku Chōsenjin no shokenri tōsō no rekishi." Unpublished typewritten manuscript.

Hitachi Shūshoku Sabetsu Saiban 30shūnen Kinen Shūkai Jikkō Iinkai. *Hitachi shūshoku sabetsu saiban 30shūnen kinen no tsudoi: Hōkokushū*. Kawasaki: Hitachi Shūshoku Sabetsu Saiban 30shūnen Kinen Shūkai Jikkō Iinkai, 2010.

Kanagawaken Kōshōbu Kokusaikōryūka. *Uchinaru minsai gaikō: Mijika na kokusai rikai no tameni*. Yokohama: Kanagawaken Kōshōbu Kokusaikōryūka, 1982.

Kawasaki City Fureaikan. *Daremoga chikara ippai ikiteiku tameni: Kawasaki shi Fureaikan 4 nenkan no ayumi, 1988–1991*. Kawasaki: Kawasaki City Fureaikan, 1993.

———. "To Let Everyone Live up to Their Potential—'Fureai' Hall." Kawasaki: Kawasaki City Fureaikan, n.d.

Kawasaki Zainichi Dōhō no Jinken o Mamorukai. *Kawasaki ni okeru chiiki undō: Minzoku undō to shite no chiiki katsudō o mezashite*. Kawasaki: Kawasaki Zainichi Dōhō no Jinken o Mamorukai, 1975.

Minzoku Sabetsu to Tatakau Renraku Kyōgikai. *Minzoku sabetsu to no tatakai: Hitachi shūshoku sabetsu kyūdan*. 1975. DVD-ROM. Ed. Kawasaki Renraku Kaigi. Kawasaki: Kawasaki Renraku Kaigi, 2008.

Nihon kōkan. *Nihon kōkan kabushiki gaisha yonjūnenshi*. Tokyo: Nihon kōkan, 1952.

Ozawa Yusaku Zemi. "Park Jong Seok-san no Jibunshi." Tokyo: Tokyo Toritsu Daigaku, 1992.

Park-kun o Kakomu Kai, ed. *Park Jong Seok shūshoku sabetsu saiban shiryōshū, no. 6*. Kawasaki: Park-kun o Kakomu Kai, 1974.

Programme to Combat Racism, World Council of Churches, Ans J. van der Bent, eds. *Breaking Down the Walls: World Council of Churches Statements and Actions on Racism, 1948–1985*. Geneva: World Council of Churches, 1986.

RAIK (Research-Action Institute for the Koreans in Japan; Zainichi Kankokujin Mondai Kenkyūjo), ed. *Gaikokujin shitei no kyōiku ni tsuiteno shomondai*. Tokyo: RAIK, 1975.

———. *Jidō teate no shikyū, kōei jūtaku nyūkyo tō no seikatsuken yōgo undō no kiroku*. Tokyo: RAIK, n.d.

Seikyusha. *Kawasaki shi Sakuramoto chiku seishōnen mondai chōsa kenkyū hōkoku*. Kawasaki: Seikyusha, 1985.

———. *Tomoni ikiru: Seikyusha sōritsu 10 shūnen kinen*. Kawasaki: Seikyusha, 1985.

———. *Tomoni ikiru: Seikyusha sōritsu 20 shūnen kinen*. Kawasaki: Seikyusha, 1995.

Seikyusha 10 shūnen Kinenshi Kankō Iinkai, ed. *Shakai fukushi hōjin Seikyusha Sakuramoto hoikuen, gakuen oyobi undō kankei nenpyō, 1969–1984*. Kawasaki: Seikyusha 10 shūnen Kinenshi Kankō Iinkai, 1984.

Tokyo Sōsharu Wākā Kyōkai. *Komyunitī kea o megutte*. Tokyo: Tokyo Sōsharu Wākā Kyōkai, 1973.

Zenkoku Shakai Fukushi Kyōgikai. *Jūmin fukushi undō o susumeru tameni*. Tokyo: Zenkoku Shakai Fukushi Kyōgikai, 1972.

Newspapers and Newsletters

El Alambre (East Los Angeles Community Union)
Arirang
Asahi shinbun
The Crisis
Eastside Sun
Economic and Youth Opportunities Board Reports
Genkainada
Kanagawa shinbun
Kawasaki kuhō
Los Angeles Sentinel
Los Angeles Times
Mainichi shinbun
Musashino shihō
Nation's Cities
New York Times
NOW!: Publication of the National Welfare Rights Organization
Park-kun o Kakomu Kai kaihō
San Luis Obispo County Telegram-Tribune

Seikyusha nyūsu (1978–82)
Tōitsu nippō
Tōyō keizai nippō
Washington Post
Welfare Fighter
Yomiuri shinbun
Youth Opportunities Board Reports

Oral Histories

Bae, Jonng Do. Interview by author, Song Kwon, and Tonomura Masaru, September 4, 2005, Kawasaki City Fureaikan.

———. Interviews by author, September 24, October 1, and November 2, 2005, Kawasaki City Fureaikan.

Choi, Seungkoo. Interviews by author, December 5, 2009, Hongo, Bunkyo-ku, Tokyo; February 16, 2010, Kawasaki-ku, Kawasaki.

Cone, James H. Interview by author, September 7, 2010, Dr. James H. Cone's House, New York.

Gillette, Michael L., ed. *Launching the War on Poverty: An Oral History*. New York: Twayne, 1996.

Henry, Mary B. Interview by author, September 30, 2002, Avalon-Carver Community Center, Los Angeles.

Jacquette, Tommy. Interview by author, August 9, 2002, Watts Labor Community Action Committee, Los Angeles.

———. Interview by author on the phone, September 27, 2000.

Kajiwara, Hisashi. Interview by author, September 20, 2009, Meieki, Nakamura-ku, Nagoya.

Karenga, Maulana. Interview by author, September 25, 2000, California State University, Long Beach.

Kimura, Hitoshi. Interview by author, January 27, 2006, Sangiin kaikan (the House of Councilors building), Tokyo.

Lee, In Ha. Interview by author, Song Kwon, and Tonomura Masaru, September 4, 2005, Kawasaki City Fureaikan, Kawasaki.

Nishio, Masaru. Interview by author, August 26, 2010, Shiseikaikan, Tokyo.

Omori, Wataru. Interview by author, December 23, 2005, Arcadia Ichigaya Shigakukaikan, Tokyo.

Park, Jong Seok. Interviews by author by mail, September 24 and 25, 2011; interview by author, September 6, 2012, Kanagawa Kenmin Sentā, Yokohama, Japan.

Song, Puja. Interviews by author by phone, February 18 and July 24, 2009; interview by author, August 14, 2012, Ms. Song Puja's House, Kawasaki.

Tillmon, Johnnie. Interview by Sherna Berger Gluck. The Women's History Collection, Oral History Archives, California State University, Long Beach.
———. Interview by Southern California Library for Social Studies and Research, October 10, 1990. Watts '65 Project, Oral History, Southern California Library for Social Studies and Research, Los Angeles.
Yamada, Takao. Interview by author, April 28, 2006, Kawasaki City, Nakahara Shiminkan, Kawasaki.

Books, Articles, and Theses

Abe, Hitoshi. "Jūmin undō to chiiki seiji." *Chiiki kaihatsu* 154 (1977): 56–69.
Abramovitz, Mimi. *Regulating the Lives of Women: Social Welfare Policy from Colonial Times to the Present.* 1988. Revised, Boston: South End, 1996.
Acuña, Rodolfo F. *A Community under Siege: A Chronicle of Chicanos East of the Los Angeles River 1945–1975.* Los Angeles: Chicano Studies Research Center, University of California, Los Angeles, 1984.
Akisada, Yoshikazu. *Buraku no rekishi—Kindai.* Osaka: Kaihou Shuppansha, 2004.
Ambrecht, Biliana C. S. *Politicizing the Poor: The Legacy of the War on Poverty in a Mexican-American Community.* New York: Praeger, 1976.
Anderson, Benedict. *Imagined Communities.* New York: Verso, 1989.
Ari, Bakuji. "Fukushi no seijika to jichitai." *Jurisuto: Rinji zōkan* (1974): 368–76.
Asai, Yoshio. "Kaihatsu no 50 nendai kara seichō no 60 nendai e: Kōdo seichōki no keizai to shakai." *Kokuritsu Rekishi Minzoku Hakubutsukan Kekyū Hōkoku* 171 (2011): 7–24.
Ashmore, Susan Youngblood. *Carry It On: The War on Poverty and the Civil Rights Movement in Alabama, 1964–1972.* Athens: University of Georgia Press, 2008.
Avenell, Simon Andrew. *Making Japanese Citizens: Civil Society and the Mythology of the Shimin in Postwar Japan.* Berkeley: University of California Press, 2010.
Bae, Joong Do. "Zainichi undo to 'kyōsei' no bunka: Kawasaki shi Fureaikan no keiken kara." *Shakai bunka kenkyū* 9 (2007): 10–17.
Bailis, Lawrence. *Bread or Justice: Grassroots Organizing in the Welfare Rights Movement.* Lexington, Mass.: Lexington Books, 1972.
Balibar, Étienne. *We, the People of Europe? Reflections on Transnational Citizenship.* Princeton: Princeton University Press, 2004.
Balibar, Étienne, and Immanuel Wallerstein, eds. *Race, Nation, Class: Ambiguous Identities.* New York: Verso, 1991.
Bauman, Robert. *Race and the War on Poverty: From Watts to East L.A.* Norman: University of Oklahoma Press, 2008.
———. "Race, Class, and Political Power: The Implementation of the War on Poverty in Los Angeles." PhD diss., University of California, Santa Barbara, 1998.

Bebout, Lee. *Mythohistorical Interventions: The Chicano Movement and Its Legacies*. Minneapolis: University of Minnesota Press, 2011.

Bender, Thomas. *A Nation among Nations: America's Place in World History*. New York: Hill and Wang, 2006.

———, ed. *Rethinking American History in a Global Age*. Berkeley: University of California Press, 2002.

Bernstein, Gail. *Recreating Japanese Women, 1600–1945*. Berkeley: University of California Press, 1991.

Bernstein, Michael A. *A Perilous Progress: Economists and Public Purpose in Twentieth-Century America*. Princeton: Princeton University Press, 2001.

Bernstein, Michael A., and David E. Adler, eds. *Understanding American Economic Decline*. Cambridge: Cambridge University Press, 1994.

Bernstein, Shana. *Bridges of Reform: Interracial Civil Rights Activism in Twentieth-Century Los Angeles*. New York: Oxford University Press, 2011.

Blum, Edward J., Tracy Fessenden, Prema Kurien, and Judith Weisenfeld. "Forum: American Religion and 'Whiteness.'" *Religion and American Culture: A Journal of Interpretation* 19, no. 1 (2009): 1–35.

Blumenthal, Richard. "The Bureaucracy: Antipoverty and the Community Action Program." In *American Political Institutions and Public Policy*, edited by Allan P. Sindler, 129–79. Boston: Little, Brown, 1969.

Bock, Paul. *In Search of a Responsible World Society: The Social Teachings of the World Council of Churches*. Philadelphia: Westminster Press, 1974.

Bollens, John C., and Grant B. Geyer. *Yorty: Politics of a Constant Candidate*. Pacific Palisades, Calif.: Palisades Publishers, 1973.

Boyle, Kevin. *The UAW and the Heyday of American Liberalism 1945–1968*. Ithaca, N.Y.: Cornell University Press, 1995.

Branch, Taylor. *Pillar of Fire: America in the King Years, 1963–65*. New York: Simon and Schuster, 1998.

Brilliant, Mark. *The Color of America Has Changed: How Racial Diversity Shaped Civil Rights Reform in California, 1941–1978*. New York: Oxford University Press, 2010.

Brinton, Mary C. *Women and the Economic Miracle: Gender and Work in Postwar Japan*. Berkeley: University of California Press, 1993.

Bullock, Paul. *Watts: The Aftermath—An Inside View of the Ghetto by the People of Watts*. New York: Grove Press, 1969.

Buraku Kaihō Kenkyūjo. "'Buraku kaihō o zen jānarisuto ni' ni tsuite: Jiko hihan to ketsui." *Buraku kaihō* 52 (March 1974): 14–17.

Burrow, Rufus, Jr. *James H. Cone and Black Liberation Theology*. Jefferson, N.C.: McFarland, 1994.

Button, James W. *Black Violence: Political Impact of the 1960s Riots*. Princeton: Princeton University Press, 1978.

Carter, Susan B., Scott Sigmund Gartner, Michael R. Haines, Alan L. Olmstead, Richard Sutch, and Gavin Wright. *Historical Statistics of the United States.* Cambridge: Cambridge University Press, 2006.

Casstevens, Thomas W. "California's Rumford Act and Proposition 14." In *The Politics of Fair-Housing Legislation: State and Local Case Studies*, edited by Lynn W. Eley and Thomas W. Casstevens, 237–84. San Francisco: Chandler, 1968.

Cazenave, Noel A. *Impossible Democracy: The Unlikely Success of the War on Poverty Community Action Programs.* Albany: State University of New York Press, 2007.

Chapman, David. *Zainichi Korean Identity and Ethnicity.* New York: Routledge, 2008.

Chappell, Marisa. *The War on Welfare: Family, Poverty, and Politics in Modern America.* Philadelphia: University of Pennsylvania Press, 2009.

Chavez, John R. *Eastside Landmark: A History of the East Los Angeles Community Union, 1968–1993.* Stanford: Stanford University Press, 1998.

Chi, Myong Kwan. *Kyōkaisen o koeru tabi.* Tokyo: Iwanami Shoten, 2005.

Choi, Seungkoo. *Gaikokujin sanseiken ni tsuite: Kore wa gaikokujin eno kenri no fuyo no mondai nanoka.* Tokyo: Yasukuni/tennōsei mondai jōhō sentā, Atarashii Kawasaki o tsukuru kai, 2010.

———. "Jinken no jitsugen ni tsuite: 'Zainichi' no tachiba kara." In *Jinkenron no saiteii 4: Jinken no jitsugen*, edited by Saito Junichi, 83–105. Tokyo: Horitsu Bunka Sha, 2011.

———. "Yugamerareta minzokukan." *Shisō no kagaku* 59 (1976): 2–8.

———. "Zainichi Chōsenjin mondai to wa nanika." *Fukuin to sekai* (October 1969): 19–27.

———. "Zainichi Chōsenjin to iu koto." *Fukuin to sekai* (February 1971): 73–74.

Choi, Seungkoo, and Kato Chikako, eds. *Nihon ni okeru tabunka kyōsei to wa nanika.* Tokyo: Shinyōsha, 2008.

Chung, Erin Aeran. "Exercising Citizenship: Koreans Living in Japan." *Asian Perspectives* 24, no. 4 (2000): 159–78.

———. *Immigration and Citizenship in Japan.* Cambridge: Cambridge University Press, 2010.

Clayson, William S. *Freedom Is Not Enough: The War on Poverty and the Civil Rights Movement in Texas.* Austin: University of Texas Press, 2010.

Cleage, Albert B., Jr. *The Black Messiah.* New York: Sheed and Ward, 1968.

Cohen, Nathan, ed. *The Los Angeles Riots: A Socio-Psychological Study.* New York: Praeger, 1970.

Colburn, David R., and Jeffrey S. Adler, eds. *African-American Mayors: Race, Politics, and the American City.* Urbana: University of Illinois Press, 2001.

Cone, James H. *Black Theology and Black Power.* New York: Seabury Press, 1969.

———, ed. *A Black Theology of Liberation.* 1970. Reprint, 20th anniversary ed. Maryknoll, N.Y.: Orbis Books, 1990.

———. *God of the Oppressed*. New York: Seabury Press, 1975.

———. *My Soul Looks Back*. Maryknoll, N.Y.: Orbis Books, 2005.

———. *The Spirituals and the Blues: An Interpretation*. New York: Seabury Press, 1972.

———. *Yokuatsu sareta mono no kami*. Translated by Kajiwara Hisashi. Tokyo: Shinkyō Shuppansha, 1976.

Cruikshank, Barbara. *The Will to Empower: Democratic Citizens and Other Subjects*. New York: Cornell University Press, 1999.

Davis, Gareth. *From Opportunity to Entitlement: The Transformation and Decline of Great Society Liberalism*. Lawrence: University Press of Kansas, 1996.

Davis, Martha F. *Brutal Need: Lawyers and the Welfare Rights Movement*. New Haven: Yale University Press, 1993.

———. "Welfare Rights and Women's Rights in the 1960s." *Journal of Policy History* 8, no. 1 (1996): 144–65.

Davis, Mike. *City of Quartz: Excavating the Future in Los Angeles*. New York: Vintage Books, 1992.

Dear, Michael J. *From Chicago to L.A.: Re-Visioning Urban Theory*. Thousand Oaks, Calif.: Sage Publications, 2002.

De Graaf, Lawrence B. "The City of Black Angeles: Emergence of the Los Angeles Ghetto, 1890–1930." *Pacific Historical Review* 39, no. 3 (August 1970): 323–52.

De Graaf, Lawrence B., Kevin Mulroy, and Quintard Taylor, eds. *Seeking Eldorado: African Americans in California*. Los Angeles: Autry Museum of Western Heritage in association with University of Washington Press, 2001.

Dudziak, Mary L. *Cold War Civil Rights: Race and the Image of American Democracy*. Princeton: Princeton University Press, 2000.

Duus, Peter. *Modern Japan*. 2nd ed. Boston: Houghton Mifflin, 1998.

Endo, Akira. "Fukushi zaigen no futan o meguru sōten." *Jurisuto: Rinzi zōkan* Tokyo: Yuhikaku, 1964: 44–50.

Endo, Fumio. "Chiikiteki rentai ishiki to komyunitī." *Chihō jichi* 294 (1972): 2–14.

Esping-Andersen, Gosta. *The Three Worlds of Welfare Capitalism*. Cambridge, Mass.: Polity Press, 1990.

———, ed. *Welfare States in Transition: National Adaptations in Global Economies*. London: Sage Publications, 1996.

Faison, Elyssa. *Managing Women: Disciplining Labor in Modern Japan*. Berkeley: University of California Press, 2007.

Feldstein, Ruth. *Motherhood in Black and White: Race and Sex in American Liberalism, 1930–1965*. Ithaca, N.Y.: Cornell University Press, 2000.

Flamming, Douglas. *Bound for Freedom: Black Los Angeles in Jim Crow America*. Berkeley: University of California Press, 2005.

Fluck, Winfried, Donald E. Pease, and John Carlos Rowe, eds. *Re-Framing the Transnational Turn in American Studies*. Hanover, N.H.: Dartmouth College Press, 2011.

Fogelson, Robert M. *The Fragmented Metropolis: Los Angeles, 1850–1930*. Berkeley: University of California Press, 1967.

———, comp. *The Los Angeles Riots: Mass Violence in America*. New York: Arno Press and the *New York Times*, 1969.

Fōramu 90s Kenkyū Iinkai, ed. *20 seiki no seiji shisō to shakai undo*. Tokyo: Shakai Hyōronsha, 1998.

Fraser, Nancy, and Linda Gordon. "A Genealogy of *Dependency*: Tracing a Keyword of the U.S. Welfare State." *Signs: Journal of Women in Culture and Society* 19, no. 2 (1994): 309–36.

Freer, Regina. "L.A. Race Woman: Charlotta Bass and the Complexities of Black Political Development in Los Angeles." Special issue (Los Angeles and the Future of Urban Cultures), *American Quarterly* 56, no. 3 (September 2004): 607–32.

Frieden, Bernard J., and Marshall Kaplan. *The Politics of Neglect: Urban Aid from Model Cities to Revenue Sharing*. Cambridge, Mass.: MIT Press, 1975.

Frühstück, Sabine. *Colonizing Sex: Sexology and Social Control in Modern Japan*. Berkeley: University of California Press, 2003.

Fujitani, Takashi. "Korosu kenri, ikasu kenri: Ajia-taiheiyō sensōka no Nihonjin to shite no Chōsenjin to Amerikajin to shite no Nihonjin." In *Dōin, teikō, yokusan* (vol. 3, *Iwanami kōza: Ajia-taiheiyō sensō*), edited by Kurasawa Aiko et al., 181–216. Tokyo: Iwanami Shoten, 2006.

———. *Race for Empire: Koreans as Japanese and Japanese as Americans during World War II*. Berkeley: University of California Press, 2011.

———. "Right to Kill, Right to Make Live: Koreans as Japanese and Japanese as Americans during WWII." *Representations* 99 (Summer 2007): 13–39.

———. "Senka no jinshushugi: Dainiji taisenki no 'Chōsen shusshin Nihon kokumin' to 'Nikkei Amerikajin.'" In *Kanjō, kioku, sensō* (vol. 8, *Iwanami kōza: Kindai Nihon no bunkashi*), edited by Chino Kaori, Narita Ryuichi, Sakai Naoki, Shimazono Susumu, and Yoshimi Shunya, 235–80. Tokyo: Iwanami Shoten, 2002.

Fujiwara Shoten Henshūbu. *Rekishi no naka no "Zainichi."* Tokyo: Fujiwara Shoten, 2005.

Fukuoka, Yasunori. *Lives of Young Koreans in Japan*. Translated by Tom Gill. Melbourne, Australia: Trans Pacific Press, 2000.

Furer, Howard B., ed. *Lyndon B. Johnson, 1908–: Chronology—Documents—Bibliographical Aids*. Dobbs Ferry, N.Y.: Oceana, 1971.

Gaines, Kevin K. *American Africans in Ghana: Black Expatriates and the Civil Rights Era*. Chapel Hill: University of North Carolina Press, 2006.

Galbraith, John K. *The Affluent Society*. Boston: Houghton Mifflin, 1958.

García, Matt. *A World of Its Own: Race, Labor, and Citrus in the Making of Greater Los Angeles, 1900–1970*. Chapel Hill: University of North Carolina Press, 2001.

Garon, Sheldon. *Molding Japanese Minds: The State in Everyday Life*. Princeton: Princeton University Press, 1997.

———. *The State and Labor in Modern Japan*. Berkeley: University of California Press, 1987.

Gayle, Curtis Anderson. *Women's History and Local Community in Postwar Japan*. New York: Routledge, 2010.

George, Lynell. *No Crystal Stair: African-Americans in the City of Angeles*. London: Verso, 1992.

Germany, Kent B. *New Orleans after the Promises: Poverty, Citizenship, and the Search for the Great Society*. Athens: University of Georgia Press, 2007.

Gilens, Martin. *Why Americans Hate Welfare: Race, Media, and the Politics of Antipoverty Policy*. Chicago: University of Chicago Press, 1999.

Gilmore, Glenda Elizabeth. *Gender & Jim Crow: Women and the Politics of White Supremacy in North Carolina, 1896–1920*. Chapel Hill: University of North Carolina Press, 1996.

Glen, Evelyn Nakano. *Unequal Freedom: How Race and Gender Shaped American Citizenship and Labor*. Cambridge, Mass.: Harvard University Press, 2002.

Gluck, Carol. *Rekishi de kangaeru*. Translated by Umezaki Toru. Tokyo: Iwanami Shoten, 2007.

Goldberg, David Theo. *The Racial State*. Malden, Mass.: Blackwell, 2002.

Goldberg, Gertrude Schaffner, and Eleanor Kremen, eds. *The Feminization of Poverty: Only in America?* New York: Greenwood Press, 1990.

Goldstein, Alyosha. *Poverty in Common: The Politics of Community Action during the American Century*. Durham, N.C.: Duke University Press, 2012.

Goodwin, Doris Kearns. *Lyndon Johnson and the American Dream*. New York: St. Martin's Griffin, 1976.

Gordon, Andrew, ed. *Postwar Japan as History*. Berkeley: University of California Press, 1993.

Gordon, Colin. *New Deals: Business, Labor, and Politics in America, 1920–1935*. Cambridge: Cambridge University Press, 1994.

Gordon, Linda. "Who Deserves Help? Who Must Provide?" *Annals of the American Academy of Political and Social Science* 577 (September 2001): 12–25.

———, ed. *Women, the State, and Welfare*. Madison: University of Wisconsin Press, 1990.

Greene, Christina. *Our Separate Ways: Women and the Black Freedom Movement in Durham, North Carolina*. Chapel Hill: University of North Carolina Press, 2005.

Greenstone, J. David, and Paul E. Peterson. *Race and Authority in Urban Politics: Community Participation and the War on Poverty*. 1973. Reprint, Chicago: University of Chicago Press, 1978.

Gunther, John J. *Federal-City Relations in the United States: The Role of the Mayors in Federal Aid to Cities*. Newark: University of Delaware Press, 1990.

Haider, Donald H. "Governors and Mayors View the Poverty Program." *Current History* 61, no. 362 (October 1971): 273–78, 302, 303.

Hall, Stuart. "Gramsci's Relevance for the Study of Race and Ethnicity." *Journal of Communication Inquiry* 10, no. 2 (1986): 5–27.

Harajiri, Hideki. *Zainichi Chōsenjin no Seikatsu Sekai*. Tokyo: Koubundou, 1989.

Harajiri, Hideki, Rokutanda Yutaka, Tonomura Masaru, eds. *Nihon to Chōsen Hikaku Kōryūshi Nyūmon: Kinsei, kindai soshite gendai*. Tokyo: Akashi Shoten, 2011.

Harrington, Michael. *The Other America*. New York: Macmillan, 1962.

Harrison, Bennett. "The Participation of Ghetto Residents in the Model Cities Program." *Journal of the American Institute of Planners* 39, no. 1 (January 1973): 43–55.

Hastings, Sally Ann. *Neighborhood and Nation in Tokyo, 1905–1937*. Pittsburgh: University of Pittsburgh Press, 1995.

Hayase, Noboru. "Fukushi to iu souchi." In *Ekkyo suru chi 4: Souchi: Kowashi kizuku*, edited by Kurihara Akira, Komori Yoichi, Sato Manabu, and Yoshimi Shunya, 199–221. Tokyo: University of Tokyo Press, 2000.

Higginbotham, Evelyn Brooks. *Righteous Discontent: The Women's Movement in the Black Baptist Church, 1880–1920*. Cambridge: Harvard University Press, 1993.

Higuchi, Hayumi, ed. *Ryūdō suru 'kokujin' komyunitī: Amerikashi o tou*. Tokyo: Sairyusha, 2012.

Higuchi, Yuichi. "Kawasaki shi Ōhin chiku Chōsenjin no seikatsu jōkyō: 1955 nen zengo o chūshin ni." *Kaikyō* 20 (2000): 62–71.

———. "Nihon no chiiki shakai to *zainichi* Chōsenjin: Kanagawa keniki o chūshin ni." *Chōsenshi kenkyūkai ronbunshū* 37 (1990): 5–20.

Hirsch, Arnold R. *Making the Second Ghetto: Race and Housing in Chicago, 1940–1960*. 1983. Reprint, Chicago: University of Chicago Press, 1998.

Hones, Sheila, and Julia Leyda. "Geographies of American Studies." *American Quarterly* 57, no. 4 (December 2005): 1019–32.

Honey, Michael K. *Going Down Jericho Road: The Memphis Strike, Martin Luther King's Last Campaign*. New York: W. W. Norton, 2007.

———. *Southern Labor and Black Civil Rights: Organizing Memphis Workers*. Urbana: University of Illinois Press, 1993.

Horne, Gerald. *Fire This Time: The Watts Uprising and the 1960s*. 1995. Reprint, New York: Da Capo Press, 1997.

Hoshino, Osami. *Jichitai no henkaku to zainichi Korian: Kyōsei no shisaku zukuri to sono kunō*. Tokyo: Akashi Shoten, 2005.

Hunt, Darnell, and Ana-Christina Ramōn, eds. *Black Los Angeles: American Dreams and Racial Realities*. New York: New York University Press, 2010.

Hyun, Mooam. "Mikkō, Ōmura shūyōjo, Saishūtō: Osaka to Saishūtō o musubu 'mikkō' nettowāku." *Gendai shisō* 35, no. 7 (June 2007): 158–73.

I, Son Jon, and Sato Yumi. "Zainichi Korian issei no gakkou keiken: Lee In Ha shi no baai." *Shokuminchi kyōikushi kenkyūkai no korekara (Shokuminchi kyōikushi kenkyū nenpō)* 10 (2007): 58–73.

Ito, Saburo. *Nomi to kanaduchi*. Tokyo: Daiichi Hōki Shuppan, 1982.

Iwasaki, Minoru, Ueno Chizuko, Kitada Akihiro, Komori Yoichi, and Narita Ryuichi, eds. *Sengo Nihon stadīzu*. Vol. 2, *"60/70" nendai*. Tokyo: Kinokuniya Shoten, 2009.

Jacobs, Ronald N. *Race, Media and the Crisis of Civil Society: From Watts to Rodney King*. Cambridge: Cambridge University Press, 2000.

James, Joy, and T. Denean Sharpley-Whiting, eds. *The Black Feminist Reader*. Malden, Mass.: Blackwell, 2000.

Johnson, Benjamin H., and Andrew R. Graybill, eds. *Bridging National Borders in North America: Transnational and Comparative Histories*. Durham, N.C.: Duke University Press, 2010.

Johnson, Chalmers. *MITI and the Japanese Miracle: The Growth of Industrial Policy, 1925–1975*. Stanford: Stanford University Press, 1982.

Johnson, Lyndon Baines. *The Vantage Point: Perspectives of the Presidency, 1963–1969*. New York: Holt, Rinehart and Winston, 1971.

Joseph, Miranda. *Against the Romance of Community*. Minneapolis: University of Minnesota Press, 2002.

Jung, Moon-Ho. *Coolies and Cane: Race, Labor, and Sugar in the Age of Emancipation*. Baltimore: Johns Hopkins University Press, 2006.

Jung, Yeong-hae. *Tamigayo seishō: Aidentitī, kokumin kokka, jendā*. Tokyo: Iwanami Shoten, 2003.

Kajiwara, Hisashi. "Daisan sekai to kaihō no shingaku." *Nagoya gakuin ronshū* 17, no. 1 (1980): 23–42.

———. "Jeimuzu Kōn no 'kokujin shingaku' ni okeru monogatari no koō ni tsuite." *Jitsuzon shugi* 86 (1979): 64–74.

———. *Kaihō no shingaku*. Tokyo: Simizu Shoin, 1997.

———. "Kaihō no shingaku ni okeru kunan no igi." *Nagoya gakuin ronshū* 20, no. 1 (1983): 97–110.

———. "The Meaning of Heaven in Cone's Theology." *Nagoya gakuin ronshū* 11, no. 2 (1974): 123–36.

———. "On the Social Responsibility of Christians: A Response to Liberation Theology." *Nagoya gakuin ronshū* 17, no. 2 (1981): 59–70.

———. "Saikin no burakku seorojī rikai eno ichi shiron." *Nagoya gakuin ronshū* 11, no. 1 (1974): 35–62.

Kamioka, Namiko. *Nihon no kōgaishi*. Tokyo: Sekai Shobō, 1987.

Kanagawa Shinbunsha Shakaibu. *Nihon no naka no gaikokujin: Hitosashi yubi no jiyū o motomete*. Yokohama: Kanagawa Shinbun Shuppankyoku, 1985.

Kanagawa to Chōsen no Kankeishi Chōsaiinkai. *Kanagawa to Chōsen*. Yokohama: Kanagawaken Shōgaibu, 1994.

Kang, Sang-jung. *Orientarizumu no kanata e*. Tokyo: Iwanami Shoten, 1996.

Karenga, Maulana. *Essays on Struggle: Position and Analysis*. San Diego: Kawaida Publications, 1978.

———. *Kwanzaa: Origin, Concepts, Practice*. Inglewood, Calif.: Kawaida Publications, 1977.

Kato, Chikako. "1970 nendai Nihon no 'minzoku sabetsu' o meguru undō: Hitachi tōsō o chūshin ni." *Jinmin no rekishigaku* 185 (2010): 13–24.

Kato, Haruko. "Kawasaki Shinyo Kinko minzoku sabetsu jiken." *Chōsen kenkyū* 180 (1978): 39–44.

Katsuyama, Masae. "Hitachi shūshoku sabetsu saiban shien katsudō ni okeru Nihonjin seinen no kenkyū: Shinriteki kattō to jiko henkaku no katei." MA thesis, Ochanomizu University, 2004.

Katz, Michael B. *In the Shadow of the Poorhouse: A Social History of Welfare in America*. New York: Basic Books, 1986.

———. *The Price of Citizenship: Redefining the American Welfare State*. New York: Henry Holt, 2001.

———. *The Undeserving Poor: From the War on Poverty to the War on Welfare*. New York: Pantheon Books, 1989.

Kawai, Katsuyoshi. "Chiiki fukushi no seisaku tenkai: Sengo Nihon no chiiki seisaku to chiiki fukushi." In *Chiiki fukushi*, edited by Makisato Tsuneji, Noguchi Sadahisa, and Kawai Katsuyoshi, 77–98. Tokyo: Yuhikaku, 1995.

Kawanaka, Niko. "Fukushi seisaku no kettei katei." In *Jurisuto: Rinji zōkan*. Tokyo: Yuhikaku, 1973: 68–72.

Kawasaki Chihō Jichi Kenkyū Sentā. *Kawasaki shimin jichi no jikken 1971–2001: Shiryō Ito/Takahashi shisei*. Kawasaki: Kawasaki Chihō Jichi Kenkyū Sentā, 2003.

Kawasaki Kyōkai. *Kawasaki kyōkai 50 nenshi*. Kawasaki: Kawasaki Kyōkai, 1997.

Kayama, Dan. "Toshi no zainichi gaikokujin komyunitī o meguru chiiki fukushi kadai ni tsuite no kōsatsu (1): Kawasaki shi ni okeru jirei o motoni." *Toyo daigaku shakai gakubu kiyō* 45, no. 1 (2007): 109–22.

Kelley, Robin D. G. "'But a Local Phase of a World Problem': Black History's Global Vision." *Journal of American History* 86, no. 3 (December 1999): 1045–77.

———. *Freedom Dreams: The Black Radical Imagination*. Boston: Beacon Press, 2002.

———. *Race Rebels: Culture, Politics, and the Black Working Class*. New York: Free Press, 1994.

———. *YO' Mama's DisFUNKtional! Fighting the Culture Wars in Urban America*. Boston: Beacon Press, 1997.

Kessler-Harris, Alice. *In Pursuit of Equity: Women, Men, and the Quest for Economic Citizenship in 20th-century America.* New York: Oxford University Press, 2001.

Kim, Chan-jung. *Zainichi Korian hyakunenshi.* Tokyo: Sangokan, 1997.

Kim, Elaine H., and Chungmoo Choi, eds. *Dangerous Women: Gender and Korean Nationalism.* New York: Routledge, 1998.

Kim, Jimi. *Fukushi kokka taisei kakuritsuki ni okeru jichitai fukushi seisaku katei.* Tokyo: Kōjinsha, 2006.

Kim, Nadia Y. *Imperial Citizens: Koreans and Race from Seoul to LA.* Stanford: Stanford University Press, 2008.

Kim, Puja. *Keizoku suru shokuminchi shugi to jendā: "Kokumin" gainen, josei no shintai, kioku to sekinin.* Yokohama: Seori Shobo, 2011.

Kim, T'ae-gi. *Sengo Nihon seiji to zainichi Chōsenjin mondai.* Tokyo: Keisō Shobō, 1997.

Kim, Yun-jeong. *Tabunka kyōsei to aidentitī.* Tokyo: Akashi Shoten, 2007.

———. "Zainichi Kankoku Chōsenjin no aidentitī keisei to tabunka kyōsei kyōiku ni kansuru kenkyū: Kawasaki shi fureaikan no setsuritsu to shakai kyōiku katsudō no tenkai o chūshin ni." PhD diss., University of Tokyo, 2006.

Kimura, Hitoshi. "Eikoku no komyunitī kaihatsu jigyō." *Chihō jichi* 302 (January 1973): 50–57.

———. "Komyunitī taisaku." *Chihō jichi* 275 (October 1970): 10–21.

———. "Komyunitī taisaku no kinkyō to kadai." *Chihō jichi* 286 (September 1971): 25–36.

———. "Komyunitī taisaku no mondaiten." *Chihō jichi* 276 (November 1970): 30–36.

———. "Shōwa 47 nendo no komyunitī taisaku ni tsuite." *Chihō jichi* 295 (June 1972): 56–71.

Klaus, Alisa. *Every Child a Lion: The Origins of Maternal and Infant Health Policy in the United States and France, 1890–1920.* Ithaca, N.Y.: Cornell University Press, 1993.

Klein, Norman M., and Martin J. Schiesl, eds. *20th Century Los Angeles: Power, Promotion, and Social Conflict.* Claremont, Calif.: Regina Books, 1990.

Kobayashi, Takao, ed. *Kawasaki minshū no ayumi: Meiji, Taishō, Shōwa.* Kawasaki: Tamagawa Shinbunsha, 1995.

Komagome, Takeshi. "Nihon no shokuminchi shihai to kindai: Orikasanaru bōryoku." *Toreishīzu (Shisō, bessatsu)* 2 (August 2001): 159–97.

Kondo, Atsushi. *Gaikokujin sanseiken to kokuseki,* new ed. Tokyo: Akashi Shoten, 2001.

Kornbluh, Felicia. *The Battle for Welfare Rights: Politics and Poverty in Modern America.* Philadelphia: University of Pennsylvania Press, 2007.

———. "To Fulfill Their 'Rightly Needs': Consumerism and the National Welfare Rights Movement." *Radical History Review* 69 (Fall 1997): 76–113.

Koseki, Shoichi. *Nihonkoku kenpō no tanjō*. Tokyo: Iwanami Shoten, 2009.

Koshiro, Yukiko. "Beyond an Alliance of Color: The African American Impact on Modern Japan." *positions: east asia cultures critique* 11, no. 1 (Spring 2003): 183–216.

Kotz, Nick, and Mary Lynn Kotz. *A Passion for Equality: George A. Wiley and the Movement*. New York: W. W. Norton, 1977.

Koven, Seth, and Sonya Michel, eds. *Mothers of a New World: Maternalist Politics and the Origins of Welfare States*. New York: Routledge, 1993.

———. "Womanly Duties: Maternalist Politics and the Origins of Welfare States in France, Germany, Great Britain, and the United States, 1880–1920." *American Historical Review* 95, no. 4 (October 1990): 1076–1108.

Kubic, Micah W. "Between Malcolm and Martin: James Cone's Black Theology as Pragmatic Ideological Alternative." *Souls* 11, no. 4 (December 2009): 448–67.

Kurasawa, Susumu. *Komyunitī ron*. Tokyo: Open University of Japan (Hōsō daigaku) Press, 1998.

Kurasawa, Susumu, and Akimoto Ritsuo, eds. *Chōnaikai to chiiki shūdan*. Kyoto: Minerva Shobo, 1990.

Kurashige, Scott. *The Shifting Grounds of Race: Black and Japanese Americans in the Making of Multiethnic Los Angeles*. Princeton: Princeton University Press, 2010.

Kurokawa, Midori. *Ika to dōka no aida: Hisabetsu buraku ninshiki no kiseki*. Tokyo: Aoki Shoten, 1999.

———. *Kindai burakushi: Meiji kara gendai made*. Tokyo: Heibonsha, 2011.

Kusmer, Kenneth L. "African Americans in the City since World War II: From the Industrial to the Post-Industrial Era." *Journal of Urban History* 21, no. 4 (May 1995): 458–504.

Kwak, Nancy Haekyung. "A Citizen's Right to Decent Shelter: Public Housing in New York, London, and Singapore, 1945–1970." PhD diss., Columbia University, 2006.

Kwon, Young-Joo. "Chōnaikai no sengo kaikaku (1)." *Hōgaku ronsō (Department of Law, Kyoto University)* 135, no. 1 (1994): 45–67.

———. "Chōnaikai no sengo kaikaku (2)." *Hōgaku ronsō* (Department of Law, Kyoto University) 135, no. 6 (1994): 67–89.

Ladd-Taylor, Molly. *Mother-Work: Women, Child Welfare, and the State, 1890–1930*. Urbana: University of Illinois Press, 1994.

Laslett, John H. M. *Sunshine Was Never Enough: Los Angeles Workers, 1880–2010*. Berkeley: University of California Press, 2012.

Lee, Changsoo, and George De Vos, eds. *Koreans in Japan: Ethnic Conflict and Accommodation*. Berkeley: University of California Press, 1981.

Lee, In Ha. *Asuni ikiru kiryū no tami*. Tokyo: Shinkyō Shuppansha, 1987.

———. "Jinshu sabetsu to tatakau kyōkai." *Chōsen kenkyū* 100 (1970): 41–46.

———. *Kiryū no tami no sakebi*. Tokyo: Shinkyō Shuppansha, 1979.

———. *Rekishi no hazama o ikiru*. Tokyo: Nihon Kirisuto Kyōdan Shuppankyoku, 2006.

———. "Seikyusha: Minzoku sabetsu to tatakai ningen shutai no kakuritsu o mezashite." *Kaihōkyōiku* 135 (April 1981): 56–68.

Leonard, Kevin Allen. *The Battle for Los Angeles: Racial Ideology and World War II*. Albuquerque: University of New Mexico Press, 2006.

Levenstein, Lisa. *A Movement without Marches: African American Women and the Politics of Poverty in Postwar Philadelphia*. Chapel Hill: University of North Carolina Press, 2009.

Levitan, Sar A. *The Great Society's Poor Law: A New Approach to Poverty*. Baltimore: Johns Hopkins Press, 1969.

Lichtenstein, Nelson. *The Most Dangerous Man in Detroit: Walter Reuther and the Fate of American Labor*. New York: Basic Books, 1995.

Lie, John. *Multiethnic Japan*. Cambridge: Harvard University Press, 2001.

———. *Zainichi (Koreans in Japan): Diasporic Nationalism and Postcolonial Identity*. Berkeley: University of California Press, 2008.

Lieberman, Robert C. *Shifting the Color Line: Race and the American Welfare State*. Cambridge: Harvard University Press, 1998.

Ling, Peter J., and Sharon Monteith, eds. *Gender and the Civil Rights Movement*. New Brunswick, N.J.: Rutgers University Press, 1999.

Lipsitz, George. *American Studies in a Moment of Danger*. Minneapolis: University of Minnesota Press, 2001.

———. *A Life in the Struggle: Ivory Perry and the Culture of Opposition*. Philadelphia: Temple University Press, 1988.

———. *Midnight at the Barrelhouse: The Johnny Otis Story*. Minneapolis: University of Minnesota Press, 2010.

———. *The Possessive Investment in Whiteness: How White People Profit from Identity Politics*. Philadelphia: Temple University Press, 1998.

———. *Rainbow at Midnight: Labor and Culture in the 1940s*. Urbana: University of Illinois Press, 1994.

Long, Charles H. "Perspectives for a Study of Afro-American Religion in the United States." *History of Religions* 11, no. 1 (August 1971): 54–66.

MacDonald, Dwight. "Our Invisible Poor." *New Yorker*, January 19, 1963, 82–132.

Mackie, Vera. *Feminism in Modern Japan: Citizenship, Embodiment and Sexuality*. Cambridge: Cambridge University Press, 2003.

Majima, Masahide. "Komyunitī to jichitai nai bunken: Jūmin jichi no kiso tani no saikouchiku." In *Kōiki to kyōiki no gyōsei seido*, edited by Ito Yuichiro, 347–69. Tokyo: Gyōsei, 1997.

Mansbridge, Jane, and Aldon Morris, eds. *Oppositional Consciousness: The Subjective Roots of Social Protest*. Chicago: University of Chicago Press, 2001.

Marable, Manning, and Vanessa Agard-Jones, eds. *Transnational Blackness: Navigating the Global Color Line*. New York: Palgrave Macmillan, 2008.

Marshall, Dale Rogers. *The Politics of Participation in Poverty: A Case Study of the Board of the Economic and Youth Opportunities Agency of Greater Los Angeles*. Berkeley: University of California Press, 1971.

Martin, Marguerite V. *Social Protest in an Urban Barrio: A Study of the Chicano Movement, 1966–1974*. Lanham: University Press of America, 1991.

Massey, Douglas S., and Nancy A. Denton. *American Apartheid: Segregation and the Making of the Underclass*. 1993. Reprint, Cambridge, Mass.: Harvard University Press, 1996.

Masur, Katherine. *An Example for All the Land: Emancipation and the Struggle over Equality in Washington, D.C.* Chapel Hill: University of North Carolina Press, 2010.

Matsubara, Haruo, ed. *Jūmin sanka to jichi no kakushin*. Tokyo: Gakuyō Shobō, 1974.

———. *Komyunitī no riron to jissen*. Tokyo: Gakken, 1976.

———. *Komyunitī no shakaigaku*. Tokyo: University of Tokyo Press, 1978.

McMillian, John, and Paul Buhle, eds. *The New Left Revisited*. Philadelphia: Temple University Press, 2003.

Melnick, R. Shep. *Between the Lines: Interpreting Welfare Rights*. Washington, DC: Brookings Institution, 1994.

Michiba, Chikanobu. *Senryō to heiwa: "Sengo" to iu keiken*. Tokyo: Seidosha, 2005.

Mieno, Takashi, and Koichi Hiraoka, eds. *Fukushi seisaku no riron to jissai: Fukushi shakaigaku kenkyū nyūmon*. Tokyo: Toshindo, 2000.

Mikuni, Keiko. "Kawasaki shi no zainichi Kankoku Chōsenjin: Shūjū katei to jinkō." *Josai daigaku daigakuin kenkyū nenpō* 16, no. 1 (1999): 5–17.

Minagawa, Masaki. "Neoriberaru Tokyo: Toshi to 'shimin' ni tsuiteno hōhōronteki oboegaki." *Rekishigaku kenkyū* 886 (November 2011): 42–52.

Mink, Gwendolyn. *The Wages of Motherhood: Inequality in the Welfare State, 1917–1942*. Ithaca, N.Y.: Cornell University Press, 1995.

Mitchell, Richard H. *The Korean Minority in Japan*. Berkeley: University of California Press, 1967.

Miyazawa, Hiroshi. "Komyunitī ni tsuite." *Chihō jichi* 266 (1970): 2–9.

Mohanty, Chandra Talpade. *Feminism without Borders: Decolonizing Theory, Practicing Solidarity*. Durham, N.C.: Duke University Press, 2003.

Molina, Natalia. *Fit to Be Citizens? Public Health and Race in Los Angeles, 1879–1939*. Berkeley: University of California Press, 2006.

Morimura, Michiyoshi. *Komyunitī no keikaku gihō*. Tokyo: Shokokusha, 1978.

Morris-Suzuki, Tessa. *Borderline Japan: Foreigners and Frontier Controls in the Postwar Era*. Cambridge: Cambridge University Press, 2010.

———. *Exodus to North Korea: Shadows from Japan's Cold War*. Lanham, Md.: Rowman and Littlefield, 2007.

———. *Hihanteki sōzōryoku no tameni: Gurōbaruka jidai no Nihon*. Tokyo: Heibonsha, 2002.

———. *Re-Inventing Japan: Time, Space, Nation*. Armonk, N.Y.: M. E. Sharpe, 1998.

Moynihan, Daniel P. *Maximum Feasible Misunderstanding: Community Action in the War on Poverty*. New York: Free Press, 1969.

Mun, Gyong-su. "Kōdo keizai seichōka no zainichi Chōsenjin." *Kikan Seikyū* 22 (1995): 44–52.

———. *Zainichi Chōsenjin mondai no kigen*. Tokyo: Crane, 2007.

Muse, Benjamin. *The American Negro Revolution: From Nonviolence to Black Power 1963–1967*. Bloomington: Indiana University Press, 1968.

Nadasen, Premilla. *Welfare Warriors: The Welfare Rights Movement in the United States*. New York: Routledge, 2005.

Nadasen, Premilla, Jennifer Mittelstadt, and Marisa Chappell. *Welfare in the United States: A History with Documents, 1935–1996*. New York: Routledge, 2009.

Nagano, Shiro. "Kūsō chihō jichi ron: Kōiki gyōsei to komyunitī." *Chihō jichi* 230 (1967): 4–13.

Nakadaira, Kenkichi. "Zainichi Kankokujin mondai to kirisutosha no sekinin." *Fukuin to sekai* 11 (1969): 43–52.

Nakamura, Kiichi. "Jūmin undō no soshiki to kōzō." *Chiiki kaihatsu* 154 (1977): 22–32.

———. *Jyūmin undō "shi"ron: Jissensha kara mita jichi no shisō*. 1976. Reprint, Tokyo: Soudosha, 2005.

Nakamura, Rika. "What Asian American Studies Can Learn from Asia: Toward a Project of Comparative Minority Studies." *Inter-Asia Cultural Studies* 13, no. 2 (2012): 251–66.

Naples, Nancy A., ed. *Community Activism and Feminist Policies: Organizing across Race, Class, and Gender*. New York: Routledge, 1998.

———. *Grassroots Warriors: Activist Mothering, Community Work, and the War on Poverty*. New York: Routledge, 1998.

Narita, Ryuichi. *Sensō keiken no sengoshi: Katarareta taiken, shōgen, kioku*. Tokyo: Iwanami Shoten, 2010.

Neubeck, Kenneth J. *When Welfare Disappears: The Case for Economic Human Rights*. New York: Routledge, 2006.

Neubeck, Kenneth J., and Noel A. Cazenave. *Welfare Racism: Playing the Race Card against America's Poor*. New York: Routledge, 2001.

Nicolaides, Becky M. *My Blue Heaven: Life and Politics in the Working-Class Suburbs of Los Angeles, 1920–1965*. Chicago: University of Chicago Press, 2002.

Nihon Shakai Jigyō Daigaku. *Shakai fukushi no gendaiteki tenkai: Kōdo seichō ki kara tei seichō ki e*. Tokyo: Keisō Shobō, 1986.

Nishio, Masaru. "Chiiki fukushi to shimin jichi: Jakkan no ronten teiki." *Shakai fukushi kenkyū* 24 (April 1979): 50–55.

———. *Kenryoku to sanka: Gendai Amerika no toshi gyōsei* [Power and Participation: Municipal Administration in Contemporary America]. Tokyo: University of Tokyo Press, 1975.

Noble, David W. *Death of a Nation: American Culture and the End of Exceptionalism*. Minneapolis: University of Minnesota Press, 2002.

Ochiai, Emiko. *21 seiki kazoku e: Kazoku no sengo taisei no mikata/koekata*. Tokyo: Yūhikaku Sensho, 1994.

O'Connor, Alice. *Poverty Knowledge: Social Science, Social Policy, and the Poor in Twentieth-Century U.S. History*. Princeton: Princeton University Press, 2001.

Oguma, Eiji. *A Genealogy of "Japanese" Self-Images*. Melbourne: Trans Pacific Press, 2002.

———. *"Minshu" to "Aikoku": Sengo Nihon no nashonarizumu to kōkyōsei*. Tokyo: Shinyōsha, 2002.

———. *Nihonjin no kyōkai: Okinawa, Ainu, Taiwan, Chōsen: Shokuminchi shihai kara fukki undō made*. Tokyo: Shinyōsha, 1998.

———. *1968*. Tokyo: Shinyōsha, 2009.

———. *Tanitsu minzoku shinwa no kigen: "Nihonjin" no jigazō no keifu*. Tokyo: Shinyōsha, 1995.

Omori, Wataru, ed. *Chiiki fukushi to jichitai gyōsei*. Tokyo: Gyōsei, 2002.

———. "Gendai gyōsei ni okeru 'jūmin sanka' no tenkai—1960 nendai Amerika ni okeru 'komyunitī katsudō jigyō' no dōnyū to henyō." In *Gendai gyōsei to kanryōsei*, vol. 1, edited by Taniuchi Yuzuru, 267–325. Tokyo: University of Tokyo Press, 1974.

———. "Jūmin undō no tenkai katei." *Chiiki kaihatsu* 154 (1977): 13–21.

———. "Jūmin undō to chihō seiji katei." *Chiiki kaihatsu* 134 (1975): 15–27.

Ong, Paul, ed. *The Widening Divide: Income Inequality and Poverty in Los Angeles*. Los Angeles: University of California, Los Angeles, Graduate School of Architecture and Urban Planning, 1989.

Onuma, Yasuaki. *Zainichi Kankoku/Chōsenjin no kokuseki to jinken*. Tokyo: Tōshindō, 2004.

Orleck, Annelise. *Storming Caesar's Palace: How Black Mothers Fought Their Own War on Poverty*. Boston: Beacon, 2005.

Orleck, Annelise, and Lisa Gayle Hazirjian, eds. *The War on Poverty: A New Grassroots History, 1964–1980*. Athens: University of Georgia Press, 2011.

Orloff, Ann Shola. "Gender and the Social Rights of Citizenship: The Comparative Analysis of Gender Relations and Welfare States." *American Sociological Review* 58, no. 3 (June 1993): 303–28.

Pagán, Eduardo Obregón. *Murder at the Sleepy Lagoon: Zoot Suits, Race, and Riot in Wartime L.A.* Chapel Hill: University of North Carolina Press, 2003.

Pak, Kyŏng-sik. *Kaihōgo zainichi Chōsenjin undōshi*. Tokyo: San-ichi Shobō, 1989.

———. *Nihon teikokushugi no Chōsen shihai*. Tokyo: Aoki Shoten, 1973.

Park, Chong-Myong, ed. *Zainichi Chōsenjin: Rekishi, genjō, tenbō*. 2nd ed. Tokyo: Akashi Shoten, 1999.

Park-kun o Kakomu Kai, ed. *Minzoku sabetsu: Hitachi shūshoku sabetsu kyūdan*. Tokyo: Aki Shobō, 1974.

Patterson, James T. *America's Struggle against Poverty 1900–1994*. Cambridge: Harvard University Press, 1994.

Payne, Charles M. *I've Got the Light of Freedom: The Organizing Tradition and the Mississippi Freedom Struggle*. Berkeley: University of California Press, 1995.

Payne, J. Gregory, and Scott C. Ratzan. *Tom Bradley: The Impossible Dream*. Santa Monica, Calif.: Roundtable, 1986.

Pearce, Diane. "The Feminization of Poverty: Women, Work, and Welfare." *The Urban and Social Change Review* 11, nos. 1 and 2 (1978): 28–36.

Pease, Donald E., and Robyn Wiegman, eds. *The Future of American Studies*. Durham, N.C.: Duke University Press, 2002.

Peterson, Paul E., and J. David Greenstone. "Racial Change and Citizen Participation: The Mobilization of Low-Income Communities through Community Action." In *A Decade of Federal Antipoverty Programs: Achievements, Failures, and Lessons*, edited by Robert H. Haveman, 241–78. New York: Academic Press, 1977.

Pierson, Christopher. *Beyond the Welfare State?* Oxford: Basil Blackwell Limited, 1991.

Piven, Frances Fox, and Richard A. Cloward. *Poor People's Movements: Why They Succeed, How They Fail*. 1977. Reprint, New York: Vintage Books, 1979.

———. *Regulating the Poor: The Functions of Public Welfare*. New York: Pantheon Books, 1971.

Plant, Rebecca Jo. *Mom: The Transformation of Motherhood in Modern America*. Chicago: University of Chicago Press, 2010.

Pritchett, Wendell. *Brownsville, Brooklyn: Blacks, Jews, and the Changing Face of the Ghetto*. Chicago: University of Chicago Press, 2002.

Pulido, Laura. *Black, Brown, Yellow, and Left: Radical Activism in Los Angeles*. Berkeley: University of California Press, 2006.

Quadagno, Jill. *The Color of Welfare: How Racism Undermined the War on Poverty*. New York: Oxford University Press, 1995.

———. "Promoting Civil Rights through the Welfare State: How Medicare Integrated Southern Hospitals." *Social Problems* 47, no. 1 (February 2000): 68–89.

Quadagno, Jill, and Catherine Fobes. "The Welfare State and the Cultural Reproduction of Gender: Making Good Girls and Boys in the Job Corps." *Social Problems* 42, no. 2 (May 1995): 171–90.

Ragsdale, Bruce A., and Joel D. Treese. *Black Americans in Congress, 1870–1989*. Washington, DC: U.S. Government Printing Office, 1990.

Rekishigaku Kenkyūkai, Nihonshi Kenkyūkai. *Nihonshi kōza*. Vol. 10, *Sengo Nihon hen*. Tokyo: University of Tokyo Press, 2005.

Roberts, J. Deotis. *Liberation and Reconciliation*. Philadelphia: Westminster Press, 1971.

Roediger, David R. *The Wages of Whiteness: Race and the Making of the American Working Class*. 1991. Revised, London: Verso, 1999.

Rose, Elizabeth. *A Mother's Job: The History of Day Care, 1890–1960*. New York: Oxford University Press, 1999.

Rosenthal, Nicolas G. *Reimagining Indian Country: Native American Migration and Identity in Twentieth-Century Los Angeles*. Chapel Hill: University of North Carolina Press, 2012.

Rowe, John Carlos, ed. *Post-Nationalist American Studies*. Berkeley: University of California Press, 2000.

Ryang, Sonia. "Inscribed (Men's) Bodies, Silent (Women's) Words: Rethinking Colonial Displacement of Koreans in Japan." *Bulletin of Concerned Asian Scholars* 30, no. 4 (1998): 3–15.

———. *Korian diasupora: Zainichi Chōsenjin to aidentitī*. Tokyo: Akashi Shoten, 2005.

———. *North Koreans in Japan: Language, Ideology, and Identity*. Boulder: Westview Press, 1997.

———. *Writing Selves in Diaspora: Ethnography of Autobiographics of Korean Women in Japan and the United States*. Lanham, Md.: Lexington Books, 2008.

Ryang, Sonia, ed. *Koreans in Japan: Critical Voices from the Margin*. London: Routledge, 2000.

Ryang, Sonia, and John Lie, eds. *Diaspora without Homeland: Being Koreans in Japan*. Berkeley: University of California Press, 2009.

Sakuma, Kosei. *Zainichi Korian to zaiei Airisshu: Ōrudo kamā to shimin to shite no kenri*. Tokyo: University of Tokyo Press, 2011.

Saruhashi, Junko. "Tagengo kyōseigata gengo keikaku to sono hattendankai shosō no shakai gengogakuteki kenkyū: Nihon no teijū gaikokujin ni yoru gengo iji doryoku to gyōseifu tono sōgo sayō o jirei to shite." PhD diss., Aoyama Gakuin University, 2004.

Sato, Atsushi. *Jūmin sanka o meguru mondai jirei*. Tokyo: Gakuyō Shobō, 1979.

———. "Jūmin undō to jichitai gyōsei." *Chiiki kaihatsu* 154 (1977): 43–55.

———. *Komyunitī o meguru mondai jirei*. Tokyo: Gakuyō Shobō, 1980.

Scott, Allen J., and Edward W. Soja, eds. *The City: Los Angeles and Urban Theory at the End of the Twentieth Century*. Berkeley: University of California Press, 1996.

Sears, David O., and John McConahay. *The Politics of Violence: The New Urban Blacks and the Watts Riot*. Boston: Houghton Mifflin, 1973.

Self, Robert O. *American Babylon: Race and the Struggle for Postwar Oakland*. Princeton: Princeton University Press, 2003.

Serizawa, Kiyoto, and Machii Hiroaki. *Ningen toshi e no fukken*. Tokyo: Gōdō Shuppan, 1975.

Shakai Hoshō Kenkyūjo, ed. *Gendai kazoku to shakai hoshō*. Tokyo: University of Tokyo Press, 1994.

Shimada, Shuichi. "Chihō jichi to jūmin no shutai keisei." *Kagaku to shisō* 32 (1979): 686–702.

Shinohara, Hajime. *Gendai toshi seisaku II: Shimin sanka*. Tokyo: Iwanami Shoten, 1973.

———. *Shimin sanka*. Tokyo: Iwanami Shoten, 1977.

Shriver, Sargent. *Point of the Lance*. New York: Harper and Row, 1964.

Sides, Josh. *L.A. City Limits: African American Los Angeles from the Great Depression to the Present*. Berkeley: University of California Press, 2003.

———, ed. *Post-Ghetto: Reimagining South Los Angeles*. Berkeley: Huntington-USC Institute on California and the West by University of California Press, 2012.

Singh, Nikhil Pal. *Black Is a Country: Race and the Unfinished Struggle for Democracy*. Cambridge, Mass.: Harvard University Press, 2004.

Sitton, Tom, and William Deverell, eds. *Metropolis in the Making: Los Angeles in the 1920s*. Berkeley: University of California Press, 2001.

Skocpol, Theda. *Protecting Soldiers and Mothers: The Political Origins of Social Policy in the United States*. Cambridge, Mass.: Harvard University Press, 1992.

Smethurst, Richard J. *A Social Basis for Prewar Japanese Militarism: The Army and the Rural Community*. Berkeley: University of California Press, 1974.

Soja, Edward W. *Postmodern Geographers: The Reassertion of Space in Critical Social Theory*. London: Verso, 1989.

———. *Thirdspace: Journeys to Los Angeles and Other Real-and-Imagined Places*. Cambridge: Blackwell, 1996.

Soja, Edward, Rebecca Morales, and Goetz Wolff. "Urban Restructuring: An Analysis of Social and Spatial Challenge in Los Angeles." *Economic Geography* 59 (1983): 195–230.

Somers, Margaret R. *Genealogies of Citizenship: Markets, Statelessness, and the Right to Have Rights*. Cambridge: Cambridge University Press, 2008.

Sonenshein, Raphael J. *Politics in Black and White: Race and Power in Los Angeles*. Princeton: Princeton University Press, 1993.

Song, An-jong. "'Koria kei Nihonjin'ka purojekuto no isō o saguru." *Gendaishisō* 35, no. 7 (June 2007): 225–39.

Song, Puja. *Aisuru toki kiseki wa tsukurareru: Zainichi sandai shi.* Tokyo: Sanichi Shobō, 2007.

Sugihara, Tatsu. *Ekkyō suru tami.* Tokyo: Shinkansha, 1998.

Sugrue, Thomas J. *The Origins of the Urban Crisis: Race and Inequality in Postwar Detroit.* Princeton: Princeton University Press, 1996.

———. *The Sweet Land of Liberty: The Forgotten Struggle for Civil Rights in the North.* New York: Random House, 2008.

Sundquist, James L. "Origins of the War on Poverty." In *On Fighting Poverty: Perspectives from Experience,* edited by James L. Sundquist, 6–33. New York: Basic Books, 1969.

Suzuki, Masahisa. "Kyōdan no sensō sekinin kokuhaku o ninatte," "Dainiji taisenka ni okeru Nihon kirisuto kyōdan no sensō sekinin ni tsuiteno kokuhaku." *Fukuin to sekai* 24 (1969): 1–8.

Takahashi, Mitsuru, Ishizawa Maki, and Naito Takafumi. "*Zainichi* Kankoku Chōsenjin no chiiki kyōiku undō to shakai kyōiku: Kawasaki shi 'Fureaikan' setsuritsu katei no jirei." *Tohoku daigaku kyōiku gakubu kenkyū nenpō* 44 (1996): 65–94.

Takegawa, Shogo, ed. *Shitizunshippu to Bēshikku Inkamu no kanōsei.* Kyoto: Horitsu Bunka Sha, 2008.

Takenoshita, Hirohisa. "Esunikku aidentitī no kattō to henyō: Hitachi shūshoku sabetsu saiban no Park Jong Seok shi no seikatsushi kara." *Kaihō shakaigaku kenkyū* 10 (1996): 33–55.

———. "Hitachi shūshoku sabetsu jiken o meguru *zainichi* Kankoku Chōsenjin no shakai undō: Park-kun o Kakomu Kai ni kansuru jirei kenkyū." MA thesis, Keio University, 1995.

Tamanoi, Mariko Asano. *Under the Shadow of Nationalism: Politics and Poetics of Rural Japanese Women.* Honolulu: University of Hawai'i Press, 1998.

Tanaka, Hiroshi. *Zainichi gaikoku-jin.* Tokyo: Iwanami Shoten, 1995.

Tanaka, Kakuei. "Jimintō no hansei." *Chūō kōron* 957 (June 1967): 284–93.

Tanaka, Stefan. *Japan's Orient: Rendering Pasts into History.* Berkeley: University of California Press, 1993.

Taniuchi, Yuzuru, ed. *Gendai gyōsei to kanryō sei.* Vol. 1. Tokyo: University of Tokyo Press, 1974.

Tashiro Kunijiro. "Toshi no fukushi mondai (2): Kawasakishi no doyagai to suramugai no jittai." *Fukushi mondai kenkyū* 2, no.1 (Tokyo: Dōshinsha, 1966): 2–34.

Taylor, Quintard. *In Search of the Racial Frontier: African Americans in the American West 1528–1990.* New York: W. W. Norton, 1998.

Taylor, Quintard, and Shirley Ann Wilson Moore, eds. *African American Women Confront the West, 1600–2000.* Norman: University of Oklahoma Press, 2003.

Teraki, Nobuaki, and Noguchi Michihiko, eds. *Buraku mondai ron e no shōtai*. Osaka: Kaihou Shuppansha, 2006.

Thelen, David. "The Nation and Beyond: Transnational Perspectives on United States History." *Journal of American History* 86, no. 3 (December 1999): 965–75.

Thompson, Heather Ann. *Whose Detroit? Politics, Labor, and Race in a Modern American City*. Ithaca, N.Y.: Cornell University Press, 2001.

Tillmon, Johnnie. "Welfare Is a Women's Issue." *Ms. Magazine*, Spring 1972, 11–16. Reprinted, Ms. *Magazine*, July/August 1995, 50–55.

Tokyo Daigaku Shakai Kagaku Kenkyūjo, ed. *Fukushi kokka*. Vol. 6, *Nihon no shakai to fukushi*. Tokyo: Tokyo Daigaku Shakai Kagaku Kenkyūjo, 1985.

Tomisaka Kirisutokyō Sentā Zainichi Chōsenjin no Seikatsu to Jūmin Jichi Kenkyūkai, ed. *Zainichi gaikokujin no jūmin jichi: Kawasaki to Kyoto kara kangaeru*. Tokyo: Shinkansha, 2007.

Tonomura, Masaru. *Zainichi Chōsenjin shakai no rekishigakuteki kenkyū*. Tokyo: Ryokuin Shobō, 2004.

Tsuchiya, Kazuyo. "Fukushi o meguru semegiai: Rosuanjerusu ni okeru 'hinkon tono tatakai' to jinshu, jendā." *Rekishigaku kenkyū*, taikai zōkangō (October 2009): 129–38.

———. "'Hinkon tono tatakai' to komyunitī soshiki no hatten: 1960 nendai kōhan no rosanzerusu no jirei o chūshinni." *Amerikashi kenkyū* 24 (2001): 51–68.

———. "'Jobs or Income Now!': Work, Welfare, and Citizenship in Johnnie Tillmon's Struggles for Welfare Rights." *Japanese Journal of American Studies* 22 (2011): 151–70.

———. "Jones, Opal C.," "National Welfare Rights Organization, 1966–1975," "Tillmon, Johnnie," "Wiley, George Alvin." BlackPast org.: An Online Reference Guide to African American History. http://www.blackpast.org.

———. "1964 nen Amerika keizai kikaihō ni okeru hōsetsu to haijo: 'Kanō na kagiri saidaigen no sanka' jōkō o megutte." *Rekshigaku kenkyū* 858 (October 2009): 18–32.

———. "Race, Class, and Gender in America's 'War on Poverty': The Case of Opal C. Jones in Los Angeles, 1964–1968." *Japanese Journal of American Studies* 15 (2004): 213–36.

Tyler, Bruce Michael. "Black Radicalism in Southern California, 1950–1982." PhD diss., University of California, Los Angeles, 1983.

Tyrrell, Ian. *Transnational Nation: United States History in Global Perspective since 1789*. Basingstoke: Palgrave Macmillan, 2007.

Uchikoshi, Ayako, and Uchiumi Mari, eds. *Kawasaki shisei no kenkyū*. Tokyo: Keibundo, 2006.

Ueno, Chizuko. *Nationarizumu to jendā*. Tokyo: Seidosha, 1998.

Umezaki, Toru. "Breaking through the Cane-Curtain: The Cuban Revolution and the Emergence of New York's Radical Youth, 1961–1965." *Japanese Journal of American Studies* 18 (2007): 187–207.

Uno, Kathy. *Passages to Modernity: Motherhood, Childhood, and Social Reform in Early Twentieth Century Japan*. Honolulu: University of Hawai'i Press, 1999.

Valk, Anne M. "'Mother Power': The Movement for Welfare Rights in Washington, D.C., 1966–1972." *Journal of Women's History* 11, no. 4 (Winter 2000): 34–58.

———. *Radical Sisters: Second-Wave Feminism and Black Liberation in Washington, D.C.* Urbana: University of Illinois Press, 2008.

Vargas, João H. Costa. *Catching Hell in the City of Angeles: Life and Meanings of Blackness in South Central Los Angeles*. Minneapolis: University of Minnesota Press, 2006.

Villa, Raúl Homero, and George J. Sánchez, eds. *Los Angeles and the Future of Urban Cultures: A Special Issue of American Quarterly*. Baltimore: Johns Hopkins University Press, 2005.

Wada, Jun. "Park-kun no 'shūshoku sabetsu saiban' no keika to mondaiten." *Chōsen kenkyū* 106 (1971): 18–29.

Wakita, Haruko, and S. B. Hanley, eds. *Jendā no Nihon shi: Shutai to hyōgen, shigoto to seikatsu*. Tokyo: University of Tokyo Press, 1995.

Waldinger, Roger, and Mehdi Bozorgmehar, eds. *Ethnic Los Angeles*. New York: Russell Sage Foundation, 1996.

Ward, Deborah E. *The White Welfare State: The Racialization of U.S. Welfare Policy*. Ann Arbor: University of Michigan Press, 2005.

Watanabe, Osamu. *Kōdo seichō to kigyō shakai (Nihon no jidaishi 27)*. Tokyo: Yoshikawa Kōbunkan, 2004.

Watanabe, Toshio. *Burakushi ga wakaru*. Osaka: Kaihou Shuppansha, 1998.

Weiner, Michael, ed. *Japan's Minorities: The Illusion of Homogeneity*. 2nd ed. New York: Routledge, 2009.

Weir, Margaret, Ann Shola Orloff, and Theda Skocpol, eds. *The Politics of Social Policy in the United States*. Princeton: Princeton University Press, 1988.

Weissman, Stephen R. "The Limits of Citizen Participation: Lessons from San Francisco's Model Cities Program." *Western Political Quarterly* 31, no. 1 (March 1978): 32–47.

West, Guida. *The National Welfare Rights Movement: The Social Protest of Poor Women*. New York: Praeger, 1981.

White, Deborah Gray. *Too Heavy a Load: Black Women in Defense of Themselves, 1894–1994*. New York: W. W. Norton, 1999.

White, Richard, and John M. Findlay, eds. *Power and Place in the North American West*. Seattle: University of Washington Press, 1999.

Widener, Daniel. *Black Arts West: Culture and Struggle in Postwar Los Angeles*. Durham, N.C.: Duke University Press, 2010.

———. "'Perhaps the Japanese Are to Be Thanked?' Asia, Asian Americans, and the Constructions of Black California." *Positions* 11, no. 1 (Spring 2003): 135–81.

Wild, Mark. *Street Meeting: Multiethnic Neighborhoods in Early Twentieth-Century Los Angeles.* Berkeley: University of California Press, 2005.

Willard, Michael Nevin. "Urbanization as Culture: Youth and Race in Postwar Los Angeles." PhD diss., University of Minnesota, 2001.

Williams, Rhonda Y. *The Politics of Public Housing: Black Women's Struggles against Urban Inequality.* New York: Oxford University Press, 2004.

Wilmore, Gayraud S. *Black Religion and Black Radicalism: An Interpretation of the Religious History of African Americans.* Garden City, N.Y.: Doubleday, 1972.

Wilmore, Gayraud S., and James H. Cone, eds. *Black Theology: A Documentary History, 1966–1979.* Maryknoll, N.Y.: Orbis Books, 1979.

Wilson, James Q., ed. *City Politics and Public Policy.* New York: John Wiley and Sons, 1968.

Wilson, William Julius. *The Truly Disadvantaged: The Inner City, the Underclass, and Public Policy.* Chicago: University of Chicago Press, 1987.

———. *When Work Disappears: The World of the New Urban Poor.* 1996. Reprint, New York: Vintage Books, 1997.

Wolfinger, Raymond E., and Fred I. Greenstein. "The Repeal of Fair Housing in California: An Analysis of Referendum Voting." *American Political Science Review* 62, no. 3 (September 1968): 753–69.

Yaguchi, Yujin. "War Memories across the Pacific: Japanese Visitors at the Arizona Memorial." *Comparative American Studies* 3, no. 3 (September 2005): 327–42.

Yamada, Takao. "Kawasaki ni okeru gaikokujin tono kyōsei no machi zukuri no taidō." *Toshi mondai* 89, no. 6 (June 1998): 53–66.

———. "Shokuminchi shugi kokufuku no igi to genjō." MA thesis, Hosei University, 2005.

Yamamoto, Eiji. "Jūmin undō no hassei yōin." *Chiiki kaihatsu* 154 (1977): 2–12.

Yamanouchi, Yasushi, J. Victor Koschmann, and Ryuichi Narita, eds. *Total War and "Mobilization."* Ithaca, N.Y.: East Asian Program, Cornell University Press, 1998.

Yasuda, Tsuneo. "Gendaishi ni okeru jichi to kōkyōsei ni kansuru oboegaki: Yokohama shinkamotsusen hantai undō no 'keiken' o tōshite." *Hogaku shimpo* 109, nos. 1, 2 (April 2002): 353–76.

———, ed. *Shakai o tou hitobito: Undō no naka no ko to kyōdōsei.* Tokyo: Iwanami Shoten, 2012.

Yasuhara, Shigeru. "Jūmin undō ni okeru rīdā sō no seikaku." *Chiiki kaihatsu* 154 (1977): 33–42.

Yoneyama, Lisa. *Hiroshima Traces: Time, Space, and the Dialectics of Memory.* Berkeley: University of California Press, 1999.

Yoon, Keun-cha. *Nihon kokumin ron: Kindai Nihon no aidentitī*. Tokyo: Chikuma Shobō, 1997.

———. *Shisō taiken no kōsaku: Nihon, Kankoku, Zainichi 1945 nen ikō*. Tokyo: Iwanami Shoten, 2008.

Yoshihara Naoki. *Sengo kaikaku to chiiki jūmin soshiki*. Kyoto: Minerva Shobo, 1989.

Yoshioka, Masuo. *Zainichi Chōsenjin to jūmin undō: Chiiki, minzoku, shakai hoshō*. Tokyo: Shakai Hyōronsha, 1981.

———. *Zainichi Chōsenjin to shakai hoshō*. Tokyo: Shakai Hyōronsha, 1978.

———. *Zainichi gaikokujin to shakai hoshō: Sengo Nihon no mainoritī jūmin no jinken*. Tokyo: Shakai Hyōronsha, 1995.

Yui, Daizaburo, ed. *Ekkyō suru 1960 nendai: Beikoku, Nihon, Seiō no kokusai hikaku*. Tokyo: Sairyusha, 2012.

———. *Naze sensōkan wa shōtotsu surunoka: Nihon to Amerika*. Tokyo: Iwanami Shoten, 2007.

Zainichi Daikan Kirisuto Kyōkai. *Senkyō 90 shūnen kinenshi, 1908–1998*. Tokyo: Zainichi Daikan Kirisuto Kyōkai, n.d.

Zarefsky, David. *President Johnson's War on Poverty: Rhetoric and History*. Tuscaloosa: University of Alabama Press, 1986.

Index

Note: The italicized *f* and *t* following page numbers refer to figures and tables, respectively.

Abraham, K. C., 127
activism, 2, 4, 6, 14, 82, 122–28, 139, 154–57, 160, 165; labor, 10; transnational, 132
Addonizio, Hugh J., 39
AFDC. *See* Aid to Families with Dependent Children
affirmative action, 33, 196n13
Affluent Society, The (Galbraith), 16
AFL-CIO. *See* American Federation of Labor and Congress of Industrial Organizations
African Americans: activists, 9, 32, 164; Christian gospel and, 128; discrimination against, 134; history of, 14, 59; Latinos and, 204n30; political status of, 59; *zainichi* Koreans and, 169
African Methodist Episcopal Church, 124–25
Agyeman, Jaramogi Abebe, 124
Aid to Dependent Children (ADC), 107
Aid to Families with Dependent Children (AFDC), 37, 107, 111–12, 113, 114, 115, 167; NWRO and, 112; welfare/women and, 111
Aid to Needy Children (ANC) Mothers Anonymous, 8, 81, 82, 107, 167; jobs/income and, 106–15; maximum feasible participation and, 99–115; welfare/women and, 106, 115
Alien Registration Law, 57, 135
Alien Registration Ordinance, 146
All Student Joint Struggle Councils. See *Zenkyōto*
American Federation of Labor and Congress of Industrial Organizations (AFL-CIO), 8, 61, 82, 99, 195n10
ANC Mothers Anonymous. *See* Aid to Needy Children (ANC) Mothers Anonymous
Anderson, Benedict, 179n19
Anderson, Samuel, 94
anti-Communism, 15, 196n16
anti-imperialist movements, 32, 33
antipoverty institutions, 72, 74, 81, 93, 96, 110, 114
antipoverty programs, 7, 18, 20–24, 30, 32, 33, 36, 37, 38, 39, 66, 69, 75–76, 77, 79, 88–91, 93, 94, 95, 97, 98, 115, 166, 189n78, 203n11, 203n18; development of, 22; diverse, 26; federal, 109; funding of, 41; impact of, 40; implementation of, 71, 78; nature of, 182–83n10; neighborhood residents and, 114; riots and, 189n81; women and, 34, 35
antipoverty struggles, 6, 31, 108

antipoverty workers, 40, 81, 89, 109, 110; critique of, 90, 91, 92*f*; WLCAC and, 104
antiracist alliances, 14, 137, 169, 170
Arai, Shoji. *See* Park, Jong Seok
Armed Forces Qualifications Test, 30
Ashmore, Susan Youngblood, 4
assimilation, 131, 147, 155
Association of Mothers Watching Out for Children, 139, 141; human rights and, 150–54
Association surrounding Mr. Park, 130, 132, 136, 141, 214n48
Association to Protect *Zainichi* Koreans in Kawasaki (Kawasaki Zainichi Dōhō no Jinken o Mamorukai), 141
Avalon-Carver Community Center, 61, 68, 88, 96; photo of, 68

Bae, Joong Do, 129, 156
Baker, Donald M., 28
Baker, John, 185n34
Balibar, Etienne, 163, 179n19
Barnes, Wilma, 101
Basic Education Policy toward Resident Non-Nationals (*Zainichi-gaikokujin kyōiku kihon hōshin*), 153–54, 157, 158, 159
Bauman, Robert Alan, 4, 180n21
Bearden School Board, lawsuit by, 124
Beheiren (Japan "Peace for Vietnam!" Committee), 129, 131
Berry, Theodore, 35
Big Four Pollution Diseases cases, 44, 190n6
black liberation struggles, 2, 10, 14, 19, 27, 33, 37, 48, 72, 124, 125, 127, 134, 137, 155
Black Nationalism, 73, 74, 96, 102, 103, 125
Black Panther Party, 74, 103
black power, Christianity and, 126
"Black Power Statement," publication of, 125
black theology, 11, 14, 124; Korean activism and, 2, 122–28
Black Theology and Black Power (Cone), 125, 126
Black Theology of Liberation, A (Cone), 126, 127
Blumenthal, Richard, 22, 182n10
Board of Public Works (Los Angeles), 98
Boone, Richard, 25, 27, 109, 185n33
Bradley, Thomas, 1, 66, 68, 70, 78, 79, 89, 93, 164, 166; Hawkins and, 95; Human Relations Board and, 76; Yorty and, 71
Brookins, Hamel Hartford, 71, 72, 97
Brown, Edmund G. "Pat," 61, 66, 71, 73, 75, 79
Brown, George E., Jr., 69, 72
Bunch, Lonnie G., 60
Buraka Liberation League, 155
Buraku, 126, 150, 155, 156
Buraku kaihō, 156
Buraku Kaihō Domei, 155
Buraku Kaihō Kenkyūjo, 156
Buraku liberation movement, 154–57
Burakumin, 139, 155, 156, 157
Bureau of Inter-American Affairs, 18
Bureau of Pollution (Kawasaki), 121–22
Button, James W., 39, 189n78
Byrd, Robert C., 189n79

CAA. *See* Community Action Agency
Califano, Joseph, 77
California Apartment Owner's Association, 61
California Real Estate Association, 61, 195n9

"Californians against Proposition 14," 195n10, 196n11
California State Legislature, 65
California Supreme Court, 60
Cannon, William B., 22, 24, 25, 27, 33
CAP. *See* Community Action Program
Capron, William M., 21–22, 23
Cary, W. Sterling, 136
Catholic Social Justice Committee, 195n10
Cazenave, Noel A., 4, 37, 178n13
CCAP. *See* Citizens' Crusade against Poverty
CEA. *See* Council of Economic Advisers
Central Avenue (Los Angeles), 60, 61; photo of, 103
Chamber of Commerce (Los Angeles), 77, 82
Chicano movement, 37
Child Allowance Law (1971), 143
child care, 106, 107, 108, 156
child welfare, 83, 142, 145, 167
Child Welfare Law (1947), 176n5
Chinese-American Citizens Alliance, 195n10
Cho, Kyong-hi, 159
Choi, Seungkoo, 131, 132, 159, 160
Chōnaikai/burakukai, 53, 54, 55, 157, 193n46
Chongryun (Sōren: Zai Nihon Chōsenjin Sōrengōkai, or General Association of Korean Residents in Japan), 12–13, 122, 129, 131, 132, 147, 158
Chōyō, 119
Christianity; black power and, 126; as theology of liberation, 126
Chung, Erin Aeran, 175n4
"Church Struggling for Liberation of the People, The" (workshop), 127
Citizens' Crusade against Poverty (CCAP), 108, 109, 110
citizenship, 2, 4, 7, 12, 134, 158, 160, 167, 168, 180n27; boundaries of, 164; civil rights struggle and, 27; community and, 53–58, 163; definition of, 13, 118, 122, 137, 145, 148, 155; ethnonational identity and, 13; inclusion/exclusion and, 29–42; reinventing, 6–14, 117, 164; second-class, 75, 163, 168; struggle over, 2, 10, 13, 118, 132, 139, 153, 161, 169; technology of, 3, 163; visions of, 13, 59, 137, 140, 142, 149, 169; welfare and, 5, 10, 42, 165, 166, 169
citizenship rights, 10, 121, 123, 134, 145, 152, 153, 160, 169; advance in, 12; struggle over, 14
civil rights, 19, 20, 31, 32, 74, 75, 91, 181n30; citizenship and, 27
civil rights movement, 65, 72, 73, 74, 129, 195n10
Clark, Ramsey, 75, 201n65
class, 7, 41, 114, 169
Cleage, Albert. *See* Agyeman, Jaramogi Abebe
Cloward, Richard, 18, 19, 177n9, 178n9; African American voters and, 20; antipoverty efforts and, 182n10
Cohen, Wilbur, 185n33
COINTELPRO. *See* Counterintelligence Program of the Federal Bureau of Investigation
Collins, Leroy, 77, 78
Communism; war on, 15, 31, 32, 33, 37; War on Poverty and, 33
community, 9, 47, 50, 179n16; approach, 5, 17, 46; boundaries of, 53–58; building, 5, 46, 49, 53, 55, 56; citizenship and, 163; defining, 46, 56; disintegration of, 43, 46

community (*continued*); imagined, 179n19; model, 12, 49; national, 5–6; sense of, 44, 51, 52, 100; vision of, 117, 154, 163; women and, 55, 56
community action, 5, 21, 29, 108, 182n10; concept of, 24–25; violence and, 39; War on Poverty and, 185n37
Community Action Agency (CAA), 1, 3, 7, 15, 32, 38, 47, 69–72, 75–79, 89, 104, 108, 164, 177n8, 202n1
Community Action Program (CAP), 18, 21, 25, 26, 28, 32, 35, 42, 43, 59, 66, 68, 69, 70, 77, 79, 111, 114, 121, 166, 167, 177n8, 177n9, 178n9, 180n21, 183n10, 184n28, 185n40; African Americans and, 4, 5, 164; attacking, 40; characteristics of, 37–38; community approach and, 6, 46; contents of, 23, 24; contradictions in, 37; creation of, 4, 9, 22–23; definitions for, 29; Green Amendment and, 40; inclusion/exclusion and, 4; innovative policies of, 47; maximum feasible participation and, 3, 4, 15, 41, 48, 49; MCP and, 6, 9, 14, 49, 52–53, 57, 163, 164; NAPP and, 7; openings in, 37–41; political participation and, 3–4, 38; recasting, 82–83, 85, 88–91, 93–99; spending by, 41; violence and, 39; War on Poverty and, 5, 27, 29, 37, 41; Watts uprising and, 7
Community Anti-Poverty Committee (Los Angeles), 78
community centers (Japan), 49, 193n35; establishing, 5, 12, 154, 155
Community Conservation Corps, 99, 100, 101, 104, 207n60
Community Development Group, 51
Community Development Program, 18
community programs, 6, 42, 47, 52, 56, 169, 179n16; creation of, 46, 51, 57, 58
Community Service Organization, 71
Community Study Group (Japan), 48, 49–50, 191n13, 192n25
Community: The Recovery of Humanity in Everyday Life (National Life Council), 46, 50, 55
Community War on Poverty Committee, 71
Cone, James H., 137, 212n31; black theology of, 125, 128; photo of, 128; theology of, 126; youth of, 124–25; *zainichi* Koreans and, 127–28
Conference of Negro Elected Officials, 95
Congressional Record, 16
Congress of Racial Equality, 110
Conway, Jack T., 37, 188n75
Copeland, Evelyn, 96
Council of Economic Advisers (CEA), 20, 21, 33
Counterintelligence Program of the Federal Bureau of Investigation (COINTELPRO), 65
crime, youth, 18, 67
Crook, Bill, 34, 35
Cruikshank, Barbara, 3, 17

Debs, Ernest, 67
deindustrialization, 61, 105, 106
delinquency, 18, 67
Delinquency and Opportunity (Cloward and Ohlin), 18
Democratic National Committee, 75, 76
Democratic Party, 20, 177n9, 178n9, 196n10
Democratic Party of Japan, 222n14
discrimination, 20, 119, 129, 132, 133, 168; educational, 150, 158;

employment, 131, 141, 158; ethnic, 14, 134, 141, 150, 153; fighting, 61, 123, 140, 142; poverty and, 89, 90, 156; racial, 14, 19, 27, 60, 90, 98, 127, 134
Du Bois, W. E. B., 59, 60
Dudziak, Mary L., 31
Dymally, Mervyn, 65–66, 66, 76

East Los Angeles, 95, 207n61
East Los Angeles Community Union, 104, 207n61
Economic and Social Development Plan, 56
Economic and Youth Opportunities Agency of Greater Los Angeles (EYOA), 1, 7, 70, 72, 77, 81, 82, 89, 90, 91, 94, 95, 96, 102, 104, 114, 115, 166, 180n21, 202n1, 203n11; establishment of, 78; funds from, 86–87*t*; health districts and, 85*f*; jobs and, 83; Jones and, 81–99; NAPP and, 97; poverty/racial issues and, 88; programs by, 84*t*, 85; reorganization of, 98; vision of, 164–65; Yorty and, 93; youth development and, 83
economic growth, 6, 9, 15, 20, 37, 44, 52, 56, 121, 152, 176n5, 207n61
economic miracle, 45, 119–20, 179n16, 194n50
Economic Opportunity Act (1964), 1, 25, 27, 38, 68, 71, 177n8, 182n1; CAP and, 3, 15
Economic Opportunity Federation (EOF), 7, 69, 70, 75, 77, 79, 82
economic problems, 8, 9, 27, 110, 114, 115
education, 2, 104, 117, 150, 159, 165, 176n5, 194n51, 200n50; compulsory, 146, 147, 167; contestations over, 140–48; ethnic, 140, 156, 158; welfare and, 154
educational policy, 145, 146, 150, 154, 160
educational programs, 76, 140, 149, 158, 167, 187n53, 202n3
educational rights, 1, 2, 122, 124, 140, 148, 151, 157, 158, 169
Elderly Law (1963), 176n5
Emancipation Decree (1871), 155
employment opportunities, 1, 36, 44, 117, 131, 141, 158, 160, 176n5
Endo, Fumio, 57, 58
environmental issues, 47, 193n35, 194n51
EOF. *See* Economic Opportunity Federation
equality: class, 7, 169; ethnic, 132; gender, 7, 169; racial, 7, 14, 132, 169
equal rights, 58, 117, 122, 135, 139, 160, 167
ethnicity, 12, 134, 146, 150, 154, 156
ethnic nursery, 123, 124, 140
Examination of the War on Poverty, 89, 202n5
exclusion, 15, 58; inclusion and, 29–42
Executive Order 8802, 60
EYOA. *See* Economic and Youth Opportunities Agency of Greater Los Angeles

Fair Employment Practices Commission (FEPC), 61, 195n8, 195n9
Family Assistance Plan, 112
Federal Anti-Poverty Program, 109
Feminist movement, poverty and, 113
FEPC. *See* Fair Employment Practices Commission
Flamming, Douglas, 60
Flores, Frances, 35
Fobes, Catherine, 34
Ford Foundation, 17, 18
Ford Motor Company, 99
Foster Grandparents, 166
Frazier, E. Franklin, 18

Frelinghuysen, Peter H. B., 27
Frye, Marquette, 72
Frye, Ronald, 72
Fujitani, Takashi, 13, 222n17
Fukuoka, Yasunori, 175n4
Fureaikan, 12, 129, 139, 158; establishing, 117, 149–54, 154–57
Furukawa, Kojun, 179n16

Galarza, Ernesto, 95
Galbraith, John Kenneth, 16, 17
Gardner, Carolee, 101
Garon, Sheldon, 52
gender, 64, 114, 169; community and, 53–58; inclusion/exclusion and, 29–42
gender relations, 4, 6, 44, 56; welfare state and, 34
General Association of Korean Residents in Japan. *See* Chongryun
General Watts Transportation, 115
Gilens, Martin, 221n9
God of the Oppressed (Cone), 126
Goe, Robert, 67, 71, 93
Goldstein, Alyosha, 4
Gordon, Kermit, 23, 185n34
Graham, Frank P., 109
grassroots, 26, 68, 69, 78, 88, 104; activism, 66, 169; alliances, 14; mobilization, 2; organizations, 2, 106
Gray Areas project, 17, 18
Greater Los Angeles Community Action Agency, 115
Great Society, 31, 176n5
Green, Edith, 40, 187n53
Green Amendment (1967), 40, 177n8
Greene, Christina, 4
Green Hill Association. *See* Seikyusha
Guess Who's Coming to the Ghettos? (Jones), 90
Gutierrez, Ursula, 94

Hackett, David, 18, 182n10
Hamachō district, 121, 148; Korean population of, 118, 119
Hamachō kyōkai, 122
Harding, Bertrand, 40
Harrington, Michael, 16, 17, 18, 185n33
Hawkins, Augustus F., 1, 65, 66, 68, 69, 70, 76, 79, 89, 91, 93, 97, 164; Bradley and, 95; OEO and, 72; Shriver and, 78; War on Poverty and, 78; Yorty and, 71, 98
Hawkins, Ed, 98
Hayes, Frederick O'R., 24, 26
Head Start, 18, 34, 35, 36, 38, 83, 166
Height, Dorothy, 35
Heller, Walter, 20, 21, 22, 23, 185n33
Henry, Mary, 88, 95–96
Herald-Dispatch, 94
HEW. *See* U.S. Department of Health, Education, and Welfare
Higasa, Tadashi, 54, 192n25
Hitachi, 1–2; battle against, 130, 132, 136; challenges at, 159, 160; consultative committee and, 136; differentiation by, 10, 169; Park and, 130–31, 159; trade unions at, 160
Hitachi Employment Discrimination Trial, 10, 117–18, 139, 142, 151, 159, 160, 164, 213n42; alliance for, 135; democratization movements and, 132; impact of, 129–37; as labor issue, 214n47; organizations formed during, 140–41; victory at, 2, 137; *zainichi* Koreans and, 11
Hitachi Trial Victory Rally, photo of, 135
Horne, Gerald, 64–67, 70, 72–73, 103, 105
Horowitz, Harold, 25, 26, 185n40

House Education and Labor Committee, 186n51, 187n53
House Loan Corporation (Japan), 57
housing, 89, 176n5; contestations over, 140–48. *See also* public housing
Housing and Home Finance Agency (U.S.), 20
Housing Bureau (Ministry of Construction, Japan), 143
Human Relations Board, 76
human rights, 144, 150–54, 165
Humphrey, Hubert, 38

identity, 175n4; ethnic, 141; ethnonational, 9, 13; Korean, 130, 135, 151, 152; national, 42
Ikegami district, 141, 148; Korean population of, 118, 119; pollution in, 120–21; poverty in, 120
Imperial Rule Assistance Association. See *Taisei yokusan kai*
inclusion, 15; exclusion and, 29–42
inequality, 119, 196n13; class, 9, 166; ethnic, 9, 14; gender, 5, 9, 34, 165, 166; racial, 4, 5, 9, 14, 20, 27, 37, 81, 165, 166
Intellectually-Disabled Welfare Law (1960), 176n5
International Convention on the Status of Refugees, 168, 194n56
International Covenant on Civil and Political Rights, 167–68
Ishida, Yorifusa, 192n25
Ita-itai disease, 190n6
Ito, Saburo, 148; administration of, 121–22, 144, 154–55; progressive agenda of, 10, 152, 165
Ito, Shigeru, 192n25
Iwai, Tomiko. *See* Song, Puja
"I Wonder Why Some People Don't Like Me?" (Jones), 96

Jacquette, Tommy, 96, 102, 103, 104
Jamal, Hakim, 74
Japan Communist Party, 47, 121, 152, 222n14
Japanese-American Citizens League, 195n10
Japanese nationals, 58, 146; non-nationals and, 143
Japanese Supreme Court, 222n14
Japan Housing Public Corporation, 143
Japan-North American Commission on Cooperative Mission, 136
Japan "Peace for Vietnam!" Committee. See *Beheiren*
Japan Socialist Party, 47, 121, 152
Jeffries, Vincent, 200n50
Jenkins, Walter, 69
Job Corps, 25, 30, 34, 35, 166, 186n51
Johnson, Charles S., 18
Johnson, Lyndon B., 35, 75, 176n5, 186n47; CAP and, 22–23; Heller and, 22; Moynihan and, 31; poverty and, 23, 27; War on Poverty and, 3, 29, 30; Watts uprising and, 76; Yorty and, 196–97n16
"Joint Powers Agreement," 67
Jones, Opal C., 68, 81, 82, 83, 88, 89, 109, 112, 114, 164, 203n18; antipoverty programs and, 90, 91, 94; CAP and, 37; critique by, 92*f*; dismissal of, 93, 94, 95, 97; Maldonado and, 91, 94, 95–97; NAPP and, 1, 7, 78, 97, 108; pamphlet by, 96, 203n11; photo of, 68; support for, 95–96, 97; War on Poverty and, 98–99; Yanez firing and, 204n30
Jordan High School Alumni Association, 102
Joseph, Miranda, 9
Jūminhyō, 119
Jung, Yeong-hae, 13
juvenile delinquency, 18, 19, 47, 67, 149

Kajimura, Hideki, 132
Kajiwara, Hisashi, 124, 126
Kanazashi, Fujitaro, 121
Kang, Sang-jung, 13
Karenga, Maulana, 74, 96, 102, 103, 104
Katz, Michael B., 19, 176n5
Kawasaki Association for Promoting *Zainichi* Koreans' Education, 12, 139; establishment of, 149–54
Kawasaki Board of Education, 145
Kawasaki City, 10, 117, 148, 169, 176n6; activism in, 122–28, 160; as alternative model, 149–54; black theology in, 122–28; coastal areas of, 11*f*; industrial belt and, 137; Korean merchants in, 120*t*; Korean population of, 118, 119, 120*t*, 129; Korean workers in, 10, 161; revisiting, 118–22; welfare policies of, 12
Kawasaki City Board of Education, 148, 150
Kawasaki City Representative Assembly for Foreign Residents, 158, 168, 222n15
Kawasaki Korean Christian Church, 10, 118, 123, 127, 131, 136, 140, 142, 151, 153, 154, 156, 159, 160; African American church leaders and, 124; citizenship and, 137; *zainichi* activism and, 137
Kawasaki system, 12, 117, 139–40, 142, 145, 149, 157, 167
KCCJ. *See* Korean Christian Church in Japan
Keihin industrial belt, 10, 119, 137
Kelly, William P., Jr., 186n51
Kennedy, John F., 24, 65, 66; antipoverty programs and, 20; Harrington and, 16; Heller and, 21, 22
Kennedy, Robert F., 104
Kessler-Harris, Alice, 15, 36
Kim, Puja, 13
Kimura, Hitoshi, 53, 54, 56, 57
King, Martin Luther, Jr., 72, 76, 126, 137; black liberation and, 124, 127; civil rights and, 74
Kōgai, 6, 42
Konoe, Fumimaro, 53
Korea Museum, establishment of, 219n38
Korean activism, 154–57; black theology and, 122–28
Korean Christian Church in Japan (KCCJ, or Zainichi Daikan Kirisuto Kyōkai), 117, 122, 123, 127, 132, 136; black theology and, 11, 128
Korean merchants, business types of, 120*t*
Korean Residents Association in Japan. *See* Mindan
Korean Student Christian Federation (KSCF), 132
Koseki system, 119, 130, 180n27
Kuramochi, Yoshio, 122–23
Kurasawa, Susumu, 51, 53, 54, 182n25
Kyōsei. *See* "Living together" slogan

Labor Standard Supervision Office, 130
Ladd-Taylor, Molly, 178n13
Lampman, Robert, 20, 30
LAPD. *See* Los Angeles Police Department
Latinos, 7, 66, 85, 94–95, 104, 167, 204n30
Law on Special Measures for Dōwa Projects (1969), 155
LDP. *See* Liberal Democratic Party
League of Cities (Los Angeles), 77, 82
League of Koreans in Japan, 146
League of Mexican-American Women, 35
League of Women Voters, 183n19

Lee, In Chok, 214n48
Lee, In Ha, 123, 126, 127, 131, 132, 150–51, 152, 156, 214n48; African American church leaders and, 124, 133–34; citizenship and, 137; Hitachi and, 129, 134; liberation theology and, 128; PCR and, 134; photo of, 128; religious leaders and, 132
Legal Defense Committee for Mr. Park. *See* Association surrounding Mr. Park
Levenstein, Lisa, 4
Lewis, Oscar: poverty and, 18, 182n6
Liberal Democratic Party (LDP), 5, 6, 51, 144; economism policy for, 45; electoral districting system and, 191n11; MCP and, 43; *zainichi* activists and, 121
liberation theology, 2, 128
Lindsay, Gilbert, 66
Lipsitz, George, 14
Living Protection Law (1946), 176n5
"Living together" slogan (*Kyōsei*), 139, 157–60, 161
Long, Charles H., 124
Los Angeles City Council, 207n60
Los Angeles Community Action Agency. *See* Economic and Youth Opportunities Agency of Greater Los Angeles
Los Angeles Community Action Program, 81, 115
Los Angeles County: African American population in, 60–61, 62–63*f*; health districts of, 85*f*; population characteristics of, 86–87*t*
Los Angeles County Board of Supervisors, 72
Los Angeles County Commission on Human Relations, 61, 102, 103, 196n10
Los Angeles County Federation of Coordinating Council, 82
Los Angeles County Schools, 82
Los Angeles County Southeast General Hospital. *See* Martin Luther King Jr. General Hospital
Los Angeles Federation of Settlement and Neighborhood Centers, 97, 98
Los Angeles Police Department (LAPD), 65, 76
Los Angeles Sentinel, 68, 71, 76, 93, 94, 96, 100, 102
Los Angeles Times, 76, 207n60
Los Angeles Unified School District, 72, 82
Los Angeles War on Poverty, 7, 59, 64, 73, 78, 82, 94, 98–99, 166, 180n21, 202n3; beginning of, 75, 85; contestations over, 66–72; poor and, 79; racial inequality and, 81; women and, 89; YOB and, 67
Lŭ, Xùn: slaves and, 218n31
Ludlam, James E., 70
Luevano, Daniel, 97, 98

MacDonald, Dwight, 17
Majima, Masahide, 48
Malcolm X, 74, 124
Maldonado, Joe, 82, 93, 203n18; Jones and, 91, 94, 95–97
Mankiewicz, Frank, 25–26
Manpower Development and Training Program, 30, 115
March on Washington, 60
Marshall, Dale Rogers, 83, 180n21
Martin, Louis, 75, 76
Martin and Malcolm and America (Cone), 126
Martin Luther King Jr. General Hospital, 105, 107
Masur, Kate, 222n19

Maternal, Child, and Widow Welfare Law (1964), 176n5
Matriarchal black families, poverty and, 33, 101
Matsubara, Haruo, 50–51, 52, 55, 182n25
Matsukuma, Hideo, 46
maximum feasible participation, 7, 8, 9, 15, 25, 26, 27, 28, 39, 41, 49, 81, 82, 96, 99–115, 164, 167
McCone, John: appointment of, 73
McCone Commission, 73
McCoy, Delores, 101
McKee, Guian A., 26, 186n47
MCP. *See* Model Community Program
McPherson, Henry, 30
Mexican American community, attention for, 95
Mexican-American Political Association, 195n10
MFY. *See* Mobilization for Youth
Mikaiho Buraku. *See* Buraku
Mills, Billy G., 66, 71, 76, 79, 97–98
Minamata disease, 190n6
Mindan (Zai Nihon Daikanminkoku Mindan, or Korean Residents Association in Japan), 12, 122, 129, 131, 132
Ministry of Agriculture, Forestry, and Fisheries (Japan), 193n35
Ministry of Construction (Japan), 143
Ministry of Education (Japan), 146, 147, 192–93n35
Ministry of Health and Welfare (Japan), 192n35
Ministry of Home Affairs (Japan), 5, 42, 46, 51, 52, 54, 57, 140, 154, 191n13, 191n18; community-building program by, 53; Community Study Group and, 49–50; technology of citizenship and, 163
Ministry of Labor (Japan), 193n35
Ministry of the Environment (Japan), 45
Mink, Gwendolyn, 178n13
Minobe, Ryokichi, 45, 121, 152
Minobe, Tatsukichi, 45
Mintōren (Minzoku Sabetsu to Tatakau Renraku Kyōgikai, or the National Council for Combating Discrimination against Ethnic Peoples), 135, 141, 156
Miyazawa, Hiroshi, 51, 57
Mobilization for Youth (MFY), 18
Model Community Program (MCP), 5, 6, 43, 46, 48–49, 51, 58, 191n13, 191n18, 194n51; CAP and, 6, 9, 14, 49, 52–53, 57, 163, 164; community and, 54, 55; community centers and, 49; creation of, 44; goals of, 56; LDP and, 42; political participation and, 48; rationalizing, 50; types/numbers of facilities creation through, 50*t*; urbanization and, 44; women and, 55
Montgomery Bus Boycott, 124, 129
Morris, Richard T., 200n50
Morris-Suzuki, Tessa, 13, 168
Mother's Day march (1968), photo of, 113
Moynihan, Daniel Patrick, 30, 31, 39, 109, 185n33; CAP and, 177n9; poverty and, 18, 33
Ms. magazine, Tillmon in, 113
multiculturalism, 159, 168
Multicultural Society Promotion Guide (Kawasaki), 158
Myrdal, Gunnar, 18
Myths and Facts about OEO (OEO), 40

NAACP. *See* National Association for the Advancement of Colored People
Nagasu, Kazuji, 152
Naples, Nancy A., 4, 36, 114, 176–77n6
NAPP. *See* Neighborhood Adult Participation Project

National Association for the Advancement of Colored People (NAACP), 59, 65, 102
National Christian Council in Japan, 123
National Citizens Advisory Committee, 96
National Committee of Negro Churchmen (NCNC, later NCBC, National Committee of Black Churchmen, and then National Conference of Black Christians), 125
National Council for Combating Discrimination against Ethnic Peoples. *See* Mintōren
National Council of Churches (NCC), 133, 136
National Council of Negro Women, 35
National Health Insurance, 57
National Land Agency (Japan), 193n35
National League of Cities, 38
National Life Council (Japan), 46, 48, 191n13
National Organization for Women (NOW), 113
National Sharecroppers Fund, 109
National Urban League, 102
National Welfare Rights Organization (NWRO), 1, 8, 107, 110, 167, 222n12; AFDC and, 112; welfare and, 111, 112, 115; women and, 111, 112, 113, 115
nationality, 13, 150, 154, 168
nationality clause, 143, 144, 160; abolishing, 12, 117, 122, 145, 148, 168
NCC. *See* National Council of Churches
NCNC. *See* National Committee of Negro Churchmen
Negro Family: The Case for National Action, The (U.S. Department of Labor), 33
Neighborhood Adult Participation Project (NAPP), 8, 81, 82–83, 85, 88–91, 93–99, 104, 203n11; CAP and, 7; EYOA and, 97; Jones and, 1, 7, 78, 97; welfare rights and, 108
Neighborhood Youth Corps, 25, 34, 99, 101, 104
Neubeck, Kenneth J., 37, 178n13
New Deal, 5, 165, 166, 176n5, 221n6
New Komeito Party, 222n14
New Look in Community Service, A (Jones), 90
New York Times, 125
Nickerson Garden Planning Organization, 106
Nihon Kirisuto Kyōdan (United Church of Christ in Japan), 133
Nihon Kirisutokyō Shingaku Senmon Gakkō, 123
Nihon Kōkan Kabushikigasha (NKK), 118, 119
Niigata Minamata disease, 190n6
Nikkei Brazilians, 158
Nippon Chisso Corporation, 44
Nishio, Masaru, 47–48, 191n18
Nixon, Richard, 65, 112
NKK. *See* Nihon Kōkan Kabushikigasha
noncitizens, 2, 9, 13, 57
non-nationals, 13, 145, 154, 161, 167, 168; Japanese nationals and, 143
NOW. *See* National Organization for Women
NWRO. *See* National Welfare Rights Organization

Ochiai, Emiko, 44
O'Connor, Alice, 6, 18, 19
OEO and the Riots (OEO), 40
Office of Economic Opportunity (OEO), 3, 7, 8, 38, 41, 42, 65, 68, 69,

Office of Economic Opportunity (OEO) (*continued*), 70, 71, 72, 74, 79, 81, 83, 93, 94, 95, 97, 102, 104, 105, 109, 114, 115, 164, 185n34, 189n78, 189n81, 203n11; antipoverty programs and, 40; CAP and, 15; criticism of, 39; educational programs and, 76; grant from, 84*t*; poverty workers and, 40, 110; requests by/authorization for, 28*t*; War on Poverty and, 36; WLCAC and, 99, 101; women and, 34, 35–36
Oguma, Eiji, 13
Ohlin, Lloyd, 18, 182n10
Okuda, Michihiro, 48
Old-Age, Survivors, and Disability Insurance, 16
O'Loane, Glenn, 207n61
Omori, Wataru, 49, 55, 56, 57, 194n51, 194n57; CAP and, 47, 48
On the Development of Community Care in Tokyo, 46
Onuma,Yasuaki, 180n27, 181n27
Orleck, Annelise, 4, 167
Other America, The (Harrington), 16
"Our Invisible Poor" (MacDonald), 17
Ozawa, Yusaku, 131, 214n48

Pak, Kyŏng-sik, 118–19, 132
Park, Chung Hee, 132
Park, Jong Seok, 140, 144, 159; citizenship rights and, 160; discrimination against, 134, 141, 142; Hitachi and, 130–31, 134, 135, 136, 159; photo of, 135; suit by, 1–2, 132
Parker, William, 65, 73–74, 76
participation, 25, 43, 46, 47, 163; citizen, 43–53, 55, 191n18; labor force, 33; of people of color, 4, 166; political, 3–4, 8, 38, 48; of the poor, 3, 4, 7, 8, 15, 26, 28–29, 38–39, 40, 41–42, 71, 76, 77, 78, 79, 81, 82, 83, 90, 91, 93, 109, 114, 164, 165, 166, 180n21; technology of, 49; War on Poverty and, 5, 29; women and, 33, 34. *See also* maximum feasible participation
patriarchal families, 19, 36
PCJD. *See* President's Committee on Juvenile Delinquency and Youth Crime
PCR. *See* Program to Combat Racism
Peace Corps, 24, 25–26
Pearce, Diane, 33, 64, 196n13
Perrin, C. Robert, 28–29
Physically-Disabled Welfare Law (1949), 176n5
Piven, Frances Fox, 19, 20, 177n9, 178n9
political power, 48, 76; African American, 8–9
Political Stability, National Goals and [the] Negro Veteran (National Strategy Information Center), 32
pollution: environmental, 120–21, 149, 157; regulation against, 122
poverty, 8, 16, 37, 40, 98, 101, 104, 114, 115, 149, 176n5, 202n3; alleviating, 19, 20, 186n51; culture of, 17, 18, 182n6; definition of, 17, 21, 83; discrimination and, 89, 90, 156; feminization of, 33, 34, 59, 64, 196n13; fighting, 7, 19, 21, 22, 27, 36, 89, 142, 183n20; inequality and, 4, 81, 165, 196n13; issues, 88, 90; level, 64, 85; matriarchal black families and, 33, 101; persistence of, 120; products of, 30; rediscovery of, 16, 17, 43; understanding, 47; unemployment and, 165; as women's issue, 113
poverty programs. *See* antipoverty programs

Power and Participation (Nishio), 47–48
prejudice, 157, 168, 196n13
President's Committee on Juvenile Delinquency and Youth Crime (PCJD), 17, 18, 19, 25, 66
Program to Combat Racism (PCR), 133, 134, 136
progressive policies, 10, 117, 144, 155
Proposition 14, 61, 195n9, 196n10
Public Affairs Program, 17
public assistance, 45, 120, 221n6
public housing, 139, 142, 143, 160, 167; right to, 144–45, 148
Public Officials Advisory Council, 38, 40

Quadagno, Jill, 4, 34, 165, 178n13

race, 4, 6, 114, 196n13; community and, 53–58; inclusion/exclusion and, 29–42; question of, 27, 169
racial inequality, 5, 9, 14, 20, 27, 37, 165, 166; poverty and, 4, 81
racism, 13, 19, 37, 88, 95, 134; polite, 222n17; poverty and, 27; sexism and, 13; struggles against, 155; welfare, 178n13
Randolph, A. Philip, 60
Reagan, Ronald, 75, 110–11
"Regarding the Treatment of Foreign Applicants for Public Housing" (bulletin), 143
Republic of Korea-Japan Normalization Treaty (1965), 147
Reuther, Walter P., 108
Richard, Pablo, 127
Rios, Tony, 71, 95
Riviera, Bill, 93
Roberts, J. Deotis, 124
Roby, Pamela, 110
Romo, Al, 95
Roosevelt, Franklin D., 60, 71
Roosevelt, James, 69
Roth, George Knox, 202n5
Roybal, Edward, 66, 69, 72, 95
Rumford, W. Byron, 61
Rumford Fair Housing Act, 61, 75, 195n8
Ryang, Sonia, 13

Sakai, Sachiko, 123; photo of, 128
Sakuramoto district, 123, 148, 154, 155, 156, 157; described, 121; Korean population of, 118, 119
Sakuramoto Nursery School, 123, 124, 149, 150, 152, 154, 159, 160; expansion of, 140; *zainichi* activism and, 137
Sakuramoto School (Gakuen), 139, 140, 142, 145, 149, 156, 157
San Francisco Peace Treaty (1952), 9, 57, 147, 180n27
Sanrizuka struggle, 44
Sato, Atsushi, 48, 51, 52, 182n25
Sato, Eisaku, 46
Sato, Katsumi, 214n48
SCAP. *See* Supreme Commander for the Allied Powers
Schlei, Norbert A., 25, 26, 185n33, 185n40
Schultze, Charles L., 16, 19, 185n33
segregation, 8, 60, 89, 124; racial, 19, 61; residential, 61, 64, 98
Seikyusha (Green Hill Association), 10, 11, 117, 124, 139, 148, 149, 150, 153, 154, 156, 157, 158, 160; citizenship rights and, 12; formation of, 140; victories for, 159
self-determination, 78, 88, 126
self-help, 56, 88, 183n20, 207n61
Self Leadership for All Nationalities Today (SLANT), 102
Senate Select Subcommittee on Poverty, 28
Shimada, Shuichi, 6

Shimizu, Keihachiro, 50, 51
Shimoebisu, Miyuki, 194n50
Shriver, R. Sargent, 28, 34, 35, 102, 185n34; CAP and, 24; criticism of, 27; Economic Opportunity Act and, 25; Hawkins and, 78; Jones and, 97; keynote address by, 108–9; War on Poverty and, 184–85n33, 185n37; women/antipoverty programs and, 34; Yorty and, 77
Smith, Rosa, 101
social change, 4, 83, 127, 153
social crisis, 8, 17, 44
social movements, 6, 37, 163, 179n16
social security, 13, 32, 56, 144, 194n50; citizenship and, 10; noncitizens and, 194n56; programs, 57, 140, 181n30; responsibility of, 194n50
Social Security Act (1935), 176n5
social welfare, 16, 49, 57, 120, 122, 168, 176n5, 179n16; citizenship and, 5; expansion of, 143
Social Welfare Council (Tokyo), 46
Social Work Bureau (Kawasaki), 148
sojourner theology (*kiryūno tami no shingaku*), 128
Somers, Margaret R., 169
Song, Eoun-ok, 13
Song, Puja, 140, 218n31; educational rights and, 152, 153; human rights and, 150–54; Korea Museum and, 219n38; photo of, 151; *Zainichi* mothers and, 2
Sōren. *See* Chongryun
South Central Los Angeles, 8, 65, 66, 73, 81, 82, 88, 105, 106, 114, 115, 169, 176n6
South Los Angeles, 61; African Americans/unemployment in, 63*t*; income in, 64*t*; poverty in, 64; unemployment in, 64
Steadman, John, 25
"Strategic Missionary Meeting on Minority People," 136
"Strategy and Strategists" (Jones), 89
Sugarman, Jule, 18
Sundquist, James L., 24, 25, 28, 184n23, 185n33
Supreme Commander for the Allied Powers (SCAP), 54, 146, 147, 181n30
Suzuki, Masahisa, 133

Taft-Hartley Act, 65
Tagawa, Kenzo, 214n48
Taisei yokusan kai, 53
Tamagawa ballast railway, 118
Tanaka, Kakuei, 45, 56, 176n5
Tashiro, Kunijiro, 121
Task Force on Manpower Conservation, 29
Teen Post, 202n3
Tennō system, 126
"Thinking about Tomorrow's Youth," 152; photo from, 151
Thompson, Heather Ann, 8–9
Thurmond, Strom, 39
Tillmon, Johnnie, 1, 8, 81, 90, 106, 112, 114, 164, 167; AFDC and, 114; article by, 113; CAP and, 37; CCAP and, 109; death of, 222n12; maximum feasible participation and, 108; NWRO and, 110, 222n12; photo of, 113; War on Poverty programs and, 82; welfare and, 111, 112, 115; women's movement and, 113
Toma, Takeshi, 130
Torres, Esteban, 207n61
Totsuka factory branch, 130, 159
transnational networks, 14, 32, 118, 129, 136, 137, 177n7
transnational perspectives, 5–6, 14, 133
Tyler, Bruce M., 103

UAW. *See* United Automobile Workers
Ueno, Chizuko, 44
unemployment, 8, 64, 67, 75, 212n6; insurance, 16; poverty and, 165; Watts uprising and, 76
unemployment rate, 61, 63, 63*t*, 64
unions, 65, 99, 121
United Automobile Workers (UAW), 37, 99, 104, 108, 207n61
United Church of Christ in Japan. *See* Nihon Kirisuto Kyōdan
United Civil Rights Committee, 71, 97
United Presbyterian Church, 102
United Way, 82
Unruh, Jesse M., 66, 74–75, 79
Upward Bound, 166
urbanization, 43, 44, 46
Us (organization), establishment of, 102
U.S. Bureau of the Budget, 20, 21, 22, 24, 185n34
U.S. Conference of Mayors, 38
U.S. Department of Defense, 29
U.S. Department of Health, Education, and Welfare (HEW), 20, 23, 67, 107, 184n28
U.S. Department of Labor, 8, 20, 23, 99, 112
U.S. Department of State, 18
U.S. Information Agency, 31

violence, 39, 40, 125
"Violence in the City: A End or a Beginning?," 73
volunteers, women as, 33–37, 55–56
Volunteers in Service to America (VISTA), 25, 34, 111, 166
voting rights, 222n14, 222n15

warfare, welfare and, 29–33, 41
War on Poverty, 7, 8, 18, 20, 21, 22, 24, 30, 31, 32, 38, 61, 65, 68, 69, 70, 72, 85, 89, 90, 103, 105–6, 108, 109, 110, 115, 178n9, 180n21, 183n10, 183n19; attacking, 39, 40; CAP and, 5, 27, 29, 37, 41; communism and, 33; community action and, 185n37; controlling, 97; described, 15; education/training and, 165; funds for, 77; implementation of, 3, 76, 81; legacy of, 42; local, 66; OEO and, 36; organizations from, 166–67; poor and, 88; programs, 82, 97, 177–78n9; race and, 4; urban insurrections and, 16; violence and, 39; visions of, 4, 59; WLCAC and, 99, 104; women and, 15, 34–35, 36; youth and, 83, 104
War on Poverty Task Force, 49, 95, 184–85n33
Watkins, Ted, 8, 81, 99, 101, 207n60; War on Poverty and, 82, 105; WLCAC and, 104, 105, 106
Watts, 1, 61, 65, 72, 88, 115; political participation in, 8; poverty in, 64; transformation of, 104, 105; unemployment in, 75; welfare in, 106, 107; WLCAC and, 99–106
Watts Community Action Group, 76
Watts Labor Community Action Committee (WLCAC), 8, 81, 82, 207n60, 207n61; maximum feasible participation and, 99–115; OEO and, 99, 101; parade float of, 103*f*; programs by, 102, 166–67; War on Poverty and, 99, 104; Watkins and, 104, 105, 106; Watts and, 99–106
Watts Summer Festival, 96, 102, 103, 167; parade of, 103*f*
Watts uprising, 39, 65, 72–78, 81, 85, 102, 104, 196n13; CAP and, 7; impact of, 75; unemployment and, 76
Weine, Maurice, 76

welfare, 6, 24, 42, 45–46, 56, 98, 114, 118, 121, 139–40, 149, 150, 152, 167, 194n51; backlash against, 166; *burakumin*, 155; citizenship and, 42, 165, 166, 169; contestations over, 140–48, 157, 160; cut from, 112; dehumanizing effects of, 106; education and, 154; expansion of, 169; narrow definition of, 110–11; policies, 4, 9, 12, 46, 137, 161, 178n13; programs, 12, 34, 142, 166, 169; racialization of, 221n9; struggle for, 136; vision of, 169; warfare and, 29–33; women and, 106–7, 111, 112; work and, 112, 115
welfare activism, 2, 4, 6, 14, 82, 165
welfare dependency, 110–11, 114
"Welfare Is a Women's Issue" (Tillmon), 113
Welfare Planning Council (Los Angeles), 69, 70, 82
welfare rights, 1, 2, 7, 12, 42, 108, 110, 112, 122, 140, 144, 151, 155, 158, 159, 165, 169, 222n12; struggle for, 137, 148, 167
welfare state, 2, 4, 5, 14, 58, 115, 164, 165, 166, 221n6; expansion of, 176n5; gender relations and, 34; Japanese, 2, 5, 46, 56, 58, 117, 164, 176n5; U.S., 1, 2, 4, 5, 29, 31, 33, 34, 41, 115, 165, 165, 166, 167, 176n5, 178n13, 221n6; warfare state and, 33, 41; women and, 56
West, Guida, 111
Westminster Neighborhood Association, 102
White, Deborah G., 98
white supremacy, 126, 134
Whitfield, Josephine, 101
"Why Should Conservatives Support the War on Poverty?," 31
"Widening Participation in Prosperity" (Heller), 21, 183n10
Wilcox, Preston R., 109
Wiley, George, 110, 111, 112, 222n12
Williams, Earline A., 76
Williams, Rhonda Y., 4
Williams, Ulis, 104
Wilmore, Gayraud S., 124, 125–26
WIN. *See* Work Incentive Program
Wirtz, W. Willard, 30, 185n33
WLCAC. *See* Watts Labor Community Action Committee
Wofford, John, 6
women: antipoverty programs and, 34, 35; community and, 55, 56; economic status of, 34; MCP and, 55, 56; NWRO and, 111, 112, 113, 115; OEO and, 33, 34, 35–36, 41; participation and, 33, 34; as volunteers, 33–37, 55–56; War on Poverty and, 15, 34–35, 36, 89; welfare and, 56, 106–7, 111, 112, 115
Women in Community Service, 34
Women in the War on Poverty, 35
Work Incentive Program (WIN), 111, 112
World Council of Churches (WCC), 2, 11, 118, 127; Program to Combat Racism and, 133, 136
World War II, 121; disconnection/continuity with, 53–55

Yamada, Takao, 144
Yamaguchi, Yasushi, 6
Yamashita, Masanobu, 214n48
Yanez, Gabrile, 204n30
Yarmolinsky, Adam, 24, 26, 185n33, 185n35
Yette, Samuel F., 93
Ylvisaker, Paul N., 17, 182n10, 185n33
YOB. *See* Youth Opportunities Board

Yoon, Keun Cha, 13
Yorty, Samuel, 66, 69, 70, 73–74, 75, 89, 91, 93, 121; antipoverty program and, 7, 166; black residents and, 65; board plan and, 72; Bradley and, 71; confronting, 79, 81; EYOA and, 93; Hawkins and, 71, 98; Johnson and, 196–97n16; Jones and, 97; King and, 74; merger plan and, 76, 77; Shriver and, 77; YOB and, 67
Young, Andrew J., Jr., 133
Youth Opportunities Board (YOB), 66, 67, 69, 70, 71, 75, 77, 82

Zainichi activists, 10, 121, 137, 140, 148, 149, 154, 165, 169; black liberation theology and, 2; equal rights and, 122; foreign registration law and, 122; human rights and, 145; letter from, 143–44; struggles of, 132, 144; welfare programs and, 42, 145
Zainichi children, 131, 148, 151, 158; educational rights of, 145, 146, 147, 152, 153; programs for, 140, 142, 143, 144, 145
Zainichi Christians, black Christians and, 128
Zainichi Daikan Kirisuto Kyōkai. *See* Korean Christian Church in Japan
Zainichi Koreans, 11, 13, 127–28, 148, 152, 156, 159, 175n3, 175n4, 214n47; African Americans and, 169; assertion by, 140; citizenship and, 2, 9, 118, 131, 145, 153; discrimination against, 131, 132, 134, 141; educational rights for, 139; financial aid for, 143; history of, 14, 129, 150, 151, 152, 154, 158; liberation of, 157; mobilization of, 14; non-nationals and, 161; political influence of, 13, 167; public housing and, 144–45; struggles of, 10, 12, 117, 129–30, 149, 150, 157; welfare rights and, 136
Zainichi mothers, 2, 145; struggles of, 148, 150
Zarefsky, David, 29, 178n9
Zenkyōto (All Student Joint Struggle Councils), 129

KAZUYO TSUCHIYA is associate professor of American history and culture at Kanagawa University, Japan.